We've filled the book with step-by-step projects, such as a faux painting technique on the right called color wash. The projects are organized into seven sections—following **Color and Style**—that explore decorative possibilities for each interior surface and how each surface relates to the others in your home.

Walls includes prep work, painting, papering, and faux finishes—such as marbling and sponging, and molding trim.

Ceilings involves lighting, ceiling fans, unique installations (such as tin ceilings, faux plaster moldings, and rosettes), and textured wallpaper.

Windows tells you how to paint and stain, how to put up blinds and shutters, and how to install several types of window coverings.

Doors explains painting and staining doors and trim, hanging prehung doors, installing salvaged or freestanding doors, installing trim and molding, and installing door hardware.

In **Floors**, you'll learn how to sand and refinish an existing floor and how to put in several types of new floors, including wood inlay, tile, and laminate. You'll also get step-by-step directions on some time-tested floor finishes—pickling, painting, stenciling, and painted floorcloths.

Furniture Refinishing helps you make your furniture compliment the rest of the room. It includes directions for painted, stained, and clear finishes, as well as special effects such as tortoise shell and faux graining.

And Finally... is full of information and projects about finishing touches large and small, including salvage and reproduction, bathroom accessories, painting window glass, and projects to dress up sinks, countertops, and tubs.

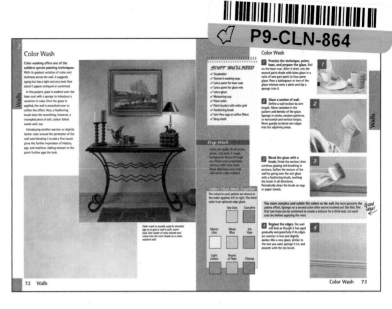

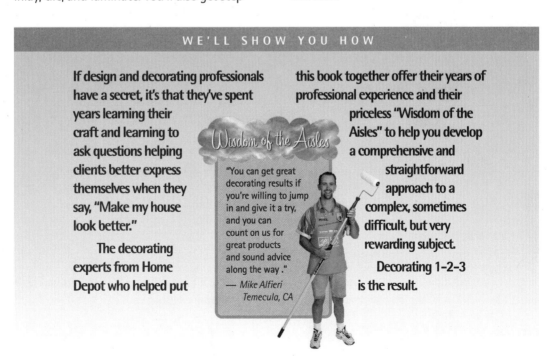

WE'LL SHOW YOU HOW

If design and decorating professionals have a secret, it's that they've spent years learning their craft and learning to ask questions helping clients better express themselves when they say, "Make my house look better."

The decorating experts from Home Depot who helped put this book together offer their years of professional experience and their priceless "Wisdom of the Aisles" to help you develop a comprehensive and straightforward approach to a complex, sometimes difficult, but very rewarding subject.

Decorating 1-2-3 is the result.

Wisdom of the Aisles

"You can get great decorating results if you're willing to jump in and give it a try, and you can count on us for great products and sound advice along the way ."
— *Mike Alfieri Temecula, CA*

Decorating 1-2-3™

Meredith Book Development Team
Project Editor: John P. Holms
Art Director: John Eric Seid
Editor/Writer: Jeff Day—Heartwood Books
Photographer: Lark Smothermon—Woolly Bugger Studios
Designer: Ann DuChaine—Ann DuChaine Creative
Copy Chief: Catherine Hamrick
Managers, Book Production: Pam Kvitne, Marjorie J. Schenkelberg
Contributing Writers: Tony O'Malley, Roger Yepsen, Jr.
Contributing Copy Editors: Margaret Smith, Carol Boker
Contributing Proofreaders: Colleen Johnson, Gretchen Kauffman, Susan J. Kling, Ron Lutz, Debra Morris Smith
Indexer: Donald Glassman
Electronic Production Coordinator: Paula Forest
Editorial Assistants: Renee McAtee, Karen Schirm

Meredith® Books
Editor in Chief: James D. Blume
Managing Editor: Gregory H. Kayko
Executive Editor, Home Depot Books: Benjamin W. Allen

Director, Retail Sales and Marketing: Terry Unsworth
Director, Sales, Special Markets: Rita McMullen
Director, Sales, Premiums: Michael A. Peterson
Director, Sales, Retail: Tom Wierzbicki
Director, Sales, Home & Garden Centers: Ray Wolf
Director, Book Marketing: Brad Elmitt
Director, Operations: George A. Susral
Director, Production: Douglas M. Johnston

Vice President, General Manager: Jamie L. Martin

Meredith Publishing Group
President, Publishing Group: Christopher M. Little
Vice President, Finance & Administration: Max Runciman

Meredith Corporation
Chairman and Chief Executive Officer: William T. Kerr

Chairman of the Executive Committee: E. T. Meredith III

The Home Depot®
Senior Vice President, Marketing and Communications: Dick Hammill
Project Director: Hugh Miskel

Copyright©2000 by Homer TLC, Inc.
All rights reserved. Printed in the United States of America.
First Edition—00
Library of Congress Catalog Card Number: 00-132132
ISBN: 0-696-21107-6 Distributed by Meredith Corporation

Note to the Reader: Due to differing conditions, tools, and individual skills, Meredith Corporation and The Home Depot assume no responsibility for any damages, injuries suffered, or losses incurred as a result of following the information published in this book. Before beginning any project, review the instructions carefully, and if any doubts or questions remain, consult local experts or authorities. Because codes and regulations vary greatly, you always should check with authorities to ensure that your project complies with all applicable local codes and regulations. Always read and observe all of the safety precautions provided by any tool or equipment manufacturer, and follow all accepted safety procedures.

Information on Color: We have made every effort to duplicate paint colors used in this book as exactly as the printing process allows, however, there will be some variation between colors as represented on the page and as they will appear on paint chips at your store.

The editors of *Decorating 1-2-3*™ are dedicated to providing accurate and helpful do-it-yourself information. We welcome your comments about improving this book and ideas for other books we might offer to home improvement enthusiasts.

Contact us by any of these methods:

1 Leave a voice message at (800) 678-2093

2 Write to Meredith Books, Home Depot Books; 1716 Locust St; Des Moines, IA 50309–3023

3 Send e-mail to hi123@mdp.com. Visit The Home Depot website at **homedepot.com**

Decorating 1-2-3™

Faux Painting
Wallpapering   Window Treatments
Floors   Molding & Trim   Lighting
STEP-BY-STEP

Decorating 1-2-3

TABLE OF CONTENTS

Table of Contents

Section 1

Color and Style

Decorating your home is a challenge, an adventure, a labor of love, and hopefully one of the most satisfying experiences you will ever have as a homeowner. Creating a living space that accurately reflects your lifestyle, personality, and sense of taste is all about learning what you want, trusting your instincts, and getting expert advice when you need it. A designer's or decorator's objective with clients is to help them understand what they like and use that information to help them put the pieces of the decorating puzzle together. Thinking like a decorator is about asking the right questions and combining all the answers into a cohesive scheme. In order to get those answers for yourself, you need a place to start. So we'll begin by talking about color and style and how they affect every design and decorating choice you make.

Color and Style

Color and Style—Beginning the Design Process

A wise interior designer once said there are three rules to decorating a home. It's just that nobody is quite sure what they are.

He was joking, of course, but it's easy to understand what he was talking about when you consider the vast array of choices and the volumes of information in magazines and on television about decorating and design. Look, style, taste, flow, mood, action, balance, contrast—how do you bring together all the home decorating elements to truly express and reflect your personality? How do you decide on the right color for the dining room walls, or the right molding and trim for the study, or curtains for the windows in the bedrooms, or the perfect floor covering for your living room? How do you make your grandmother's treasured blanket chest fit in the same room with your brand-new sofa? How do you overcome your dependence on "white-on-white" and take a chance on a more complex color scheme? After you've put all the pieces together, how can you be sure you'll like living in what you've worked so hard to create?

Many sources of color are present in this elegant living room—rich fabrics, lush wall and floor treatments, and a variety of ambient lighting. All these elements work together to create a sense of style, comfort, and well-being.

Warm the room with creamy hues. Popular color choices in the 1800s and still popular today, creams create intimacy in large rooms or rooms with north-facing windows.

By asking yourself these questions, you're doing what designers or decorators do as they begin to formulate a plan for a client. Questions, and the ideas that evolve in answering them, are the tools designers use to create a look for a home that is focused, attractive, comfortable, and an expression of the taste and style of the people who live there. Pros are well paid to figure this out. But you don't have to spend a fortune on advice to learn how to make the most of your home's charm.

Decorating pros know following a rigid set of design rules doesn't work. Every house is different—a mixture of great features and others that are inconvenient or don't coordinate at all. Instead, they focus on the pluses in a house—big windows, interesting moldings, wood floors, an expansive floor plan, or a quirky but cozy layout. Then they combine the decorative elements and styles best suited for the setting and the homeowner's preferences.

Creating a Design Strategy That Works

The first decorating lesson is learning to trust your gut feelings. You know more about what you like and what you want than anyone else. What you may be unsure about is how to turn those feelings into a plan. Start by jotting down adjectives that clearly express and summarize the look and feeling you want to achieve. Words like calm, energetic, mysterious, spartan, alluring, efficient, uninhibited, and cozy all evoke emotional responses that could become keys to your decorating scheme.

CONSIDER COLOR. For most of us, including interior designers, the decorating process begins with color. What colors come to mind as you think about the adjectives you've listed? Color directs the eye and influences mood and action. Muted greens soothe and make a nice background color for a bedroom. Red, however, stimulates the senses and works well in dining or living areas. Choice of color is the boldest decorating statement you'll make.

CONSIDER STYLE. Style comes into play once you've thought through color and the mood it creates. When we think of style we think of looks that define a period in history such as Colonial or Victorian or a sense of location such as Southwestern or Country.

CONSIDER THEME. Designers don't want to limit themselves to a single style and often use a mix of styles to create themes in a home. Themes incorporate elements of particular styles that reoccur from room to room to create transitions and to unify the entire scheme. For instance, a geometric border along a dining room ceiling might be repeated in pillows and curtain treatments in the living room. Color schemes can move from room to room in the same fashion.

Most Decorating Schemes Are a Mix of Styles

Few of us are interested in decorating our homes strictly according to the dictates of a particular style. Even if we could strip the house to the bare walls and start over, what would we do with the pieces we already own and love but don't fit in the new look? That's why most of us want a plan that will get us the look we want and still allow us to enjoy the things we love. To make informed design choices, we need to know a little bit about color and then about how the dominant styles in American decorating emphasize certain colors, furnishings, and accessories.

After we talk about color and how color choices affect design schemes, we'll delve into styles. The seven major styles we're going to talk about are Country, Colonial, Southwestern, Traditional, Victorian, Arts and Crafts, and Contemporary. Once you have a sense of the basic elements of each of these styles you can begin creating a design that reflects your personal taste and makes good use of the objects you love.

1

Begin with Color

Hot Reds

Understanding COLOR

The world around us is full of information about color. Every day we see combinations that please and surprise us. Natural and artificial light both affect our perception of color. Look at a room over a 24-hour period. You'll see that the color differences can be radical. That's why painters suggest painting a large test swatch on the wall and seeing how light affects the choice.

COLOR Makes Us Feel

Warm colors are associated with heat—the yellow sun, orange flames, and red-hot coals. They make us feel comforted and energized. Warm colors tend to make rooms feel smaller and more intimate, an advantage in rooms that feel too large for conversation or for curling up on a sofa with a good book. A range of red—from raspberry to plum to earth tones—has been traditionally and effectively used in studies and dining rooms. Warm-hued paint schemes counteract the cool light of rooms with north-facing windows. Be careful, though, fluorescent lighting can make certain reds look harsh.

COLOR Changes Rooms

Cool colors remind us of forest glens, crystal blue lakes, purple shadows, and dusky foliage. We even feel somewhat cooler in rooms painted shades of green, blue, or violet. Cool colors have another effect—they create the illusion of distance. Look at the horizon and observe how the landscape seems to mute to blue or violet. A far-off mountain forest isn't leafy yellow-green; rather, it is green chilled with the mixture of blue or violet. Cool colors will suggest distance, just as they do in nature, and make a cramped room appear larger. Make a ceiling look taller by painting it cool white. For a greater illusion of height, continue the ceiling paint down the wall a foot or more, and cover it with a picture rail that runs around the top of the room.

Cool Blues

Choosing COLOR

We each experience color differently. Discuss the palettes you're choosing with everyone who'll be living with them. You'll have to make the decision, but eveyone should have a say. Cool colors possess varying degrees of coolness, and not all warm colors are equally toasty. Warm yellow tends toward orange and has an open, peachy cheerfulness while lemon yellow leans toward green. Choosing a scheme is a matter of research and experimenting until you get it right.

COLOR Combinations

Warm and cool combinations may seem an odd couple but think of cherry red and lime green. There is tropical energy in this complementary relationship. Think of Christmas red and green, Easter lavender and yellow, and school pennant blue and orange. Bold palettes will create strong, dynamic looks and force visual movement from room to room—they're real attention grabbers.

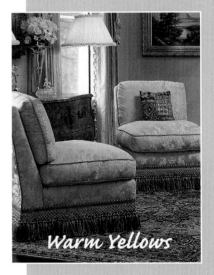

Warm Yellows

The warm-cool game can be played with lighter and whiter shades as well. For example, roll walls with a slightly warm white and the ceiling with a cool white. Both colors look white in the can, but they will assert their personalties in the room. Use warm and cool shades to transition from room to room. For example, a warm living room may be adjacent to a cool dining room. A warm hallway may lead to cool bedrooms. If the transitions are subtle, the effect is subliminal and calming.

The Color Wheel and How to Use It

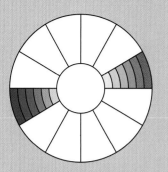
Complementary

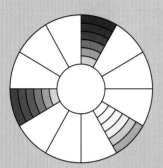
Triad

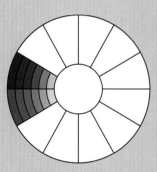
Analogous

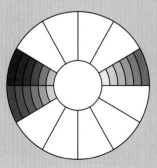
Analogous with complementary accent

Painting a room white is easy. But you can confidently devise a more ambitious color scheme once you understand how colors work together. The color wheel organizes colors to help you make choices. The **PRIMARY** colors—red, blue, and yellow—are always the same distance apart and in the same order. Mix two primary colors, you'll get a **SECONDARY** color—red and yellow make orange; blue and red create violet. **TERTIARY** colors occur when a primary is combined with any secondary color adjacent to it on the wheel—red and violet make red violet and green and yellow make yellow green.

How do you pick a color scheme? By combining colors on the wheel. Take a lesson from nature. Think of a brick sidewalk running through a green lawn or a field of marigolds along a bright blue lake. They both have something in common. They're **COMPLEMENTARY**—meaning that they're opposite each other on the color wheel.

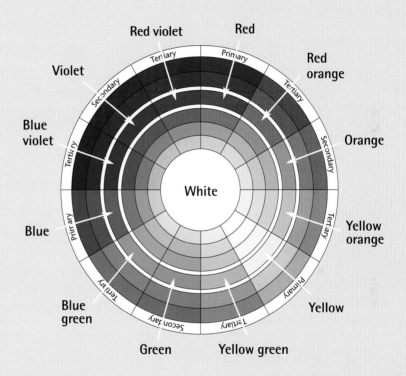

Start with your favorite color—say it's blue—and build some color schemes around it. The basic choice is various shades or tints of blue. Designers call this **MONOCHROMATIC**. You can combine blue with its opposite on the wheel—orange—to create a **COMPLEMENTARY** scheme. When you bring the other primary colors into the scheme, it's called a **TRIAD** because all three are equidistant from each other. Blue also goes well with blue violet and blue green, the **ANALOGOUS** colors on either side of it. Add a color from the opposite side, like orange, and you get a **COMPLEMENTARY ACCENT**. Use the color wheel to create any color scheme you choose.

A few general theories: Neighboring colors will create softer, less intense palettes. Combinations from opposite sides of the wheel will give you bold schemes. Neutral colors are low-intensity mixtures (nearer the middle of the circle) of two or more colors. Finally, black is the presence of all color, and white is the absence of all color.

Color and Style   9

Begin with Color *continued*

Consider every component of the room when choosing your color palette—walls, ceilings, trim, doors, and windows. Each plays a distinctive role in the final result.

What about gloss? Although gloss or sheen is not a factor in color, the impression of surfaces is influenced by light reflection. Glossy walls and trim attract attention because they reflect more light. Gloss paints highlight baseboard molding and trim or frame-and-panel doors. Use less glossy sheens for restful areas of your home.

Blending COLOR and Style

Every style uses color differently. Colonial and contemporary styles use tints and shades of the three primary colors—a triad. Traditional styles focus on an analogous scheme based on neighboring bands of color, such as secondary and tertiary colors. Still others, such as Victorian, use an analogous scheme with complementary accents. The color palettes in this chapter will give you basic combinations for each style.

Floral upholstery on the dining room chairs accents the muted green of the wainscoting.

Find Colors You'll Love to Live With

If you're interested in bold color combinations and standard paint chip palettes or photos of interiors aren't doing the trick, take a trip through some full-color travel guides. As shown in these photographs—a brightly colored Southwestern blanket, the soft blue pastel of a Spanish Colonial wall niche, richly red English cabinetry, checked curtains in a French country-style window, the dusty rose of a Victorian entryway—the dynamic use of color will surely spark your imagination. Each culture has its own palette—influenced by tradition, available materials, landscape, and sunlight.

It might surprise you to discover that the doors of Scotland's stone train depots are vivid chartreuse. The walls of the Majorelle gardens in Marrakesh, Morocco, are intense ultramarine blue inspired by the French laborers' overalls. Ancient buildings in Rome run the color range from ruddy earth tones to tawny yellows. In India, buildings are painted with vibrant candy-color pastels.

For a touch of local color, gather a palette from nature in your neighborhood. Create paint colors from trees, bushes. stones, pieces of wood, and dried leaves.

Hue, Tone, and Intensity

The great thing about taking a chance with color, especially on the walls and ceilings, is that if you don't like the results you can repaint. And, if you do like it, you've taken a bold step into the decorating world. Sure, you probably won't go wrong with off-whites; but choosing the perfect color scheme for a room is one of the joys of decorating. After a while success won't come by accident but by choice. As a way to start planning your color scheme, think about its impact or effect on the room and the people who will be using it. When designers begin to pick a color scheme they consider three color variables—hue, tone, and intensity.

Hue

When we talk about colors in simple terms, we usually speak of hue. The three primary hues of yellow, red, and blue are enhanced by the secondary hues of green, orange, and violet. These six hues make up the colors in elementary school paint boxes and can be mixed to produce an infinite number of tertiary shades with names such as chartreuse, periwinkle, burnt orange, and turquoise. Dark hues may may feel constricting in small rooms. They can also feel cozy and intimate. Even black can be used effectively on baseboards, floor tiles, countertops, tables, and upholstery.

Tone

It's generally safe to keep colors within the same tonal range—colors that would be the same shade of gray if you took a black-and-white photo of the room. Since colors that appear wildly different may have the same tone, tonal unity allows you to be adventurous. In a Victorian den, a bold maroon balances a bright green. In a blonde pared-down Contemporary living room, several shades of taupe and beige are combined. As with any color rule, there is a risk—if the tone in a room is too much the same, the overall effect can be heavy or bland.

Intensity

Intensity refers to the "pureness" of a color and where it falls between pure white and black. Pure, primary hues are "neutralized" or softened by adding white; one or more secondary hues can be added to heighten the effect. Add a little of a darker hue to intensify the color—add a lot for a dramatic change. Truly custom colors are created by experiment. If you're mixing color on your own, keep track of the proportions as you go so you can recreate the color as needed.

A warm terra-cotta hue on the walls accented with neutral gray-green window treatments is repeated as accents in the choice of the throw and pillows on the sofa.

Intensity and Style

Intense hues are found in every style. In Country homes, they might be the unrestrained palette of a folk painting or the bold patches on a quilt. Strong colors on Colonial walls define spaces from room to room. Contemporary walls are often punched up with bursts of full-intensity primary colors. Complex colors and combinations tend to be more visually interesting. They demand focus. Muted hues create more neutral backgrounds and draw attention to accessories, furniture, and window treatments. The goal is to choose colors that harmonize and complement all the other design elements in the room.

Seven 7 Basic Styles

Mention a Country kitchen, a Victorian parlor, Traditional living room, or a Colonial dining room and the person you are speaking to is very likely to have a strong visual impression of what you are describing. In recent years more people are using interior decorating as a way to express personal taste and sensibility.

The names of major North American decorating styles are a central part of the language of interior decorating. Decorating elements—everything from wall treatments to floor coverings, furniture to windows—are categorized and defined to a large degree by their style. Within each of these basic decorating styles are countless variations. However, understanding the fundamentals of these seven styles will help you learn the language of decorating and, more importantly, help you make decisions about your own very personal decorating plan. To help clarify, we've picked seven styles: Country, Colonial, Victorian, Arts and Crafts, Traditional, Southwestern, and Contemporary because they are the most popular and commonly used stylistic influences on interior design in North American decorating. Draw on them for inspiration and ideas. Use them as a resource and a starting point. The only rule: Don't be bound to style at the expense of your personal vision. Be open. Be flexible. And you'll confidently evolve your distinctive look.

As with most decorative themes, Country works best when it expresses a way of life rather than a momentary trend.

Country

The touchstone of Country is simplicity and practicality—a comfortable home that serves equally well when times are good and times are lean. Images of wood-frame houses surrounded by lush gardens, dense woodlands, waving fields, and shady lanes—Country draws not on a historically based architectural style, such as Victorian or Arts and Crafts, but on other centuries, other countries, distant places, and longing for simpler times. Country style, whether American or European, rises out of an interest in the simple life and the attraction of rural pleasures. The popularity of Country style is a reaction to the hectic pace of city life and the onslaught of technology.

Country style is highly personal, offering a wide variety of interpretations and allowing for great freedom of expression. Hallmarks are easy to spot: fresh herbs hung to dry, unfinished (or barely finished) wooden furniture, and a simple, warm color palette. You'll find reminders of the Old World in bold folk painting or a long trestle table with caned chairs. Today's Country style showcases the trappings of Americana—from Colonial times through the Industrial Age to the present. The modern trend expresses a lively mix-and-match spirit, rather than a historian's zeal for accuracy. High-end antiques and yard sale treasures mix with ease.

Country–From the Ground Up

Floors are typically wide unfinished, painted, or clear-finished boards. Area rugs are scattered on the floors near beds, wooden benches and high-backed chairs. Walls are paneled or plastered. Simple baseboards are painted to contrast with whitewashed surfaces. Wainscoting and chair rails are common, and moldings have a simple profile—often hand-planed 1-inch stock, with single bead ornamentation along the top edge or small beads along both long edges of chair rail.

Windows are often double-hung with six panes in each sash. Doors, a focal point of a Country room, are frame-and-panel; or in a more rural vein, they are simply vertical boards backed by Z-shape bracing and hand-wrought hinges and handles. Overhead, exposed beams support the floor above and serve as a place to hang drying herbs or kitchen implements. A massive stone fireplace might be the center of both the kitchen and the sitting room.

Keep window treatments simple. Hang tab curtains from rods either at the top or midway across the window. Use fabric-covered custom roller shades with delicate print or broad stripes on off-white linen. Or, skip window treatments and showcase windows, window frames, or deep windowsills.

Furniture tends to be handcrafted and practical. It is clear-finished, painted simply, or highly decorated in Old World folk styles. Characteristic items are dry sinks, trestle tables, pie safes, and blanket chests. Seating is less luxurious. Supplement ladder-back chairs and wall benches with a lightly padded camelback sofa covered in traditional plaid.

Don't overdo it. Country houses were workplaces—a place for everything and everything in its place. Let efficiency generate good decorating ideas by hanging braided garlic from the ceiling, line favorite china along a plate rail, leave cupboards open to display kitchen tools, hang pots and pans from hooks, and show fresh produce in wicker baskets. Open the space and let the beauty of everyday objects—they are a dominant feature of Country style.

The Country Palette

Until the mid 1800s, paint colors came from basic ingredients. Earth, soot, blood, and milk were principal materials used to produce paint. Painters created blue-green by exposing copper to vinegar fumes. This pickling treatment was also used to make white lead paint. *Terre verte*, French for "green earth," was a subtle, somewhat transparent shade. Barn red was based on iron oxide, also known as rust. The few available ingredients created warm, subtle colors; the oil base caused ambering over time; and some pigments changed with exposure. White was added to create pastels, while black from soot or animal bones was added for depth.

Walls were typically white. One primary color was chosen for the trim and another for the doors. Ceilings were painted as well, with barn red a common country choice, making an already low room seem more intimate.

The opposition of long expanses of perfectly painted white walls and well-used, even battered, Country furniture can create an exciting Contemporary or Country look. For a feeling that is older, homey, and more comfortable, "wash" the walls with rags dipped in several translucent, watered-down layers of color to build up a depth that imitates decades of constant use.

Winter Solstice

Green Gable

Crystal Light

Sweet Butter

Drama Red

Khaki Shadow

Cranberry Mist

Dry Twig

Wedgewinkle

Knoll Green

Antique Blue

Farm Fence

Colonial

Throughout the 18th century, America was caught up in the exciting and often difficult process of inventing itself. America's coming of age is seen in Colonial style. Mount Vernon, George Washington's gracious family home, comes to mind when most Americans think of Colonial style. Homes of the mid-to-late-18th century in the United States are noted for the sense of proportion, simplicity, and serenity of their interiors. The sense of calm and gentility hints at a deep worldly concern for logic, comfort, and visual order. Furnishings and underlying structure reveal sophistication and an interest in all things scientific. The highly-engineered Windsor chair, a symbol of the period, makes this point with spare lines and perfect proportions.

Country style reflects the rural world. Colonial style proudly speaks of global involvement, fascination with philosophy, science, and the flow of ideas. Libraries were prized showcases. Wealthy homeowners graced their rooms with luxurious Oriental carpets, a benefit of international trade. Middle-class families made do with simpler alternatives—painted floor cloths or stenciled flooring in imitation of inlaid woods.

Colonial rooms of Washington's time were larger in scale than their Country cousins. Wood paneling and wainscoting on walls were common. Decorative chair rails grounded tall ceilings and protected the walls. Stenciled patterns as borders and simulated wallpaper were an economical means of ornamentation. Dining rooms often showcased murals of the surrounding landscape framed in wood paneling above the wainscoting.

Bulit-in clothes closets became a standard part of the home after the Colonial period. Families in the 18th century used armiores or hung their possessions on wooden pegs tapped into picture and chair rails. Today, we use similar pegs to display art objects and collectibles.

Low ceilings on the upper floors, multi-paned windows with shutters, wide-plank flooring covered with a woven area rug, and simply designed but elegantly upholstered furniture are all major elements of Colonial style.

Well-heeled colonists appreciated and took pride in displaying fine handmade and upholstered furniture. Although American styles followed those in Europe, furniture styles on this side of the Atlantic were, for the most part, marked by restraint and simplicity. People could not afford to redecorate on a whim; therefore several types of period furniture—Jacobean (1600-1700), William and Mary (1700-1725), Queen Anne (1725-1750), and Chippendale (1750-1775)—usually passed from generation to generation, existed side by side in Colonial homes.

Light Colonial rooms with ginger jar or vase lamps topped with off-white shades to represent the absence of natural gas or electric light. Cluster groups of small lamps to suggest the ambience of candlelight.

Window treatments are prim, spare, and tidy, with linen and calico curtains hung by tabs from rods. Draw curtains away from the window and hold in place with tiebacks.

The Colonial style in architecture and interior design has weathered many movements and remains extremely popular across the country to this day.

The Colonial Palette

Colors of Colonial homes are straightforward and bold—and almost universally attractive. The modest number of pigments, made from fewer than a dozen pulverized ores, clays, and household ingredients, insured against excess and disharmony.

Colonial homes were painted slate blue, salmon, apple green, and apricot yellow—each with its own warmth and complexity. Prussian blue, developed in Europe in the early 1700s, found its way to the walls of George Washington's Mount Vernon home. These weren't the tame shades that you see on paint chips. Dimly lit interiors needed visual punch to compete with the hot, open flames of fireplace, candles, and lanterns. The pigments were often applied in patterns that we would consider outrageous—bold Xs and polka dots that make today's stenciling look timid in comparison. Interestingly, colors were at their boldest about the time of the Revolution and then softened through the 1800s.

Barbizon

Melted Wax

Merlin

Golden Straw

Ruby Amber

Heather Dusk

Wild Cattail

Plum Dusk

White Silence

Terrestrial

Softly Silvered

Talisman

Southwestern

Spanish culture in the Southwest was so pervasive that it left a strong imprint on the region's architecture and interior decor. Spanish Colonial and Native American influences combine themselves into a style more generally known as Southwestern.

The most notable feature of Southwestern architecture is its thick adobe walls. Bricks are made from mud formed in wooden molds and sun dried, then coated with stucco. The result is a form both fluid and sensual, yet extremely practical. Ceiling beams, or vigas, are peeled pine logs. Latillas, narrow pole supports, are used in dramatic, geometric criss-cross patterns.

Today's Southwestern style, both interior and exterior, retains these fluid forms. Main rooms are anchored by adobe, kiva-style fireplaces. The fireplace and the walls are hand-finished in tinted plaster. Floors are covered with thick, unglazed clay tiles or wide-plank boards.

The built-in nature of Southwestern style creates rooms that are at their best with simple decoration and furnishings.

Unlike the milled lumber, brick, and quarried stone used elsewhere in North America, the elements of Southwestern interiors are rounded and sensual. Thick walls, deep window and door recesses, and generous roof overhangs contribute to the hushed, secure, and inviting interiors.

The kiva-style fireplace (above) is an updated signature of Southwestern sytle. Buckskin upholstery, complete with fringe, on a classically styled side chair enhances the theme. The handmade ceramic tile on the countertop and backsplash links the Spanish Colonial past to a modern working kitchen (below).

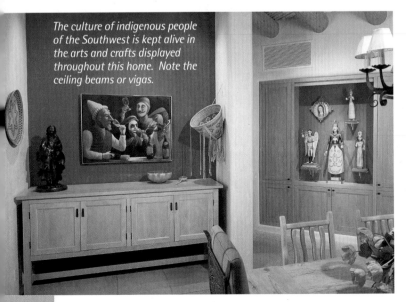

The culture of indigenous people of the Southwest is kept alive in the arts and crafts displayed throughout this home. Note the ceiling beams or vigas.

Characteristic Southwestern furniture and appointments include boldly patterned Navaho hand-woven rugs and saddle blankets, found objects (cattle skulls collected by New Mexico artist Georgia O'Keefe are a famous example), stylized regional art, religious icons, Pueblo pottery, and heavily carved Spanish Colonial furniture. Daybeds replace sofas. Heavy doors have sturdy hardware and tall windows have large divided panes and brightly painted frames, floor-to-ceiling window treatments are avoided so as not to conceal simply appointed windows.

Sturdy, simply upholstered furniture and brightly painted regional furniture work well with Southwestern design. Use earth tones and pastels to feature curves or display niches and to accent expanses of neutrally-hued plaster walls.

Suggest the effect of plastered adobe walls by applying textured paint—with or without sand. For a more ambitious project, trowel on finish plaster and work it into dramatic peaks and swirls.

The Southwestern Palette

The sun-baked earth and open skies of the Southwest are accented by green desert plants and brightly painted religious artifacts. White or bisque interior walls complement the impact of color. For this reason, tone down wall color with white to suggest sun bleaching. Include cool colors and earth tones for visual relief. Taos Blue, a regional hue, is often seen on doors.

Color samples: Shilo Blue, Lupine, Lighthouse, Wood Blue, Stallion, Aqua Foam, Petite Nina, Sandpiper, Autum Cornfield, Echo Canyon, Choctaw, Plum Scent

Rounded, hand-formed surfaces of traditional adobe are reproduced in modern materials. This home retains the distinctive pole-supported beam ceiling.

The small corner fireplace keeps this room cozy on cool desert nights. Native American pottery, hand-woven baskets, and the brightly-colored primitive area rug are essential decorating accents for Southwestern style.

Traditional

Traditional style is a decorator's elegant catch-all, largely referencing 18th- and 19th-century periods with staying power, such as Chippendale (Georgian), Federal (neoclassic), Empire, Classical Empire, and the Greek, Gothic, and Rococo revivals as well as taking the best elements of fads and fancies that appeared over the succeeding decades such as Art Deco.

Traditional style is a link with the past, a blending of popular trends, adjusting and softening highly-decorative and elaborately visual concepts to create comfortable and timeless interior designs. The aim is not to reproduce looks of the past, but to rethink or reinvent them for the modern home. At its best, Traditional style marries echoes of the past with a contemporary flair.

The scale of Traditional style is large, so it has tended to reach full flower in times of prosperity, when the American middle class could afford the luxury of redoing an interior. While there are many options, decorating in the ultra-traditional style is a challenge in modern homes with 8-foot ceilings. A richly detailed Rococo chair from an 1800s parlor, for example, may overpower the spare style and low ceilings found in the living room in a typical ranch-style home. However, two overstuffed wing-back chairs in front of a brick fireplace, an Oriental area rug, and a wooden sidetable with a tall, brass candlestick lamp might serve the same space quite effectively and still lend a traditional sensibility and flair.

Traditional style rooms are airy and open. Large windows, though heavily curtained, admit lots of light. Inexpensive species of wood can be stained or faux painted to resemble more valuable species, such as mahogany and walnut. These techniques are widely used on doors and furniture made from pine and poplar. As an alternative, woodwork and trim are often painted to match walls and ceilings.

Elegant and complex window treatments are popular, including valances,

The Traditional bedroom above is influenced by Victorian style, especially in terms of scale, but not dominated by it. The color palette is softer and the juxtaposition of pattern is subtle. Note the oversized bed and the matching of fabric and wallpaper.

Boldly upholstered, oversized furniture mixes comfortably the generous architectural detailing of traditional interiors. Match the scale of furniture and ornamentation to the rooms in which they will be placed.

High ceilings and large windows allow an abundance of natural light. The scale of the windows and the room offer opportunities for detailed window treatments and a complex garland wallpaper pattern in a classical European style.

swags, and asymmetrical jabots installed over layers of sheer curtains. Draperies are ornamented with tassels, fringes, and elaborate rosettes, brackets, and finials.

Comfortably upholstered furniture boasts rich-looking velvet, moiré silk, brocades, and damask fabrics.

Wallpapers feature complex Classical motifs drawn from patriotic symbols—columns, wheat sheaves, and eagles. Designs often comprise murals to suggest familiarity with the Golden Ages of Rome and Greece or links with grand European styles, such as Georgian, Empire, and Edwardian.

Color schemes, in general, and color transitions from room to room are often bold in concept and application. Use colors and patterns to unify the overall look of a traditional style home.

The Traditional Palette

Greek temples inspired early traditional homes. White paint, suggestive of Mediterranean masonry buildings, was used plentifully inside and out. Visiting New England, Charles Dickens wrote that "every house is the whitest of the white." In bold contrast, Venetian blinds were "the greenest of the green." The simple classicism of Greek Revival soon lost its hold, and homeowners turned for inspiration from one quasi-historical period to another. Colors schemes became rich, bold, and highly romantic—deep reds and greens were paired, as were yellow and lavender. Black was used in combination with gilding. Designers continue to draw on the sophisticated Traditional color palette.

Holland Blue

Equator

White Thunder

Vermouth

Pastel Yellow

Drama Red

Blue Marble

Pine Branch

Ashes of Roses

Silver Mushroom

Pale Taupe

Woodleaf Green

Style: Traditional   19

Victorian

The Victorian era is defined as a period of excess. In full flower, Victorian style was oppressively dark, cluttered, and embellished. Victoriana drove designers and decorators toward the simpler forms and open spaces of the Prairie and Arts and Crafts movements that rose up in reaction to perceived excesses. Not until entire blocks of Victorian homes were leveled during urban renewal did Americans come to appreciate and reinvent the quirky boldness of this romantic time.

Scale was large in every aspect—big rooms, coffered ceilings, ornate moldings, highly carved, darkly stained furniture and woodwork, dense wallpaper patterns, heavy ornamentation of all kinds, ornately stained glass, oversized fringes and tassels, potted ferns, and knickknacks. Paintings with very romantic themes, photographs, mirrors, prints, and drawings, all with heavily embellished frames, were packed floor to ceiling, rather than placed at regular intervals along the walls.

The movement was named after England's Queen Victoria who ruled from the mid-19th to early-20th century. Victorian influence was felt into the 1920s. Several movements within the Victorian era were embraced by the popular imagination.

Most were revivals of historical styles. Gothic Revival, inspired by medieval times, was marked by carved tracery, dark wood, pointed-arch windows, and rigidly tall chairbacks. The Rococo and Renaissance Revivals brought increases in comfort, a less theatrical appearance, and softer color palettes. These revivals gave way to the lighter touch of the Eastlake style, which places far less emphasis on ornamentation.

The Victorian house was the homeowner's temple and expected to be an extension of the family's class and status in the community. Less was certainly not more, and no surface was left bare of objects. Even Tiffany lamps were festooned with glass beads.

Victorian style is all in the details, and there are a lot of them. Every surface sports an embellishment. Note the ornate staircase, the highly carved side chairs, the stained glass window, the criss-cross molding in the archway, the Oriental rug, and the paneled molding on the stairwell (left). The tall corner windows in the living room (below) with their single swags of sheer curtain are a lighter, more modern Victorian treatment, allowing ample light into the room while maintaining a 19th century feel.

Victorian bedrooms and bathrooms were a retreat from the world at large and the formality of the downstairs living spaces. Colors are softer and outside light plays an important part in the general ambiance.

Windows were elegantly dressed in layers of draperies, scarves, sconces, and shears.

Wallpapers were bold in color and pattern. Combinations of wainscoting, chair rails, walls and ceiling borders were popular. Ceilings were commonly papered as well.

Floors and woodwork in the main area of the house most often had natural finishes with elaborate inlays. Upstairs, walls, floors, and woodwork were painted.

Modern interior decorators and designers have distilled Victorian lavishness and scale to fit more comfortably in modern homes. Large vintage pieces are carefully selected and used sparingly for accent and effect. Paint, wallpaper, and fabric, when selectively used, can become elegant reminders of a time when excess was everything.

The Victorian Palette

Rich, somber paint colors include dark green, terra-cotta, and dark brown. Bolder salmon and lilac are used as accents. Darkly painted ceilings made the heavily furnished Victorian rooms seem even more cloistered. As a reaction to the harshness of early electric light which tended to empahsize the dark, and somewhat opressive color schemes, white paint for walls gained popularity late in the 19th-century.

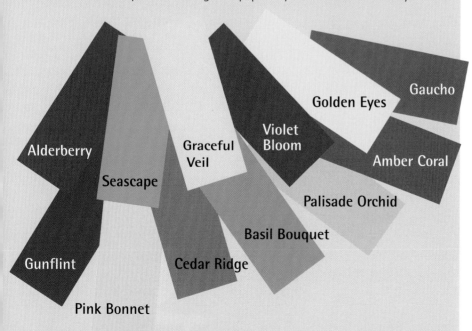

Gaucho

Golden Eyes

Violet Bloom

Alderberry

Graceful Veil

Seascape

Amber Coral

Palisade Orchid

Basil Bouquet

Gunflint

Cedar Ridge

Pink Bonnet

Arts and Crafts

The designers behind the Arts and Crafts movement (also known as Craftsman) were on a mission—to cure society of the excesses of Victorian style. The reactive movement, with its emphasis on simplicity and use of natural elements, caught the public imagination for about 15 years at the turn of the 20th century but is seeing renewed interest today.

Arts and Crafts style room layouts are open, with emphasis on horizontal lines. The interiors display sturdy columns and exposed beams, similar to the obvious joinery on Mission style and Arts and Crafts furniture produced by Gustav Stickley and other manufacturers. Fireplace faces are often tiled and commonly flanked with sitting niches, or Inglenooks—each with a bench. Doors are often massive and clearly handmade with large strap hinges and hardware.

The furniture is a clear break from the past, appearing strikingly functional and squarish rather than flowing and fanciful. In a show of honesty, pieces reveal huge mortise-and-tenon joints. Favored wood is oak—boards often quarter-sawn to emphasize grain. Clear finishes were used for Arts and Crafts style furniture, and character was further coaxed from the wood by fuming (smoking) to exaggerate the grain. The adjustable back Morris chair is the best known piece in the style. Cabinets with lead-glass doors are another distinctive example. Upholstery is typically leather, or geometric with highly stylized nature motifs influenced by Native American weaving. Fabrics include taffeta, chintz, and printed cotton.

White walls are at odds with the Arts and Crafts style. Paint or colorwash them with earth colors or cover them with grass cloth, burlap, or canvas. Wallpapers with themes related to nature are often used as a frieze. Indicative of the popularity of handcrafts during this period, stenciling played an important role. Decorative tiles with simple motifs adorned fireplaces.

Curtains made of sturdy fabrics, conspicuously hand-stitched, decorate windows. Unobscured windows again allow occupants to feel closely connected to nature.

Simplicity in detail and execution is the hallmark of the Arts and Crafts movement. Form and function are inseparable. Note the massive oak mantel above and its geometric supports. Geometry is also evident in the patterned mixed-wood border below.

Natural elements—
varnished oak,
ceramic tiles in a
color palette of earth
tones exude warmth
and comfort. Gently
tapered columns
frame the tub and
add an almost
classical sensibility.

Lighting casts a warm glow similar to candlelight of Colonial times. Well-known period lamps have shades of translucent mica, a naturally occurring mineral that creates a filtered amber light when light shines through. Bamboo and wicker shades create a similar effect.

Arts and Crafts' straightforward practicality has been called an early form of Modernism, but its intention was to present an alternative that was more human in scale and more in touch with the elements of nature. Arts and Crafts was, in truth, a reaction to Victorian style and a call to a simpler way of living.

The palette in this bedroom is muted and comfortable. The two basic colors are echoed throughout the scheme in the walls and trim as well as the striped fabric used for the bedspread and window treatments.

The Arts and Crafts Palette

Throughout the 1800s, homeowners became sophisticated in color choices. Options were broader than ever, as large paint companies produced standard paint colors with trendy trademarked names. Paint charts were common sales tools. And yet Arts and Crafts interiors drew from a relatively constrained palette. Because Arts and Crafts took its inspiration from the natural world and Native American handiwork, paint needed to look as if it came from the earth, herbs, and berries. For color ideas, look through fabric samples at stores that carry Arts and Crafts-inspired furniture; match the colors you like with paint samples.

Chartreuse

Briny

Mauve Nougat

Rice Cake

Fried Banana

Medallion

Claytile

Butter Crisp

Toscana

Saddle Soap

Trailblaze

Gray Comet

Contemporary

Like Traditional, Contemporary style embraces several waves of interior design, including Art Nouveau and Art Deco, which flourished in France and America during the first half of the 1900s, and the influencial Bauhaus movement in Germany. Architects and designers pared away centuries' worth of accessories and ornament and created a functional minimalism yielding a house famed architect Le Corbusier called "a machine for living."

In a clear break from the past, Contemporary homes use straightforward materials. Metal looks like metal, and plastic looks like plastic. Wood is clear finished without an effort to dress it up with stains, fuming (smoking), or graining. When patterns figure into the interior, they are geometric. Molding may be absent along the floors and around doors and windows. Architect Frank Lloyd Wright declared molding obsolete earlier in the century. Windows are large openings covered with plate glass, without muntins to define the break between indoors and out.

Uncluttered Contemporary rooms serve as settings to highlight a few prized art or antiques pieces; furniture is chosen for sculptural value and utility; beds rarely have head- or footboards. While framing art is common, pictures are often hung

White walls become showcases for works of art in contemporary settings. Uncluttered by molding and trim, tables and mantels become neutral spaces for display.

The Contemporary Palette

Similar to art gallery and museum walls, the walls of Contemporary homes are often painted relatively stark white or soft neutral—think of sand or unbleached muslin. The high-tech association with black turns up in the use of leather, plastic, slate, and lacquered wood, working particularly well in kitchens. The cool, calm moods of Contemporary rooms can be snapped to attention with loud, cheerful bursts of primary colors—in the manner of a Mondrian painting with red and yellow squares on a grid of black over white.

Ultra Pure White
Royal Turquoise
Knockout Red
Arrowroot
Radiant Daisy
Newtowne Brown
Warm Chinchilla
Bluebeard
Vivid Lime
Plum Paradise
Green Court
Dark Platinum

without frames. Some Contemporary homes draw on the high-tech look—commercial fixtures and furniture, retail store lighting, office chairs, conference tables, metal shelving, and restaurant equipment.

Interiors of sparsely furnished rooms with understated paint schemes can play a starring role. Open floor plans call attention to architecture, emphasizing the relationship between rooms and between the home and its environment. Walls may stop short of the ceiling or make use of wall cutouts and roof skylights to alleviate boxed-in rooms.

The simplicity can be restful. Quiet colors, horizontal lines, low-slung furniture, and muted colors are easy to live with. To further soften Contemporary rooms, mix friendly '50s-style furniture pieces with modern furniture and use nubby industrial-style carpeting on stark bare floors. Use carpeting either wall-to-wall, or small geometric design area rugs and bold dhurries to complement Contemporary rooms.

Alternating geometric forms define interior space and provide complex surfaces for strong color palettes.

If you find yourself dispensing with curtains altogether for a clean appearance, add narrow horizontal blinds for privacy and to keep the simple horizontal theme. For warmth, use wood slat blinds or select a color for the tape that holds the blinds together.

Lighting is high-tech and concealed—tiny halogen fixtures suspended from wires, metal trapezes, or airport runway fixtures. Tuck lighting into the ceiling, conceal it behind soffits, or direct it upward through oversized foliage.

Contemporary interiors are absent of clutter, though there may be a neat stack of art books on the floor or a folk art collection on the shelf. Rooms typically make excellent use of storage space, much as beds and tables are tucked away in traditional Japanese rooms. To arrange homes with clear, open spaces, plan adequate closets and cabinets. Unlike the complex and cluttered Victorian approach to display, place objects in a Contemporary setting minimally and give careful thought to the role each object plays in the overall look.

Walls

Section 2

Walls

Walls set the tone, mood, and style for your house. Off-whites create a modern look; wallpaper provides a Traditional, Victorian, or Colonial feeling; and painted trim says Country.

Paint has countless personalities—from a single rolled-on color to faux marble. Using wallpaper ranges from a simple border to a wallpaper chair rail to a whole-wall combination of patterns and colors. The possibilities are endless.

Moldings make a wall look elegant, old-fashioned, Country, or Victorian. Beaded-board wainscoting dresses up a Country kitchen or bath and creates a formal dining room. The vast variety of tile options offers a Southwestern, retro, or Arts and Crafts look.

This book starts with walls, and your decorating plan should as well.

Walls

Wall Prep and Priming

When it comes to painting walls, beauty is more than skin deep.

No amount of paint, whether it's the best quality or most expensive, will cover the flaws beneath it. There are no shortcuts. There is nothing more discouraging than noticing every ding, dent, or gouge on your living room wall after you roll on that can of expensive designer paint.

This chapter is the first step toward getting a good paint job. For the paint to stick, clean the walls thoroughly. Dust and dirt may not be noticeable, but they will prevent the formation of good bond between the new paint and the old. Mold, mildew, and stains that aren't sealed into the wall will bleed from one coat of paint into the next. Scrape flaking paint and fill the resulting dips along with other cracks and chips on the wall.

The same is true for wallpapering. Imperfections in the wall telegraph through the paper—a crack will appear as a wrinkle and a dent will appear as a wallpapered indentation.

Apply primer even if there's already paint on the walls. Primer is specifically designed to stick to the walls below and provide a surface for the new paint or paper to adhere to. Primers are formulated for different jobs; check with your paint supplier and make sure you use the right one.

Remind yourself that there aren't any preparation shortcuts and that if you want a good job, it's worth the time.

To guarantee a finished job you'll be proud to display, spend time and effort to prepare and prime the surface. Professional painters and plasterers suggest that preparation is 90 percent of successful and long-lasting jobs.

Prepping for Wallpaper

Good preparation is basic for good wallpapering. Remove grime; clean smoky or greasy surfaces; and patch, sand, and prime the walls before applying new wallpaper.

Removing old wallpaper will guarantee a good job. If the surface is in good condition, professionals frequently paper over the old. Painters often recommend painting over existing paper. If you decide to leave paper on the wall, make sure it is firmly attached to the wall, free of seams and dents, and generally in good repair. Clean vinyl and vinyl-coated paper the same way you clean painted walls. Remove nonvinyl papers—cleaning will do more damage than good. Although several products make removal easier, taking off wallpaper is an inexact science. Be prepared for a labor-intensive few hours and then be pleasantly surprised if the job is easy.

Good quality wallpapers hide many blemishes, but cracks and bumps aren't among them. Because wallpaper conforms to the surface beneath it, patch and sand the wall well after it's cleaned.

Prime the wall after it has been cleaned, patched, and sanded. Use a wallpaper primer tinted with a color close to the background color of the wallpaper to help hide slight mismatches in seams. Wallpaper primer is formulated especially for wallpaper applications; it gives the paper a better surface to grab onto and keeps the wall from absorbing water from the wallpaper paste. Neither wallpaper sizing nor regular primer does both jobs; choose the right product to prime the walls before rolling out the wallpaper.

Remove the old paper, repair cracks and holes, and hang a few rolls of wallpaper to make the room as good as new.

Walls

Prepping for Wallpaper

1 **Shut off power to the room at the service panel.** After the power is off, remove switch and outlet cover plates and any surface-mounted electrical equipment. **Remove as much dry paper as you can easily peel off.** Before you apply wallpaper, place masking tape over receptacles and light switches to keep out water and paste.

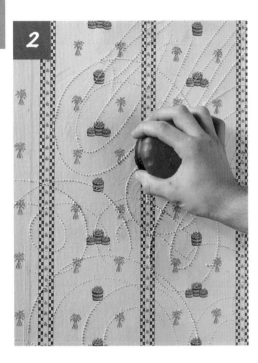

2 **Perforate the wallpaper.** Remove the old paper with the help a wallpaper removal solution that dissolves the paste. Some papers prevent the remover from getting through the paper to the adhesive, and some papers are held up by particularly strong paste. A perforating tool, such as the one shown, left, punctures the paper to allow the removal solution to do its job. Be careful. Run the tool over the surface just hard enough to perforate the paper. If you press too hard, you will gouge the drywall or plaster underneath, which will require repair before you begin to hang new paper.

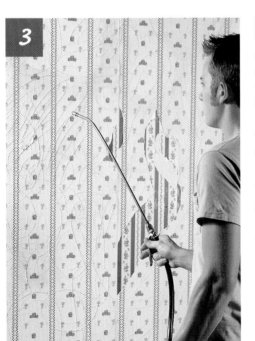

3 **Apply wallpaper remover.** To apply the remover quickly, easily, and least wastefully, spray it on with a garden sprayer. Or, apply the remover with a sponge or brush; in small areas, use a plant mister. Mix the remover with hot tapwater and pour it in the sprayer. Start in a corner of the room and work from the ceiling down. Spray the walls until they are soaking wet, but not dripping. Take your time to do a good job; the remover needs about 15 minutes to work. Spray the entire room again.

STUFF YOU'LL NEED

✔ Remover solution and sprayer for stripping wallpaper
✔ TSP cleanser, or equivalent, for greasy walls
✔ Paint primer
✔ Wallpaper primer
✔ 120-grit sandpaper
✔ Screwdriver
✔ Masking tape
✔ Newspapers or drop cloth
✔ Perforating tool
✔ Bucket
✔ Rubber gloves
✔ Sponge
✔ Broad blade putty knife
✔ Paint roller or broad brush

Wallpaper Remover Gel

Wallpaper remover gels are especially good for working in tight spaces. If you work near kitchen cabinets, for example, you can wipe on the gel without getting remover on the cabinets and possibly damaging the finish. Some people prefer the gel over the liquid and use it most of the time. Do not use wallpaper remover gel on vinyl paper; it doesn't soak through well enough to dissolve the paste.

Planning to put up wallpaper, and paint the ceiling and trim, too?
Paint the ceiling first to avoid getting paint on the fresh wallpaper. Then paint the trim. If you get a little paint on the wall, the wallpaper will cover it.

4 Peel off the paper. Start removing paper immediately after you spray the second coat. Depending on the paste and paper used, you may be able to pull off entire strips with your hands. On some paper, the paper will lift off in smaller sections. (See right.) Use a plastic putty knife or one of the many specialty wallpaper scraping tools to scrape off wide strips. (Be careful with metal putty knives and wallpaper scrapers with sharp blades; they can damage the wall.) After the paper is removed, wash the wall again and then patch, sand, and prime. (See "Cleaning and Repairing Walls," page 32.)

Good idea!

Wallpaper that has been applied over unprimed drywall usually pulls at least some of the paper facing from the drywall when it is removed. If this happens, there's little you can do to prevent it. Soak the wall thoroughly, and keep trying. If the damage is minor, apply joint compound over the damaged areas. If it's major, apply wallpaper liner—a thick, patternless paper that is applied horizontally across the wall. Paper over the joint compound or liner the same as you would an undamaged wall.

Patch, Sand, Clean, and Prime

Cracks and gouges in the wall will show through new paper.

Fill them with spackle or joint compound, spreading the material with a putty knife. Bridge wide cracks with fiberglass mesh sold for this purpose; then cover with spackle. (See "Drywall Repair," page 36, and "Plaster Repair," page 40.)

Lightly sand the patches and the entire wall to remove bumps.

Clean painted walls with Trisodium phosphate (TSP), the traditional cleaning solution. There also are cleaners that are phosphate-free. Cover the floor and baseboard heating units with a drop cloth. Protect your hands with rubber gloves, mix the TSP in water according to the directions on the box, and sponge the walls. Rinse until the rinse water is clear. (See "Trisodium Phosphate," page 35.)

When the wall is thoroughly dry, apply wallpaper primer. (See "Priming Walls, Ceilings, and Trim," page 49.)

Cleaning and Repairing Walls

Two of the most important jobs in the painting process are also the least dramatic. A painting or papering job is only as good as the prep that precedes it. Fresh paint reveals every shortcut you took, and no matter how much you pay for the store's best one-coat paint, cracks, dings, poorly patched areas, and paint-repelling grime will come back to haunt you. The bottom line is that there are no shortcuts.

First, wash the wall to remove grime that prevents the paint from sticking. Next, examine the wall surface carefully under the beam of a 100-watt trouble light. Fill dings and cracks with lightweight spackling compound and scrape loose paint. Lightly sand high spots, rough areas, and glossy surfaces with 220-grit sandpaper. When the walls are clean and dry, you're ready to prime. (See "Priming Walls, Ceilings, and Woodwork," page 49.)

Cleaning walls is similar to cleaning floors. Use soap, water, a sponge, and maybe even a scrub brush. Patching comes next; then the wall is ready for primer.

Walls

Cleaning and Repairing Walls

1 **Wash walls and scrape loose paint.** Put a tarp on the floor, wear rubber gloves, and wash the walls with a solution of TSP, or a similar phosphate-free product. This step is especially important if the room has been exposed to grease, smoke, soap, and handprints. Rinse well with clean water.

When the wall is dry, scrape off loose or flaking paint with a paint scraper or wide putty knife. The uneven surface left by scraping will show through the best new paint job. Fill depressions caused by scraping with a thin layer of surfacing compound. Sand lightly when dry.

2 **Fill the cracks.** Fill fine cracks with surfacing compound. Use paintable caulk, which retains flexibility, to fill cracks caused by substantial movement between walls or between walls and doors or window jambs. Cover wider cracks with self-adhesive mesh tape, spread surfacing compound over them, and sand to smooth the area.

Good idea!
→ **If you're not a caulking artist,** buy an inexpensive caulking tool. It's a small blade of plastic that is drawn along a bead of caulk to remove excess and to leave a consistent, professional-looking seam.

3 **Sand the walls.** Sand lightly to remove surface bumps, to smooth patches, and to lessen the sheen of glossy paint. Wrap the sandpaper around a commercial block, as shown, or fold the sandpaper and hold it against the palm of your hand. To hold the paper, rip a full sheet in quarters and then fold the quarters in thirds. Refold to expose new areas as each surface clogs with sanding dust.

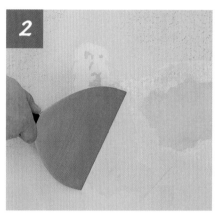

STUFF YOU'LL NEED

- ✔ Primer
- ✔ Oil-based stain blocker (to cover water stains and mildew)
- ✔ Trisodium phosphate (TSP)
- ✔ Surfacing compound
- ✔ Paintable caulk and caulk gun
- ✔ Bleach
- ✔ Tarp
- ✔ Rubber gloves
- ✔ Sponge
- ✔ Paint scraper
- ✔ Putty knife
- ✔ Self-adhesive mesh wall repair tape
- ✔ 120-grit sandpaper
- ✔ Masking tape
- ✔ Bucket

Wisdom of the Aisles

"Try the new lightweight surfacing compound for repairs. They don't shrink, they dry quickly, and they sand easily."

— *Mike Alfieri*
Temecula, CA

Cleaning and Repairing Walls

4 **Treat mildew and stains.** Washing doesn't remove stains left by mildew and water damage, and mildew will reappear if it isn't entirely removed. Sand the area and then scrub it with a mixture of half bleach and half water. Wear gloves to protect your hands from the bleach. To prevent water stains from bleeding through the paint, seal them with one of several types of stain blocker. Several types, including some aerosol products, are available in paint departments. Allow the stain blocker to dry on the wall for at least 24 hours.

5 **Spot prime and apply stain sealer.** Apply primer over plaster or drywall patches to seal off the porous surface and to provide the paint a good surface to adhere. If there are water or mildew stains in the wall, seal them with an oil-based stain sealer to keep them from bleeding through subsequent coats of paint.

TOOL TIP

Necessary sanding creates dust. To eliminate the dust, smooth drywall and plaster repairs before they set with a drywall wet sander. This tool is a sponge that has a coarse abrasive on one side and a fine abrasive on the other. When the drywall compound is firm and almost set, wet the sponge and ring it out until damp. Use the coarse side to level high spots; blend and smooth with the fine side.

Reappearing Cracks

If you have a problem with a recurring plaster or drywall crack, it's probably caused by the house settling on its foundation or by the wall flexing. If you live on the West Coast, seismic activity may be the culprit.

Enlarge small cracks in a plaster wall with a church key-style can opener or scraping tool. Create more surface area for the patching compound to bond with the wall by digging away some of the plaster beneath the finish surface, creating a wider groove near the lathe than on the finish surface.

For cracks more than $1/16$ inch wide, apply a flexible patch kit, available at home centers. A typical kit contains fiberglass tape, a paintlike patching compound, and a disposable putty knife or applicator. Apply the flexible patch by brushing the patching compound over the crack and 2 to 3 inches on both sides. Or, spray flexible compounds into the crack to help hold it together.

While the compound is still wet but has set, cut the tape to size and lay it into the patching compound. Push the tape flat against the wall with a wide putty knife or with the applicator supplied with the kit. Feather the edges for a smooth transition from wall to patch.

Most flexible patch systems require two coats. Let the patch dry about one-half hour before brushing on a second coat. Smooth it with the applicator. If the surface has taken on the texture of the mesh tape, wait one-half hour and apply a third coat to smooth it out. Finish with a drywall wet sander (See "Tool Tip," page 34.)

Walls

Trisodium Phosphate

Trisodium phosphate—or TSP—has long been the painter's cleaner of choice. It's effective, inexpensive, and easy to use. But, what is it?

It's soap—a very strong straight phosphate, nonsudsing soap. Too strong for the laundry, tough on hands, and great for walls. Soap has cleaning agents. (In hand soap, it was originally lye.) The agent in TSP is phosphate. Dishwasher detergent, for example, usually lists the amount of phosphate contained in the detergent. The higher the phosphate, the stronger the soap. Dishwasher repair personnel tell homeowners who have trouble getting dishes clean to use a higher phosphate detergent. Because phosphates are also fertilizers that cause algae

blooms in lakes, ponds, and streams, phosphate use has been restricted in some states, and manufacturers have created alternatives to phosphates in cleaning products.

TSP cuts through grime and soot, and it bonds with lead dust, making it easier to clean up. It's strong enough to damage varnish, so use it sparingly around woodwork. Because it's a soap, remove it entirely from the walls in order for the paint or wallpaper paste to adhere. Rinse the walls with clean water and a sponge or a sponge mop, and continue rinsing until the water runs clear. Use the sponge to get into the corners and edges, making sure that all the TSP residue is removed.

Drywall Repair

Traditional plastering was a messy, high-skilled job that required the house to dry out for weeks before painting. Then along came drywall, a thin manufactured sheet of gypsum sandwiched between two layers of paper. Although drywall sheets are notoriously vulnerable to breakage and crumbling, once you nail or screw them fast to studs and joists, they are largely out of harm's way. However, the chalky material will get dinged with exposure. You can fill small dents with lightweight drywall compound, then sand before repainting. Repairing larger problem areas involves cutting a drywall patch.

Wallboard walls look solid, but they're vulnerable to bumps, bangs, gouges, and dings. Repair is easy and, done properly, will make an old wall as good as new.

Drywall Repair

^^^^^^^^^^^^^^^^^^^^^^^^

STUFF YOU'LL NEED

✔ 2×4 scrap wood

✔ 3-inch drywall screws

✔ Drywall scrap

✔ Self-adhesive fiberglass drywall tape

✔ Lightweight drywall compound

✔ Fine-grit sandpaper

✔ Framing square

✔ Drywall saw

✔ Utility knife

✔ Electric drill or screw gun

TOOL TIP

When you hang drywall, the depth that the screw is driven is critical. Screw heads that break the paper facing have no holding power. If the screw isn't driven deep enough, the joint compound over it won't stick. Drywallers use a screw gun drill to make sure the screw is set just right. Spend less and achieve the same results with an inexpensive dimpler tool. The dimpler fits into the chuck of a standard drill to hold the screw and act as a depth stop, preventing the screw from breaking the paper and ensuring that each screw will leave a small dimple to fill with joint compound.

Prep Work

Fix the problem before you repair the damaged area. This may appear obvious for a doorknob that creates a hole in the wall. It is less obvious for damage caused by leaky roofs, for example. Solve the problem before patching to avoid continued repatching.

1 Outline the damaged area. Draw a rectangle around the area. The top and bottom of the rectangle should be an inch or so outside the damaged area. The sides should be centered over the studs on both sides of the hole.

2 Cut the top and bottom of the rectangle. Cut along the top and bottom lines with a drywall saw. The saw comes to point so that you can start the cut by forcing the tip through the drywall. It's easier to drill a hole inside the lines and start the cut at the hole.

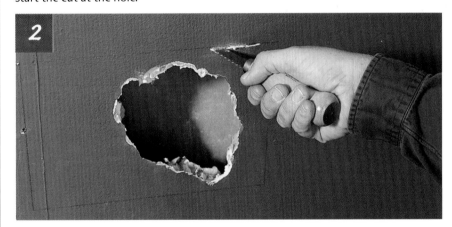

3 Cut out the sides. When the saw blade runs into the studs, make a mark and measure over $3/4$ inch. This is the center of the stud, and the line should be directly over it so both the existing drywall and the patch will have support. If necessary, redraw the line. Cut along the line with a utility knife. Don't try to cut through the drywall in one pass. Make several cuts, each one slightly deeper than the previous cut.

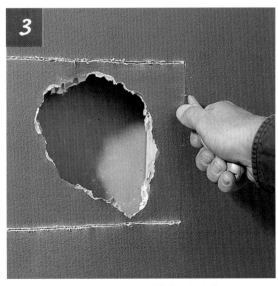

Drywall Repair

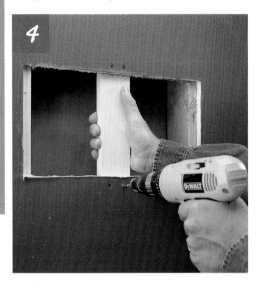

4 Cut supports. To keep the patch from flexing—and then cracking at the seams—screw wooden supports vertically across the opening. 1x3 or plywood scraps make excellent stiffeners. Cut them about 2 inches longer than the patch is high. Feed the support into the opening. Hold the support in place, and drive drywall screws through the drywall and into the wood. Be careful not to press the drill too hard; avoid driving the screw through the drywall. Now you are ready to cut the patch.

5 Cut the patch to size. Carefully measure the hole you've made, and use the framing square to lay out a same-size rectangle on a scrap of drywall. Use the utility knife to cut out the patch.

6 Install the patch. Use 1¼-inch drywall screws to attach the patch to the studs and to the board. Position the screws as far as possible from the edges to avoid splitting or crumbling the drywall.

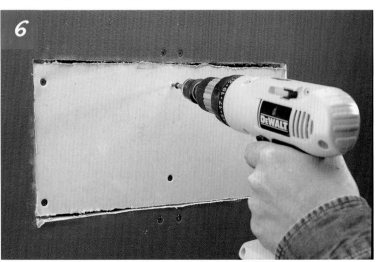

Carpenter's Secret

Fixing Nail Pops

Nails have a tendency to pop out as the stud holding them dries out. Nail pops, as carpenters call them, may reveal the head of the nail or may appear as if a small disk has been slipped under the drywall paper.

If you have a nail pop and can remove the nail from the wall without damage, do it. Drive a drywall screw an inch or so above and below the pop to secure the wall.

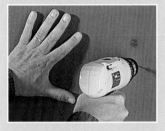

If the nail won't come out, drive it back in place with a hammer. Drive the nail just far enough so that the last tap of the hammer puts a slight dent in the drywall without tearing the paper surface.

Fill the dents or screw holes with joint compound. When the compound is dry, usually 24 hours later, sand or wipe the patch with a damp sponge to smooth it out. Prime and paint.

TOOL TP

Check out metal patch kits sold at most home improvement centers. They have a small metal plate that you screw over the hole. A thin skim coat of joint compound hides the plate—and between the two of them you have a patch that's as strong as it is easy to install.

7 Tape the joints. The seam between two pieces of drywall cracks unless reinforced. Run strips of self-adhesive fiberglass drywall tape around the patch, centering the tape on the seam. Spread joint compound across the patch and tape to create a smooth, flat surface. Let the compound dry overnight, and spread a second coat with a 9-inch knife. For the smoothest patch, spread a third coat with a 12-inch knife. Sand the surface to smooth out any irregularities.

Drywall Crack Repair

When you repair drywall, you have to make the situation worse in order to make it better. To fill a narrow drywall crack, widen it slightly to prepare a permanent fix.

1. Scrape along the crack with a cold chisel or an old screwdriver.

2. Fill the widened crack with lightweight surfacing compound, using your finger to apply it.

3. Smooth the area by applying one or more thin coats of the surfacing compound. When the patch is dry, sand and prime it.

Plaster Repair

The older your home, the more likely it is to have plaster walls. Depending on its age, the original plaster may have a horsehair binder.

A plaster wall is actually three layers of plaster meticulously applied over wooden strips called lath. Plastering an entire wall is highly skilled work, but with the right materials, repairing a plaster wall is well within a homeowner's skill.

Invest in good tools and the right materials. Surface and joint compounds are designed for other jobs and make a good plaster repair job next to impossible. For the best results use a powdered material called plaster patch. This compound has specially added adhesives that bond easily with the existing plaster to make a seamless repair.

A good plaster repair requires patience. Apply the compound in thin (1/8- to 1/4-inch) layers and let each layer dry thoroughly before you add the next. This will keep the compound from cracking and make the repair permanent.

Plaster walls were built to last centuries, but they aren't indestructible. Fortunately, the skills involved in patching holes and cracks are few. Make sure you have the right materials on hand.

1 Remove plaster from the damaged area. You can pry away most of the loose and cracking plaster with your fingers. Check to see if the remaining plaster is attached to the lath by trying to gently slip a 1-inch putty knife between the lath and plaster. (Be careful; pushing too hard may loosen more plaster, creating a larger area to repair.) If the knife slips under the plaster, pry gently to remove the plaster above it.

STUFF YOU'LL NEED

✔ Church key-style can opener
✔ Paint can opener
✔ Plaster scraping tool
✔ Spray bottle
✔ Plaster patching compound
✔ Cup or plaster pan
✔ Dust mask
✔ 4- or 6-inch broad knife or putty knife
✔ Nail
✔ 10- or 12-inch broad knife
✔ 150-grit sandpaper
✔ Drywall scrap (optional)

Plaster Repair

Planning Ahead

When Good Plaster Goes Bad

• Cracks and broken plaster are often signs of other problems—usually a settling house. Settling is normal. If the house continues to settle after you patch the wall, the wall will crack again, probably in the same place. If so, basement floor jacks near or underneath the recurring crack may eliminate the problem. Ask for advice from a pro at your home center.

• Brown spots or crumbly plaster usually indicate water damage—sometimes from the roof or a leaky pipe. Find and correct the problem before repairing the plaster to avoid having it happen again.

• When you repair a plaster wall, be prepared to remove all the loose material you find. Whatever is easily removed must be removed. This may mean removing a much larger section than you intended. If the hole is larger than the size of a broad knife (10 to 12 inches) fill it with a piece of drywall, as shown on page 43.

2 **Undercut the hole.** Using a church key-style can opener, paint can opener, or plaster scraping tool, undercut the edges of the hole to make it wider as it approaches the lath. This creates a void or notch under the good plaster, which will help anchor the plaster patch when you apply it later. Remove dust and debris.

3 **Spray the area with water.** Plaster and lath will draw water out of the patching compound, leaving you with a crumbling mass that won't stick. Soak the lath and the surrounding area with water to keep the patching compound from drying too quickly.

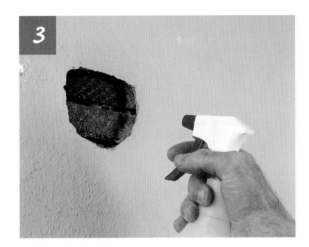

4 **Mix the plaster patch.** Wear a dust mask and avoid splashing the compound on your skin or in your eyes. If the hole to be patched is small, mix the compound in a cup. For larger holes, mix the compound in a pan made for holding plaster or joint compound. Put in the powder and stir in just enough water to form a paste. Stop stirring when the paste is smooth; overstirring causes the compound to set too quickly for easy application.

Plaster Repair

5 **Apply the patch.** Using a broad knife or putty knife, work the compound into the damaged area and press it through the spaces between the lath. Apply compound until the layer is about half as thick as the plaster.

6 **Score the surface of the wet compound with a nail.** The next coat will lodge in the grooves to create a mechanical bond in addition to the chemical bond that exists between coats. Let the patch dry thoroughly before applying the second coat.

7 **Apply the second coat.** After the first coat is dry, mix another batch of compound. Apply a second coat, filling about half the space between the first coat and the wall surface, leaving no more than a 1/4-inch recess. (See inset, right.)

Plasterer's Secret

Surface compound, joint compound, and plaster patch are easily confused with one another. Make sure you get the right one. Drywall compound is meant to be applied in thin layers between sheets of drywall, requires drywall tape as reinforcement, and will crack in thicker layers. Surface compound expands at a different rate than plaster and is less likely to crack. Use surface compound to fill small holes. Plaster patch is a combination of plaster and glue that bonds to existing plaster and lath. It sets quickly and doesn't crack even when applied in large areas.

Wisdom of the Aisles

"It's hard to know how much plaster to remove in order to make a repair around damaged areas. As a guideline, I remove plaster two inches in each direction beyond the hole. Unless you have a highly damaged wall, the damage seldom goes much farther."

— *Greg Korczak*
Lodi, NJ

8 Apply a final layer of compound. Let the second coat dry; then mix and apply a third coat. Smooth it with a 10- to 12-inch broad knife. Extend the edges of the compound beyond the edge of the original hole, feathering (tapering) and blending the edges flush with the wall. Wear a dust mask and sand lightly to complete the smoothing.

Patching Plaster with Drywall

Most plaster repair is a process of building up layers of plaster until the patch is thick enough to match the original wall. Work in layers $1/8$-to $1/4$-inch thick. Borrow a technique from drywall repair for large holes. Square off the damaged area with a hammer and cold chisel. Tap gently to remove only the damaged area. In the example shown, left, the lath is missing because the patch will be applied over an outlet opening that is no longer used. Unless the lath is already missing, leave it intact to provide extra support for the patch.

Get a scrap of drywall that is as thick as the plaster. Lay out a rectangle that is bigger than the opening in the wall by about 2 inches in each direction. Cut out the patch with a utility knife and snap it off.

Find the center of the patch and draw a rectangle slightly smaller than the opening in the wall. **Ⓐ**

Score along the line with a utility knife and pick away the plaster, leaving a 2-inch paper flange around the edge of the patch. **Ⓑ**

Test fit the drywall in the opening; make necessary adjustments. Lay plaster patch in the hole and trowel a layer on the wall larger than the flange on the patch. Put the patch in the hole, and screw it in place with drywall screws. Trowel the flange tightly against the wall with patching compound. Feather the edges and sand smooth when the patching compound is dry.

Choosing a Good Brush

You may have noticed the wide price range between cheap paintbrushes and top-of-the-line offerings. Expensive brushes have benefits that the bargain brushes don't.

Better brushes and rollers make painting go faster because the tools perform a superior job of distributing paint. You will spend less time dealing with loose bristles and roller fibers, and there will be less splattering, which means less cleanup. Most important, the final results look better.

A good, expensive brush will last a lifetime if you clean and store it well. (See "Cleaning a Brush," page 54.)

An angled sash brush, left, lays down a fine line of paint, as long as the short bristles are on the leading edge of the stroke. A trim brush, center, brushes in either direction, but lays down a wider swath of paint. Synthetic brushes, below, are for latex paint.

Anatomy of a Good Brush

Brushes have hundreds of moving parts—the bristles—which collectively draw paint from the can and release moderate amounts with each stroke. The bristles of good brushes are firmly anchored. For better control, they're tapered to a chisel point rather than a blunt end. Close inspection reveals that they have split ends to help carry paint.

Look closely at a brush before you buy it. A good brush has a reinforced, rustproof ferrule. Wooden spacer plugs separate the fibers. Flagged ends, which look fuzzy, help spread the paint. The ends have a chisel top that helps to control the paint.

The choice between bristle materials is simple. Use synthetic (nylon or polyester) bristles to work with water-based finishes; use natural bristles for alkyd-based finishes. Although foam brushes don't work as well as traditional bristle brushes, the low cost makes them good for touch-up areas.

Brushes are available in many shapes and sizes. For interior work, buy a 3-inch trim brush for painting the areas the roller doesn't reach (cutting in). Also select a 2- or 2½-inch brush for trim and windows. Trim brushes have either a square or angled end, and the choice between them is a matter of preference. Square brushes apply paint to the wall more quickly. Sash brushes, designed for painting window sashes, provide finer control when you lead the stroke with the shorter edge bristles.

Good idea! →

Using a Brush

You won't need special instructions in order to use a paintbrush.
Minutes after you start painting you'll begin to develop a technique that
suits you. A few tips will help produce better results and extend the life of
the brush as well.

Even a good brush is apt to shed a few bristles when it's new. To
avoid having to pluck them out of the wet paint, give the dry brush a few
good slaps against the palm of your hand.

**Don't dip the brush more than one-third of the way into the paint
or finish.** You won't speed up with a deep dip, and you will clog the base
(or heel) of the bristles—making it hard to clean and shortening its life. Tap
the loaded brush against the side of the bucket or can to shed excess.

Then Brush Away

Follow the wood grain when painting trim so that any texture left by
the brush is inconspicuous. Paint during the day; the higher light level
shows flaws, such as drips and bare patches, allowing you time to correct
them immediately. Supplement natural light with work lights as necessary.

Wisdom of the Aisles

"Shopping for
a roller is all
about nap.
Shopping for a
paintbrush is the
only time when
split ends are a
good thing."

— *Mel Sanders
Totowa, NJ*

"Use the best tools.
If you buy expensive
paint and a cheap
applicator, the result
will be bad-looking
expensive paint."

— *Jerry Allen
Tustin, CA*

*In addition to the usual types,
you'll find a few specialty brushes
in the paint department. Clockwise
from the top: a stencil brush, a
feathering brush, a stippling brush,
a dragging brush, and a small
stenciling brush. These are needed
for specialty finishes, rather than
for most paint projects.*

BRITISH MADE
3"

Walls

Spotting a Good Roller

Unlike purchasing a brush, buying a roller is a two-step operation. You need both the roller handle and the roller cover. It's easy to discover a quality roller handle. It fits comfortably in your hand and has a threaded hole in the base for an extension. Give the wire cage a spin; it should spin easily. Well-made rollers use bearings for less resistance. For most jobs, use the standard 9-inch-wide roller.

To choose a roller cover, look at the price and the appearance. Rub your hand over the roller. A good cover doesn't shed lint, and you should feel no obvious seam through the nap; seams can leave a pattern on the wall. Better covers are beveled at both ends instead of ending abruptly. The nap angles toward the roller core over the last fraction of an inch. Bevels prevent the edges of the roller from laying down an unwanted bead of paint.

The shape of the bar on a roller handle makes a big difference. The pressure from a bar that turns at 90-degree angles, such as the roller on the left, helps keep the roller cover from slipping off as you paint. An angled roller handle, such as the roller above, applies pressure unevenly and can push the roller cover off the handle as you paint. Flex the bar, as well as looking at its shape. The stiffer the bar, the better the roller.

Choosing a Roller to Match the Job

Note that the nap on rollers varies from $1/16$ of an inch to 1 inch or more. The fluffier the roller, the more obvious the texture it leaves on the wall. The choice of nap is also influenced by the surface you paint. Longer naps ($3/4$ inch or more) are recommended for textured walls, stucco, and poured concrete; short-napped rollers ($1/8$ to $1/4$ inch) are better for smooth walls and glossy paints.

Roller covers are available in several materials. For latex, choose a nylon roller. Nylon, wool, and lambskin blends are intended for alkyd finishes. For easy cleanup, purchase less expensive roller covers to toss after each use.

Spotting a good roller

Wisdom of the Aisles

"Even good roller covers shed some lint. Go over new covers with strips of clear packing tape until it stops picking up lint."

— *Lonnie D. Siemons*
Crystal Lake, IL

"Use the roller to flatten ridges made by the brush when cutting in. This means doing only a section of the room at a time so that the edges will still be wet when you roll."

— *Jerry Brennan*
Westminster, CA

Using a Roller

You can't just dip a roller in a can of paint the way you would a brush. There has to be some way of evenly applying paint all around the cover. The most common roller pan has a well for paint at its deep end and a ribbed surface over which the cover is run a couple of times to distribute the paint.

To save time when you have a lot of wall area to paint, use a 5-gallon bucket with a roller grid. Less time is spent pouring paint into the pan, and the grid is better for cleaning off excess paint.

Reach upper walls and ceilings with a roller handle extension. Also use the extension to reach lower sections of walls without leaning over.

Painting around the edges of the room is time-consuming. To speed up the job, use a beveled corner roller. This specialty tool looks like a doughnut on a handle, and it makes quick work of painting the tight spots that conventional rollers can't reach.

There's a roller for every job, even though they aren't named as brushes are. Find these as well as many other rollers at your home center. From left to right, the thin, tight-napped roller is for getting a smooth finish; the small roller is for tight spots. The blue foam roller is for use with textured paint. Next is a roller used to achieve special effects in faux finishing. Finally is the yellow general purpose, medium-napped roller.

Spotting a Good Roller   47

Walls

Painting Checklist

Painting is like any other home improvement project. If you're going to do the job, you must have the tools. You won't need everything on this list—you won't need a ladder to paint the floor, for example. Before you go to the home center, however, review the list, and double-check it against your shopping list.

Ladder	Fiberglass is strong and nonconductive—a plus if you're going to be doing some wiring, too. Wood is generally less expensive, lighter, and is also nonconductive. Aluminum ladders cost slightly more than wood and weigh less than wood or fiberglass. Don't use them for electrical work, however. They conduct electricity.
Drop cloths	Newspapers will do the trick, but not very well. Plastic-lined, paper drop cloths absorb spills and keep the paint from bleeding through to the floor. Canvas cloths are slightly more expensive but will last a lifetime.
Brushes	Use synthetic fibers for latex and bristle fibers for oil. You'll want a 2-inch brush for painting around the edges of a room. A sash brush is made for painting trim and around the edges of the room. An angled sash brush is easier to control than a standard sash brush. If you brush broad expanses, such as floors, use a 4-inch brush.
Rollers	Rollers make fast work of painting wide areas. Get a thicker nap for rough surfaces. A donut-shape corner roller makes quick work of painting an area you would otherwise have to paint with a brush.
Roller pan	Pans are available in plastic and metal. Plastic won't rust if you put it in a damp basement.
Roller bucket and grid	The bucket holds more paint than a roller pan; the grid is more aggressive when you roll off excess paint. You'll spend less time pouring (and spilling) paint out of the can, and buckets are harder to knock over than roller pans.
Roller handle	An extension that screws into the roller handle simplifies ceiling painting.
Plaster patch, surface, or joint compound	Plaster patch is for patching big holes in plaster; surface compound is for small holes and cracks. If the surface is drywall, patch with joint compound.
Glazing compound	It's the putty they make for holding glass in a window. Painters use it to patch nail holes because it's easy to use and dries quickly.
Putty knife or drywall knife	You'll need it to apply patch material. The wider the repair, the wider the knife you'll want.
Sandpaper	Get 120- or 180-grit for sanding repairs smooth.
TSP, sponge, bucket	If you don't wash the walls before you paint, the paint won't stick well. TSP is the traditional cleaner but can cause algae blooms once it travels from your drain to the water supply. Some states require the use of a phosphate-free alternative, which can be found in paint departments.
Wallpaper remover and garden sprayer	If you take down wallpaper, get an enzyme-based wallpaper remover. It soaks through the paper, dissolves the paste, and eliminates the need for steaming and heavy-duty scraping. Use a garden sprayer to apply it.
Masking tape	Look around the paint department—there are more kinds of masking tape than you ever imagined possible. Tapes for wallpaper, paint, short-term use, long-term use, and some with adhesive down only half the surface. Read the labels or ask for help if you have questions.
Stain blocker	Most primers cover a wall, but allow stains to seep through. If you've got any patches, water stains, smoke stains, or even sap that's bleeding through a wooden surface, apply a stain sealer.
Paint	No doubt you'll need paint if you're painting. Cleanup is easier with latex, which is water-based, and produces fewer fumes than oil-based paint.
Paint comb or pocket comb	When you clean brushes, clean paint buildup out of the area near the ferrule by dragging a comb through the bristles.

Priming Walls, Ceilings, and Trim

The first step to a good paint job is applying primer. It goes on like regular paint—and can even be tinted to match the top coat. Primer makes applying the final coat easier and can reduce the number of top coats required.

Although priming is vital to a lasting finish and a great-looking room, there are also sound economic reasons for a good priming job. If you spend $30 for a gallon of designer paint, you don't want to see stains or discoloration bleeding through because you didn't take the time to prime and seal the wall.

Primer isn't just a watery paint. It is formulated to adhere well to a variety of surfaces and seals them to prevent stains and discoloration from bleeding through the final coat. The finish coat sticks more effectively to a primed surface than it does to plaster, wood, or an earlier coat of paint. Priming not only adds to the durability of the paint job, it may prevent you from rolling on a second coat of finish paint—especially if you have the primer tinted the same as the color you've chosen.

Priming and painting will be more efficient if you follow a logical sequence. First, apply stain and varnish to any new trim to protect it from paint. (See "Natural Finishes for Woodwork," page 272.) Next, prime and paint the ceiling, proceed to the walls, and conclude with any trim that needs to be painted. Careful masking at each stage will allow you to work quickly and freely, saving time in the long run.

Sponging Off

Sponging off—like its partner ragging off (page 67)—is a subtractive technique in which a base coat is applied to the wall and allowed to dry. Then a glaze mix is rolled on and removed by blotting it away with a sponge until the desired effect is achieved. Sponging off is a great way to work a delicate pattern across a wall. Practice on a sheet of drywall that has primer and base coat added.

Remember, a hint of the base wall color will show through: this is a two-color or two-tone effect. Coordinate the two layers with some care. The closer the colors or shades of the base and top coats are to each other, the quieter the treatment. You can add more complexity and depth to the wall by lightly sponging on a second coat of glaze mix. Choose a third color, or mix up a different shade of the same color, by stirring in a different proportion of either glaze or white paint.

A base coat that has some gloss will give you more time to work. Prepare by masking the room's ceiling, trim, and adjacent walls so you can work freely and quickly.

Sponging off offers a more delicate and subtle finish because you see less of the base coat than you do with an additive application, such as sponging on.

Sponging Off

Walls

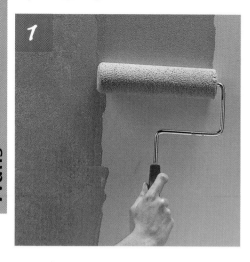

1 Test, prime, and base. Prepare the glaze mixture. You'll get both translucency and a longer working time by mixing glaze in the second coat. Manufacturers usually recommend mixing one part paint to four parts glaze, but you can add more glaze to increase the drying time.

After the base coat has dried, begin by rolling glaze on a small floor-to-ceiling section of wall, covering no more area than you can sponge off before the glaze mixture dries.

2 Lift the glaze with the sponge. Begin removing glaze by pressing the sponge against the glaze. Continually turn the sponge by rotating your wrist to avoid creating a repetitive pattern. Be sure to lift the sponge directly from the wall so that you don't smudge its distinctive effect. To reach into edges, use a torn piece of sponge to lift off glaze. Continue rolling and sponging off in sections. If a section starts drying out before you sponge it, mist the glaze with water from a spray bottle.

Good idea! →

If you sponge off a little too eagerly, the wall may end up with bald spots. Step back from the completed dry wall and look for spots that need paint. To fix the problem, lightly dab glaze on the areas with the same sponge you used to take off the glaze.

3 Clean and blot the sponge. A glaze-saturated sponge is less effective at making a pattern. Blot the sponge frequently with a lint-free rag or coffee filter. Sponge off the glazed area, blot the sponge as necessary, and then roll more glaze into an adjoining area. Rinse the sponge as necessary

STUFF YOU'LL NEED

- ✔ Low-tack masking tape
- ✔ Latex paint
- ✔ Latex glaze
- ✔ Measuring cup or paint bucket with measurements
- ✔ Roller
- ✔ Paint bucket and grid
- ✔ Natural sea sponge
- ✔ Lint-free rags or coffee filters

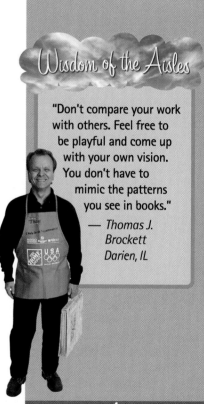

Wisdom of the Aisles

"Don't compare your work with others. Feel free to be playful and come up with your own vision. You don't have to mimic the patterns you see in books."

— *Thomas J. Brockett Darien, IL*

Prep Work

Sponging off requires a base coat that is rolled on the wall and allowed to dry. Make sure you have patched, sanded, and primed trouble spots before applying the base coat. It usually takes two coats of paint—or a coat of tinted primer followed by a coat of paint—to completely cover the painted wall. Don't rush this part of the job—your work will look only as good as the surface it covers.

Ragging Off

Ragging off is a subtractive technique and a traditional way of applying a two-color surface. You achieve the look by rolling a rag through a wet glaze to reveal the color underneath.

Ragging provides a great finish for hiding rough or uneven surfaces—though it doesn't hide bad prep work. Scrape, sand, and clean the walls as you would for any other paint job.

Rolling creates different effects depending on the selected colors and the wrinkles in the rag. While you can use any rag, a clean cotton material, similar to that in T-shirts, handles well and absorbs the glaze nicely. Like all faux techniques, ragging is labor intensive. Be patient and pace yourself as you work.

Practice, as always, makes perfect. Before you commit to painting a large wall, experiment on several sheets of poster board taped together or an extra sheet of drywall or hardboard.

Ragging off is a great choice for rooms with natural light. The technique adds richness to almost any wall. If you like the look, practice the technique to gain confidence before tackling the project.

Ragging Off

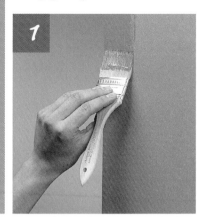

1 **Brush the glaze mixture into corners.** Brush a two- to three-inch wide strip in places where the roller will not reach—the corners, near the ceiling, and along the woodwork, for example. Cut in about 5 to 10 feet at a time and then roll on the paint, as described in Step 2, so the cut-in area and the rolled have the same effect. Rolling into a dry cut-in strip results in an obvious difference between the brushed and rolled sections.

2 **Roll on the glaze.** Put some glaze in a paint tray, use a short-napped roller, and roll a two-foot wide section of wall from floor to ceiling. Work the roller into cut-in areas, removing as many of the brush marks as possible. The glaze can become too dry to work in as few as 15 minutes. For more efficient results, use two people—one to roll and one to rag.

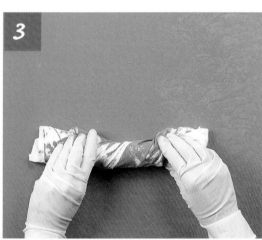

3 **Roll the rag along the wall.** Loosely roll the rag into a cylinder, leaving it partially wrinkled. (See photo, left.) The amount and size of the wrinkles aren't crucial, as they change while you roll. Practice on a scrap of painted and freshly glazed drywall to get the feel for the best way to handle the rag.

Start at the bottom of the wall and roll the rag through the fresh glaze toward the top. The surface of the rag will fill with paint as you work. When the entire surface of the rag is wet, turn it inside out. When the rag becomes saturated, replace it.

For more depth and texture, allow the first coat to dry and then apply a second glaze color over the first coat.

STUFF YOU'LL NEED

- ✔ Low-tack masking tape
- ✔ Semigloss latex base coat
- ✔ Latex in second color to mix with glaze
- ✔ Latex glaze
- ✔ 2-inch synthetic fiber trim brush
- ✔ Roller and handle
- ✔ Roller tray
- ✔ Clean, lint-free cotton rags
- ✔ Drop cloth

Painter's Secret

If you run into isolated spots that dry too quickly, spray a fine mist of water onto the glaze with a spray bottle. If the mixture dries too quickly, add more glaze.

*Designer's Tip

For a subtle look, use colors that are close in tone.

For impact, use high contrast colors. Experiment and practice on old boards or cardboard to achieve the combination and technique you prefer.

For more visual depth, use a third color.

Colors That Work Together

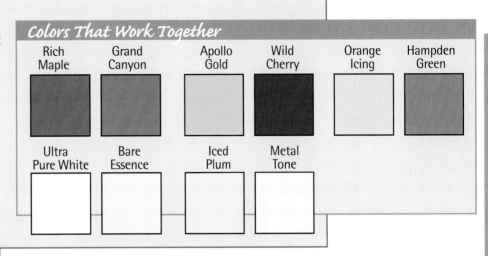

Rich Maple	Grand Canyon	Apollo Gold	Wild Cherry	Orange Icing	Hampden Green

Ultra Pure White	Bare Essence	Iced Plum	Metal Tone

Original Idea – Frottage

1 Roll the glaze mix on the wall; cover a section that is a little larger than a section of newspapers.

2 Press the newspaper onto the wall. Smooth out the newspaper, and let it absorb some of the paint.

3 Peel off the newspaper to reveal the final look.

Frottage is one of the oldest and most dramatic variations of ragging on and ragging off. Begin with a base coat, just as you use for ragging off. Use newspaper pages to create pattern and texture. Make the glaze mixture by mixing two parts paint and one part water.

Ragging On

Ragging on is an additive technique, which is the opposite of ragging off. Instead of removing paint by rolling a dry rag along the wall, you add a glaze mix by rolling a paint-filled rag along the wall.

There's a less labor-intensive technique for both ragging on and ragging off. Instead of working the rag with your hands, wrap it around a paint roller, fix it with rubber bands, and work the rag and roller across the wall. To rag on, coat the rag with the glaze mix and roll it along the wall—changing it when the rag becomes too wet. To rag off, apply a base coat, and after it dries, apply a second color. While the second color is still wet, move the roller across the surface, replacing the rag when it becomes saturated with glaze mix.

Any texture of rag will work, but it's easiest to use a clean, lint-free cotton rag—old T-shirts or cheesecloth are perfect.

The base color of this wall breaks through the glaze to mimic stone. Use a rag-wrapped roller and change base or glaze colors to create the look.

STUFF YOU'LL NEED

✔ Latex base color
✔ Latex second color
✔ Latex glaze
✔ Measuring cup and container for mixing
✔ Rag
✔ Paint roller or roller core and roller handle
✔ Rubber bands
✔ Paint tray

Colors That Work Together

The colors in each palette are shown in the order you apply them, left to right.

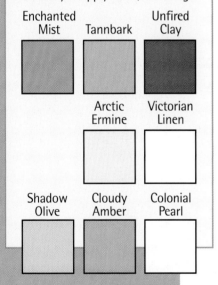

Enchanted Mist	Tannbark	Unfired Clay
	Arctic Ermine	Victorian Linen
Shadow Olive	Cloudy Amber	Colonial Pearl

Prep Work

Clean, repair, and prime the wall before you apply the base color, using either latex or oil-based (alkyd) primers. Sand the primer to get a smooth base. Oil sands easier than latex, but is more difficult to clean up, takes longer to dry, and has a stronger smell. Most homeowners prefer latex. After the primer has dried, apply the base color. See "Colors That Work Together," above, to choose colors for the ragging.

Ragging On

1 **Wrap a T-shirt or other cotton rag around a low-nap roller made for applying contact adhesives.** Wet the rag and twist it as you wrap it around the roller, wrinkling it as much as you can. Slip rubber bands around the roller and rag and conceal them into the rag creases to keep them below the surface.

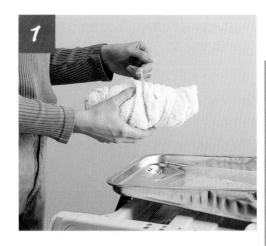

Good idea! ↙

A slightly damp rag will absorb the glaze mix better than a dry rag. Dip the rag briefly in water and then roll it along the wall to remove excess water. (Do this on a section of wall that will be ragged last, and allow that section of the wall to dry before ragging.) Put the roller in the pan and load it with paint the same way you would load a regular roller.

2 **Dip the roller in the glaze.** Similar to other special paint effects, the second coat—the ragged coat—consists of a glaze-thinned paint. The glaze makes the second color more translucent and slows the drying time of the paint. Mix one part paint to four parts glaze, and pour it into a roller pan.

3 **Roll glaze onto the wall, working from top to bottom.** To avoid painting stripes or columns, roll at a slight angle (below) and occasionally step back to look at the wall, making sure you do not create roller patterns.

Color Wash

Color washing offers one of the subtlest special painting techniques. With its gradual variation of color and darkness across the wall, it suggests aging but has a light and airy look that doesn't appear antiqued or contrived.

In this project, glaze is washed over the base coat with a sponge to introduce a variation in color. Once the glaze is applied, the wall is smoothed over to soften the effect. Here, a feathering brush does the smoothing; however, a crumpled piece of soft, cotton fabric works well, too.

Introducing another warmer or slightly darker color around the perimeter of the wall and blending it to add a fine touch gives the further impression of history, age, and tradition. Adding texture to the paint further ages the look.

Color wash is usually used to simulate age or to give a wall a soft, warm look. One shade of color blends and mixes into the next shade on a color-washed wall.

Color Wash

STUFF YOU'LL NEED

✔ Stepladder
✔ Painter's masking tape
✔ Latex paint for base coat
✔ Latex paint for glaze mix
✔ Latex glaze
✔ Measuring cup
✔ Paint roller
✔ Paint bucket with roller grid
✔ Feathering brush
✔ Lint-free rags or coffee filters
✔ Drop cloth

Prep Work

Clean the walls, fill all cracks, prime, and sand. A rough background shows through any finish and is especially obvious with color wash. Mask adjoining areas that will not be color washed.

Colors That Work Together

The colors in each palette are shown in the order applied, left to right. The third color is an optional edge glaze.

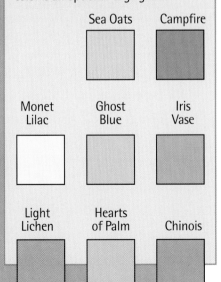

Sea Oats	Campfire	
Monet Lilac	Ghost Blue	Iris Vase
Light Lichen	Hearts of Palm	Chinois

1 **Practice the technique, prime, base, and prepare the glaze.** Roll on the base coat. After it dries, mix the second paint shade with latex glaze in a ratio of one part paint to four parts glaze. Pour a tablespoon or two of the glaze mixture onto a plate and dip a sponge into it.

2 **Glaze a section of wall.** Define a wall section by arm length. Allow variation in the pattern and density of the glaze. Sponge in circles, random patterns, or horizontal and vertical stripes. Work quickly to blend wet edges into the adjoining areas.

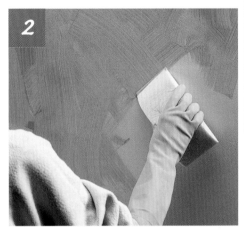

3 **Blend the glaze with a brush.** Finish the section; then continue glazing and brushing in sections. Soften the texture of the wall by going over the wet glaze with a feathering brush, working the brush in all directions. Periodically clean the brush on rags or paper towels.

The more complex and subtle the colors on the wall, the more genuine the patina effect. Sponge on a second color after you've brushed out the first. The first two hues can be combined to create a mixture for a third coat. Let each coat dry before applying the next.

Good idea!

4 **Reglaze the edges.** The wall will look as though it has aged gradually and gracefully if its edges are warmer in hue and slightly darker. Mix a new glaze, similar to the one you used, sponge it on, and smooth with the dry brush.

Walls

Dragging

Although some decorative paint finishes consist of unusual techniques or materials, dragging simply involves pulling a paintbrush through wet glaze to create fine parallel lines. These lines reveal the background wall color, typically a lighter shade. The closer the paint and glaze are in color, the quieter the effect.

You can buy a special-purpose dragging brush, or use a new, high-quality paintbrush. The work goes more smoothly if you have a helper—one rolls on a vertical strip of glaze, while the other drags a brush through the previous strip. Because it can be tricky to drag a continuous course from floor to ceiling—unless the ceilings are very low or you are very tall—you might consider dragging only the portion of the wall below a chair rail (see Step 4, page 76). This spares you the trouble (and exercise) of going up and down a stepladder. Before rolling paint, mask the ceiling and trim. Also, mask any adjacent walls that you are not dragging.

Dragging is a subtle technique. To make a more dramatic pattern in the wet glaze, see "Combing," page 77.

Dragging a dry brush through a wet glaze leaves a subtle pattern if the base color and the glaze are similar and a stronger pattern if the colors are farther apart.

Walls

Dragging

1 **Test the technique, prime and base coat the walls, and prepare the glaze mix. Apply the glaze mixture over the base coat.** The lighter color shown is the base coat. Use a semigloss paint that absorbs the next glaze coat slowly and allows longer time for dragging. (See "Colors That Work Together," page 73, for suggested color schemes.) After the base coat has dried, mix one part glaze to two parts paint. Roll the mixture on a limited area of the wall—only what you can drag before the mixture dries. Begin with a floor-to-ceiling strip the width of the roller until you become comfortable with the process.

Have the store tint the primer the color of the top coat. Primer won't hold as much color, so it will look lighter. Even so, the top coat usually covers tinted primer in just one coat.

Good idea!

2 **Drag a long-bristled brush through the glaze.** Start at the top of the strip and drag a dry brush through the wet glaze. Apply enough pressure so the bristles bend as you drag the brush. Although slight unsteadiness of hand adds pattern interest, avoid having the brush stray too far from the vertical.

3 **Start the next strip.** Remove excess glaze from the dragging brush by wiping it on a lint-free rag or paper towel. Roll and drag the area next to the first, working across the wall. Dry the brush on a lint-free rag after each pass, or as necessary.

STUFF YOU'LL NEED

✔ Semigloss latex paint for base coat
✔ Flat latex paint for second color
✔ Latex glaze
✔ Stepladder
✔ Painter's masking tape
✔ Measuring cup or paint bucket with measurements
✔ Paint roller
✔ Paint bucket with roller grid
✔ Wide paintbrush
✔ Paper towel or lint-free rags

Wisdom of the Aisles

"Relax and have fun when you drag paint. If you don't think about what you're doing, you'll get better results."

— *Josephine Jackson Bronx, NY*

Prep Work

Don't let a bad prep job ruin your work. Wash the walls, repair all problems, apply a primer, sand, and apply two coats of the base color.

Glaze Paint Ratios

There are varying opinions about the glaze to paint ratio for dragging. Glaze manufacturers recommend one part glaze to four parts paint. Some experienced painters prefer eight parts glaze to one part paint because the ratio slows the drying, allowing more time to work. Other painters prefer one part glaze to two parts paint for a thicker mixture and pronounced brush strokes. Experiment with different mixtures on scraps of hardboard, drywall, or cardboard to find the mixture you like best.

Walls

Dragging

Painter's Secret

Does your handiwork look a little too harsh? While the glaze is still wet, go over the dragged areas again. This time, hold the brush nearly perpendicular to the wall and move it at a slight angle to the dragged lines.

4 **Brush upward when working below a chair rail.** Hold the brush as shown and drag upward to drag the area below a chair rail.

5 **Brush horizontally for a fabric effect, if desired.** Achieve a woven fabric look by going over wet, just-dragged areas with horizontal strokes. Because this added dragging takes more time, you may want to increase the proportion of glaze to paint to extend the mixture's drying period.

Wisdom of the Aisles

"When doing faux finishes, you'll have more consistent results if the same person works with the brush, rag, or sponge for the whole job. If you use a helper, make the change on adjacent walls. You'll get a nicer blend."

— *Dale Solomon San Diego, CA*

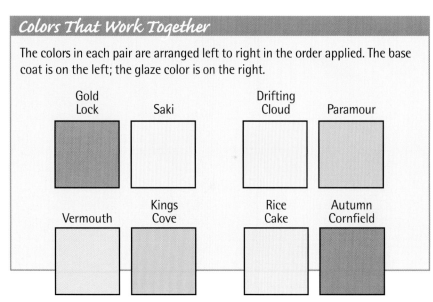

Colors That Work Together

The colors in each pair are arranged left to right in the order applied. The base coat is on the left; the glaze color is on the right.

Gold Lock	Saki	Drifting Cloud	Paramour

Vermouth	Kings Cove	Rice Cake	Autumn Cornfield

Combing

Combing tools were developed to mimic wood grain. They also lend themselves to dragging evenly spaced lines into a coat of glaze or paint to create geometric designs, stripes, plaids, checkerboards, and weaves.

In this mudroom, combing is used on alternating bands down the wall to the chair rail. (Small areas are easier to comb, especially if you are inexperienced with this technique.) The darker bands are the semigloss base coat to which nothing else has been done. The lighter bands were rolled with a lighter paint, and a comb was dragged through them. A single pass with the combing tool creates a simple ribbon effect; additional curving passes create the optically dazzling moiré effect, below.

Buy specialized combing tools with notches of various sizes and spacing; look for them in paint departments and art supply stores. Or, make your own durable comb from a window squeegee. (See "Painter's Secret," page 79, for details.) Experiment. The look you want is up to you.

Walls

This sophisticated moiré effect is simpler than it looks. Most faux painting techniques work well for creating stripes.

Combing

1 Test the technique, prime, and lay out the bands. Roll on a semigloss base coat and allow it to dry thoroughly; the sheen absorbs the next coat of paint

more slowly for added time in combing. Use the width of the squeegee to lay out the width of each band, starting in a corner. Or, measure the width of the wall and divide it into even vertical spaces. Narrower bands are easier to comb because they are smaller areas to work before the paint dries. For marking, use a pencil color that is almost the same color as the base coat.

2 Draw the lines between bands. Working from the marks you made to determine the band widths, use a level to lay out vertical lines.

When laying out a decorative painting project, use a pencil that is the same color as the paint; the lines will disappear. Don't use pens and grease pencils; the marks will bleed through.

Good idea!

STUFF YOU'LL NEED

- ✔ Stepladder
- ✔ Low-tack masking tape
- ✔ Semigloss paint for base coat
- ✔ Carpenter's level
- ✔ Glaze
- ✔ Measuring cup or paint bucket with measurements
- ✔ Paint roller
- ✔ Paint bucket with roller grid
- ✔ Roller pan
- ✔ Window-washing squeegee or comb
- ✔ Razor knife
- ✔ Lint-free rags

TOOL TIP

Commercially made combs are great tools.

Triangular combs have different size teeth on each side. Others look like traditional combs.

Although professionals use commercial combs, they also make their own. Use a squeegee and a piece of cardboard, or try whatever works—including real combs.

Colors That Work Together

The colors in each pair are arranged left to right in the order you apply them. The base coat is on the left; the color on the right is the top coat.

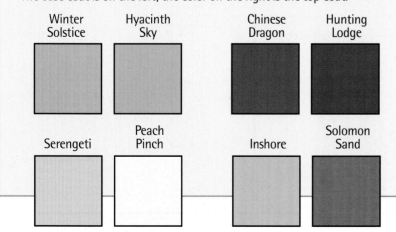

Winter Solstice	Hyacinth Sky		Chinese Dragon	Hunting Lodge

Serengeti	Peach Pinch		Inshore	Solomon Sand

Prep Work

The more complicated the paint job, the more important it is that the surface is smooth and defect-free. Paint doesn't hide irregularities—they show through, interrupting the pattern you're creating. Patch, prime, and sand before applying two coats of the base color.

Painter's Secret

Making a Custom Comb

Purchase a standard window squeegee from a hardware store or home center; they come in several different widths. Use a ruler to mark off the teeth and the spaces between them. Cut the notches with a razor knife. Typically, the notches are V-shaped with narrow teeth between them. Although the teeth and spaces are usually consistent, irregular cuts create a different look.

3 **Tape off the strips.** Use low-tack masking tape along the outside edges of every other band. Painters prefer low-tack tape because it doesn't pull off paint like conventional masking tape. Low-tack tape is usually blue, but it often comes in white and different grades. Some are designed for wallpaper while others are designed to be taken down within a day. Read the label, and select tape that can be left up for awhile. If you don't finish the job immediately, you won't have to retape. The tape should be the widest you can find to prevent accidentally rolling paint onto adjacent strips.

4 **Roll on the paint.** Use a roller to apply paint that contrasts with the base coat. (See "Colors That Work Together," page 78, for suggested color schemes.) If you wish, mix glaze with the paint to slow drying, add translucency, and provide luster to the finished effect. Work one square at a time, rolling on the paint and combing one square before rolling paint on the next.

Combing

5 **Comb the first pass.** Use a commercial combing tool or a notched squeegee to drag a continuous course from floor to ceiling. To guide your hand in making a straight line, run the tool along a board that is cut to the height of the wall. The combing should allow the base coat to show through (right). After each pass, remove the paint from the comb with a lint-free rag.

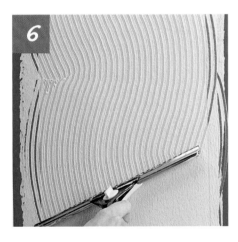

6 **Comb the second pass.** Begin again at the top of the wall and drag the tool in a series of even curves.

7 **Comb the third pass.** For an intricate moiré pattern, make a series of curves the mirror opposite of those just completed. When you finish, move on to the next square.

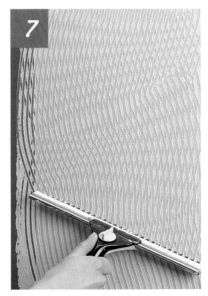

Wisdom of the Aisles

"Have a rag handy to wipe the paint from the comb after each pass."
— *Edna Atkins*
  Willow Grove, PA

Planning Ahead

Plan ahead as you comb. A horizontal pass from one corner to another is easy—just walk along the wall. A pass from floor to ceiling usually involves a ladder, and keeping the pattern consistent as you climb up and down is impossible without a guide. To comb from floor to ceiling without a guide, devise a freehand pattern that doesn't demand definite vertical lines.

Combing a Traditional Basket Weave

By combing squares horizontally and vertically, you can create a basket weave or checkerboard that effectively ornaments small areas. The wall below a chair rail is shown.

1 **Use a level to draw a grid for the squares of the design.** Make the sides of each square equal in length to the combing tool you use. Use low-tack masking tape to mark the top and bottom horizontal lines on the wall. **A** Mark the top run of tape for a guide for combing the squares, and use the level **B** to draw the verticals from the top run to the bottom run.

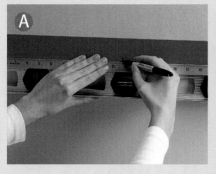

2 **Roll on the paint** and draw the comb vertically through every other square. Clean the comb frequently. Concentrate to avoid dragging the comb past the masking.

3 **While the paint is wet,** drag horizontal lines in the remaining squares. Use the comb length to define the size of the squares, making it easy to control the comb as you drag out the design.

Combing a Traditional Basket Weave

4 **For smaller spaces,** or for squares that leave part of the space unfinished, make a smaller comb from cardboard and drag a narrow row of rectangles. To match the pattern created in the adjoining larger areas, use the teeth in the longer tool as a guide.

5 **Cut the notches carefully with sharp scissors or a utility knife.** Make the cuts as precise as possible; otherwise, paint will leak through.

6 **Run the cardboard in** alternating directions as for the full-size squares. Plan to replace the comb if you work in a large area. The paint causes the comb to flex and the teeth to soften.

Stippling

Stippling is a subtractive finish. You apply glaze and then take some of it off—in this case by pouncing or bouncing the ends of a finely bristled stippling brush through the wet glaze. It's in the same family as sponging off and ragging off but creates a more finely textured surface. It also takes more work because it requires pouncing the brush over every square inch of the freshly glazed wall.

A stippling brush has long bristles that cover a good bit of area with each pounce. Stippling brushes are relatively expensive, but to get the right effect there is really no substitute. An edge stippler, another special-purpose tool, has a narrow design that makes it easier to pounce along the edges of the wall.

For the more adventuresome, stippling also can be an additive effect. A brush is dipped into the glaze mix and applied to the wall by lightly slapping the bristles against the palm of your hand, splattering tiny drops of paint on the base coat.

A stippled finish owes its looks to two coats of finish. The second coat is partially removed while it's wet, by pressing the ends of a brush into it.

Stippling

Walls

1 **Practice and prime. Apply a semigloss base coat.** Mask off adjoining walls, the ceiling, and trim. Brush on semigloss paint near the masked areas, and roll paint over the remaining walls. For best results, brush short sections, and then roll out as many of the brush strokes as possible. Finish rolling the area, and paint more of the edges with the brush.

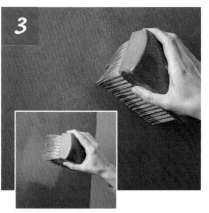

2 **Roll on the glaze.** Mix paint and glaze (see "Using Glazes," page 64). Roll a section of the wall with the mixture, covering only as much area as you can stipple before the surface begins to dry. Brush on the glaze near the edges. Apply it elsewhere with a 3/8-inch roller or with a foam roller. For a lighter finish, use less glaze and apply it in random swirls with a paintbrush. For a two-tone finish, with the main wall color shading into another hue around the edges, follow the technique given for "Color Wash," pages 72-73.

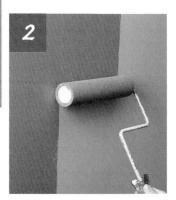

3 **Stipple the glaze.** Work from top to bottom of the wall, pouncing the brush, so that you feel a rebound from the bending bristles (inset). Push gently to finely freckle the existing layer of glaze. The overall effect on the wall should be even. Turn your wrist between each application of the brush to avoid creating a pattern.

4 **Remove excess glaze from the brush.** A loaded brush won't leave a finely textured surface. Use a rag frequently to absorb excess finish from the bristles and to lighten the overall effect of the wall. Clean the brush after every five or six pounces.

5 **Stipple the corners.** Move along the wall, rolling and stippling, section by section. When you get to the corners, use a small, stiff-bristled brush to stipple around the edges of the wall, where the large brush can't reach.

STUFF YOU'LL NEED

✔ Stepladder
✔ Low-tack masking tape
✔ Latex paint
✔ Latex glaze
✔ Measuring cup or paint bucket with measurements
✔ Edging brush
✔ Roller
✔ Paint bucket and grid
✔ Stipple brush
✔ Edge stippler
✔ Lint-free rags

Colors That Work Together

The colors in each palette are shown in the order applied, left to right.

Red Rockies	Tyrian Pink
Cottonfield	King Neptune
Graceful Veil	Saki
Cream Sash	Spiced Peach

Work Smarter

This technique is time-consuming for an entire room. To prevent the finish from drying before you stipple, ask a helper to roll on the glaze in the area just ahead of you. If you switch positions mid-job, make the change on an adjacent wall.

Faux Marbling

Marble paneling in homes has been a statement of luxury and elegance for centuries. For most homeowners, marble has been beyond their means, especially for large-scale use.

Faux marbling is an affordable way to create the look of fine stone. The depth and variety of color in natural marble allows faux painters a great deal of freedom to create looks that range from striking and dramatic to simple and understated. Marble tiles possess many different colors and much variety of combination embedded in the stone. The wainscoting treatment shown here creates dark green marble panels set in a green limestone frame. Wainscoting, which refers to the siding on a wagon, was applied to protect walls from everyday wear and tear.

Faux marbling is a simple technique, especially if you practice. The most common is to sponge on layers of color. The method in this project uses a sheet of plastic—a variation of a classic paper technique called frottage. (See "Frottage," page 69.) The directions suggest a couple of variations that add color and depth to the finished look. The frame around the panels has been stippled to resemble limestone, and the wainscoting has been capped with a chair molding.

The key to imitating marble is to capture the stone's natural colors and diagonal veining. In the faux marble at left, glaze was applied over the base color and then blotted off with a plastic sheet. The veins were handpainted and softened with a feathering brush.

Walls

Faux Marbling

1 **Practice the technique. Paint the frame and lay out the panels.** Prepare and prime the walls and nail a chair rail in place. (See "Installing Chair and Picture Rails," page 132.) Base coat the chair rail, baseboard, and walls. The stippled frame is a two-coat process. First apply the base color over the entire area. When the base color dries, mix paint and a latex glaze, and roll it on the walls. Wet a stippling brush in water and push it into the wet paint to get the look you want. Stipple the area in and around the stiles, but not the entire wall. (See "Stippling," page 83.)

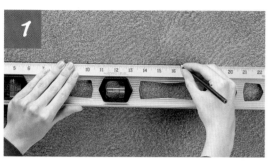

Let the paint dry completely; then lay out the marble panels with a pencil and level. The panels shown are 5 inches below the chair rail, 20 inches wide, and 22 inches high, with a 6-inch-wide stile separating them.

After laying out the panels, mask the stiles. Use a low-tack tape around the panel, aligning the inside edge with the outside panel edge.

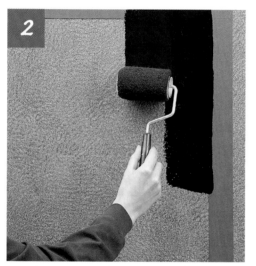

2 **Apply the marble base color.** Marbling begins with a base coat of color that peeks through subsequent coats. Select the color, roll it on the panels, and let it dry thoroughly.

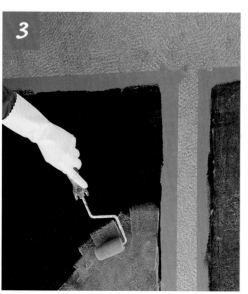

3 **Mix and apply the glaze.** The glaze mixture applied over the base is one part paint to four parts glaze. Roll it on only one panel at a time so that the glaze doesn't dry out before you finish working with it.

STUFF YOU'LL NEED

- ✔ Latex semigloss paint for frame base coat
- ✔ Latex paint for second color of frame
- ✔ Latex semigloss paint for marble base
- ✔ Latex paint for second color of marble
- ✔ Latex paint for veining
- ✔ Latex glaze
- ✔ Chair rail
- ✔ Construction adhesive and 8-penny nails
- ✔ Hammer and nail set
- ✔ Level
- ✔ Paint roller, trim roller, and tray
- ✔ Plastic drop cloth
- ✔ Stippling brush
- ✔ Feathering brush
- ✔ Synthetic brush for polyurethane
- ✔ Painter's masking tape
- ✔ Turkey feather (for veining)

Wisdom of the Aisles

"When it comes to marbling, the best teacher is the real thing. Buy 12-inch marble tile to use as a model when practicing marbling techniques on poster board or scraps of drywall."

— *Diane Collins*
Woodland Hills, CA

Walls

Colors That Work Together

Each of the palettes shown here is applied left to right, first to last.

MARBLE BASE	MARBLE FINISH	STIPPLE BASE	STIPPLE GLAZE
Ink Black	Woodsman Green	Fox Hollow	Smoky Emerald
Ink Black	Tiger Eye	Ink Black	Brandy Cherry
Coral Snow	Briar Patch	Argo	

Painter's Secret

Although feathers are the traditional veining tool, brushes also are used. Use a fine point artist's brush such as those that come with children's paint sets. Roll the brush between your finger and thumbs as you paint to give the line shape and direction.

Whether you use a brush or a feather, little paint is needed. Dip the feather or brush in the paint on the lid of the can. For added depth, dip the feather in a second color.

4 Marbleize the glaze mixture. Use a plastic drop cloth to give the glaze a mottled appearance. Cut the drop cloth about an inch wider and longer than the marble panel. Place the plastic on the wall against the wet glaze, wrinkling it randomly. The wrinkles create sharp lines in the glaze, similar to the color shifts in marble. With your hands, push the plastic against the wall and mush it around to create a mottled marble look. Remove the plastic and discard it. Use fresh plastic for remaining panels.

Faux finishers often add a second or third coat of glaze. To try this, start with the lightest glaze, apply, and mottle it. Let it dry thoroughly. Apply and mottle a darker glaze. Repeat with a slightly darker glaze for a third coat.

5 Apply veining. Create the veins with a turkey feather. If you have difficulty locating one, check in a costume shop or a fly-fishing shop. Stroke the feather from tip to tail to create individual clumps of fibers. Dip the feather lightly into the veining paint. Drag the feather along the wall to make thin meandering lines diagonally across the tile. Twist the feather to vary the width and quality of the veins as you draw the feather along. (See "Painter's Secret," left.)

Finishers often let the first lines dry, then drag another series of fine lines at diagonals to them. If you do this, don't soften the new lines with a brush as described in the next step. Leave them sharp so they appear to run along the surface, increasing the illusion of translucency.

6 Brush the veining to create the illusion of the vein continuing below the surface. Draw a feathering brush along one side only of a wet line to feather the distinct vein edge.

Faux Marbling 87

Faux Marbling

7 Repeat on the next section of wall. When you finish one panel, move on to the next.

8 Mask to paint the border. The dark green band around the marble panel furthers the three-dimensional illusion. Remask the wall to create the band. Gently remove the existing tape and wait until the paint is thoroughly dry, which can take as long as a week.

After the paint has dried, measure 1 1/2 inch up from the panel, lay out a line with a level, and run tape the entire length of the wainscoting. Apply tape along the line. Measure the same amount all around the panel and mask the areas to be protected.

*Designer's Tip

Stand back occasionally to look at your work. Faux-painting techniques require concentration, and it's easy to get lost in the details. Keep the big picture in mind. Close your eyes to clear your mind, and step back to look at the individual panels. Note if there are bare spots or areas to improve.

Take time to look at the job as a whole. Walk out of the room, have a cup of coffee, look out the window, and come back with fresh eyes. Why? The more you marble, the better you get at it. Make sure that as your skills develop, the panels look like they belong together.

9 Paint the border. Roll paint onto the border area using a small trim roller. Work carefully to avoid getting paint beyond the masked areas. Remove the masking tape while the paint is still wet.

To protect the finish and increase the effect of depth, allow the marbling to dry thoroughly before applying one or more coats of untinted glaze. Water-based polyurethane makes removal difficult if you change the look and color of the wall later.

Faux Leather

The richness and variety in the grain and texture of leather wallcovering lend a warm and rustic look to a family room or home office. The standard technique involves laying down a base coat and applying a darker glaze mixture with a glazing brush. The surface is then textured while still wet by dabbing with a clean rag. Finally, it is spattered with glaze by slapping the handle of a brush against the palm of the free hand.

Another technique is much simpler, but just as effective. After applying a base coat and glaze mixture, a plastic drop cloth is pressed into the wet glaze to texture the surface.

Leather provides the inspiration for the color and the texture, but don't restrict yourself to brown. Vary the colors to imitate leather found in shoes, coats, and other clothing.

Parchment panels are another popular faux technique. The process is the same as faux leather, but the look is softer and less dynamic.

Use either technique by yourself on panels. Whole walls require helping hands.

The beauty of leather lies in its imperfections. There are many options for color combinations, but keeping the variations subtle will achieve both nostalgic richness and comfortable warmth.

Faux Leather

1 **Practice, prime, and base coat, then lay out the panel width.** Traditionally, leather walls are done in panels because few animals have hides large enough to cover an entire wall. After the wall has been base-coated and allowed to dry, lay out the wall in equal-width panels—roughly 3 feet wide (not more than 4 feet to avoid rushing later steps while the finish dries). Lay out the sections from floor to ceiling with light pencil lines and a level. Panels may wrap around corners, with a portion on each adjoining wall.

2 **Mark the panel heights.** If you don't have a chair rail, lay out a horizontal break between panels at chair-rail height. Place taller panels above shorter ones

to create a pleasing appearance. Equal-size panels tend to divide the wall in half. Lay out the break with horizontal pencil lines and a level, slightly varying the line from one panel to the next. To mimic natural materials, variation is expected between panels.

3 **Mask the first set of panels.** Because masking one panel covers adjacent panels, you will paint every other panel at a time. Mask the outline of every other panel, running tape along the outside of the pencil lines. Where strips of tape meet at a corner, tear the tape along a putty knife to get a clean, sharp edge. For remaining panels, remove the tape and remask. Where panels end in a corner, run the tape along the adjoining wall.

STUFF YOU'LL NEED

- ✔ Latex leather-color paint
- ✔ Latex base coat
- ✔ Latex glaze
- ✔ Painter's masking tape
- ✔ Level
- ✔ Putty knife
- ✔ Roller with fine-napped sleeve
- ✔ Paint tray or paint bucket with roller grid
- ✔ Rubber gloves
- ✔ Lightweight plastic drop cloth
- ✔ Scissors
- ✔ Artist's brush (for parchment)
- ✔ Cotton rags (for parchment)

Painter's Secret

Leather is not always brown. For the look of a light leather, use an off-white base coat. For brown leather, use a tan base coat to avoid too much contrast between paint layers.

Prep Work

For best results, prepare the surface well. Faux leather will not hide existing imperfections. Clean, patch, and prime the wall. When the primer is dry, sand, then roll on the base coat.

4 **Roll on the finish.** Experiment on one of the sections before you begin the entire wall. When you feel comfortable with the technique, roll out the first panel and proceed with the technique.

Good idea!

To keep track of where to roll the glazing mixture, place tape Xs in each panel to roll later.

✳ Designer's Tip

After you master the technique of working with plastic, do an entire wall. Collect a large plastic drop cloth and several friends. Put the large plastic on the wall, working it the way you would smaller sheets. Your helpers also can pull off and deposit the plastic in a trash container.

"Don't press too hard when you're working the plastic against the wall. The idea is to leave texture, not handprints. Once you get the plastic on the wall, pat it lightly, slide it gently around, and then pull it off."

— *Dale Solomon*
San Diego, CA

5 **Texture the surface.** Cut a piece of plastic drop cloth slightly wider and longer than the rolled panel. (Wear rubber gloves.) Press the sheet against the wall so that it contacts the entire panel. Peel off the sheet—it will pull off paint the same way plastic food wrap pulls the glossy surface from a pumpkin pie. If you want more patterning, put up another piece of drop cloth and repeat the process. Create the scrapes and abrasions found on hides by crumpling a paper bag and twisting it on small areas of the panel.

Faux Leather   91

Faux Leather

6 **Repeat for the remaining panels.** Remove the tape before the panels dry. Dried paint on the tape pulls off neighboring paint on the wall. After the paint is dry, mask the walls for the remaining panels, applying tape on the opposite side of the layout lines.

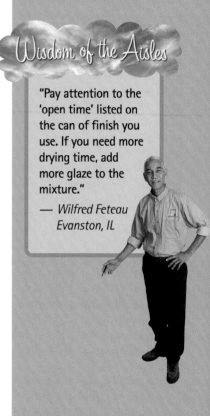

Wisdom of the Aisles

"Pay attention to the 'open time' listed on the can of finish you use. If you need more drying time, add more glaze to the mixture."

— *Wilfred Feteau Evanston, IL*

Colors That Work Together

The palettes shown are applied left to right, first to last. The first color is the base; the color to the right is the color mixed with the glaze. Follow by texturing with the plastic sheet.

| Mustard Grain | Unfired Clay | | Salted Ash | Gaucho |

| Stratosphere | Merlin | | Kestral Blue | Casbah |

Practice, Practice

Leather has natural imperfections that add character to indvidual hides. Perfect the technique before you begin the walls to guarantee the look you want.

Mix small amounts of leather-color paint and glaze, experimenting with different proportions. Roll the different mixtures onto primed and base-coated drywall scraps. While the glazes are wet, mottle the finish by pressing it with a crumpled and then smoothed paper bag. Let the glazes dry, and place the scraps in the room you are painting to see how they look.

Faux Parchment

The faux parchment technique is similar to faux leather. Instead of manipulating the paint with plastic, however, use a soft cotton rag. For a traditional look, choose colors found in nature. Mix yellow and earth tone semigloss paints with the glaze to achieve traditional parchment. For a bold look, combine colors that appeal to you; and for a bold parchment, pick the colors that are found in handmade papers at custom stationery stores.

1 **Apply a base coat.** (See "Faux Leather," page 90.) Mark the wall into a grid of panels and mask. Roll a glaze-and-paint mixture onto as many sections of wall as you can comfortably texture in about 15 minutes.

2 **To create the fibrous look of parchment,** use a thin artist's brush to apply short lines and flecks of a darker color to the wet glaze.

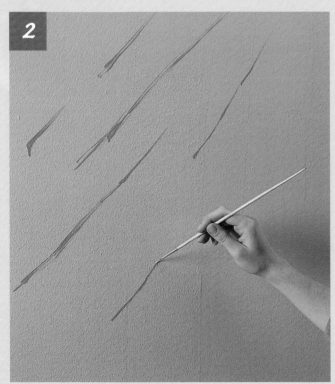

3 **Rag off the wet glaze** with a bunched-up cotton rag or T-shirt (see "Ragging Off," page 67). As you dab a panel, turn your hand frequently and rebunch the material to avoid developing patterns. Create a subtle directional effect that suggests the natural graining of parchment by dabbing along at roughly a 45-degree angle on some panels, then at the reverse angle on others.

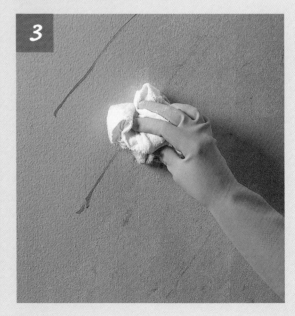

Southwestern Texturing

Walls

Settlers to the Southwest United States applied tinted plaster veneer to interior walls of their homes to soften the harshness of the desert. The smooth, shiny, natural stonelike surface has become the identifying signature of contemporary Southwestern interiors. Professional plasters re-create the look with a veneer plastering technique—a ⅛-inch base coat of finishing plaster followed by another ⅛-inch layer of burnished finishing plaster. Homeowners who have some drywall experience can also master this technique.

To create the wall texture, do-it-yourselfers must understand a few basics. Professional plasterers working on a 20-foot wall may have as many as five people working at the same time: one to mix batches of plaster and four to "butter" the walls. The working time for each batch is approximately 45 minutes. An entire wall must be completed at one time because the seams between dry coats and wet coats will crack. Depending on the area you need to cover, you may have to recruit a few helpers. Until you get the hang of it though, choose a manageable area, such as a small accent wall, the surface around a fireplace, or the walls of a powder room. After you feel comfortable with the technique, you can teach your friends to help you.

Although this process can be applied to painted and plastered surfaces, blue board is used in new construction for the wall surface. An alternative (and the old-fashioned method) is to mount drywall with the back facing out. The paper on the back is thicker and rougher, which makes the plaster application easier. To practice, begin with a trial run on the back of a sheet of drywall. Screw it to a garage or basement wall with the 8-foot edge parallel to the floor. Mix a batch of plaster, follow the directions, and work the technique until you're comfortable.

The final finish color will be much lighter when it's dry than it looks as it's being applied. It's important to test to get the exact finish you want.

Southwestern texturing, also called veneer plastering, produces a smooth, even surface that follows the curves and round shapes of these living room walls.

Southwestern Texturing

1 **Test the color.** The color is determined by the tint added to the plaster. There are many possibilities; experiment with amounts of tint and plaster to find one you like. Cut a test piece of drywall into12-inch squares. Mix small batches of plaster according to the instructions below, using a different tint for each square. Keep notes on proportions of tint to plaster. You may need to use more than the specified measure to achieve more color saturation—less for a subtle look. The color saturation you choose dictates the proportion of tint to plaster and must be consistent throughout the plastering process.

After you apply the first coat, try a variety of treatments with the second coat. For example, add a different tint to the top coat, and allow the bottom coat to show through in some areas. Once the top coat is on, stop at any time. However, the more you work it the smoother it gets. Experiment, have fun, and you'll be rewarded for your efforts.

When mixing the plaster in a plastic bucket, be sure to avoid scraping the sides. Certain types of mixers can remove bits of plastic from the sides and mix them into the plaster. The plastic bits prevent the plaster from being smooth. If this happens, make up a fresh batch and consider the first batch a practice run.

Good idea!

2 **Mix the plaster, water, and tint.** Add one part plaster to two parts water. The consistency should resemble soft serve ice cream or pudding. After you have the desired consistency, mix in tint based on your test. Mix thoroughly with a drill and a paddle. Overmixing can result in plaster that dries too

quickly; undermixing can result in an unworkable or lumpy plaster. As a result, manufacturers give specific instructions for mixing—the manufacturer of the plaster used here specifies a ½" drill that operates at 900 to 1000 rpm, in combination with a cage-type plaster mixer. The directions you receive may differ; follow them exactly.

STUFF YOU'LL NEED

✔ Finishing plaster

✔ Universal tints (available at paint centers)

✔ Clear acrylic sealer in eggshell

✔ 600-grit sandpaper

✔ ½" drill, 1000 rpm

✔ Mixing cage (mixing bit for plaster)

✔ 10" finishing trowel with a rubber handle

✔ Mason's hawk

✔ 5-gallon mixing bucket

✔ Plastic auto body putty burnishing trowel (available at automotive supply stores)

✔ Spray water bottle

Prep Work

New construction: Blue board, a porous gypsum sheet that installs like drywall is the preferred wall backing. Veneer plaster can also be applied over drywall (back face out). Tape the joints and inside corners with pressure-sensitive tape and put metal edging on the outside corners; it is not necessary to prime the tape with a plaster coat. Apply the first coat of plaster over the entire wall.

Over existing paint surface: Clean the walls with a TSP solution, and let dry. Paint an acrylic bonding agent on the walls according to the manufacturer's instructions. Add an acrylic glue powder to the plaster at the mixing stage. Check the manufacturer's mixing instructions.

*Designer's Tip

About textures

This technique produces a flat shiny surface. You also can create an adobe look by mixing texture, such as sand, into the paint to roughen the surface.

About tints

Buy tubes of universal tints from the paint department. Some stores let you pick a color you like from the color palette and will dispense the proper tints from their machine.

Keep in mind when you choose tint colors that the plaster dries lighter than it appears when applied.

Southwestern Texturing

3 **Trowel on the base coat.** Spread the plaster over the entire section you work—whatever size it is. Dump a dollop of plaster on a mason's hawk with the trowel.

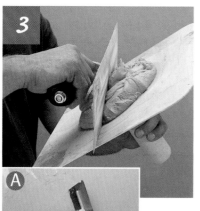

A cut off plastic milk carton works well to transfer the plaster onto the hawk. Transfer a small mound onto the trowel by sliding the trowel away from you while tilting the hawk toward you.

Ⓐ Place the bottom edge of the trowel on the drywall and apply the plaster in sweeping strokes. Work across the wall, picking up fresh plaster for each stroke. Don't worry about getting the plaster smooth at this point; it's more important to get it on the walls. The motion is similar to frosting a cake or buttering bread.

Ⓑ "Butter" the entire wall, then go back to the beginning and work the trowel back and forth to create a smoother surface, adding more plaster as you trowel, building up to a ⅛-inch layer.

4 **Apply the second and final coat.** Mix a second batch of plaster the same as the first. Butter the walls with the second coat, working the plaster vertically, rather than horizontally (insets), to a uniform ⅛-inch layer. Remove excess plaster from the trowel onto the hawk and then into the trash. Keep the trowel clean as you work to enable you to create a smooth surface. Stop at any point during the final coat, depending on the final look you plan to achieve. The more you work the plaster, the smoother it becomes.

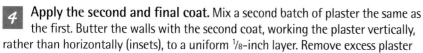

Plasterer's Secret

The cooler the environment you work in, the longer time you have to apply the plaster. Professionals often set the thermostat to 60 degrees to slow the drying and to increase the plaster's working life.

It's not important to achieve a perfectly uniform surface at this stage. Try to get the first coat as even as possible, working quickly across the wall. Then step away from it and allow it to set. At this time, tidy the edges with the burnishing trowel. Pull excess plaster away from the corners, floor, and ceiling and toss it in the trash. The plaster is not reusable.

The plaster is ready for the second coat when you can pass your hand over the surface without leaving fingerprints, only picking up powder or dust on your fingers.

Give the surface extra texture by pressing tiny pieces of straw, leaves, or sea shells into the plaster before it sets. Randomly spread and set items or cluster them around doors or window frames.

Warm and Cozy

The smoothness, density, and richness of color that Southwestern texturing offers makes it a perfect choice for a powder room or entryway. Ambient light reflects warmly off the surface and creates a comfortable and intimate space.

*Designer's Tip

More tinting techniques

Apply a light tint to the sealer to create even more depth to this technique. Experiment first on a sample piece before you attempt the whole wall.

Use a powdered sugar shaker to sprinkle the wall with powdered tint before you apply the sealer. This technique imparts an aged look to the finish. Experiment first on a sample piece before you attempt the whole wall.

5 Smooth the plaster. As the plaster sets, continue to work it with water and trowel. Use a spray bottle to apply the water. Plaster sets from the inside out, allowing you to continue to work the surface. Keep it moist to achieve a uniform surface and to create the mottled look in the finished texture. You'll learn how quickly the plaster sets as you continue to work it. When the plaster dries to the point that it can't be pushed around, you're ready for the next step. Fine trowel lines will disappear during the burnishing process.

6 Burnish the plaster. The final sheen and texture of the wall come from working it with a plastic trowel made for applying auto body putty. The trowel—available at auto supply stores—is smoother and more flexible than a metal trowel and provides a tighter, shinier surface. Work the trowel top to bottom across the wall, spraying the surface with water as you go. Burnishing the wall with this trowel polishes the surface. The more you burnish, the smoother and shinier the surface will be. If you apply a protective coat, you won't need to spend as much time burnishing, except to get a smooth finish. The gloss in the protective coating makes the wall shine.

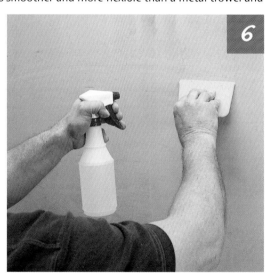

7 Apply a protective coat (optional). To protect the surface of the plaster from dirt and grease, apply a protective plaster sealer. Lightly sand the wall by hand with a 600-grit paper and wipe off the dust. Apply a clear acrylic-base plaster sealer, which is formulated differently from wood sealers. Ask for a clear eggshell finish specifically designed for application over plaster.

Apply most sealers the same way you apply paint. Cut in along the corners with a brush, and then roll the broader surfaces.

Stenciling a Wall

Available in a wide range of patterns, stencils can highlight any room style. They are attractive on solid-color walls and can provide special effects on sponge-painted or rag-rolled walls. Stencils employ one color or several and can be hand-designed and cut. (See "Making Your Own Stencil," page 101).

A popular stenciling approach is to apply a patterned border along the walls around the entire room—at chair-rail height, close to the ceiling, or along the base molding. Once you attempt border stencils, more elaborate stenciling is only a small step away, such as entire wall surfaces.

Depending on the design and color scheme, patterns may consist of more than one stencil. In the following project, the commercially available pattern requires three stencils for the border and two for the wall treatment. Each stencil is clearly marked from the manufacturer to indicate the sequence, complete with registration marks. These marks enable you to line up subsequent stencils easily and accurately.

Softly understated and inviting, the stenciled pattern on the walls of this bedroom lends an air of elegance and ease.

Stenciling a Wall

STUFF YOU'LL NEED

✔ Level
✔ Stepladder
✔ Stencils
✔ Acrylic paints
✔ Stenciling brushes
✔ Paper plate or palette
✔ Paper towels
✔ Stencil adhesive
✔ Low-tack masking tape

A Little Stenciling History

Stenciling, the technique of brushing color onto a wall through a cut pattern, has been used for centuries. It was widely used in the Middle Ages as wall decoration in places of worship and royal residences to add color, texture, and design to plain walls. In most cases, entire rooms were stenciled in pigment, such as terra-cotta, umber, ochre, or verdigris, then embellished with gold leaf. Patterns reflected the family's coat of arms and other family symbols. The design was repeated throughout the room and framed with ornate borders, such as chevrons, architectural details, or mottoes.

1 **Test the pattern.** Stencil kits frequently have a suggested color palette, which may or may not work with your color scheme. Test the stencil design, paint colors, and brush techniques before beginning your project. Test the colors and design in the room, either on a discreet corner of the wall or on poster board taped to the wall. Try different colors, brush techniques, and get acquainted with the positioning of each stencil to complete the design. It is important to understand how the stencils work together before you begin stenciling the wall.

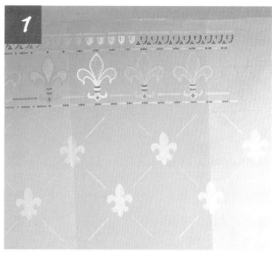

In this project, we achieve a tone-on-tone appearance to the entire room by starting with a base color, which is then color-washed in subtle stripes the width of the stencil pattern. This technique adds depth and texture to the design.

2 **Draw level lines.** Measure the height of the border stencil. Measure down from the ceiling and make pencil marks every 2 feet to indicate the bottom position of the stencil. Using a level, extend a light pencil line around the room to mark the bottom edge of the border stencil. In older homes where the ceiling may not be straight, the level line may not connect all the dots. In this case, use the lowest mark to redraw the level line.

Good idea! → A vinyl eraser helps get rid of the evidence in most cases. If you used a satin enamel base, scrub lightly with a mild all-purpose cleaner to remove the pencil marks.

3 **Apply repositionable adhesive spray mount to the stencil.** Artist's spray enables you to line up the registration marks and prevents paint from seeping under the stencil. Use masking tape to adhere the stencil to the wall as you work—spray adhesive does not work for that. Apply a light coat of adhesive to the back of the stencil, and reapply adhesive as it loses its tackiness.

Stenciling a Wall

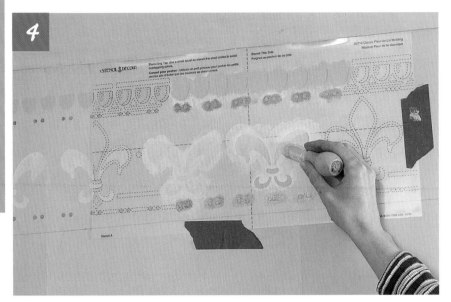

A dinner plate or paper plate makes a good paint palette. Squeeze a small amount of paint on the plate. Dip your stencil brush in the paint and dab off the excess.

4 **Tape the stencil to the wall and paint the first colors.** Begin in the most visible corner of the room, usually opposite the entry. Position the stencil on the level line drawn in Step 2. Press the stencil to the wall so the adhesive grabs; fix the stencil to the wall with masking tape. Apply the paint with a dabbing or swirling motion (each achieves a slightly different appearance).

From the corner, stencil one of the adjoining walls, continuing halfway around the room. Return to the corner and finish the other half of the room (working in the opposite direction). This technique creates an attractive corner in the most visible part of the room. As the pattern wraps around the room, it eventually meets in the least visible corner, where pattern mismatch is less noticeable.

With some stencils, one color is applied around the entire room; then the process is repeated with another stencil to apply additional colors. On others, more than one color is applied before moving the stencil. When the paint dries to the touch (in seconds), remove the stencil and reposition it along the wall, lining up the registration marks with the previously stenciled pattern and the level line. Repeat the process halfway around the room, ending in the least visible corner.

5 **Start the second wall.** Position the stencil at the starting corner on the opposite wall. Depending on the pattern, you may need to bend the stencil into the corner, as shown. Align the stencil registration marks with the appropriate painted parts. Continue around the other half of the room, ending in the least visible corner. This completes the first pass.

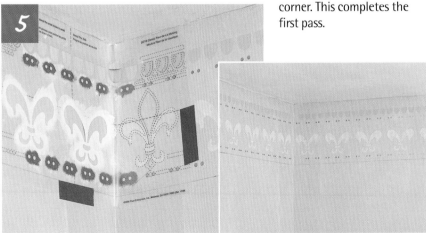

Stenciler's Secret

When you cut stencils from scratch, make an extra copy. A spare may be handy for adding extra colors. Use light-tack spray adhesive to hold the material together, and tape around the outside edges to keep the pieces from sliding. Use a sharp blade and make careful deliberate cuts, staying within the lines.

Most purchased stencils are computer designed and cut. Thousands of uniform, precisely cut patterns are available. If you want your own creation, make your own stencil. Copy a pattern found elsewhere in the room—on the curtain fabric or the carpet, for example. Or you may want a truly original pattern that springs from your own experience.

1 Start with a drawing of the design to photocopy. Make a trial copy—repositioning, enlarging, or shrinking the pattern as needed. Replace the paper in the machine with photocopier transparency film—sold in office supply stores for making transparencies for overhead projectors. Copy the image onto the film.

Add registration marks to the pattern to align the stencil on the wall as you work. A center mark along each edge works for most applications.

2 Make the photocopy and cut out the stencil with a fine tapered crafts knife that has a new, sharp blade. Practice on a scrap piece first, using a portion of the design. To protect your work surface, place the work over a piece of foam board as you cut. For the cleanest cuts:

- Hold the knife like a pencil, and always draw it toward you to make cuts. Either turn the transparency film as you work, or move yourself around the work table.
- Make two distinct cuts in corners—cutting into them, not out of them.
- Use a continuous motion without lifting the blade to make curved cuts.
- Use a straight edge to guide straight line cuts.

3 To make stencils for multiple-color patterns, make separate stencils for each color. The stencils are identical except for the cut out areas. The stencil for blue, for example, would have only the blue areas of the pattern cut out; the stencil for black would have only the black areas cut out. Registration marks are crucial in multi-color patterns: Make the marks on the original so that they are identically positioned on each photocopy.

Good idea!

Make an Extra Stencil

Stencils become used as they are bent to fit in corners. If you make your own stencils, make an extra set for use in corners. Stick two pieces of stencil material together with low-tack spray adhesive (high-tack adhesive is too strong). Transfer the pattern to the stencil material, and then cut through both pieces at the same time.

Walls

Stenciling a Wall

6 **Add secondary elements and colors.** In this design, the second stencil adds highlights and the third stencil adds shadows. To get this look, some colors were repeated. The painting process is the same as the first layer, and the registration marks make it easy to align the design with the previous stencil. Follow the direction of the first stencil to paint one-half of the room; reverse the stencil to paint the other half of the room.

7 **Apply the third stencil or accent color.** A third stencil is used to apply the shadow detail, above. In this design, color is applied directly over color by lightly dabbing, adding interest by allowing the color beneath to peak through. To add second and third colors, whether using single or multiple stencils, align the registration marks so the pattern maintains its continuity and crispness all the way around the room.

Stenciling Around a Window

1 **Lay out the design.** Arrange photocopies of the stencil on the wall. Adjust spacing, and check for a noticeable front and back. Arrange the stencil so the image flows naturally around the window—flowers should be right side up. Center single images at the top of the window.

2 **Start above the window.** Apply the stencil along the top first. Align the stencil to create an attractive corner between the top and side rows of stenciling. If possible—and it isn't always—the corner stencil should contain a full image. The spacing between images should remain constant as the stencil turns the corner. Apply paint.

3 **Position the stencil along the side of the window, and apply paint.** On this stencil, all the colors are applied without repositioning the stencil. On others, apply the first color all around the window; apply the second color next.

Keep It Clean

As the stencil pattern fills with paint, it prevents a clear image on the painted surface. Clean the stencil every 10 to 15 feet of use with a mild detergent and a sponge. Be gentle to avoid bending the pattern—sponging in one direction. Rinse thoroughly with water and pat the stencil dry with paper towels.

*Designer's Tip

What's Old Is New

In the early 1900s the Arts and Crafts movement revived stenciling with a rich and varied color palette. Walls became canvases that promoted color, design, and poetry. The art of stenciling is even more popular today; and fortunately, you don't need to be an artist to accomplish excellent results. It's one of the easiest painting techniques for adding color and interest to rooms.

TOOL TIP

Use the Right Brush

Stencil brushes come in two sizes. For speed, use the larger brush for large images. Put the paint on smaller details with the smaller brush. You'll use less paint and make less of a mess.

8 **Position the wall stencil.** With the border completed, it's time to stencil the rest of the wall. Position the wall stencil in the original corner, aligning the top of the design with the level line drawn earlier. Paint the first section. Reposition the stencil, using the registration marks and level line as your guide; then continue across the wall in rows. Finish one wall at a time rather than continuing a row all the way around the room. Paint one-half of the room first, then start in the original corner and finish the other half. The first wall stencil in this project lays the entire design on the wall. The second will overlay the highlights—in this case, a glaze mix (four parts glaze to one part paint) of the highlight color to achieve the desired effect.

9 **Stencil in rows.** Full wall stencil patterns like this usually are stencilled in rows. Others require either vertical or random placement. The test performed at the beginning of the project determines the best placement and the direction to follow.

10 **Stencil the second half of the room.** Start in the original corner and place the top of the design on the level line. Work in rows right to left and top to bottom, completing one wall at a time.

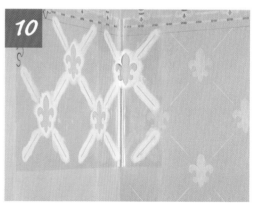

11 **Apply highlights.** Begin at the starting point and work in horizontal rows, top to bottom, checking registration marks on every section. The highlight color shown is used at full strength. The stencil applies the highlight color on top of the glazed color. Even though wall surfaces are greater, stenciling them may take less time than doing a complex border.

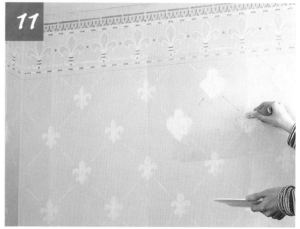

Stamping

Stamping and stenciling produce similar effects. Stenciling is precise, while stamping is free form and forgiving of mistakes. Stamping allows for variation—no two impressions are identical, and you can break the pattern any way you like. Impressions can face in different directions, and the relationship between overlapping patterns can change so that the background stamp becomes the one in the foreground. Though stamping is usually applied to cover an entire wall, it is not a fixed rule. In a child's room, for example, stamps create a path populated by teddy bears; in a family room, stamps can create a border or a chair rail.

Make stamps yourself, as we have done here, or buy premade stamps.

Once you have your stamps and paint, test your technique on poster board or a piece of scrap drywall. If the stamp slides when pressed, you're probably too generous with the paint. When you feel confident, move on to the project. There is no need to reapply paint after each impression. Variations in the stamping are part of this technique's effect.

With stamping, create any pattern you can imagine—from anchors and sails to lilacs and lilies. Stamping goes quickly and allows you to play with patterns. The anchors on this wall, for example, cover parts of the sail, while each sail faces a different direction.

∧∧∧∧∧∧∧∧∧∧∧∧∧∧∧∧∧∧∧∧∧

STUFF YOU'LL NEED

✔ Blocking glaze, or latex paint and glaze
✔ Disposable plates
✔ Paint applicator (brush or small foam roller)
✔ Stamping blocks
✔ Drop cloth

Wisdom of the Aisles

"You don't have to buy stamps. Your home is probably full of them—tennis balls, the sole of a toddler's sneaker, and scraps of plastic foam—to name a few."

— Greg Korczak
Lodi, NJ

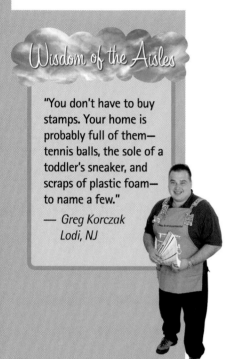

Adding Highlights

Add detail to your work by painting the stamp with a fine-tipped artist's brush. Add shading or highlights to objects or add depth by changing the color as you move from one edge to the other. It's easy, once you get the hang of it. Until you do, practice on a piece of poster board, drywall, or hardboard until you get the look you want.

Stamping

1 **Paint and apply each stamp.** If you don't use a prepared stamping paint, mix your own from half glaze and half latex paint. Place some paint on a plate. Use a brush or foam roller to pick up paint from the plate and distribute it on the face of the block. Here, the paint is rolled on one element of the sailboat design. The wall has already been randomly scattered with sail shapes.

2 **Overlap design elements.** Parts of a design scheme can be overlapped after the first prints have dried. You don't have to use an opaque paint for the second prints—a translucent glaze helps to blend the colors.

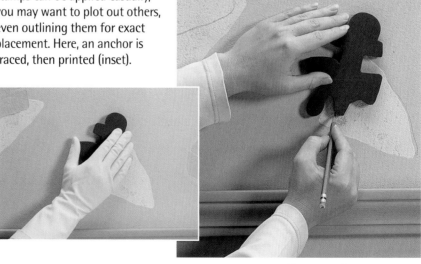

3 **Trace around stamps to be placed with more regularity.** Although some stamps can be applied casually, you may want to plot out others, even outlining them for exact placement. Here, an anchor is traced, then printed (inset).

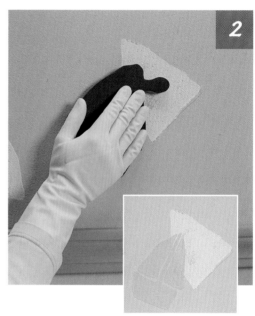

Making Your Own Stamp

You're not confined to premade stamps. Any flat object that holds paint can be an interesting pattern for your walls. Flea market vendors may have fabric stamps. Or use the foam from a computer mouse pad, which has the perfect density to hold paint. Trace a pattern and cut it out with a utility knife to create custom stamps.

1 Find a pattern. Any simple image can become a stamp. Use wallpaper books, pattern books, and children's coloring books to find patterns to photocopy.

Good idea! ←

For a running border, combine two or more elements. Use three blocks to make a grapevine, for example—one for the vine, one for the leaf, and one for the grape. If you are timid about stamping a border around the walls, practice using the blocks on the back of old wallpaper or a roll of kraft paper cut into several lengthwise strips.

2 Transfer design. Cut out the outline of your pattern and put it on the mouse pad. Trace around it with a marker or transfer it to the pad with transfer paper.

3 Cut out the pattern. Cut out the shapes with scissors or a utility knife. For a handle, either run a large safety pin just under the top surface or glue the stamp to a larger scrap of foam.

*Designer's Tip

To apply patterns around windows, doors, or archways, stamps are more versatile than stencils. If you apply stamps, such as cats or sheep, for example, you can apply the stamp so that the feet continue to point downward as you move around the opening. In contrast, stencil images are repositioned. For example, flowers above a window reach toward the ceiling while the flowers along the side casing look as if they are lying down.

Allow some variation from one stamped print to the next—but not too much. Touch up rough prints with a cotton swab or small artist's brush, making sure to maintain the imperfect look that distinguishes this technique from stenciling.

Wall to Wall Color

Walls are more than places to hang pictures. They should be as interesting as the objects they frame. Sometimes a white wall is the right choice. Before you pull out the brushes, think about all the options for expression available with faux painting, stenciling, stamping, and painted trim. The next surface option is wallpaper.

Stippled bedroom

Beamed ceiling with multi-color panels

Wallpapered staircase

Color washed bathroom

Painted trim and wallpaper

Wallpaper

Wallpaper can establish the style of a room more thoroughly—and more quickly—than any other single element, including paint. If you're sure about the look you want, choosing the right paper is a cinch. If you're not sure, or you find it hard to put your thoughts into words, open up a wallpaper sample book.

Sample books are available in the majority of outlets that carry wallpaper and are organized to help make the decision process easy. After a few minutes of browsing, you'll find yourself gravitating toward a look. If you think about complex arrangements—wallpaper wainscot, chair-rail, paper above the rail, border, and frieze—the books show combinations that work together.

Most wallpaper isn't paper anymore. It's made from vinyl printed to look like paper and stands up to the dirt and stress of modern life more efficiently. It lasts longer and is easier to install. If you look for historically accurate replicas for a restoration, true paper wallpaper may be your choice. True papers are widely available as special orders through home centers and decorator showrooms, from houses specializing in reproductions, and online. They're aimed at the top-of-the-line market, are generally expensive, and can be a challenge to hang. If you like the historical look, but not historical installation and cleaning problems, find a pattern in true paper and then search the vinyl books. You'll probably find a duplicate of the paper version.

Stripes or solids, florals or prints, wallpaper sets the tone of the room.

Papering Walls

Wallpaper offers color, pattern, and texture spread out over hundreds of square feet. Before deciding on a paper, bring home a roll sample, tape it to the wall, and examine it during the day and at night. Place it next to upholstered items and the carpet to see how they match. Be picky; if you don't love it, try again.

When you make your choice, measure the walls to get the square feet you need. Home center salespeople will help you estimate how much you need. Some professionals measure the windows and doors and deduct the difference; others build in excess at the start because you want extra anyway.

Prepare the walls as you would for painting; paper won't stick to a greasy surface, and irregularities in the wall may be visible through the paper. To help the paper stick (and to ease later removal) roll on a primer-sealer made specifically for wallpaper. This step is especially important if a gloss paint has been used on the wall.

Allow the wall to dry completely before hanging paper. The wallpaper manufacturer may recommend applying a coat of sizing to further prepare the wall, but a wallpaper primer-sealer is usually sufficient. Finally, turn off the power to the room, remove the cover plates, and tape over the outlets and switches to protect them during the project.

Wallpaper adds color and character to a room. Some people find it difficult to pick bold paint colors. However, it's easier to be bold with paper because you can see the pattern before you begin.

Walls

Papering Walls

1 **Begin by looking at the pattern of the paper you select.** The type of pattern determines how the strips are cut and glued on the wall. On straight-matched papers, patterns along the left and right edges of the paper are the same,

and installation is straightforward. On drop-matched papers, such as the one shown, the elements are staggered along both edges. Aligning the pattern results in an uneven top edge, which is trimmed. This takes more time and wastes some paper but results in an interesting pattern. Cut down on some of the wallpaper waste by organizing and cutting alternating strips from two rolls of wallpaper.

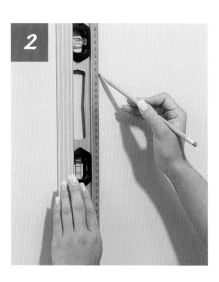

2 **Begin the job in the least-conspicuous inside corner of the room—usually behind a door.** Position the first strip so that most of the paper is on the first wall to be papered, with about 1/2 inch of the strip wrapping around the corner onto the adjoining wall. Wrapping the corner hides cracks that might develop in the corner. To lay out the strip, start in the corner and measure out a distance equal to the width of the paper minus 1/2 inch. Draw a plumb line at this point, using a level as a guide.

3 **Cut the first strip of paper to length.** To allow temporary overlap at top and bottom, add 4 inches to the height of the wall. Roll out the paper on a long work surface, and cut the strip to length with scissors.

STUFF YOU'LL NEED

- ✔ Wallpaper
- ✔ Paste (for unpasted papers)
- ✔ Vinyl-to-vinyl adhesive (for edges only of vinyl and vinyl-coated papers)
- ✔ Tape measure
- ✔ Scissors
- ✔ Water tray (for prepasted paper)
- ✔ Paint roller or brush (for paste)
- ✔ Wallpaper brush
- ✔ Seam roller
- ✔ Utility knife
- ✔ Trimming tool (also called a broad knife)
- ✔ Sponge

Paperhanger's Secret

Wallpaper is printed in die lot batches, and the color can vary from lot to lot. Ask your retailer for rolls from the same lot, and check to make sure you get them.

Write down the lot number when you get the paper. If you need to repair wallpaper in years ahead, you'll be able to give the manufacturer the lot number, and they will try to match it. It may not be perfect, but it's guaranteed to be better than if you didn't have the number.

Designer's Tip

Want to hide some ugly plywood paneling? One of the best ways is with wallpaper. First wash the paneling with TSP and rinse thoroughly. When dry, scuff with sandpaper to take off any shine in the finish.

Papering is a two-step process. Hang strips of wallpaper liner horizontally across the paneling before hanging the wallpaper.

TOOL TIP

Staying Sharp

Many paperhangers use single-edge razors mounted in a special handle. They change the blade after each cut. A utility knife works well, and you may already have one in your tool box. Whichever you choose, buy several blades and change them often.

Work Smarter

People who frequently hang wallpaper buy specially made tables that are about as wide as a roll of wallpaper. Make your own by having a sheet of plywood cut to the same width as your paper. Wrap the plywood in a old sheet to absorb excess paste, and set the plywood sheet on a pair of sawhorses or an old table covered with newspapers.

4 **Prepasted papers seem simple to hang**—soak each strip and apply it to the wall. Conditions vary, however, and the paste sometimes fails. Professional paperers and most paint departments recommend an application of paste activator instead of soaking. Brush or roll on the activator following the manufacturer's directions. If you use unpasted wallpaper, brush on wallpaper paste instead.

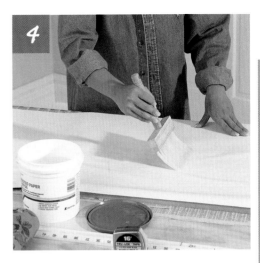

5 **Gently fold the ends toward the middle with the pattern side out.** Take care to avoid creasing the paper. Wait one minute, or as directed, so the paste has a chance to activate before hanging. This is called "booking" the roll.

6 **Hang the first strip along the plumb line.** Push the the paper against the wall with a brush or a piece of flexible plastic smoother. Work down from the top and coax bubbles out to the edges. Push the wallpaper into the corner and wrap the extra ½ inch onto the next wall.

Papering Walls

"In earthquake country, it's important to keep extra rolls of paper on hand because shifting ground causes the walls to crack. Even if you're in a stable part of the world, keep a roll or two on hand to make necessary repairs."

— *Kelly Banducci*
San Leandro, CA

7 **Trim the strip at top and bottom. Some papers shrink as the glue dries.** Hang the first strip, hang the second strip, and then go back to trim the first. Trim, as shown, placing a broad knife between the paper and the cutting knife, and guiding the cut along the edge of the broad knife.

Good idea!

Change knife blades frequently. Some pros change their blades before each cut. It's especially important on a cut such as the one shown above. It's better to use more blades than to tear wallpaper.

8 **Butt subsequent strips against each other.** After you hang a few strips, go over the seams between them with a seam roller to fix the edges in place. Don't apply so much pressure that you force much paste out from under the strips. Sponge paste from the surface with clean, warm water. Foils or flocked or embossed papers may be damaged by rolling; instead, press along the seams with the smoothing brush. (Continued on page 114.)

Try a Little Tenderness

Wallpapering can test your patience; it also can test your marriage. Although patient spouses make great helpers, so do patient friends. Choose someone who is more patient than you; it's better for both the room and the relationship.

Work Smarter

Some ceilings are covered with puffy acoustical insulation often called "popcorn." Popcorn can make it tough to get a tight seam at the ceiling. Use a can opener to scrape off a thin line, $1/16$ inch or less, of the material along the edge of the ceiling. You won't be able to see it, and the wallpaper will go on easier.

Papering Switchplates or Covers

Careful treatment of faceplates and receptacle plates plays an important part in the final look of your room.

Replacement plates come in a variety of styles and finishes, including brass, sterling silver, wood, mirrored glass, and hundreds of handcrafted and custom variations. There are even clear plastic plates to show off cross-stitch work. As long as you're hanging paper anyway, why not cover plain plastic faceplates with matching wallpaper? The steps here show you how to wallpaper a faceplate over a receptacle. The procedure is the same for papering a switch plate.

1 Remove the faceplate and align the wallpaper. Turn off the power to the switch or outlet at the fuse or breaker box. Remove the faceplate with a screwdriver and wash the faceplate with warm, soapy water. Dry; then sand the sheen from the front surface with 120- or 180-grit paper.

Cut a piece of wallpaper larger than the faceplate so you can match the pattern. Put the paper over the open outlet and move it to align the pattern with the paper on the wall. Tape it in place with low-tack masking. Rub to emboss the outline of the receptacle on the paper. (To paper a switch plate, cut a slit in the wallpaper to slip over the switch before taping the paper in place and rubbing it.)

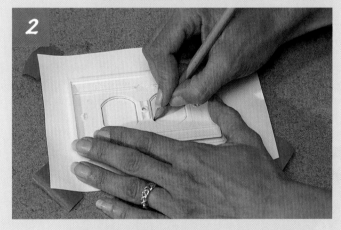

2 Trace around the plate. Take the paper off the wall, put it face down on a table, and align the opening in the faceplate with the embossed marks. Trace around the plate with a pencil, and then trim the paper so that it's about $1/2$ inch wider than the plate on each side.

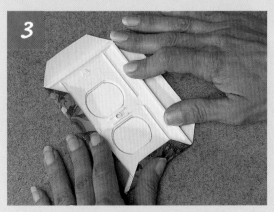

3 Cover the faceplate. Brush vinyl-to-vinyl adhesive on the front of the plate and on the back of a piece of wallpaper. Press the paper onto the plate, and place the front of the plate on a work surface.

Trim off the "ears" of the paper at each corner to permit folding over along the sides, as shown. Allow the adhesive to dry; cut out the opening with a razor knife. Use a finishing nail or other sharp object to poke holes for the screws through the paper. Screw the plate to the wall after the adhesive dries.

Papering Walls

9 **Paper over electric switches and outlets. Cut away the excess paper.**
Before cutting around an electrical box that has been covered by a strip, shut off the power to the room. Use a utility knife to make four diagonal slices through the paper, starting at the center of the box and working toward the corners. Be careful so that you don't cut into the outlet or switch. Trim the paper to make a rectangular opening, leaving enough paper to conceal the edges by the cover plate.

10 **When you come to a door or window, hang a full-length strip over it.**
Trim away the excess paper with scissors, cutting in from the edge of the strip. Work at a diagonal toward a corner of the window or door frame until you are about an inch from the outer edge of the frame. Continue doing this for each corner covered by the paper.

Walls

Paperhanger's Secret

Eventually your beautiful papering job will get a ding or a scuff that can't be rinsed off. Make a patch by placing a scrap over the affected area and moving it until it aligns with the pattern. Cut through the patch and all the way through the paper underneath. Peel away the cut piece from the installed paper, and glue the patch in place.

Work Smarter

Don't Cut Off the Clown's Head

When you cut the first strip of wallpaper to length, make sure you don't cut off an important part of the pattern. Avoid cutting off the head of a clown, the flowers in a bouquet, or the top of a medallion, for example. Take the time to get the first strip right, and the others should fall in place.

*Designer's Tip

Accents in Arts and Crafts

A signature of the Arts and Crafts movement was stylized design that reflected the harmony and geometric precision found in nature. Complement Mission-style furniture with a wallpaper frieze (or border) with geometric forms or stylized nature motifs placed above a picture rail.

Paperhanger's Secret

Double cutting adjoining strips. To create a seam between two strips, paperhangers "double cut" them. Begin by installing the first strip; then install the second strip so that it overlaps the first. Slide the paper until the patterns match, and then cut through both strips, guiding the cut along a straightedge. Peel away the excess from the overlapping strips and press the two pieces of border together to form a perfectly matched seam. Roll the seam with a seam roller and sponge away excess paste.

11 Press the paper into the edge between the frame and the wall with the trimming tool. Cut away the excess with the knife. Wipe the frame with a damp sponge to clean off the paste before it dries.

Good idea! → **You're bound to generate large wallpaper scraps** as you work your way around the room. Save them. They may be just the right size for the area above and below windows or doors, or for future repairs.

12 At an inside corner, measure the distance from the last full strip to the corner at the ceiling, floor, and halfway up the wall. Add 1/2 inch to the longest measurement; cut the strip to this width so that when you hang it, it can go around the corner, and onto the first 1/2 inch of the next wall. This provides a continuous piece of paper in the corner to cover cracks that occur in the plaster or drywall.

After you hang the last strip on a wall and wrap it around the corner, lay out the first strip on the next wall. Start at the edge of the strip that was wrapped around the corner. Measure over the width of a new strip of paper, and draw a plumb line as in Step 2. Apply activator, and hang the strip so that it butts against the previous strip, aligns with the plumb line, and matches the pattern as closely as possible. You may find a slight gap somewhere on the seam because the corner of the wall might not be plumb.

If there's a gap along part of the seam between the strips, overlap them just enough to eliminate the gap. Check to make sure the other edge remains plumb. Smooth the seam with a seam roller; then clean up with a sponge. Work your way across the wall, hanging wallpaper the same as on the previous walls.

13 At an outside corner, take measurements at top, bottom, and middle. Add at least 4 inches, and cut the strip this width. This provides a generous overlap to avoid having a seam at a vulnerable edge. As you smooth the strip into place, make cuts in the excess paper at top and bottom to allow it to round the corner. Check the new edge for plumb. If it's plumb, butt the next strip and continue hanging paper. If it isn't plumb, hang the new strip by overlapping the previous strip until the patterns match. Plumb the leading edge. Double cut the strips (see "Paperhanger's Secret," left) to create a seam. Roll the seam and proceed to the next strip.

Papering Borders

Wallpaper doesn't have to cover the entire wall. It doesn't even have to run up and down. Borders add color, focus, and dimension to a wall painted a single color.

Install borders at any height you choose. Most commonly, however, they're applied anywhere wooden moldings would be found. Borders serve as chair rails, substitutes for crown molding, trim around a door or window, or occasionally as an accent or replacement for baseboard.

Installing borders involves the same techniques used for any wallpaper installation. You'll need to draw level layout lines on the wall and follow them carefully. You'll need to piece together strips of border in order to go around the entire room. And, at corners, you'll need to match the pattern. If you run borders around doors and windows, make sure the pattern will work both horizontally and vertically. It's not good to have flowers or puppies hanging upside down.

Requiring only a fraction of the work involved in wallpapering an entire room, adding borders helps provide definition. They can function as chair rails, around windows, and along the ceiling.

STUFF YOU'LL NEED

✔ Wallpaper border
✔ Wallpaper paste or paste activator
✔ 4-foot level
✔ Drafting triangle
✔ Tape measure
✔ Scissors
✔ Broad knife
✔ Utility knife
✔ Wallpaper brush
✔ Sponge

Paperhanger's Secret

If the joints between the ceiling and the walls are level, square, and flat, the border can run right up to the ceiling. If the ceiling slopes, however, the border will call immediate attention to the problem. A border may not be the best choice. To be sure of a level ceiling, temporarily tape the border in place and determine where you can live with gaps, if any. You may not be able to return the roll, but that is a small price to pay to avoid not liking the result.

Work Smarter

Priming the area where the border will run makes removal much easier. You don't have to prime the area perfectly; you just want enough to cover most of the border surface.

Papering Borders

1 Measure the room. Measure the circumference of the room to determine how much border you need. If you run border material around doors or windows, add an extra foot for each turn you make. If the wallpaper is in 5- or 7-yard rolls, add least $1/2$ yard extra for each 5 yards you measure. If the wallpaper is in longer rolls, add 2 yards for each roll you use.

2 Lay out the border. To lay out a ceiling border, measure down the width of the border and draw a level line for your guide in installing the strip. Check to make sure the ceiling is level by measuring the distance between the line and the ceiling at several points around the room. If the measurement varies, proceed to the smallest measurement. Measure down the width of the border at this point, and lay out a new level line around the room.

Chair-rail height borders are usually centered about one-third of the way up the wall. Choose a height and use a level to extend a line around the room that marks the bottom of the border.

3 Apply paste or paste activator. Prepasted papers adhere much better if you use a paste activator instead of soaking them. Brush on the activator (or paste if the paper isn't prepasted). To make the paper easier to handle, "ribbon fold" the strip as shown so that the pasted sides face each other. Let the strip rest for a minute, or as directed by the activator manufacturer, so that the glue can come to full strength.

2

Walls

Walls (side tab)

4 Hang the strip. A strip of border may be long and awkward to handle. Ask someone to help you. Begin near the corner, and apply border on the wall (the left wall, above) adjacent to the wall to hold the first full strip. Turn the corner without cutting the paper, and press the paper into the corner with a wide broad knife. Continue applying border along the adjacent wall, aligning it with the layout lines. Smooth the strip by running along it with a wallpaper brush or a damp sponge.

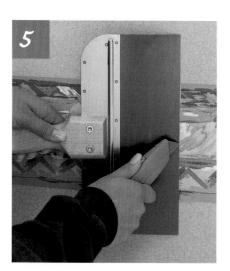

5 Double cut adjoining strips. A single strip of trim may not reach the length of a wall. To make a joint between two strips, paperhangers double cut them. Install the first strip; then install the second strip so that it overlaps the first. Slide the paper until the patterns coincide; then cut through both strips, guiding the cut along a straightedge. Peel away the excess from the overlapping strips and press the two pieces of border together to form a perfectly matched seam. Roll the seam with a seam roller and sponge away excess paste.

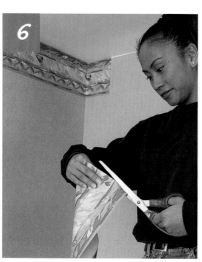

6 Turn the inside corner. When you reach the corner, cut the strip long enough to run around the corner and onto the next wall. Place the second strip over the first without applying any glue or activator. Align the patterns, and make a crisp fold in the second strip at the corner. Then cut along the fold with a pair of scissors and install the strip tight against the corner. If the paper is vinyl—and most are—regular adhesive won't hold the overlapping pieces together. Glue the overlap with vinyl-to-vinyl adhesive.

Paperhanger's Secret

If the wallpaper border has a distinct and uniform pattern, use it to hide the seam of two pieced strips. Instead of cutting along a straight edge, cut along the shapes in the pattern. The seam follows the pattern and is much harder to see.

Wisdom of the Aisles

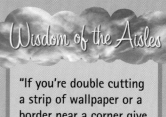

"If you're double cutting a strip of wallpaper or a border near a corner give yourself enough room on the wall to postiion the straightedge and the razor so it won't be awkward for you as you make the cut."

— *Karen Sonenson Aurora, IL*

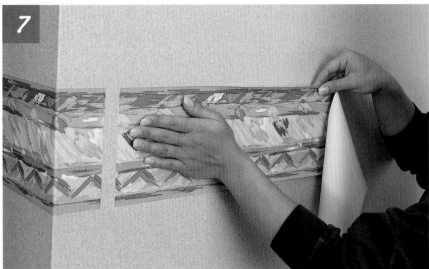

Wisdom of the Aisles

"To apply a border along the ceiling, paint the top fraction of an inch of the wall with the same paint you use on the ceiling. If dips and bumps in the ceiling result in gaps between it and the border, the extra band of ceiling paint will camouflage them."

— *Greg Korczak Lodi, NJ*

Work Smarter

How Big an Overlap?

The purpose of running the border around the corner is to have a single piece of paper covering the entire corner. This keeps the wall from peeking through if the walls settle or the corner cracks.

The amount of border that extends around the corner and onto the new wall varies. Run stiff borders a few inches past the corner. For flexible borders that stay in place easily, overlap as little as 1/2 inch.

Walls

7 Turning outside corners. Unless the corners are perfectly plumb, the border will go out of level as it turns the corner. To solve the problem, cut the paper so it's long enough to go around the corner by one or two inches. Smooth the paper onto the wall with a wallpaper brush. Pick up the cutoff, apply paste, and butt the cut edge against the strip that turned the corner.

Sometimes you'll run out of paper as you turn the corner. If this happens, the pattern on the new roll won't align perfectly with the old roll. To solve this problem, apply paste activator to the new strip, and then slide the new strip over the old strip until the patterns align. Press both strips firmly against the wall. Double cut the seams, as described in Step 5, for patterns that match perfectly at the seam.

8 Make mitered corners where the border meets doors or windows. Install the first strip right up to the door; then install the second strip over it. Cut the miter at a 45-degree angle through both strips using a utility knife and triangle. Peel away the cut off scraps and run over the cut ends with a seam roller. Sponge away excess paste.

Good idea! →

Hanging the last corner. When you finish the last wall, you'll come to the small section of border that started the job. Lay the final strip over the small section, and then cut through both about 1/2 inch from the corner, guided by a straightedge.

Papering Below Chair Rails

Papering the area below a chair rail takes about one-third the work required to paper a wall. There's less area to cover, no need for a stepladder, and the strips of paper are shorter. It's a good starting project for people with little or no experience hanging paper.

Generally speaking, wallpaper like this runs about one-third the way up the wall. Adjust the height as necessary to avoid having the top edge of the paper meet window trim at an awkward point, such as in the middle of the windowsill.

Once the paper is up, cover the top edge with a wooden or wallpaper chair rail. You may want to repaint the upper portion of the wall to complement the choice of paper. For example, a stark white may contrast too sharply with a dark-tone wallpaper. If you paint, do it before papering to avoid splattering the new paper.

Wallpaper manufacturers design borders to use at chair-rail height and with specific patterns. Complementary papers and borders or papered chair rails are usually grouped together in wallpaper books.

STUFF YOU'LL NEED

✔ Wallpaper
✔ Chair rail
✔ Tape measure
✔ 4-foot level
✔ Scissors
✔ Paste activator and wallpaper brush
✔ Wallpaper smoothing brush
✔ Seam roller
✔ Single-edge razor blades
✔ Broad knife
✔ Sponge

---

*Designer's Tip

Wallpapering chair rails and below chair rails is a good choice for children's rooms. They're easy to redo as kids' tastes change.

Work Smarter

Even professional paperhangers encounter occasional bubbles—bulges caused by trapped air. Pop these little balloons by cutting a slit with a razor knife, then squirt in adhesive with a syringe-style applicator, and apply pressure.

---

1 Lay out the rail. In this application, the wallpaper reaches only to the top of the chair rail. Make a mark at what will be the top of the rail, and extend the lines along the entire wall, guided by a level. Install the rail after the wallpaper is up.

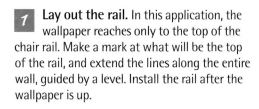

2 Cut the first strip of wallpaper. Avoid cutting off important design elements at the rail. Place a piece of the rail over a strip of wallpaper, as shown, to determine a good place to end the strip. Cut the strip to length, adding 2 or 3 inches for trimming at the bottom. Start in an inconspicuous corner so that mismatch between the pattern on the first wall and the pattern on the last wall won't be obvious. Measure a distance equal to the width of the paper minus $1/2$ inch (more if the paper is stiff) and draw a plumb line at that point to mark the edge of the first strip.

3 Hang the paper. Because the strips are short, there is no need to fold and then roll pasted papers for easy handling. Hang the first strip along the plumb line, and roll the excess around the corner. Continue hanging strips along the wall. When you are about to hang the strip that goes into the next corner, measure the distance between the corner and the top and bottom of the last strip hung. Add $1/2$ inch to the longest measurement, and cut a strip to this width. (Add up to 4 inches if the paper is stiff.) Hang the cut strip, wrapping the excess around the corner.

Hang the cutoff on the new wall, as shown. Check the far edge with a level, and adjust as necessary for plumb.

Papering Chair Rails

Wallpapering a room with floor-to-ceiling sheets can be a challenge for a beginner. A paper chair rail, however, goes up quickly and is a manageable project. Choose among rail strips that are soaked, pasted, or backed with peel-off paper. The biggest hurdle will be selecting a pattern and deciding how to use it.

A paper chair rail is often used to ornament a one-color painted wall or a wall with different shades above and below the rail. It also can act as a border for wallpaper wainscoting (see page 120), or be used as trim for the bottom edge of wallpaper that is on the top two-thirds of the wall. Use a paper chair rail as a transition between patterns or textures.

Wallpaper manufacturers take the work and worry out of selecting patterns and combinations. They provide examples of wainscoting, chair rail, and wallpaper that complement each other, and they group them together in sample books. These books are available at home centers, wallpaper outlets, and decorator showrooms. Take advantage of in-house design personnel to help you with choices.

This paper chair rail demonstrates the transition between wall treatments. Rules concerning height are few. Position borders so that furniture—cribs, dressers, and chairs—won't obscure them.

STUFF YOU'LL NEED

✔ Tape measure

✔ 4-foot level

✔ Scissors

✔ Wallpaper paste (for unpasted papers)

✔ Vinyl-to-vinyl adhesive (for a vinyl chair rail on vinyl paper)

✔ Wallpaper brush

✔ Utility knife

✔ Broadknife

✔ Seam roller

✔ Sponge

Wisdom of the Aisles

"If you apply a border over a painted wall, prime the area first. If you don't, you'll damage the wall when you eventually remove the border to repaint or repaper the room. Get a narrow roller, and apply wallpaper primer in a swath that's almost as wide as the border. (If you're nervous about drips, mask the area first.) Let the primer dry before you apply the border."

— Terri Sanders
Elgin, IL

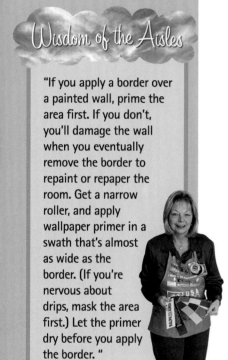

Paperhanger's Secret

Most chair rails and wallpapers are vinyl or vinyl coated. If you try to install the rail with regular adhesive, it won't stay put. Use vinyl-to-vinyl adhesive instead. It's sold right in the wallpaper department, looks like paste activator, and brushes on the same way as activator or wallpaper paste.

1 **Start in the corner.** A wallpaper chair rail, like wallpaper border, is started by placing a short section of paper on the wall adjacent to the wall holding the first full strip. (Left wall in photo.) Turn the corner without cutting the piece, and apply the paper along the wall, wrapping the corner to assure that gaps won't appear in the paper where the two walls meet.

There is no need for a layout line. Position the chair rail so that the top aligns with the top of the wallpaper.

Cut a piece of rail an inch or so longer than the wall for the first border. Apply adhesive or paste activator, ribbon fold it, as shown on page 117, and set it aside to come to full strength. (The exact time should be listed on the can of paste or activator.) When the adhesive is ready, start in the the corner and place about $1/2$ inch of rail onto one wall, running it into the corner and onto the next wall. Press the paper firmly into the corner with a broadknife. Apply the rail along the rest of the wall, aligning the top of the rail with the top of the wallpaper.

2 **Smooth the strip into place with a wallpaper brush and hang the next strip.** Smooth out the paper with a wallpaper brush as you work your way down the wall. Wash off excess paste with a damp sponge. When you reach the second corner, go around it, and then press the paper firmly in place.

3 **Hang the rail on the new wall.** Align the patterns of the new strip with those of the earlier strip. The alignment will be automatic if the new strip has been cut from the old. Apply adhesive, ribbon fold, and let the adhesive come to full strength. Butt the edges or overlap them slightly if a gap develops along the seam. Press the chair rail in place and run it along the new wall and around the corner.

If you have to start a wall with a new roll of chair rail, you may have to pattern match on the old wall, as shown. Press the paper in place; then double cut the seam on the new wall.

On the last corner, you will approach the small section of chair rail that started the job. Lay the final length of rail over the small section, and cut through both layers $1/2$ inch from the corner, guided by a straightedge.

Papering Chair Rails   123

Wallpaper—Putting It All Together

Wallpaper, borders, and chair rails can each stand on their own, but they can also reinforce one another.

The Victorians, in particular, loved to combine papers. Below the chair rail there would be a paper with a dominant image. Above the rail, a contrasting paper gave way to a wide border. Ceilings were papered. Ceiling borders and corner molding were layered on regular paper.

The current approach to wallpaper combinations is somewhat simplified in comparison, but most wallpaper pattern books do contain bold paper and border combinations designed to work well together. Homeowners can combine pattern books and their imagination to suit their sense of style and taste.

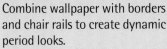

Combine wallpaper with borders and chair rails to create dynamic period looks.

The border snugs up against crown molding (above).

Matching the curtains and wallpaper presents a lush, sensual effect (upper right).

A wallpaper chair rail repeats as a border at the ceiling (right) and both can be framed between wooden chair rail and crown molding.

In the dynamic Victorian scheme (left) the border offers a bold break from the rest of the paper, framing the wall like a frieze and dramatically separating the walls and ceiling.

Walls

For the best wallpapering job, follow these guidelines from experienced paperhangers.

- Use a paste activator, as the pros do, instead of soaking prepasted papers. It's better to take time to brush on activator than to have wallpaper fall down later.

- Apply each strip from the top down.

- Choose patterns and match the seams well. Some seams match perfectly. Others, with a drop match pattern, require the adjacent strip to be slid up or down to get a match. The amount, or drop, is listed in wallpaper books and on the package or roll.

- Use a sharp blade and change it regularly. Pros often use single-edge razor blades that are held by special handles. Some pros advocate changing the blade after every cut. Demand clean straight cuts, and the only way to get them is with the right tool.

- Colors vary from batch to batch. Tell the supplier that you want paper from the same batch, and check batch numbers to confirm. Save the labels from every roll.

Molding and Trim

The demand for housing after World War II changed home-builder business. To meet the need, builders began to cut back on complexity in design to allow for quicker building, and the tract house was born. Gone was the level of interior finishing details that made houses unique. Some of the first eliminated design elements were the molding and trim that defined both style and personal taste. Elements that were traditionally used to define style, such as baseboards, picture rails, crown molding, window and door trim, and wainscoting, were replaced by simple trim pieces or eliminated altogether. Ranch trim was developed to use in the Post-war ranch-style homes that became the emblem of the '50s and '60s.

Growing interest in design and decor in recent years has produced a renewed appreciation for more complex molding and trim—baseboard, chair rails, picture rails, crown molding, wainscoting, and the trim around doors and windows. Today's homeowners are learning that trim can dramatically change the atmosphere or set the scene for a particular decor.

Though molding and trim are applied primarily for esthetic reasons, there's a practical side to them as well. They hide the cracks that inevitably develop between walls, ceilings, and floors, and they protect other surfaces from regular wear and tear.

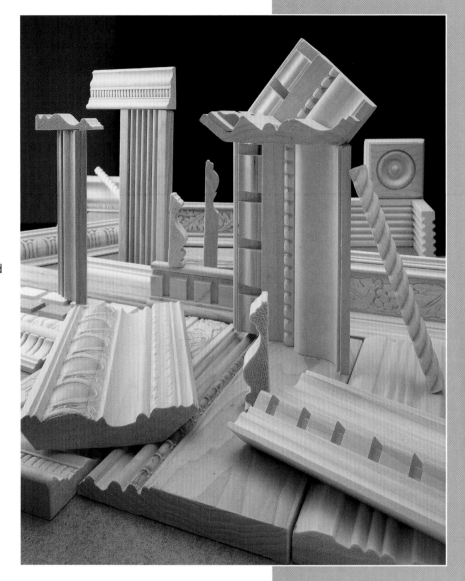

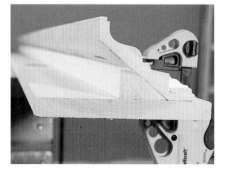

No Miter/No Cope Baseboard

Cutting miters and coping joints are two jobs that discourage homeowners from installing new molding and trim. If the walls are out of square, as they often are, there's a need to work around the angle of the miter cut or the position of the molding. Usually it's both. If the angle of the cut is off, the joint won't fit—it's that simple and that frustrating.

If you're serious about carpentry, mitering and coping are skills to learn (See "Coping a Chair Rail," page 135, and "Cutting Molding Returns," page 140.) However, there's a no miter/no cope alternative that eliminates miter and cope joints altogether. Instead of running the molding around the corners, install precut corner blocks that fit the inside and outside corners. Nail the blocks in place and make square cuts at each end of the molding to fit between them. These cuts are easily made with a fixed-angle miter box or a power miter saw. The blocks come in several sizes and styles to fit the look of your room.

No miter/no cope baseboard is easy to install. The corner blocks eliminate having to cut angles for potentially complex joints and make it easier to deal with corners that are out of square. The look above is Victorian; there are other styles available as well.

No Miter/No Cope Baseboard

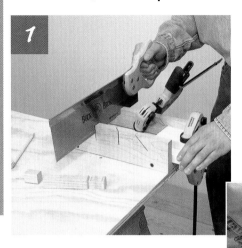

1 **Cut the corner blocks if needed.** If the corner blocks are higher than the base molding you use, cut them down. Position a corner block and straight molding to judge how much to trim (inset). Clamp a stop inside the miter box and cut all the blocks to length at the same time.

STUFF YOU'LL NEED

✔ Pry bar
✔ Wood shims
✔ Inside and outside corner blocks
✔ Hammer
✔ #6 and #8 finish nails
✔ Base molding
✔ Nail set
✔ Caulk and caulk gun
✔ Paint or wood stain and finish
✔ Miter box

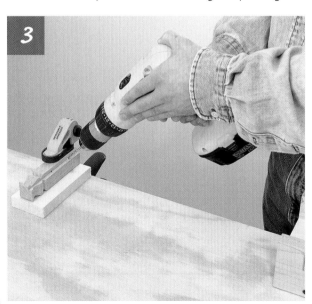

2 **Nail the inside corner blocks to the wall.** Nail into one face of the inside corner blocks with #6 finish nails, angling the nails toward the corner to draw it in. Keep the nails at least 1 inch from the top and bottom of the blocks and predrill to prevent splitting. If the corner is not perfectly square, gaps will be present on either side. Fill gaps with caulk after installation.

TOOL TIP

Hardwoods may split if you don't drill pilot holes for the nails. Carpenters use a nail as a drill bit. Tighten the nail in the chuck as if it were a drill, and drill a hole with it wherever you will drive a nail. Because the nail pushes the fibers out of the way rather than severing them like a drill does, some of the fibers spring back, leaving a perfect pilot hole, slightly smaller than the nail.

3 **Predrill the outside corner blocks.** Outside corner blocks are difficult because they need to be nailed diagonally through the corner of the block.

Predrill the holes from the inside out—it's easier to start the drill bit on the inside ledge. Clamp the block to a bench with a scrap of wood underneath and drill through. Position the corner block and drill through into the corner of the wall to break through the metal corner bead.

To find studs the high tech way, buy a stud finder—a handheld device with lights that glow when the finder is over a stud. Sometimes the old way is just as good. A few inches out from the corner, drive a nail into the wall. If the nail hits something solid, it's a stud; if not, move over an inch and try again. Repeat as often as necessary until the nail hits a stud. Plan to position holes where they will be covered by molding, and work at least 3 inches above the floor to avoid hitting framing that runs along the floor.

Wisdom of the Aisles

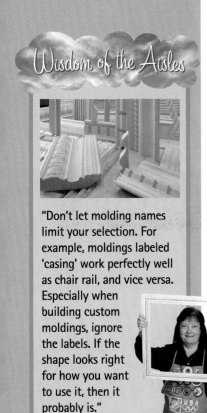

"Don't let molding names limit your selection. For example, moldings labeled 'casing' work perfectly well as chair rail, and vice versa. Especially when building custom moldings, ignore the labels. If the shape looks right for how you want to use it, then it probably is."

— *Julie Kay Lenz*
Deerfield, IL

4 Nail on outside corner blocks. Drive nails through the predrilled holes into the corner of the wall.

5 Check corners for square; scribe as needed. The corner blocks follow the prevailing contour of the walls, which usually means at least one of the joints with the base molding will be slightly out of square. This is easy to gauge before you cut the molding. Take a length of molding—a 3-foot length works well—and make a square cut on both ends. Hold this piece in position against the corner blocks to gauge whether the end cut on the molding will be square. If it's not, hold the molding in position and scribe a mark from the corner block onto the face of the molding. A metal rule, shown, is reliable, and a compass will also work. Cut the end of the molding to the scribed line. If both ends of a piece need to be scribed, repeat the process on the second end.

6 Cut the molding. Use a miter box to cut the molding. Hold the wood firmly in the box. To make a cut that is slightly off square in a fixed angle miter box, position the molding under the saw so the scribed mark lines up with the saw. Place a shim between the molding and the edge of the miter box to keep it from shifting. Hold the molding, and make the cut.

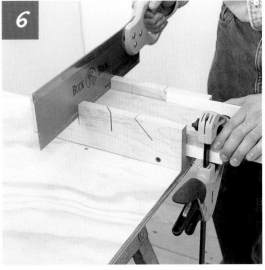

Walls

No Miter/No Cope Baseboard

7 **Nail the molding to the wall between corner blocks.** Use #6 finish nails. Locate the nails about 1 inch from the floor to catch the bottom plate of the wall. Nails higher than 1½ inches from the floor need to hit a stud or they won't hold. Studs are typically spaced 16 inches on center starting from the inside corners of the room. Drive all the nails, then set them below the surface of the wood with a nail set.

8 **Fill gaps with caulk.** Gaps are inevitable around the top of the corner blocks. Fill the gaps with with wood-tone caulk before you stain the base molding. Use plain white latex caulk if you plan to paint.

9 **Finish the base molding.** To stain, mask off the wall and floor before application. Follow up with a clear topcoat of polyurethane. Fill the nail holes with latex wood putty, then sand with 150-grit sandpaper. To paint, apply a primer first, then the topcoat.

Wisdom of the Aisles

"Sometimes a molding will flex away from the wall at a point where there's no framing to nail into. If this happens, drive a nail at an angle into the wall. Move over an inch, and drive another nail into the wall at the opposite angle. The nails will work together to help hold the molding to the wall."

— *Debi Peoples*
Rancho Cucamonga, CA

Work Smarter

Paint or stain the molding before you install it—if you have the room. If you don't have the room, carefully mask off the surrounding areas, and apply the finish after installation.

Miter Boxes & Chop Saws

To install most moldings, miter the joints at inside and outside corners. The angle of cut on each piece is one-half the angle of the corner. On a typical 90-degree corner, the moldings are each cut at 45 degrees. If you're adept at using a handsaw, lay out the angle with an adjustable square and cut the miters by hand. You'll get better results with a miter box.

Three types of miter boxes are available. The best one depends on how much molding you have to cut, how many angles you need to cut, and how much money you want to spend.

Fixed-Angle Miter Box and Backsaw

The entry-level miter box is either a solid maple box or molded plastic. There are slots at 90 degrees for straight cross cuts and 45 degrees for miters. The best saw to use with the miter box is a backsaw; it has a long rectangular blade with a solid bar of steel (brass on better models) along the back edge. A miter box and saw cost less than $20.

This simple miter box works well for cutting small moldings. It can't handle large moldings—they won't fit in the box. You're also limited to 45- and 90-degree cuts. With time and use, the slots in the miter box get wider and the cuts become less accurate. To trim only a window or door or install a room of small base molding, this setup works well.

Adjustable Miter Saw

This saw looks like a hacksaw mounted in a rigid metal frame that rotates on a stand. The saw blade locks at the desired angle between 45 and 90 degrees to either the left or right of center. There's no side-to-side play in the saw (as there is in a fixed miter box), so the cuts are smooth and clean. These saws have a larger capacity than fixed-angle miter boxes. A downside to these miter saws is that you have to supply muscle power. Unless you earn a living cutting molding or plan to trim out your whole house, this is an efficient and accurate tool for any molding job.

Power Miter or "Chop" Saw

These saws typically carry a 10-inch blade that pivots down into work held on a small table with a built-in fence. They are often called "chop" saws because of the pivoting action. Professional finish carpenters work with power miter saws, with good reason. Equipped with a good carbide blade, these saws effortlessly cut through any wood molding. The blade locks at any angle between 45 and 90 to either the left or right. Unlike manual saws, power miter saws allow you to trim just a sliver at a time from a cut to get a perfectly tight joint.

The blade on a compound miter saw tilts in two planes for more advanced cuts. There are also sliding miter saws, on which the blade pivots into the workpiece and slides along rails. These are akin to radial arm saws and can cut stock up to 12 inches wide precisely.

Power miter saws are as potentially dangerous as they are powerful and precise. A careless cut or a misplaced finger can be instantly disastrous. BE CAREFUL. Protect your eyes and ears, too. Chop saws throw dust and occasionally a large piece of wood—wear safety goggles. Wear hearing protectors to counter the noise of the chop saw.

Installing Chair and Picture Rails

Chair and picture rails dress up a room and help define period and style. Orignally used to protect plaster walls from damage, chair and picture rails also establish a border between two different wall treatments, such as a wallpapered lower section and a painted section above. Chair rails also provide a transition between paneling below and paint or wallpaper above. (See "Installing Beadboard Wainscoting," page 154.)

Even if a chair rail isn't intended to be functional, it should still be placed at a height that will protect it from damage from chair backs. Depending on the chairs in a room, the rail should be placed between 32 and 36 inches from the floor. Adjust the height as necessary to avoid awkward meetings with the bottom of window frames, as well as to suit rooms with ceilings that are unusually high or low.

Picture rails are usually installed from 10 to 16 inches below the ceiling line, depending on the height of the wall. Follow the same procedures for installing picture rails. Picture rails should be mounted securely to the wall whether they are intended to carry the weight of hanging objects or to be used as purely decorative elements.

Moldings transform a room. Here, the chair rail marks a change from wallpaper to paint. The picture rail is both functional and decorative, but in many homes, the picture rail is purely decorative.

Installing Chair and Picture Rails

Walls

STUFF YOU'LL NEED

- ✔ Chair or picture rail
- ✔ Primer or varnish
- ✔ Paintbrush
- ✔ Level
- ✔ Tape measure
- ✔ Power miter saw or handsaw and miter box
- ✔ Stud finder
- ✔ Electric drill
- ✔ Hammer
- ✔ Finishing nails
- ✔ Nail set
- ✔ Wood putty
- ✔ Caulk
- ✔ Caulk gun

1 Prime the rail. To prevent warping, paint or varnish both sides of the molding before installing it. If you plan to finish the trim after it is nailed on, apply a coat of finish to the back now.

2 Draw a layout line. Determine the height of the chair rail. Mark the wall at that height, and use a level to extend a horizontal line for the top edge of the rail.

Good idea!

Buy molding from the same bundle to make sure the pieces are as identical as possible. The molding profile changes as the cutters wear down.

3 Make miter cuts at corners. Moldings with simple profiles can meet at 45-degree miter joints for both inside and outside corners. Complex moldings meet better at inside corners if joints are coped. (See "Coping a Chair Rail," page 135.)

Wisdom of the Aisles

"Check your level to make sure the layout line on one wall is level with the layout line on the other. Start a couple of feet from the corner, and put one end of the level on the line. Put the other end of the level on the line on the other wall. It's okay that only the ends of the level touch the wall. If you get a level reading, the lines are level. If not, redraw one of the lines."

— *Ed Czar*
Landsdale, PA

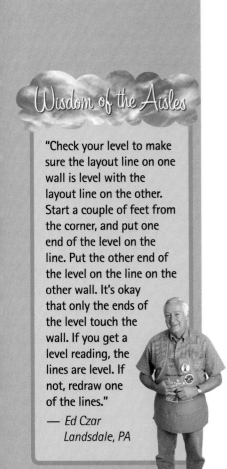

Installing Chair and Picture Rails

4 Make square cuts at door and window casings. At doors and windows, end the molding with a square cut. If the molding is thicker than the casings, make a transition by cutting a bevel on the portion that protrudes. Along walls that can't be spanned with a single length of rail, scarf two or more pieces. (See "Carpenter's Secret," page 139 and Step 3, page 142.)

Good idea! → **Make finishing nails less conspicuous.** Drive them at an angle into a crevice in the profile.

5 Nail the chair rail. Locate the studs with a stud finder or by tapping a nail through the wall where the holes will be concealed by the trim. Studs are almost always spaced every 16 inches on center. Hold the chair rail in place and transfer the stud locations to the rail. Drill pilot holes at each mark and attach the molding with finishing nails. Countersink the nails, putty the holes, and smooth outside corners by sanding the exposed edges.

Installing Picture Rails

Picture rails protect walls as chair rails do, although they are higher on the walls.

The purpose, other than to add visual interest or historical pedigree to a room, is to allow pictures and other objects to be hung without hammering nails into the wall. Picture rails are installed the same way as chair rails; they have a cove along the top edge to hold specialized hardware from which pairs of wires descend to support pictures. If the trim is purely decorative it can be nailed in place. If the trim will be used to hang pictures, however, screw it to the studs, countersinking the screws and covering them with putty.

Good idea! → When installing molding around a room, always start with the longest wall and work in the direction of the shorter ones if possible. If you make an error and cut a piece slightly short, you can still use it for shorter lengths of wall.

Coping a Chair Rail

When miters work, they're great, but when they're bad, they're horrid. If the room is out of square, if there is a buildup of drywall compound in the corners, or if the moldings are slightly different thicknesses, putty will not fix the gap. Learning how to cope a joint, which is all about trimming a profile in one piece of molding so that it will butt against its mate without needing an angled joint, will save you many headaches. (See "Installing Crown Molding," Step 5, page 143.)

1 **Miter with the piece flat on the miter box.** This is a normal mitering operation, with the miter cut as it would be for an inside corner. In the next step, however, part of the stock will be cut away, so a longer piece than the finished length is needed. Miter the piece so it's longer than needed by at least the thickness of the stock. If you cope both ends, the stock should be longer by at least twice the thickness.

2 **Follow the outline with a coping saw.** The miter reveals a crisp profile of the molding. Cut along the profile, creating a socket that fits over the face of a similar piece of molding. Angle the saw as you cut, creating a gentle point that will be the only part of the joint to touch the neighboring molding.

3 **Test-fit the cut.** Check the joint by fitting it against a cutoff. Don't be surprised or dismayed if the fit isn't perfect. Even experienced carpenters fine-tune the joint. Sand and file to get a good fit.

The forerunner of the cupboard, the galley shelf can display objects that complement the walls the way this china mimics the wallpaper.

Alternatives to Picture Rails

Picture rail molding is the classic solution to hanging pictures on a wall without damaging it, but every style presents its own possibilities. Hang pictures from 1-inch-thick branches for a rustic scheme. Use a brass foot rail for a loose interpretation of Victorian style. Plastic and copper pipes, black gas pipe, and electrical conduit can serve in contemporary settings. Imitate the picture rail found in country homes by nailing wood strips about 6 feet from the floor and around the perimeter of the room. Search hardware stores and flea markets for dowels, graphite chimney brush rods, or other unusual alternatives.

Shaker pegs that were designed to hold clothes and furniture also hold pictures.

In this Southwestern-style home, a weathered wood rail displays local artifacts.

For a contemporary look, hang art from a copper pipe screwed to the wall or hang it from a picture rail.

Creating Custom Moldings

Home centers and lumberyards carry large selections of wood moldings. Look closely and you'll notice that there are usually two or three choices with slight variations—mostly the same profiles, in different widths. If it's variety you want, create custom molding yourself. Complex moldings and trim are usually built from several pieces. Traditional baseboard is a good example. The main piece is often 1× stock. The top profile is a separate base cap molding. There's a quarter-round shoe molding against the floor. When painted, it looks like one piece.

This chair rail is a combination of simple profiles found on the sample boards at home centers. Each molding is identified in "Stuff You'll Need" by a number assigned by the Wood Moulding and Millwork Association. The upper rail, for example, is based on an $^{11}/_{16}{\times}2^5/_8$-inch chair rail called WM390. The lower rail is built around WM298, an $^{11}/_{16}{\times}2^1/_2$-inch chair rail. The rest of the stock is either 1× or cove molding.

If all this molding talk seems like a foreign language, ask an associate at your home center or lumberyard to take you on a tour of the molding and trim area.

Molding combinations are limited only by your imagination. This combination, made of stock pieces found in most lumber stores, creates an intricate and interesting double chair rail.

Creating Custom Moldings

Walls

1 **Make a sample profile.** Determine from the molding profiles on page 139 which molding you want to create. Sketch the molding and then make a full-size drawing to take to the store. Purchases samples—you may be able to buy 1-foot samples of the moldings, and use these to create short sample assemblies. Before you purchase the molding you need, hold a sample in place in the room to get a sense of the scale and fit.

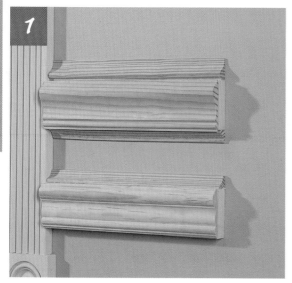

STUFF YOU'LL NEED

✔ 1×3 pine; twice room perimeter plus 8 feet

✔ ¹¹/₁₆×2⅝ chair rail, WM 390; room perimeter, plus 8 feet

✔ ¹¹/₁₆×2½ chair rail, WM 298; room perimeter, plus 8 feet

✔ ¹¹/₁₆×¹¹/₁₆ cove molding, WM 100; twice room perimeter, plus 16 feet

✔ Chalk line

✔ 4-foot level

✔ Saw

✔ Hammer

✔ #4, #6, and #8 finish nails

✔ Nail set

✔ Masking tape

✔ Paint or stain

✔ Miter box or chop saw

✔ Wood form

2 **Draw a layout line on the wall.** The foundation of the double chair rail molding is a pair of 1×3s. Determine the height of the chair rail; 30 to 40 inches from the floor is the typical range. For a true chair rail that protects the walls from chair backs, place the bottom molding the same height as the chair backs. Draw a level line where the bottom edge of the lower 1×3 will be. You need only this one line. Position the top 1×3 by placing a spacer against the lower one.

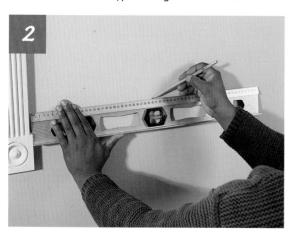

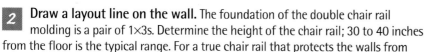

Wisdom of the Aisles

"When you make a cut in a miter box, never try to cut right along the line on the first try. Make a cut that you know leaves the piece a bit long, and then edge the piece over to make another cut. Keep cutting and edging until the piece is the right length. If you want the piece to fit tightly between two walls, cut it ¹/₃₂ to ¹/₁₆ inch on the long side, flex it into place, and nail it down."

— *Debi Peoples*
Rancho
Cucamonga, CA

3 **Cut the lower 1×3 to length.** Butt the 1×3s at the inside corners, and miter the outside corners. Nail the 1×3 to the wall, driving #6 or #8 finish nails into the studs. Or use screws, since most of the surface is covered by molding.

Molding Profiles

Top Rail

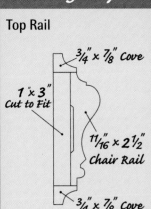

3/4" x 7/8" Cove

1" x 3"
Cut to Fit

11/16" x 2 1/2"
Chair Rail

3/4" x 7/8" Cove

Bottom Rail

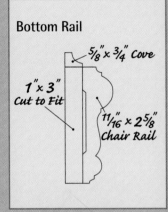

5/8" x 3/4" Cove

1" x 3"
Cut to Fit

11/16" x 2 5/8"
Chair Rail

Carpenter's Secret

Piecing Molding

Although walls may be 12 or more feet long, moldings are available only in 8- or 10-foot lengths. No problem. Just splice or scarf a shorter length onto the long one to complete the wall. Make a splice joint by mitering the end pieces and overlapping them. The angle is not crucial (although between 35 and 45 degrees is best). Cut the first piece, with the molding on one side of the box. Put the second molding against the other side of the box when you cut it. Overlap the first piece with the second piece.

---

4 **Use a spacer to position the second 1×3.** Cut a short length of 1×3 and rest it on top of the piece nailed to the wall. Position the second 1×3 on top of the scrap and nail it to the wall. Use the scrap as a spacer to keep the second 1×3 parallel with the first. If the boards are short, cut the top piece to stagger the joints.

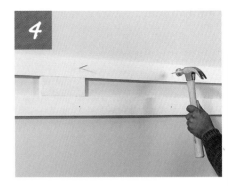

5 **Nail on the additional moldings.** Before you nail the top trim in place, bevel the edges where the molding will fit window or door frames. This will provide a cleaner look. (See "Cabinetmaker's Secret," page 161.) Nail moldings to the face and edges of the two 1×3s.

Good idea! To install molding around a room, start with the longest wall and work in the direction of the shorter walls, if possible. If you make an error and cut a piece slightly short, use it for shorter lengths of wall.

6 **Miter molding at inside and outside corners.** Use a miter box or chop saw to cut all the inside and outside corners. You may have to piece moldings together for the right lengths. (See "Carpenter's Secret," left). Wherever possible, miter the end of the first piece, and nail it in place. Hold the second piece in place, and mark it to meet the first piece. Miter at the mark, and put the molding in place. It's faster and more reliable than measuring. If you're in doubt about the length, err on the side of cutting the piece long, and trim it to fit.

7 **Prime and paint the molding.** Mask the wall at the top and bottom edges of the molding. Set all the nails and fill the holes with latex wood putty. Prime and paint the new molding. An alternative to painting in between the moldings is to run a strip of wallpaper that matches other decorative elements in the room.

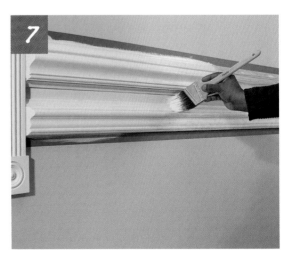

Cutting Molding "Returns"

In most rooms, moldings go along the wall and end when they run into door or window trim. The termination looks neat and clean. Not all doors and windows have trim. Often molding is thicker than the trim it meets so that it protrudes into the room, calling attention to itself.

To end a molding at an untrimmed doorway (a common scenario), make a square cut or a slightly angled cut, and round the end of the profile with sandpaper. Professional carpenters handle this situation by cutting what's called a molding return.

A return is a small mitered piece that allows the profile to turn (or return) back to the wall, much the way it wraps around an outside corner. This eliminates abrupt endings and exposed end grain.

1 **To cut and fit a molding return, first cut a 45-degree miter on the molding** that runs along the wall, cutting it a bit short of the door or window. Nail the molding in place.

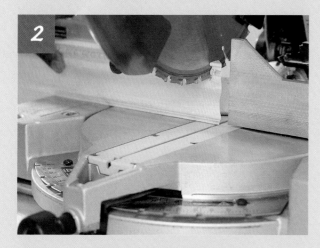

2 **To cut the actual return, cut another outside miter** that will mate with the one already cut. When they fit together, they will form a 90-degree angle. This is one end of the return. To cut the return to length, make a square cut that frees just the mitered section of molding from the rest of the stock. If you use a power miter saw, make sure this piece falls freely away from the blade, and not back into the blade.

3 **To attach a molding return,** dab white or yellow wood glue onto the mating surfaces and press it into place. Do not use a nail. Hold it for a few seconds or wrap masking tape around it until the glue sets up. Lightly sand as necessary to clean the joint.

Walls

Installing Crown Molding

Though carpet, paint, and furnishings receive more attention, crown molding sets the tone for formality and grace in traditional spaces by highlighting and finishing the upper areas of a room.

Why bother with crown molding? Aside from its beauty, it artfully conceals gaps that can open up between wall and ceiling. Crown molding is also a visual transition from one surface to another. Not every house requires this treatment—crown molding might simply clutter a contemporary design. But it's an asset in homes that draw on traditional styles, adding a touch of refinement and formality.

Installing crown molding requires cutting some coped and mitered joints, and you may want to ask a helper to hold long pieces in place. You can hire a carpenter for the installation, or—if you want to do the job yourself but can't cope with coping—buy no miter/no cope molding that uses plinth blocks in the corners. (See "Faux Plaster Rosettes and Crown Molding," page 200.)

Before shopping for molding, decide whether to use a clear finish on natural wood or to save money with finger-jointed stock or medium density fiberboard (MDF) and paint it. As you walk the aisles, look for ways to build an impressive molding by combining common types of stock; store personnel can help suggest combinations.

Walls

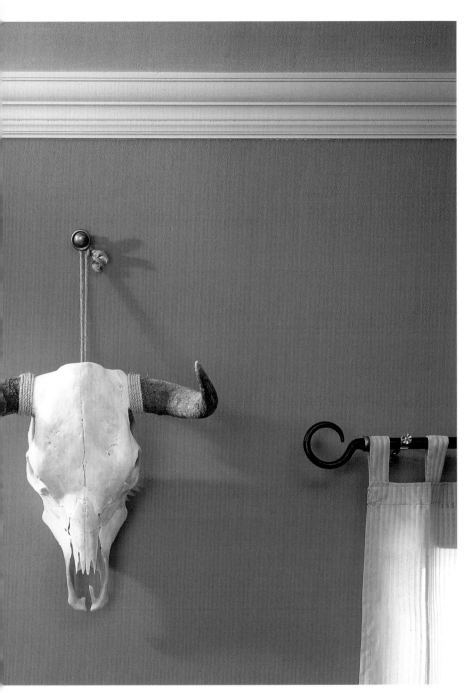

Crown molding enhances almost any decor—from elegant colonial to this rustic Southwestern look.

Installing Crown Molding

Walls

1 **Prime the molding.** Molding will be less likely to warp if it is finished front and back. Either completely apply finish before installing the trim, or at least brush a coat of primer or varnish on the back.

STUFF YOU'LL NEED

✔ Crown molding
✔ Primer or varnish
✔ Paintbrush
✔ Tape measure
✔ Stepladder
✔ 4-foot level
✔ Power miter saw
✔ Stud finder
✔ Electric drill
✔ Hammer
✔ Finishing nails
✔ Nail set
✔ Wood putty
✔ Caulk
✔ Caulk gun
✔ Coping saw
✔ Clamps

Good idea! →

Combine two moldings to make a third molding. One of the easiest combinations starts with nailing a baseboard to the wall along the ceiling. Nail it upside down so that the decorative edge faces the floor. (Baseboards with a bead along the edge work well.) Then attach a crown molding to the baseboard, positioning it to expose the decorative edge.

2 **Measure the room and mark the stud locations.** The molding will be nailed into the wall studs. Find them with a stud finder, and make faint pencil marks high on the wall (where they won't be covered by molding) to guide the nailing. Draw a pencil line along the wall to lay out the bottom edge of the molding.

3 **Make scarf joints for long runs.** Where you need two or more strips of molding to span a wall, have them meet at an angled scarf joint cut. Because the strips overlap, the combined length must be greater than that of the wall width. Mark the strips for 45-degree cuts that will position the joint over a stud. Make the cuts with a miter saw.

Painter's Secret

Nervous about cutting tight joints? For first-timers, plan to paint crown molding. You'll be able to caulk and paint any gaps.

✱ Designer's Tip

Size the molding to suit the room. Wide molding can lower the ceiling too much in a small room, and narrow molding disappears in a room with high ceilings.

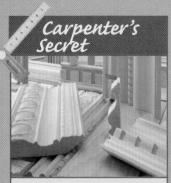

Carpenter's Secret

To match the look of your home's molding, ask to see a store copy of Wood Moulding Association's *Wood Moulding* booklet. If the molding you're after isn't in the booklet, order custom-made molding from a cabinetmaker or architectural mill house. Be prepared to place a large minimum order.

Wisdom of the Aisles

"Don't have a stud finder? All you need is a hammer and a finishing nail. Start by driving the nail into the wall a couple of inches out from the corner. Make sure you work high enough that the trim will cover the holes, but stay at least 2 ½ inches from the ceiling to avoid framing along the top of the wall. Drive a series of holes at 1-inch intervals, until you hit something solid—it's a stud. The center of the next one will be 16 inches away from the center of the one you've found."

— *Steve Smith*
 La Quinta, CA

4 **Drill pilot holes.** To prevent molding from splitting, drill pilot holes the diameter of the finishing nails you'll use. Mark the locations of pilot holes by holding the molding in place and transferring the wall stud marks onto the molding. Drill holes at the angled ends of scarfed pieces, too.

Good idea! **When you cut pieces that are square on one end and** cut the piece long, and then cut it to length after you're happy with the coped joint. By initially cutting the pieces long, you have the luxury of botching one or two coping attempts without having to throw out the molding.

5 **Make coping cuts at inside corners.** Crown molding isn't mitered at inside corners. It's coped—the end of one piece is cut to nestle into the profile of another. For this to work, cut and install the molding in the sequence shown here. In a room with four walls, the first wall's molding is square at both ends. Cut and install it now. On the second wall, the molding is square at one end and coped at the other. (Cut the joints as explained on the following page). The third wall is treated the same way. The molding on the fourth wall is coped at both ends. (Continued on page 145.)

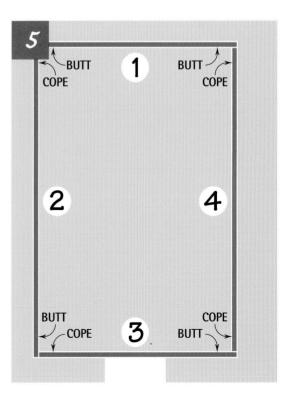

Installing Crown Molding   143

Coping Crown Molding

Because crown molding slopes between the ceiling and the wall, coping it is different from coping a flat molding, such as a chair rail. The purpose is the same, however—to create nesting joints that mimic a miter, but that won't be affected by wall irregularities.

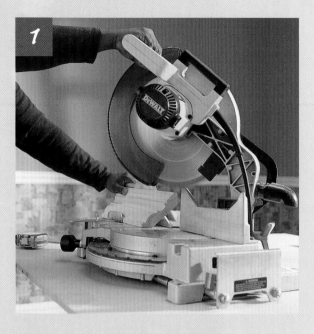

1 Set up the saw. Part of the challenge of coping is orienting the molding in the miter box. Mark the bottom edge of the molding with tape to avoid confusion. Then rest the top of the molding on the bottom of the miter box. Lean the molding back so the bottom is against the back fence of the miter box. Set the saw to cut at 45 degrees, and miter as if cutting a miter for a normal inside corner. Set the piece so that the top is flush with the saw fence.

2 Cut the profile. When you look at the face of the molding, you'll see that the miter cut exposed the profile of the molding, outlined here in red. Cutting along the profile creates a joint that will nest against a similar piece of molding.

3 Test fit the cut. The coped piece should nest tightly against the molding on the adjoining wall, as shown. If it doesn't, file high spots with a rat-tail file.

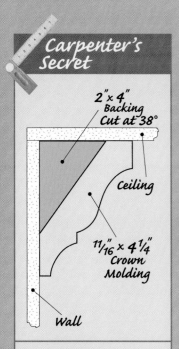

*Designer's Tip

When choosing paint for crown molding, remember** that a dramatic color can cause the ceiling to look low or make the molding look too ornate.

Carpenter's Secret

2" x 4"
Backing
Cut at 38°

Ceiling

11/16" x 4 1/4"
Crown
Molding

Wall

When nailing crown molding, nail the bottom edge into the wall studs. On the two walls perpendicular to the ceiling joists, nail the top edge of the molding into the joists. On the other two walls, there's nothing in the ceiling to nail into. On these walls, cut 2x4s to make triangular nailing blocks, such as the one shown, above. Nail the infills into the studs and into the plate at the top of the wall. When you install the molding, nail it to the nailing block.

6 **Make mitered joints at outside corners.** If there are outside corners, the moldings meet at 45-degree miter joints. Mitering, like coping, requires you to put the molding in the saw with the top edge on the floor of the box. Mitering is explained on page 146.

7 **Nail the molding.** Hold the strips in place and nail them in place. Once all the molding is up, drive the heads below the surface with a nail set, and fill the holes with putty. If you will apply a clear finish over stain, use a putty that matches the stain or that will take stain. If you paint the walls, fill the holes with glazing compound—the putty that's used around windows. It dries quickly and paints well.

8 **Caulk the seams.** Dark, gaping seams can become obvious if you paint the molding a light color. Fill gaps between the molding and the ceiling and between the molding and the wall with paintable caulk or one that matches the stain you use. Apply the caulk with a caulk gun, and smooth out the surface with a moist finger. If you paint the molding, caulk gaps in the joints.

Walls

Installing Crown Molding 145

Installing Crown on Outside Corners

Mitering outside corners—such as those that go around a chimney or cabinet that juts into a room—is simpler than coping inside corners.

An outside corner is a true miter; the key is to position the molding correctly in the saw. Put the molding in the saw so the top of the molding is against the floor of the saw. Then, lean the molding back so that the bottom of the molding is against the fence. Putting the top of the molding against the floor of the saw may seem backward. The other way creates a gap in the joint. Mark the bottom of the molding with a piece of tape for proper orientation. Follow these steps to make molding cuts for a chimney that juts into the room. The directions begin with the left side, work across the front, and finish on the right side.

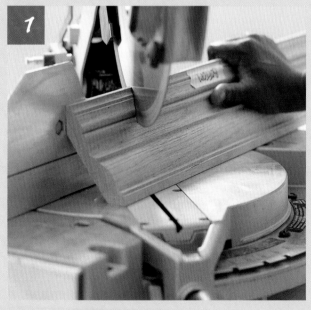

1 Miter the molding for the left side. Start with a piece of molding longer than you need, and put it in the miter saw, as shown. The bottom of the molding is against the fence, and the top of the molding is against the floor of the saw. The piece leans back; only two surfaces actually touch the saw, and there is a triangular gap between the rest of the molding and the saw. Set the saw handle 45 degrees to the left, and slide the molding so that the scrap will be to the left of the blade. Cut through the molding to create the miter. Set the saw to make a square cut, and cut the piece to length from the other end.

2 Cut the left corner of the front molding. Set the saw handle 45 degrees to the right, and put the molding in place so the scrap piece will be to the right of the blade. Cut a piece about 6 inches longer than you need. Once you make the cut, you should have two parts of a corner. Set them in place on the wall to see how they fit, and have a helper draw a line marking where the bottom of the untrimmed molding meets the wall.

3 Cut the right corner of the front molding. Set the saw handle to the left, with what will be the scrap to the left of the blade. Carpenters like to sneak up on this cut in order to make sure that they don't cut the piece too short. Here's how to do it. Position the molding so that it's obvious that the piece you cut will be too long. Make a cut that just touches the molding, so that you can see where the blade will hit it and how far that is from the layout line. Slide the molding toward the blade, enough to get close to the mark. Take another trial cut. Keep cutting and sliding until the trial cut is at the layout line, and then cut the piece to length.

4 Cut the molding for the right side. Put a new piece of molding in the saw; set the saw handle to the right with the scrap to the right of the blade. Miter the stock, then set the blade square, and cut it to length from the other end.

Crown Molding

The fancy and elegant trim along the ceiling in a frame-and-paneled Colonial parlor is what often comes to mind when we think of crown molding. While crown is a decorative element, it has a practical purpose as well. It masks the line between the ceiling and the wall, which is a prime candidate for cracking. Many decorating styles have embraced crown molding as a result. To help you decide on a look, bring home some molding samples from your home center and see how they look on the wall in your room. No matter what the profile, style, or use, crown molding adds focus and dimension to almost any room.

A lightweight crown rail can complement a picture rail, creating a wide composition with a feeling of grace.

The Arts and Crafts home almost always had a band of trim around the top of the wall, tying the rooms together and making the ceiling seem lower. Sometimes the trim was simplified crown molding or a strip of wood tucked between exposed beams; sometimes it was two strips of wood separated by a few inches to create the feeling of a frieze.

In a Country home, crown molding was often painted to match the rest of the trim and to bring color into poorly lit interiors (above). Crown molding also creates a transitional element between a papered wall and a painted ceiling (below).

Lighted Crown Molding

Installing lights in crown molding combines a classic decorative element with a modern, functional purpose. Though most lighting is focused downward, some lights (sconces and torches, for example) are designed to reflect light off the ceiling and wall surfaces. Uplights in crown molding provide warm, subtle, indirect light in a room and augment other primary lighting sources.

Cable lights provide the simplest approach to installing lights in crown molding. They are made up of tiny long-life bulbs strung together and encased in clear, flexible PVC tubing. Individual cable lengths join together at the ends with screw-together fittings and can be strung as long as 150 feet. They also can be cut every 18 inches along any cable to fit a given space.

Part of the job of adding lighting to crown molding is to install a new outlet near the ceiling to provide power to the lights. (See, "Wiring Crown Molding Lights," page 151.)

Adding lighting to crown molding creates a subtle sense of warmth and accents the molding.

Lighted Crown Molding

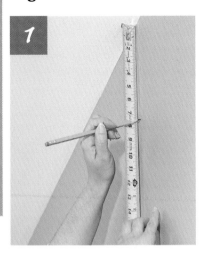

1 **Find and mark the wall studs.** The backer board, which supports the crown molding, needs to be attached to the wall studs for support. Use a stud finder or tap on the wall with a hammer to find the studs—the sound pitch will go up and become less hollow at the studs. Wall studs are typically spaced 16 inches on center, so that once you've found one, you'll know approximately where to look for the others. Mark the locations on the wall just below where the bottom edge of the backer board will be.

2 **Cut the backer boards to length.** If you don't have access to a radial arm saw or a sliding miter saw, make the cuts with a circular saw guided by a square, such as the one shown. Lay out the cut, position the saw, and put the square against it before making the cut.

3 **Nail or screw the backer boards to the wall.** If you install a new outlet for the wall, cut an opening for it as explained in "Wiring Crown Moldings Lights," page 151. After you cut the opening, install the backer board by driving drywall

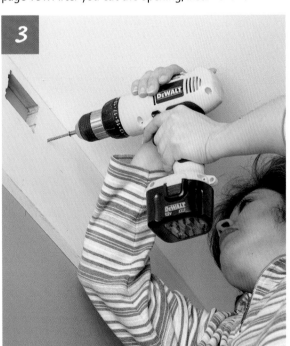

screws along the bottom half of the board and into the studs. The crown moldings, when they are attached, conceal the screws. Drive finish nails or finish screws into the upper half of the backer board, which will be visible. Inside corners can be butted one piece to the other. Outside corners should ideally be mitered. Set nails and drive screws that will be visible so they're below the surface of the wood. Fill the holes with wood putty.

STUFF YOU'LL NEED

- ✔ Crown molding
- ✔ 1×6 or wider backer board
- ✔ 2×4 for nailer block
- ✔ Stud finder
- ✔ Circular saw
- ✔ Square
- ✔ Tape measure
- ✔ Drill
- ✔ Screwdriver
- ✔ Cable lights
- ✔ Receptacle and cover
- ✔ Hammer
- ✔ Nail set
- ✔ Finish nails and screws
- ✔ Paint or varnish
- ✔ Trim brush
- ✔ Saber saw
- ✔ Fish tape

Carpenter's Secret

Prefinish the molding components as far as practical before installing them. This means priming painted molding and applying all but the final coat on stained and clear-coated molding.

Wiring Crown Molding Lights

Cable lights usually have a standard power cord and plug. Though the manufacturer may suggest the cord run to an outlet near the floor, the dangling lamp cord generally ruins the effect. It's better to hide an outlet for the cord somewhere behind the crown molding. (Keep the outlet low in the wall so that it won't be seen.)

Running wires from floor to ceiling usually involves cutting holes in the wall. Fortunately, with this job there's almost no wall repair. Cut the hole for the new outlet directly above one along the floor. Connect new cable to the outlet, and fish the wire up the wall to the new outlet. Run more cable from the outlet to the switch. If you remove the baseboard and cut out part of the wall behind it, you can run the wire and then replace the baseboard to cover the work. (For specifics, see "Running Wire for a New Ceiling Fixture," page 205.)

1 **Determine the position of the crown and nailer block** on the backer board, and cut a hole in the backer board for the outlet box so it is above the level of the nailer block. Drill a ³/₈-inch or ¹/₂-inch diameter hole at each corner, and cut along the layout lines with a saber saw.

2 **Use the hole in the backer board to mark and cut the hole through the drywall.** Install the backer board.

3 **Fit the outlet box in the opening,** feed the wiring to the outlet box, and install the outlet.

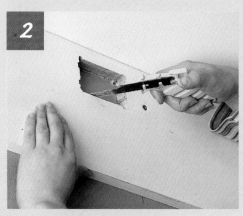

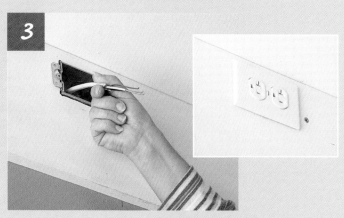

Lighted Crown Molding   151

Lighted Crown Molding

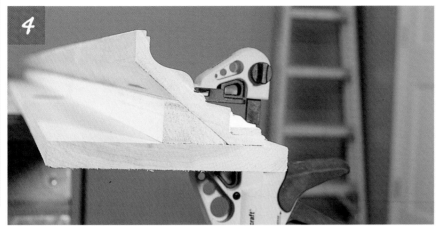

4 Cut a continuous nailer block. A nailer block, shown here clamped between the molding and the backer board, gives the molding support necessary because the molding is not nailed along the top edge. The block needs to be cut at an angle that matches the angle of the molding. Determine this angle by making a full-scale drawing of the molding and backer board. Rip the nailer blocking from straight pieces of 2×4 material or have it cut at a home center. Decide on the location of the molding and strike a line to show where the nailer block will go. Test the fit of the nailer block by clamping the backer board, nailer block, and crown molding together on a bench. Nail the blocking to the backer board on the wall.

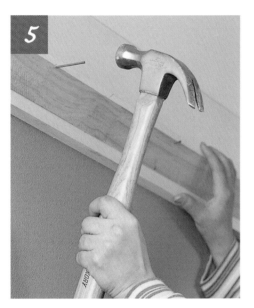

5 Attach the nailer block. Before you nail the nailer block, determine the location of the light cable. The light cable can be attached to the backer board or to the top of the nailer block, whichever is easier. You may want to temporarily nail up a short piece of the crown molding and hold the light cable in place with the power on to determine the best position for the lights. Small adjustments in position change the amount of light that is cast against the ceiling. In general, the light cable should be an inch or so below the top level of the installed crown molding.

6 Attach mounting clips for cable. Attach the cable mounting clips to the backer board or nailer block. Some nail in place; others are screwed on. Locate the clips every 18 to 24 inches.

Choosing Crown Molding

The larger the molding, the wider the swath of light projected against the ceiling. A small crown molding does not allow much light to project from behind the molding. A 4½-inch-wide crown is the smallest to consider. The one used in the installation here is almost 5 inches wide across its face.

For proper lighting, leave at least 2½ inches of space above the top edge of the crown molding.

Wisdom of the Aisles

"Make sure you install the crown molding in a straight line along both the ceiling and the wall. If you don't, the straight lines and edges in the molding will appear to wander. Put the molding in a framing square, as if one arm of the molding were the ceiling and the other, the wall. Notice where the molding hits the 'ceiling arm' and where it hits the 'wall arm.' Draw corresponding lines along the wall and ceiling at these distances, and follow the lines when you put up the molding."

— *Joe Pelligrini Jericho, NY*

Lighted Crown Molding

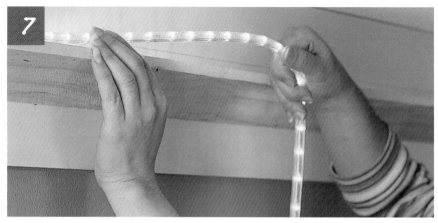

7 **Attach the light cable.** Press the light cable into the mounting clips. Bend the cable gently around corners. Connect additional lengths of cable as needed. With the cable lights in place, connect the power and check that all lights work.

8 **Cut and fit the crown molding.** Now you're ready for a typical crown molding installation. Cope-cut the inside corners and miter-cut the outside corners. If the molding will be painted, attach it to the backer board and nailer block by driving finish head screws along the bottom edge of the molding. If the molding is stained and varnished, attach it with finish nails, which leave smaller holes. (See "Installing Crown Molding," page 141, for a full treatment of crown molding installation.)

9 **Set nails, fill, and paint the molding.** Sink all the nailheads below the surface of the wood with a nail set. Fill all the nail or screw holes with a latex filler that matches the finish. Paint the molding.

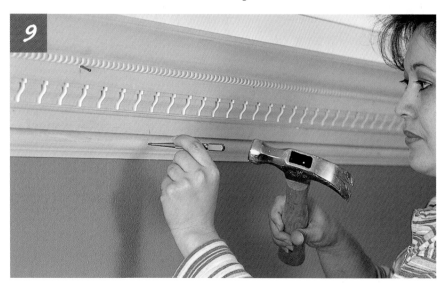

---

*Designer's Tip

The bottom edge of the backer board is flat, square, and dull. Dress it up with a piece of molding. Check sample boards at the home center and pick one that you think will work well. It doesn't have to be specifically designed to work with crown molding. Try base cap molding designed to go on a baseboard. Other possibilities include chair rail, door trim, or window trim. Cut and install the molding, coping the inside corners as explained on page 135.

Installing Beadboard Wainscoting

Wainscoting—partial paneling used on the lower part of a wall—served for centuries as protection for the plaster and added a decorative touch as well.

Wainscoting provides an intimate, traditional feeling in dens, bedrooms, and bathrooms, as well as a somewhat formal look for dining rooms. Installation is typically 32 to 36 inches off the floor, or roughly one-third of the room height. You can also create real drama in a dining room by reversing that proportion and making the wainscoting the main feature of the room as we have done here. Whichever proportion you choose, raise or lower the top edge to avoid running into windowsills or other trim in the room. Select wainscoting that is thinner than door and window casing to avoid building up the thickness of existing door and window trim.

The most common version is the tongue-and-groove beadboard shown in this project. The edges between boards are subtly ornamented with a ridge or bead. Wainscoting can also be built from a horizontal series of panels set in frames, similar to a row of traditional cabinet doors. There also may be a bead running down the center of each board so that a single board looks like a pair. Plywood wainscoting sheeting is a modern, easy-to-install alternative.

Home centers sell kits with all the pieces—beaded boards (or plywood panels), cap rail, and baseboard. They also can special order frame-and-panel wainscoting, custom-made to fit a room. (See, "Frame and Panel Wainscoting," page 158.)

Typically wainscoting is at the height of a chair rail. Here, it reaches almost to the ceiling, with the top rail doubling as a plate shelf.

Installing Beadboard Wainscoting

STUFF YOU'LL NEED

✔ Tongue-and-groove beadboard
✔ Cap rail
✔ Baseboard (optional)
✔ Varnish or paint, and brush
✔ Pry bar
✔ Level
✔ Stud finder
✔ Miter box or power miter saw
✔ Tape measure
✔ Construction adhesive
✔ Notched trowel for adhesive
✔ Hammer
✔ #6 and #8 finish nails
✔ Paintable caulk
✔ Caulk gun
✔ Hand plane (optional)
✔ Nail set
✔ Rubber gloves
✔ Saber saw
✔ Combination square

*Designer's Tip

No Baseboard?

In some older homes, wainscoted rooms didn't have baseboard because the beaded boards provided protection for the lower wall.

If you opt for baseboard, reuse the existing board, if possible. It will match the rest of the baseboard and help to tie the room together.

Smart Start

Start installation in the most obvious corner of the room. Little errors will be hidden in less obvious parts of the room.

1 **Remove the baseboard and outlet covers.** Coax the baseboard from the wall with a pry bar. Avoid damaging the wood if you plan to reinstall it. You may prefer to use new baseboards with a rabbet to hold the lower ends of the wainscoting boards. The wainscoting will create a well around the outlet covers; install box extension rings, inexpensive metal collars that allow you to bring the outlet to the wainscoting surface.

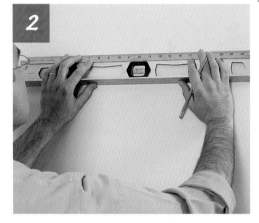

Good idea!

A pry bar has an enormous wallop. Put a piece of wood between it and the wall to gain leverage, distribute the force, and avoid damaging the wall.

2 **Draw a line for the top edge of the wainscoting.** Determine the height for the wainscoting, measure up from the floor, and with a level, extend a line around the room.

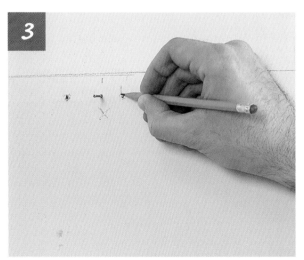

3 **Locate the studs.** The top and the bottom of the wainscoting are held in place by a cap rail and a baseboard that are nailed into the studs. Use a stud finder to locate the studs or use the low-tech method. Begin 16 inches out from an adjacent wall (studs typically are spaced 16 inches apart measured from center to center) and drive a nail into the wall. Make the hole low enough that it will be concealed by the wainscoting or cap rail, and keep it at least 5 inches above the floor—any lower and you may be misled by other framing that doesn't extend to the ceiling. Keep trying until the nail hits something solid: It's a stud. (Don't drive nails near electrical outlets or switches.) Mark the stud both at floor level and just above the level line, move 16 inches along the wall, and drive nails to find the next stud.

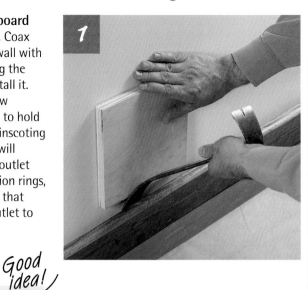

Installing Beadboard Wainscoting

4 **Prefinish all components.** Finish the back of the wainscoting as well as the front in order to minimize possible warping. Finish the back while you can still

get to it. If you wish, you can finish the front, as well as the cap rail and baseboard, at this time, too. Keep in mind that you'll have to fill nail holes at the end of the job, so make sure to have matching putty.

5 **Install baseboard.** What you do at this point depends on what you're working with. **If the baseboard you use has a rabbet** that houses the beaded boards, cut it to length and install it now. Nail it to the studs with #6 finish nails, and countersink the nailheads. When splicing two lengths of baseboard to span a wall, achieve an inconspicuous seam by overlapping them with a scarf joint, as shown on page 142.

If the baseboard isn't rabbeted and it will be nailed on top of the boards, install the beadboard first, as described below.

6 **Cut the wainscoting to length.** Begin at either end of the wall, and measure to determine the length of the wainscot boards. If you have a rabbeted baseboard, measure from the bottom of the rabbet to the line marking the top of the wainscoting. If the baseboard will go on after the wainscoting is installed, measure between the line and the floor. For now, cut two or three boards to this length with a handsaw, circular saw, or miter saw. The length of the boards may change as you move along the wall, due to uneven or unlevel floors.

7 **Glue the wainscoting in place.** Butt the grooved end of a board into a corner and nail it in place. Place the next board upside down on a drop cloth or newspapers, run a waving line of construction adhesive along the back, and spread

the adhesive with a notched trowel. Apply adhesive to several boards before proceeding to the next step. Spread glue as you slip the boards into place. Slide the tongues in the grooves, leaving a ¹⁄₁₆-inch space between the visible edges of the boards to allow for expansion in humid weather. Align the top edges with the level line, check the edge for plumb with a level, and make necessary corrections. Press the boards with the heels of your hands to help bond the boards with the wall.

To accommodate electrical outlets, cut rectangular notches in the beaded boards. Lay out the hole by rubbing lipstick or chalk onto the edges of the electrical box holding the outlet. Position the board on the wall and press it against the box. Put the board on a work surface and drill ¹⁄₂-inch holes just inside each corner. Cut along the line with a saber saw to make the cut.

Scribing to Fit

If you install the first board plumb, then discover the wall isn't plumb, it can create a gap. Carpenters deal with this by cutting or scribing the board to fit.

To scribe a board, hold it in the corner with its edge against the problem wall. Plumb the board with a level so that it is perfectly vertical. Lay out the cut with the help of a simple compass. Set the distance between pencil and point to the width of the gap. Run the metal point along the wall and the pencil along the board to lay out the cut. (Make sure the compass setting doesn't change while you do this.) Cut along the pencil line with a saber saw.

8 **Once you install the boards you've cut to length,** measure for the next two or three boards, and cut and install them. Whenever a board is over a stud, nail it in place. If possible, hide the nail in the groove along the bead or drive it through the tongue. Cut or plane as much of the last board as necessary to make it fit. Install it by slipping it down from above with its groove engaging the tongue of the previous board.

9 **Approaching an out of plumb corner.** If you are working toward a corner that isn't plumb, you may be able to deal with it by making small adjustments several boards away. Measure the distance between the last board and the corner at both the top and bottom of the wainscoting; divide the difference by the number of boards remaining to be installed along

the wall. If it's within 1/16 of an inch, install the remaining beaded boards slightly out of plumb so that the last board will be flush with the adjoining wall. If the distance is more than 1/16 inch, scribe the last board to fit.

10 **Install the cap rail and baseboard.** Nail the cap rail in place with 6-penny nails if they'll reach about 1/2 inch into the studs, or with 8-penny nails if they won't. Miter it at inside and outside corners. If the rail is especially large or complex, cope inside corners as shown for chair rails. (See "Coping a Chair Rail," page 135.) **If the baseboards go on top of the beaded boards,** nail them in place, using #8 finish nails in order to reach the studs. Fill all nail holes. If you paint the wainscoting, seal any gaps with paintable caulk. Countersink the nailheads.

 It may take getting used to, but you can do a smoother job of caulking if you push the cartridge gun rather than pull it. The caulk penetrates tight corners better, and you'll make a less-conspicuous bead.

Frame-and-Panel Wainscoting

In Colonial homes wainscoting elegantly protected walls from dings, dents, and daily wear. Installing wainscoting, however, was time-consuming work that required skilled labor.

The frame-and-panel look, without the intensive labor, is now available to do-it-yourselfers. Check home centers and magazines about home renovation for companies that, based on room measurements, make frame-and-panel walls. The wainscoting usually is shipped unassembled and is installed piece by piece on the wall.

Before placing an order, determine whether the panels are solid wood or built over medium density fiberboard. Wood is traditional, of course, but fiberboard costs less and is more stable. After the panels are on the wall, no one will know the difference.

Take the measurements for coved chair rail, beaded stiles, and panels that slope to follow the stairs. Have a well-equipped shop build them for you and tackle the installation yourself.

Traditional painted panels lighten this room while providing substantial looking walls.

Creating a Custom Bookcase

You'll probably find two extremes when shopping for bookcases— beautifully finished expensive units and unfinished, bare-bones units that cost less and don't look as good. Even the best bookcases tend to have an institutional look—cases lined up against a wall, one next to the other. Functional, yes; attractive, not necessarily.

With basic carpentry skills, however, you can turn inexpensive, basic bookcases into an attractive integrated unit. The key is to use stock moldings to blend the separate cases into well-composed pieces of furniture.

The project shown here connects two bookcases side-by-side, raising them slightly on a base (or plinth) and adding a face frame, base molding, column-like trim called pilasters, and crown molding. All the moldings are off-the-shelf profiles, commonly available at home centers and lumber stores.

Because inexpensive bookcases are often made of several different species of wood, getting a smooth, consistent stain is difficult. Finish the bookcase with paint; you'll save money because painting allows you to use less expensive paint-grade moldings.

Creating a Custom Bookcase

1 **Screw two (or more) bookcases together.** Nestle the bookcases side-by-side and hold them together with clamps. Make sure the front and top edges align. It may help to slide shims under the cabinets if the floor is uneven. Predrill holes for screws through the side of one case and partway into the other; countersink the holes with a countersink bit. Space the holes evenly along the front and back of the side, drilling a hole every foot or so. Drive 1¼-inch drywall screws into the holes to hold the cabinets together.

2 **Build a plinth base.** Most bookcases have a nondescript base—a recessed "toe kick" at the front and nothing along the sides. A plinth base raises the assembled bookcases to create a base at least as high as the baseboard in the room. Choose 1×3-inch or 1×4-inch material, depending on the height of the baseboard. If the baseboard in the room is low (3½ inches or less), build a plinth base in any event. (The bookcase will look better sitting on it.) Nail the plinth base together with #6 finish nails.

3 **Remove the existing baseboard.** Bookcases should be attached to the wall to prevent them from tipping over. To attach the bookcase, remove the existing baseboard. Hold a wood shim between a prybar and the wall to prevent damaging the wall, and push the prybar down behind the baseboard. Pry the baseboard away from the wall. The baseboard may be built from several pieces of molding. Cut off a few inches from each, take them to a home center, and buy molding to match—get enough to go around the bottom of the bookcases.

STUFF YOU'LL NEED

✔ **Pine bookcases**
Two approximately 24 or 30 inches wide by 72 or 84 inches high. Get the most basic style available—no face frame, no trim. There will be a slightly recessed toe kick 2 to 3 inches high.

✔ **Wood for plinth base**
Use 1×3 or 1×4 depending on height of base molding and height of bottom shelf on bookcases. Two 8' lengths should be plenty.

✔ **Wood for face frame**
Four pieces of 1"×3"×8'

✔ **Bottom fascia**
One piece of 1"×6"×8'. Rip to width if necessary.

✔ **Crown molding**
1 piece of 3¼"×8'

✔ **Screen molding**
Approximately 42 feet of ¼"×¾" triple-bead screen molding. (Exact amount depends on size of bookcases.) Get additional screen molding to cover the shelf edges.

✔ **Base molding**
Approximately 7 feet to match existing baseboard.

✔ **Tapered wood shims**

✔ 1¼", 2", 2½" **drywall screws**

✔ **#4 and #6 finish nails**

Tools:
✔ Clamps
✔ Electric drill, screwdriver bit, countersink or combination bit
✔ Hammer
✔ Nail set
✔ Pry bar
✔ Stud finder
✔ Level
✔ Utility knife
✔ Miter box and saw
✔ Bevel gauge
✔ Hot-melt glue gun and glue
✔ Caulk gun and paintable caulk
✔ Primer
✔ Sandpaper
✔ Paint

TOOL TIP

It's faster and easier to use a combination bit.

A countersink is a cone-shape hole in a work surface that houses the head of a screw. You can drill them with a countersink bit, although it's faster and easier to use a combination bit that simultaneously drills the countersink and a hole for the screw.

Cabinetmaker's Secret

When two boards—such as the face frames of the bookcases—meet, it's rarely a perfect match. One might be too thick, too thin, or out of square enough to cause a gap. Cabinetmakers camouflage the gaps by sanding a small bevel on the front edges of all vertical pieces and on the visible face at the end of each horizontal. (On this project, sand a bevel no more than $1/16$-inch wide.) This creates a shallow V-groove wherever two pieces meet. It looks like a decorative detail, but in fact, it's a cabinetmaker's secret.

4 **Level the plinth base and screw it to the wall.** Locate the studs in the wall with a stud finder and mark them. Use a level to extend these marks up the wall just beyond the finished height of the bookcases. Then level the plinth base, sliding tapered shims underneath it as necessary.

Screw through the back of the plinth base into the wall studs with $2^{1}/_{2}$-inch drywall screws. Trim the shims with a utility knife.

5 **Screw the bookcases to the wall.** Make sure the bookcases sit evenly on the plinth base. If there is a slight overhang (or gap), center the bookcase so the mismatch is equal on all sides. Attach the bookcase backs into the wall studs with 2-inch drywall screws. If there are gaps between the back edge of the bookcase and the wall, slide a shim into the gap and trim the shim. Caulk the gaps later.

6 **Cut and attach face-frame pieces.** Start with the vertical pieces. Cut them to the full height of the unit. When you install them, the side verticals are even with the outside edge of the bookcase. The center vertical Ⓐ overhangs the walls of the individual bookcases evenly. Nail the vertical pieces Ⓑ in place with #6 finish nails and countersink the nailheads. Next, cut the horizontal face-frame pieces to fit between the verticals. The bottom horizontal face-frame pieces, or fascia, should be flush with the top of the bottom shelf.Ⓒ Nail the pieces in place.

Creating a Custom Bookcase   161

Creating a Custom Bookcase

7 Cut and attach the crown molding. First add support blocks; these are short, 1×2-inch blocks with the end cut to 50 degrees (the angle of the crown molding). Set the miter box to 50 degrees and cut enough blocks to place one roughly every foot along the bookcase. **A**

Fix the blocks to the top of the cabinet with hot-melt glue. **B**

Cut the crown molding (see page 146). Nail the crown molding to the top edge of the cabinet, but not to the blocks—they're for positioning and added support.

Crown Molding Tip for a Perfect Fit

Once the crown molding is cut to fit, tack it in place with hot-melt glue. First, dab a small amount of hot-melt on the support blocks and then press the molding in place. Hold it for 30 seconds while the glue grabs. If it fits, nail the bottom edges of the molding to the cabinet. If it needs adjustment, pry off the molding, remove the dried hot-melt glue, and cut it again.

8 Cut and attach the base molding. The base molding is cut and fit much like the crown molding—mitered at the corners and butted to the wall along the sides. It should match the existing baseboard. Many baseboards are built up from a flat board and piece of molding, such as the cap molding shown here. Others (such as "clamshell" and "Colonial" trim) are single pieces of molding. In either case, the profiles are standard, and your home center should be able to match them.

Cut the molding and nail it in place. Reinstall the old baseboard along the wall and fit it to the new base molding on the cabinet with a scribed joint. (See page 129.)

9 Cut and nail on screen moldings. Apply two strips of beaded screen molding centered on the three vertical face frames. These pieces butt into the edge of the

crown molding at the top and into the base molding at the bottom. Cut the strips to length, and nail them onto the vertical face frames with 4-penny finish nails. Also, cut strips to fit across the front of the shelves, and nail them in place.

Seal any gaps between the bookcase and wall, or between any of the pieces of molding, with paintable caulk. Prime, sand, and apply two topcoats of paint.

Painter's Secret

For a smooth and glossy finish, fill imperfections, prime, sand, and apply two coats of finish color with a soft-bristled brush.

Using Architectural Columns

Columns are a central element in classical architecture. Over the centuries they've contirbuted structurally and aesthetically to building composition. Although the use of classical columns for structural purposes is less common today, using them to decoratively define room spaces is popular.

Use columns to define an entryway or to divide a large room into two or more distinct spaces without imposing a wall. A pair of columns can frame a prominent window or wall unit, while a single column can enliven a nondescript corner. Half columns applied directly to the wall can define space without intruding into the room.

Columns are available in many styles, sizes, and materials: round, tapered, square, fluted; full columns and half columns; wood, metal, polyurethane. All columns are made up of three parts: the base, the shaft, and the capital.

In general, the column shaft is cut to fit between the floor and ceiling, and it is secured with angled screws or metal brackets as well as construction adhesive. Some manufacturers assemble the base and capital in separate halves around the column after it is in place. Others are solid pieces that slide over the shaft before it is positioned and are then secured to the floor and ceiling after the shaft is in place.

Columns provide dimension and focus to an otherwise large and empty space. They work well to emphasize ceiling height while linking the rest of the room.

Using Architectural Columns   163

Using Architectural Columns

The column in this project is installed between a half-wall and the ceiling. The procedure is the same as installing a column from the floor to ceiling.

STUFF YOU'LL NEED

✔ Column
✔ Plumb bob
✔ Tape measure
✔ Hacksaw, crosscut, or saber saw
✔ Wood shims
✔ Latex paintable caulk
✔ Caulking gun
✔ Latex filler

1 Mark the column location on the ceiling and on the top of the half-wall. Mark the center point of the column on the top surface of the half-wall. Use a plumb bob to transfer the center mark to the ceiling. Using the centers as starting points, lay out the shape of the column base and cap on the half-wall and ceiling to make sure they fall where you want them.

2 Measure the overall height. Measure the distance between the marks on the floor and ceiling to determine the overall height of the column. Transfer the measurement onto the column. Take into account the base cap, which may or may not extend above the top of the column itself. The top of the column is usually factory cut, and any excess is removed from the bottom of the column. Don't try for a perfectly tight fit—you'll never be able to stand the column and get it in place. Follow the manufacturer's instructions for how much to trim from the bottom to get the column into place. After it's upright, shim it from the bottom. The base and cap will cover the gap.

Wisdom of the Aisles

"Columns are designed to be forgiving during installation. The cap and base are wide and will cover mistakes. Work slowly and measure carefully. Avoid making mistakes, even though you usually can make a cut up to an inch short and still install the column without visible gaps."

— *Joseph Palinsky*
S. Plainfield, NJ

*Designer's Tip

Columns don't have to be white. Faux techniques, such as stippling, marblizing, sponging, and ragging, add luster and style. Coordinate color combinations already in the room or introduce an accent color.

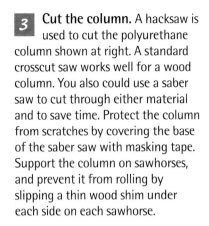

Wisdom of the Aisles

"Don't have a stud finder? All you need is a hammer and a finishing nail. Drive the nail into the wall a couple of inches from the corner. Work high enough that the trim will cover the holes, but stay at least 2½ inches from the ceiling to avoid hitting framing along the top of the wall. Drive a series of holes at 1-inch intervals until you hit something solid—it's a stud. The center of the next one will be 16 inches from the center of the one you found."

— *Steve Smith*
  La Quinta, CA

Carpenter's Secret

To mark a straight line around a circular column, make two marks on opposite sides of the column to indicate the length. Connect the marks with a piece of wide masking tape—the wider the better—wrapped around the column. Or wrap a strip of poster board around the column and position an edge along the cut by measuring down from the straight factory edge. Trace along the edge to mark a line all around the column.

3 **Cut the column.** A hacksaw is used to cut the polyurethane column shown at right. A standard crosscut saw works well for a wood column. You also could use a saber saw to cut through either material and to save time. Protect the column from scratches by covering the base of the saber saw with masking tape. Support the column on sawhorses, and prevent it from rolling by slipping a thin wood shim under each side on each sawhorse.

4 **Position base and cap moldings on the column.** The column base shown slides on before the column is stood up; it then slides into position when the column is upright. Make sure the flat part faces the floor. The neck molding was preinstalled at the factory on this column; although some neck molding is installed at this stage and the column cap is positioned on top of the column.

5 **Stand the column.** In this installation the column slides onto the top of the half-wall conveniently. Whenever possible, stand the column in an adjacent area that has plenty of headroom. Standing the column next to the kneewall, for example, gives the installer room to work without scraping the ceiling. If you can't do this, position the base of the column near the base layout marks and stand it up. If you have to scrape the ceiling a bit to get the column fully upright, make sure it's within the area that will be covered by the column cap. In the photo (right) a length of string tied around opposite corners of the column base prevents it from sliding down the column. Notice the slight gap at the ceiling.

Walls

Using Architectural Columns 165

Using Architectural Columns

6 Shim the base of the column to raise it tight to the ceiling. Nudge the column into position on the layout marks; you may want to temporarily slide the column base down to make sure it's in the right place. Apply a bead of construction adhesive (check manufacturer's instructions for the correct type) into the gap around the top of the column. Slip a pry bar under the bottom of the column to raise it up against the ceiling, then slide wood shims under the column to hold it tight to the ceiling. Use three or four shims evenly spaced around the column. Straight columns can be checked for plumb; tapered columns require that you rely on initial layout marks.

Good idea! →

Home centers and hardware stores sell small packages of shims. They're inexpensive and help you do an accurate job of squaring up.

7 Attach mounting brackets to column. Follow the manufacturer's instructions for securing the column—L-brackets are a common approach. Screw the L-brackets to the column and the half-wall base (or floor). Use angle brackets at the top of column only if you can connect to a ceiling joist. The adhesive on the top of the column and column cap should be sufficient.

Wisdom of the Aisles

"To cover an obstruction—such as pipes or a steel basement column—have the store special order a split column. Assemble the column around the obstruction, and no one will ever know it was there."

— *Jim Pellegrini Jericho, NY*

8 Attach the column base and cap. Apply construction adhesive to the flat surfaces of the column base and cap, then slide them into position. Drive screws through the column base and cap to secure them in place. For the base cap, you may need to drive the screws at an angle into the column itself. Fill all screw holes with a latex filler. Caulk any gaps around the base and cap moldings.

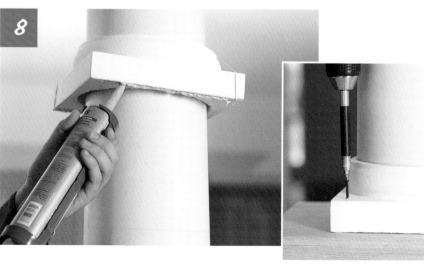

Columns

Even when not functional, columns serve as decorative elements to define and regulate room space. They create focus and break up emptiness in especially large spaces. Whether they actually hold up the wall, well-placed columns provide a sense of security and well-being in any room.

The classical column (top left) establishes formality in this Traditional entryway. In keeping with the Arts-and-Crafts belief that room elements should work together, the columns (above) are a continuation of the frame-and-panel wainscoting. The purely decorative column (below right) defines the fireplace area and echoes the mantel. The enclosed atrium columns (below left) provide visual relief.

Using Architectural Columns   167

Details

It's the details that flesh out the design and make it complete. Pay attention to details and ask yourself these questions to provide clues to your decorating style.

• How about old sconces hanging on the wall? You may want to restore them, or you may want to replace them with something more in tune with your decorating scheme.

• Pictures present two questions— where do you place them and how do you hang them so they stay up?

• How about shelfing? Built-ins are potentially expensive. Purchased racks that are screwed to the wall may not present quite the picture you'd like. You may want to consider making your own.

Explore these details and more in this chapter—tiling around a fireplace, painting tiles, choosing switch plates and outlet covers, and combining wallpaper and molding.

If you've already begun decorating, these ideas will help complete the job. If you're just beginning, start with a few of the larger details and fill in around them.

The ultimate success of every decorating project is attention to details. Decisions and choices make the difference between pleasing and fabulous.

Replacing Wall Sconces

Replacing a wall sconce is one of the simplest ways to dress up a wall, whether your reasons are practical or aesthetic.

Taking out an old sconce involves removing a couple of screws and untwisting a couple of wires. Installing the replacement is just the opposite. A couple of pointers: connect similar colored wires to each other and twist the wires together before applying the wire nut.

Be smart and safe. Before you start, turn off the power at the panel, not just at the switch.

An eye-level wall sconce—whether it's new, a reproduction, or an antique—is a small investment that makes a big difference.

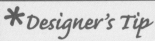

STUFF YOU'LL NEED

- ✔ Sconce
- ✔ Screwdriver
- ✔ Wire strippers or combination tool
- ✔ Electrician's pliers
- ✔ Wire nuts (if old ones need replacing)
- ✔ Nylon cord or coat hanger

*Designer's Tip

Sconces are perfect as accent lights above the mantel or beside the fireplace. They provide subtle light without taking up mantel or floor space.

1 **Remove the existing fixture.** Turn off the power to the fixture at the fuse or circuit breaker box. Remove the glass globe, shade, and bulb. Remove any nuts or screws holding the fixture in place; then carefully pull the fixture from the wall. Pull gently in case the fixture has been painted in place and to avoid yanking on the wires. After you remove the fixture, twist off the wire nuts that connect the wires.

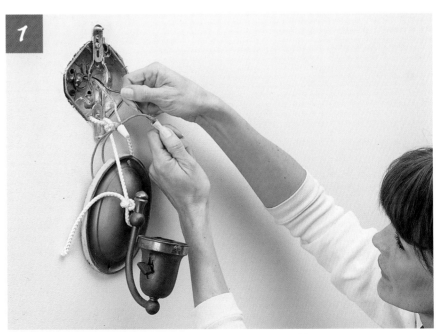

Replacing Wall Sconces   **169**

Replacing Wall Sconces

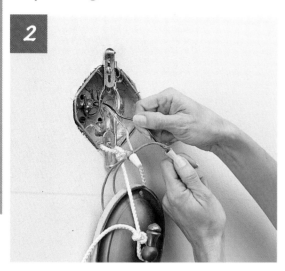

2

2 Inspect the wires and install the mounting strap. Check the condition of the wires in the electrical box. If the metal is nicked, scratched, or twisted, it may break off after you install the light. Clip the wire flush with the end of its insulation, and then strip off about an inch of insulation using a wire stripper.

Sconces mount in a couple of different ways; check the manufacturer's directions. Most mount on a strap that is attached to the junction box in the wall. The strap usually comes with the fixture. Screw the strap to the junction box.

Once the strap is in, the lamp likely is attached with either a pair of boltlike threaded studs or with a single, hollow-threaded rod, called a nipple. Twist the studs, or nipple, into the mounting strap.

Smart & Safe

Faulty wiring may send current into the body of an electrical fixture. The grounding wire in the cable safely diverts the electricity. If the box is plastic, connect the fixture's grounding wire to the one in the cable. (Grounding wires either are uninsulated copper or have a green plastic coating.) If the box is metal, attach the grounding wires to a third wire, and connect the third wire to the electrical box. Ask the home improvement store's electrical department for advice if the wiring in your home makes grounding difficult.

3

Electrician's Secret

It may require more than two hands to hold a light fixture as you twist the wire connections on or off. If you don't have a helper, temporarily support the fixture by tying a nylon cord to the mounting strap on the electrical box. If there's no mounting strap, hang the fixture on a hook made from a hanger.

3 Wire and install the new fixture. Twist the wires together with electrical pliers, connecting white wires to white wires, and black to black. Twist a plastic wire cap over the bare wires to insulate them and to keep them from coming undone. If the cap doesn't cover all the bare wire, remove the cap, trim the bare wire a bit shorter, and reattach the cap. Carefully fold the wires into the junction box, place the fixture over the studs or nipple, then attach the fixture with the ornamental nuts provided. (See inset.)

Tiling Around a Fireplace

Installing ceramic tile around a fireplace is an easy way to bring color, texture, and pattern into your home, making the fireplace the highlight of the room. Add a single course of tile around a plain fireplace or coordinate the tile with a wood mantel surround, as in this project. If conditions allow, include a tiled hearth.

Tile can be applied to drywall, plaster, and plywood, but not to wood paneling or other paneling products. The hearth has a layer of backerboard beneath the tile for added support. (The cement in the backerboard also provides a bonding surface for the mortar.) Backerboard isn't necessary on walls because they carry less weight. An organic mastic adhesive holds tile directly on drywall or plaster.

Tiling around a fireplace personalizes the centerpiece of your living room. It's also a great project to learn tiling basics.

Tiling Around a Fireplace

1 **Apply backerboard to the hearth.** Backerboard ensures a strong bond between the tile and subfloor to withstand floor traffic. Though it may not be walked on much, you will rest logs on it. Cut the backerboard to fit the shape of the

hearth. Apply mortar bed to the subfloor or existing hearth, and nail or screw down the backerboard with hardened fasteners designed for use with backerboard. Follow the manufacturer's instructions regarding adhesives and type of screws to use.

Because the wall tiles aren't subjected to weight, there's no need to put backerboard on the wall.

STUFF YOU'LL NEED

✔ Backerboard
✔ Ceramic tile
✔ Latex-portland cement mortar
✔ Organic mastic
✔ Latex-portland cement grout
✔ Tile saw or cutter
✔ Notched trowel
✔ Tile spacers
✔ Soft rubber mallet
✔ Straightedge board or 2-foot level
✔ Masking tape
✔ Sponge float
✔ Clean sponge

2 **Dry-fit the tiles.** Before you mix mortar or open a can of adhesive, know exactly how the tiles will fit around the fireplace. Start in the center of the hearth and work to the edges, positioning the tiles with tile spacers between them. Mark the tiles to be cut.

TOOL TIP

Cut edges on tile are very sharp. Soften the edges with a masonry stone, which is a sort of coarse sharpening stone. Rub the stone along the tile to remove the sharp edge.

3 **Cut tiles as needed.** There are several ways to cut ceramic tiles. A simple score-and-snap tile cutter is efficient and inexpensive. You also can rent power tile-cutting tools. Many home centers and tile specialty suppliers will cut tiles for a nominal charge. Mark the tiles at home and take them to the store for cutting. To use the scoring tile cutter, shown, mark the cut line, place the tile against the fence, and slide the scoring wheel firmly across the face of the tile. Press down on the tile using the pressure pad opposite the cutting wheel to snap it cleanly.

Mortar is a mixture of cement and sand used to hold tile in place. Latex-portland cement mortar is made with portland cement, which is stronger than other cement, plus a latex additive. Latex makes the mixture stronger and easier to work.

Grout is a fine-grained mixture of cement and sand used to fill the spaces between the tiles. Like mortar, it can be mixed with portland cement and latex for added durability.

Organic mastic is a solvent-based glue used to hold tiles in place. It works especially well bonding tile to drywall and plaster.

4 **Apply adhesive.** Mix latex-portland cement mortar as directed on the package, and apply it to the backerboard with a notched trowel. (The instructions on the package will recommend a specific notch size for specific tile sizes.) There's nothing mysterious or artistic about spreading mortar; just apply it to the surface, then run the notched trowel through at a consistent angle—about 45 degrees—to produce a uniform bed of adhesive. Since the area is small, trowel on all of the adhesive at once.

5 **Set the hearth tiles in mortar.** Press the tiles firmly into the mortar with a slight squiggle motion, but don't force them into place. Insert spacers to maintain even spaces for grout lines. Use a straightedge, board, or level to check that the tiles are level. Tap high spots lightly with a rubber mallet.

6 **Cut and fit the wall tiles.** Measure and mark the position of the wall tiles that surround the fireplace. Dry-fit the tiles with spacers to make sure of the measurements. (Use masking tape to temporarily hold the tiles in place.) Cut tiles to fit as needed.

Tiling Around a Fireplace **173**

Tiling Around a Fireplace

7 **Apply mastic and set the fireplace tiles.** Mortar is not suited for applying tile directly to drywall or plaster. Use organic mastic instead, mixing it as directed.

Trowel the mastic onto the wall, and comb it out with a notched trowel. (The size of the notch depends on the thickness of the tile; follow the mastic manufacturer's recommendations.) On small areas it may be easier to "butter" the back of the tile instead of applying the mastic to the wall. Set the tiles in place on the wall, working from the bottom up. Press the tiles firmly into the adhesive. Insert spacers between the tiles.

8 **Level the tiles.** When setting tiles (especially wall tiles) it's initially nearly impossible to get them level with one another. Use a straightedge, board, or level to check the overall surface of the installed tile. Press the high spots to set the tiles more deeply into the adhesive. Some pros use a piece of 2×4 wrapped with carpet to level the tiles.

9 **Grout the tile.** Mix the latex-portland cement grout according to the manufacturer's instructions. Spread the grout over the tile with a sponge float. Work the grout evenly into the joints by moving the float at a 45-degree angle to the joint lines. Remove the excess grout with a wet sponge, pressing lightly and rinsing the sponge frequently in clean water. The surface of the tile will glaze over with grout residue as it dries; remove this residue with a clean damp sponge.

The Keystone to Success

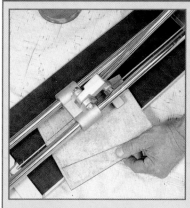

Give your fireplace tile surround a professional look by installing a keystone-shape tile at the top center. Use a bevel gauge to lay out the shape of the keystone where it will go on the fireplace wall. Use those lines as guides to mark the tiles that will go on either side of the keystone. Cut the angle on each tile and mount them in place. Mark the keystone using the adjacent tiles as guides. Cut the keystone to fit and install it last.

Painting Ceramic Tiles

When tiling a wall, countertop, or backsplash, designers often break up the runs with accent tiles. Available in many patterns, accent tiles highlight, personalize, and embellish a design.

Add an even more personal touch—and save money—by painting your own accent tiles. In addition to capturing your own artistic skills, making custom accent tiles can record special events in your family's life. Let the kids create tiles for lasting and loving mementos.

You can paint ceramic tile, but matte finish tiles are best because the paint sticks more effectively. Control the glossiness of the final product with the amount of sheen in the applied glaze.

Painting your own ceramic accent tiles for your home requires a few basic tools (above). Paint tiles several ways, including stenciling (right, top left), stamping (right, center), and copying or tracing (right, bottom).

Painting Ceramic Tiles   175

Painting Ceramic Tiles

Walls

1 **Clean and prime the tiles.** Dust, dirt, and fingerprints can ruin the bond between the paint and tile. Clean with all-purpose household cleaner, rinse, and dry thoroughly. Because the surface of ceramic tiles is slick, you need to apply a surface conditioner to prime the surface. It won't interfere with your design because it's clear, and it primes the surface to help the paint adhere to it.

2 **Paint the tiles.** Choose a design. Draw your design on paper from a template, pattern, or stencil. A simple design, such as a child's handprint (below), works best.

Buy permanent enamel paint specially formulated for use on ceramics. If it is used for handprints, read all the cautions on the label, and make sure you have the necessary materials for cleanup. Let the paint dry thoroughly.

STUFF YOU'LL NEED

✔ Matte-finish tile
✔ Ceramic air-dry enamel surface conditioner
✔ Air-dry enamel satin paint
✔ Air-dry enamel glaze
✔ Paintbrush
✔ Wide foam brush

Painter's Secret

The secret to success is using the right paint. Use an enamel that is designed for ceramics and that air-dries (as opposed to baking or firing). Check the label to determine if the enamel is designed for tile, glass, or ceramics. Whatever the label reads, if the word "ceramic" isn't there or if it isn't air-dry, it isn't the right enamel. If a paint department doesn't have it, look for it in a crafts store.

Work Smarter

Painting ceramic tile can be a family affair. Encourage everyone to express themselves, to be creative and to have fun. The project experience will spark creativity and the result will be memorable.

3 **Apply glaze to the tiles.** Protect the design so that it will not wear off or chip. A matte or gloss enamel glaze locks the paint onto the surface of the tile to make it washable and to withstand everyday use.

The glaze is the consistency of nail polish and about as tricky to apply on large surfaces. Going over the surface a second time without ruining the glaze is almost impossible. Use the widest foam brush you can, and paint the tile in the least number of strokes possible.

Let the glaze dry several days before installing the tile.

Gallery of Hand-Painted Tiles

A painted tile is a one-of-a-kind object that reflects your personality. Fortunately, skill level isn't a determining factor. There's plenty of room for skilled or struggling artists.

Hand-drawn images can be unsophisticated. The child's drawing of the house (first row) can be on the wall to greet your grandchildren. The sun drawing (third row) is simple to make and a strong wall accent.

Rubber stamps are easy to manipulate. The flower (second row) and leaf (fourth row) are made with rubber stamps. Even if you use the same stamp for each tile, the results will be slightly different, lending a handmade look to the tiles.

The fleur-de-lis (fifth row) and the musical note (third row) are produced from purchased stencil designs. They're an easy way to create uniform, sophisticated images.

Your pattern can be one-of-a-kind or a running series, like the diamonds (fifth row). These tiles were painted in a batch, with each tile having a full diamond and a half diamond. When you install the tile, turn one 180 degrees from the one preceding it, and the two will automatically match.

Open Shelving

Generic shelving systems work fine for closets or utility areas. But when you want to display something important, or just make everyday items—such as bath towels—look a little more special, you're in the market for custom shelves. The display boxes shown here are constructed of solid wood, and the good news is you don't need to be a skilled woodworker to put them together. They're made from lengths of standard 1x10 pine. The only cuts necessary are the cross cuts, and if you're not comfortable doing them, you can usually have the cuts made at the home center where you buy the wood.

Because they are so simple, you can adjust the size of these boxes to suit the objects to store or display. Each box shown requires one 8-foot length of 1x10 stock. Choose 1x8 or 1x6 for shallower boxes. Finish them any way you want. (See "Applying Stains and Clear Finishes," pages 355-363, to get ideas for finishing touches.)

An elegant set of shelves is a simple workshop project. These shelves are made of pine right off the lumber racks and held together with drywall screws.

Open Shelving

STUFF YOU'LL NEED

(For each shelf)

- ✔ One 1x10x8-foot board
- ✔ 1⅝-inch drywall screws
- ✔ 2-inch drywall screws
- ✔ Two keyhole hangers
- ✔ Two self-drilling anchors
- ✔ Safety glasses
- ✔ Circular saw
- ✔ Triangular square (12x12x12)
- ✔ Tape measure
- ✔ Clamps
- ✔ Drill
- ✔ Countersink
- ✔ Phillips bit for drill
- ✔ 150-grit sandpaper
- ✔ Level
- ✔ Screwdriver
- ✔ Paint or stain

Cutting List (for each box)

- ✔ 2 pieces at ¾x9½x18 (inches)
- ✔ 2 pieces at ¾x9½x10½ (inches)

*Designer's tip

The square, flat edges of this box are a typical modern treatment. To add decoration, rout the edge after you assemble the box. For a simple look, choose a roundover bit; for a more intricate look, choose an ogee pattern. Balance the router on the edge of the box, and work counterclockwise around it. For this type of cutting, a smaller laminate style router works well; heavier models are harder to control. Home centers sell router tables with fences that make a job such as this easy.

1 Lay out and cut the boards to size. (A 1x10 is really only ¾x9½ inches. 1x10 is the size of the board when it's cut from the tree, before it's planed smooth. Confusing, but it means your boards are already the right width and thickness. All you have to do is cut them to length.) Make the cuts with a circular saw while guiding it with a 12x12x12 square like the one shown here. Make the first cut near the end, cutting off any cracks in the wood. Measure, mark, and cut each piece to length.

2 **Predrill for the assembly screws.** Put one of the long sides and one of the short sides together to form a corner of the box. Put the long piece so it overlaps the short one, and clamp them together. Drill three ⅛-inch diameter screw holes through the face of the long side and into the short one. To prevent splitting the wood, keep the holes at least 1 inch in from the sides of the boards. Countersink the holes, as shown, so the screw heads will rest below the surface of the wood.

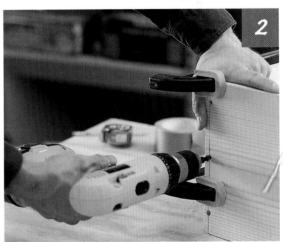

3 **Screw the boxes together.** Either drive the 1⅝-inch screws by hand or with an inexpensive bit that fits your electric drill. Screw two sets of sides together, and clamp them together to form a box. Drill and countersink at the corners that need screws, and screw the corners together as before.

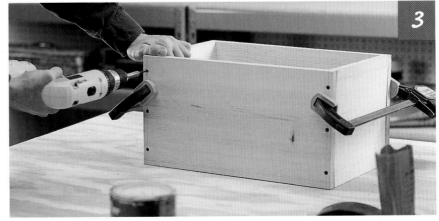

Open Shelving

4 **Install hangers.** For a clean look, the shelves hang using keyhole hangers. In order for the box to sit tightly against the wall, recess the hangers into the back edge of each vertical member. For heavy loads, at least one of the keyhole hangers should be on a stud. If you don't want to position the shelves so one of the verticals aligns with a stud, add an angle bracket on the inside top of the box and position it on a stud.

Trace around the hanger with a pencil. Remove most of the waste by drilling a small hole within the lines, making the hole as deep as the hanger is thick. Remove the rest of the waste with a chisel.

Put the hanger in the recess and make sure the narrow slot of the keyhole points toward the top of the box. Screw or nail the hanger in place, depending on the one you buy. (See inset.)

5 **Paint or stain the shelves.** Sand the wood with 150-grit paper, and round over all the corners and edges slightly so that they feel smooth and the finish won't rub off with use. The shelves are easiest to handle at this point if you apply finish to the inside first, then to the outside.

6 **Make a small mark on the outer sides** of the box to show the center of each keyhole hanger. Position the shelf, make sure it is level, and transfer the marks to the wall. Measure in from the wall marks ³/₈ inch to the center line of the hanger. Drill holes for plastic inserts, tap them into the holes, then drive a roundhead screw in each that fits the slot in the hangers. Position the shelves so the hangers are over the screws in the wall; slide the shelf downward to engage the hangers.

*Designer's Tip

Experiment with the size and arrangement of the boxes. The 18-inch boxes, such as the ones shown, are large enough so that there will be at least one stud behind them for hanging. Smaller boxes carrying smaller loads may not need studs behind them. Make the box sizes to suit your needs.

Cabinetmaker's Secret

To hang the boxes against each other, screw them together first with 1¼-inch drywall screws. It makes hanging—and aligning the boxes—much easier.

Wallpaper and Molding Combinations

Wallpaper and wood molding work together to create a more formal frame-and-panel effect than traditional beadboard-style wainscoting. Strips of molding visually anchor wallpaper, becoming a major design element in the room. Combining paper and trim has another advantage—the trim acts as a border so you don't have to cover the wall with full-length strips. The shorter the strips, the easier the papering job. Wallpaper and molding make a strong statement in Colonial or Traditional-style dining rooms. It's also a great choice for beginning paperhangers and for those getting started with molding.

Off-the-shelf lumber combines with wallpaper to create a strong alternative to traditional frame-and-panel woodwork. Installation is straightforward and easy for those who want to boost their skill levels while achieving great results.

Wallpaper and Molding Combinations

1 **Rebuild the baseboard.** There are four long horizontal boards in this project—the baseboard, the rail below the wallpaper, the rail above it, and the chair rail assembly. In order for it to align correctly, the baseboard is about twice as wide as normal. Instead of buying expensive wide board, you'll put shims between the baseboard and the wall, and then reinstall the baseboard.

Remove the baseboard with a prybar. Drive the bar behind the baseboard and slip a shim between the bar and the wall to protect the wall. Pry gently, and work your way down the wall. Once the baseboard is off, locate the studs with an electronic stud finder, and mark the locations on the wall. Use 1×2 or 1×3 shims—have the lumberyard or home center rip it to width, if necessary. Cut pieces that are slightly shorter than the baseboard width, and nail them to the studs. You'll put the baseboard back later.

2 **Lay out the project.** Determine the height for the top rail. Measure up from the floor at each end of the wall and make a mark for the top edge of the rail. Have a helper hold a chalk line at one mark, stretch the line taut between the two marks, and snap the line. Lay out the bottom rail the same way. Use the stud finder to locate studs for nailing the rail, and mark the lines at these points.

Using a level, lay out the vertical pieces, called stiles, dividing the wall equally into panels. Here the builder lays out the left side of each rail. Unless you are experienced, you may find it less confusing to mark both sides.

3 **Cut and attach the rails.** Measure for the rails above and below the wallpaper, and cut them to length. The chair rail on this wall is a piece of 1× stock nailed to the wall with molding nailed above it. Use a helper to hold the far end of the board as you work toward the helper. Make sure the board follows the layout line. If the board begins to wander away from the line, have a helper flex the board up or down as necessary. When the board is in the correct right place, nail it in place by driving two 8-penny nails through the board and into each stud.

Nail the chair rail in place.

STUFF YOU'LL NEED

- ✔ Wallpaper
- ✔ Paste for unpasted paper; wallpaper paste activator for prepasted paper
- ✔ 1×3 stiles
- ✔ Pry bar
- ✔ Shims
- ✔ Stud finder
- ✔ 1×4 for chair rail
- ✔ Tape measure
- ✔ Chalk line
- ✔ 8-penny nails
- ✔ 4-penny nails
- ✔ Hammer
- ✔ Level
- ✔ Construction adhesive
- ✔ Trowel
- ✔ Wallpapering tools
- ✔ Sponge
- ✔ ½- or ⅝-inch cove molding
- ✔ Miter box and saw
- ✔ Nail set
- ✔ Caulk gun

Wallpaper and Molding Combinations

Painter's Secret

Paint while you can make a mistake without ruining the project. In this project, paint when the stiles and rails are up. Sand, prime, and paint everything, including the yet-to-be installed molding that goes around the wallpaper. Stopping a project midstream is difficult, but in the long run, it saves time. If a little paint drips onto the wall now, you'll paper over it; but if you wait to paint until the last piece of molding is in place, the wallpaper will already be on the wall. On an intricate job, it will take a long time to work around the panels while avoidng getting paint on the wallpaper.

*Designer's Tip

Use fabric instead of wallpaper on a clean, primed wall. Brush wallpaper paste on the wall; then press the fabric in place. Remove excess paste from the wall with a damp sponge.

4 Cut and attach the stiles. The stiles are the vertical pieces of wood that divide the wall into panels. Don't assume that they all will be exactly the same length. Cut each stile to fit its location. Spread construction adhesive evenly over the backs of the stiles with a trowel, press them in place, and check with a level to make sure they are plumb. Position a stile and hold it in place by driving 4-penny finishing nails at angles into the wall. You probably won't be nailing into a stud, but it doesn't matter. When the construction adhesive is dry, it will hold the stiles in place. Follow the directions on the tube to remove any adhesive that squeezes out onto the wall. Nail the baseboard to the shims on the wall with 8-penny nails.

5 Hang the wallpaper panels. Measure the openings framed by the rails and stiles. Make it easier by cutting the wallpaper slightly smaller—about ¼ inch in each direction. The trim you apply later will cover the gaps. Working from the top down, hang and smooth the wallpaper (see pages 109–115). If you work with prepasted paper, use a paste activator instead of soaking the paper and applying it. You'll get a stronger bond when the glue is dry, and it's easier to slide the paper around while it's still wet, if necessary. Clean up visible paste with a damp sponge.

6 Cut and attach the mitered trim pieces. Carefully measure the height and width of each opening, and cut mitered trim pieces to fit. When the adhesive holding the stiles has dried, attach the trim by driving 4-penny nails at an angle into the rail and stiles. Countersink all nails, and fill all holes. Use a putty that matches the stain or one that can be painted or stained to match the finish.

Wallpaper and Molding Combinations

Investigate possible wallpaper and trim combinations before committing to a room's worth of wallpaper and molding. Take home wallpaper pattern samples and lengths of baseboard, chair rail, picture rail, or crown rail—whatever your design involves. You also may want to try two or three species of wood if you plan to apply clear finish on the trim. Buy a pint of the paint or stain you plan to use.

Apply the finish to pieces of molding, allow them to dry, and check the results. Look at the samples in the room where the work is to be done, both in daylight and under artificial light. Fine-tune the finish as necessary. Tint the trial paint to your liking. Lighten stain by diluting the can with the approved solvent; darken it by applying a second coat of stain.

A Country check paper plays off moldings with fanciful relief work.

For a Contemporary look, mix uncomplicated molding profiles with light, cheerful papers (left).

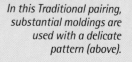

In this Traditional pairing, substantial moldings are used with a delicate pattern (above).

Victorian papers are ornate; they do not necessarily look heavy (right).

Hanging and Arranging Pictures

There is an art to hanging art. First, you have the challenge of placing objects on a wall in a pleasing way. It's similar to arranging furniture. Even hanging a single picture on a bare wall can be difficult. Experiment by taping up pieces of paper cut to the size of your pictures. Arrange them in rows, in a circle, or randomly until you find a pleasing combination. Generally, larger and darker pictures look better placed toward the bottom of a grouping. By breaking up pictures that feature particular colors, the eye is encouraged to travel around an arrangement.

Make sure your precious objects are installed securely. Use proper hanging hardware to securely hang your paintings on the wall.

Test possible arrangements directly on the wall. Cut out pieces of paper the size and shape of each picture to tape to the wall. Rearrange the pieces until you find a pleasing grouping.

STUFF YOU'LL NEED

- ✔ Screw eyes
- ✔ Picture wire
- ✔ Drill
- ✔ Coat hanger
- ✔ Picture hanger with nails
- ✔ Stud finder

1 **Group the pictures on the wall.** Juggling pictures to get the right one in the right place can be difficult; instead work with pieces of paper. Trace the outline of each frame on paper that contrasts with the wall. Cut out the shapes, place masking tape loops on the backs, and experiment with grouping the pictures. (See photo above.) For the security of anchoring heavy works and mirrors into wall studs, first locate the studs with a stud finder. To support especially large objects, drive hangers into adjacent studs.

Good idea!

To see how a picture grouping will look on the wall, first lay it out on the floor. You're getting a bird's eye view and you'll find it easier and quicker to move things around as you work out a preliminary arrangement.

Hanging and Arranging Pictures

2 **Install eyes and picture-frame wire.** Screw eyes and braided wire are sold in a range of sizes to handle framed objects of different weights. To position the eyes, measure the height of the frame, and mark pilot holes one-third of the way down the frame. Drill a hole slightly smaller than the diameter of the threaded portion of the eye. Drill carefully to avoid boring through the frame. Twist in the eyes by hand.

To determine the length of wire to cut for a picture, measure the picture width and add 50 percent. This allows enough wire to wrap each end around a screw eye and then around itself, while preventing the frame from dropping below the hanger.

Hanging Hardware

You'll find a variety of picture hangers in the hardware department. The common hangers shown above work in almost every situation.

Traditional hangers (A) have a nail that runs through the top, with a hook that acts as a hanger. They work in both drywall and plaster, but may tend to chip plaster.

Hangers sold as "professional" picture hangers (B) also work in plaster and drywall. They have a thin, sharp, hardened nail that is less likely to chip plaster. The nail is removable and reusable.

Wallboard anchors (C) are large nylon screws that house metal screws. Drive the pointed end into the drywall with a hammer; then screw the anchor into the wall with a standard screwdriver. Drive in the metal screw and hang the picture.

Anchors are available with hooks (D) to hang pictures and with special hooks to hang mirrors.

3 **Use double wire for heavy pictures.** To securely hang heavy pictures where there is no access to a stud, run two wires between the screw eyes and support each with a hanger. Space the two hangers at least half the picture's width apart.

4 **Nail a hanger to the wall.** To determine the exact position for the hanger, poke a pencil point through the paper cutout at the spot where the picture wire will be when fully stretched by the picture weight. When you find the best location

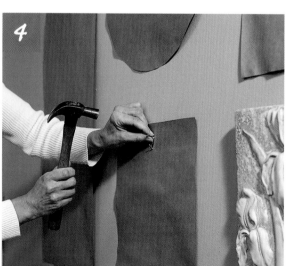

for the picture, tap a nail through the hole just enough to mark the wall.

Select a picture hanger that's the right size— the weight a hanger can handle is marked on the package. To help prevent plaster from chipping, apply a small cross of tape to the wall at the point where you are driving the nail, and nail the hanger to the wall.

Wisdom of the Aisles

"When hanging a big picture, you may not be able to see behind the picture to connect the wire on the hanger. Place a large washer over the screw or nail to give yourself a bigger target."

— *Greg Korczak Lodi, NJ*

Arranging Works of Art

Collecting art and objects you love to live with requires great care. Artfully arranging them requires the same attention. Work at the display until you get patterns and groupings exactly how you want them.

A simple method of displaying family pictures and similar works of art is to align the top edges. For a variety of shapes, sizes, and subjects, hang art with the center point a specific distance from the floor. Basing arrangements on the centers of pictures breaks the monotony of perfectly aligned top edges and puts the focus of the art on possibly the most important aspect—the center of the picture. Museums use 60 to 64 inches as a guide to hang art.

For a lively grouping, arrange the pictures within a circle or oval—aligning edges of some frames to give order to the arrangement.

When in doubt, break the pattern completely. Asymmetrical groupings are informal and work well for pictures of children or folk art. Even here, however, align the edges of some frames for a continual reference point.

✳ Designer's Tip

Think eye level. Paintings and art should be hung at, or close to, eye level. Hang art lower in dining rooms or areas where people will primarily be seated; hang art higher, for instance, in hallways.

Open staircases (above and below right) are showcases for paintings, photos, and drawings. Scale is an important consideration. Note how the size of the dancer provides an anchor for the two smaller works on each side.

Bold art (below) requires space to breathe and distance to be appreciated. The large scale traditional arrangement is placed symmetrically.

Hanging and Arranging Pictures   187

Fireplace mantels, which lend themselves to both symmetrical and asymmetrical arrangements, are used to display favorite objects. The symmetrical arrangement of plates on the Arts-and-Crafts fireplace works well because the green in the center plate draws the eye to the center of the mantel.

This collection of objects and art is asymmetry in action. No two items are the same size or shape. The comfortable, inviting asymmetrical arrangement, which allows the eye to randomly move among the objects, is a popular Country look.

❋ Designer's Tip

When you decorate a room, the most important person to please is you. You live with the art and design. The decorator, designer, or even your best friend doesn't.

Images and objects in the Traditional living room (right) reinforce one another. The collection of figures calls attention to the paintings above it, while the arrangement of shorter figures flows to the tallest center figure, echoing the arc of paintings and creating a line for the eye to follow. The result is a formal look with a touch of whimsy.

The antique wooden bracket in the South-western setting (lef), connects the two rooms to the paintings on both sides.

The wainscoting and plate rack in this Country kitchen (right) provide order and logic, while the randomly placed folk art adds rhythm, movement, and fun.

Switchplates and Outlet Covers

Incorporate switchplates and outlet covers into decorating schemes, particularly for historical looks, to call attention to them.

Brass covers, for example, are attractive in most rooms. Wood covers match many wood trims. Durable and colorful ceramic plates enhance children's rooms, kitchens, and bathrooms, and switchplates can also be covered with wallpaper.

The best thing about changing switchplates is that it's easy. Remove the screws, take off the old plate, and put on the new.

Ceilings

Section 3

Ceilings

Ceilings deserve more attention than homeowners usually give them when they redecorate—a fresh coat of white paint and that's about it. **Proper treatments for the ceiling can make a room feel taller or close in a space that feels too large.** You can take a room back in time by installing a chandelier, a tin ceiling, or faux plaster embellishments. A contemporary treatment is track or recess lighting. Ceiling fans provide accent, air flow, and fit in with many decorating schemes. Designers know that carefully chosen ceiling treatments are an integral part of a good design. Renovators work rooms from the top down so that each job covers up drips from the job before. Think like a designer, act like a renovator, and remember the ceiling.

Ceilings

Ceilings

Ceiling Treatments

Ceilings

The ceiling in most rooms is the least noticed surface. Usually white and a neutral backdrop, it is often just what's wanted. So why lavish time and effort on this part of the room?

A plain vanilla ceiling can weaken many decorating schemes. Like other surfaces in the room, the ceiling significantly influences design.

Paint is the most popular ceiling treatment, although other materials are gaining popularity. Tin ceilings, for instance, are making a strong comeback. They're fairly easy to install and they provide historical context to rooms.

There are other ways to embellish the ceiling without a complete makeover. Decorative architectural ornaments, such as ceiling rosettes and cornice moldings, are popular for do-it-yourself home remodelers. Available in pre-painted lightweight polyurethane (faux plaster), these ornaments are easier to work with than plaster or wood. With relatively little time and expense, you can install an ornate cornice detail or a Madelyn around a chandelier, completely transforming the look of a room.

Readily available decorative trims make ceilings an exciting and viable part of overall room design.

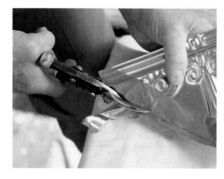

Installing a Tin Ceiling

Covering ceilings with decorative tin panels became popular in the mid- to late-1800s. Today the phrase "tin ceiling" is still used generically, but the products available include steel, copper, and brass in a variety of styles and finishes. Most can be finished with any color oil-based paint.

Typical tin ceiling installations include three components: the field panels, which cover the main area of the ceiling; the filler or perimeter panels; and the crown molding. Field panels are sold and installed in 2×2-, 2×4-, and 2×8-foot sizes. The filler panels are cut to fit between the field area and the crown molding. Provide a measured drawing of a room for most tin ceiling materials suppliers to work out a plan and to sell the component combination you need.

If you like the look but not the work involved in installation, there also are systems for suspending the tin ceiling components from a T-track grid, similar to suspended acoustical tile. You also can use embossed paper. (See "Embossed Papers," page 199.)

Before installing a tin ceiling, locate and mark all the joists on the ceiling with chalk lines. The tin ceiling components are nailed to furring strips that are nailed or screwed to the ceiling joists.

The tin ceiling installed in this old farmhouse, has been varnished instead of painted. Tin ceilings, once the height of elegance, complement Country and Victorian decorating schemes. The installation technique hasn't changed, but there are some new looks and new materials from which to choose.

Ceilings

Ceilings

Installing a Tin Ceiling

1 **Attach two furring strips for crown molding.** The first two furring strips are nailed close to the wall and run perpendicular to the joists. They're the first of several strips to install—these two are the nailing surface for the crown molding. Measure out from the wall the projected distance of the crown molding. (This dimension should be included in the materials specifications from your supplier.) Snap a chalk line representing the outside edge of the first two furring strips. Nail or screw the furring strips to the ceiling. Don't hammer the nails or drive the screws all the way in until after all the strips are installed.

STUFF YOU'LL NEED

✔ Tin ceiling components and nails
✔ Furring strips
✔ Measuring tape
✔ Chalk line
✔ Toggle bolts
✔ Hammer
✔ 8-penny nails or 2" drywall screws
✔ Brad nailer
✔ Level
✔ Shims
✔ Nail set
✔ Tin snips
✔ Stud finder
✔ Masking tape
✔ Compass
✔ Primer and paint, or clear polyurethane
✔ Paintbrush and bucket

2 **Snap lines for field area furring strips.** The main part of the ceiling—the field area—has strips installed every 12 inches on center. Since you can't see the chalk line under the center of the strip, snap chalk lines to indicate the strip edge. Snap two lines to represent the edges of the first strip across the center of the room, perpendicular to the joists. Work in both directions from these two lines, snapping lines 12 inches apart.

Carpenter's Secret

When leveling furring strips for tin ceiling tiles, don't expect perfection. Eliminate any gross bumps or valleys, but deviations of 1/8 inch or so won't be noticed in the finished job.

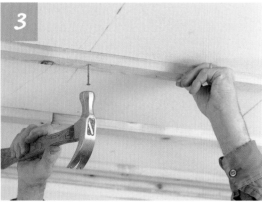

3 **Attach the main furring strips.** Align the edge of each furring strip with a chalk line; then nail it in place. The main furring strips run perpendicular to the joists. Nail into every joist.

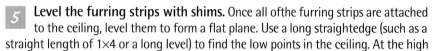

4 **Nail up short intermediate furring strips.** To complete the furring strip grid, install short strips between the long ones every 24 or 48 inches, depending on the size of the panels. These short strips are nailing surfaces for the field panels, which make up most of the ceiling. The strips run parallel to the joists, so they can't be nailed or screwed to the joists. Hang them with toggle bolts, using one near each strip. You also can cut the short strips to fit snugly between the main strips, tap them in place, and then angle-nail them to the long ones with a brad nailer, available from tool rental companies.

5 **Level the furring strips with shims.** Once all of the furring strips are attached to the ceiling, level them to form a flat plane. Use a long straightedge (such as a straight length of 1×4 or a long level) to find the low points in the ceiling. At the high

spots, slide tapered shims between the ceiling and the strips. Gradually shim the high spots down until the strips of furring are level with the low points all across the ceiling in both directions.

6 **Nail up the first panel.** To best conceal the seams between panels, the first panel should be installed at the farthest point from the main entry into the room. Holding tin ceiling tiles in place for nailing is nearly impossible without a second pair of hands—or a simple device to hold the panels for you. Start by nailing two scrap strips adjacent to where the panel will be positioned. Pivot them, as shown, to hold the panel in place while adjusting its final position. You also can use a length of furring strip cut to fit between the floor and ceiling, adding a piece of cardboard, as shown in the inset, to protect the ceiling panel. Use the nails provided with the ceiling material and nail every 6 inches along the designated nailing ridge or bead. Most panels have a central bubble or dimple in the pattern to conceal nails. Use a nail set to drive in the nails all the way without denting the metal.

Ceilings

Installing a Tin Ceiling   195

Installing a Tin Ceiling

7 Nail on adjacent sheets. The next panels to install are identical to the first—they're the field panels that make up the bulk of the ceiling. Install panels along the longer edge of the first panel. Overlap the edges and align the ends carefully. If the first two panels are misaligned, the rest of the panels will not fall squarely into place.

8 Close the seams. The seams between the panels will be imperfect—tight near the nails and slightly open between the nails. Pros have developed a simple method for blending the seams together. (They call it "caulking" though it doesn't involve caulk.) Rest a small block of wood—the thick end of a shim works well—against the metal along the seam, and tap it at an angle with a hammer. The metal will bend just enough to close gaps. Work the entire length of each seam.

9 Cut the filler panels to width. Filler panels fit in the space between the panels installed and the crown molding. Most filler panels include a transition molding that joins to the edge of the field panels. The other edge of the filler panel is nailed to the crown molding furring strip and is covered by the edge of the crown molding. First cut the filler panels to width using tin snips.

TOOL TIP

Tin snips are made in three basic styles that each do a specific job. You are likely to need more than one style when you install a tin ceiling.

Buy all three styles when you purchase all the materials so you don't have to run back and forth to the store. The three styles look similar; check the labels at the store to make sure you get the ones you want.

Straight-cutting tin snips are sufficient if you only need to make straight cuts, but they'll give you trouble if you try to cut curves.

Left- and right-handed tin snips are for cutting curves in designated directions. They cut openings in tin ceiling panels for light fixtures or outlets and cut the cope joints for the corners of the crown molding.

Power Up

Getting power to a fixture in an existing ceiling can be a challenge. The easiest (though perhaps least likely) scenario is replacing an existing light with a recessed light. If you're comfortable making basic electrical connections, this type of installation is straightforward. Installing a light in a new location means you have to tap into an existing electrical circuit—a wall outlet, for example—run a line, and put in a switch. (See "Running Wire For a New Ceiling Fixture," page 205, for more on running new electrical wiring.)

10 Install the filler panels. Fit filler panels along two opposite walls. When filler strips meet in the corner, they overlap by the width of the strip. Allow for this when cutting panels to length. If there is a molding along the edge of the filler, miter it on each end of the run so that the molding will appear to run around the room when installed. If the room is out of square, cut a stepped miter (see inset), a process that is explained in the installation directions. Nail the filler panels to the furring strips, and cut and install those on the adjoining walls.

11 "Caulk" the corner seam. The mitered corners in the filler panel transition molding can be made tighter looking by "caulking" the joint, as in Step 8, except the head of a 10-penny nail does the blending instead of a shim. Hold the nail so the edge of the head is along the seam, and tap it gently. Move the nail along the entire seam to blend the joint.

12 Lay out the crown molding. Measure down along each wall and make a mark to indicate the bottom edge of the crown molding. (The materials specifications with the tin ceiling components should include this dimension.) Snap a line around the entire room at this height.

Installing a Tin Ceiling 197

Installing a Tin Ceiling

13 Locate wall studs. The crown molding is nailed to both the ceiling furring strips and the wall. Find and mark all the wall studs in the room. A stud finder is quick and reliable. You also can find studs by nailing a series of holes through the wall until you hit wood. To find the remaining studs, measure (typically 16 inches on center) and mark them. Position the holes so that the molding will cover them up when installed.

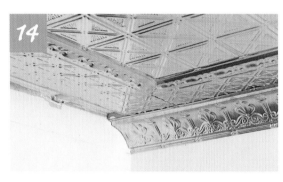

14 Install crown molding along two opposite walls. Inside corner joints are fit with coped joints. Start by cutting molding that runs from corner to corner on two opposite walls.

15 Lay out a coping template. To cut the coped half of the corner joint, make a trial piece to use as a template for cutting the final piece. Cut a 45-degree angle on a short scrap of crown molding. Put a piece of tape along this mitered edge to receive a pencil mark. Hold the template in place in the corner and scribe a pencil mark onto it by guiding the point of a compass across the face of the adjacent piece of crown, as shown in the inset.

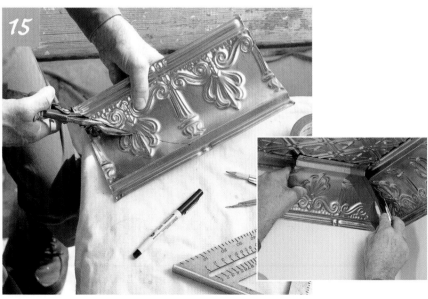

16 Cut the coping template. Cut along the scribed pencil line with tin snips to get an accurate template for the coped side of each corner joint.

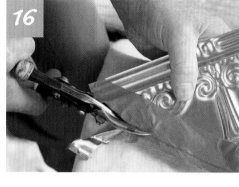

17 Cut the cope on the crown and install. Using the coping template, trace the profile of the corner onto the crown molding pieces, and cut the miters with tin snips. To get a tighter joint in the crown, cut the molding about ¼ inch longer, and then cut ⅛-inch deep snips into the coped edge. Nail the crown molding pieces to the ceiling furring strip and to the wall studs. Then "caulk" the miter joint as shown in Steps 8 and 11.

18 Prime and paint the ceiling. Tin ceilings can be clear-coated with oil-based polyurethane or painted with oil-based paint. Do not use latex paint or water-based polyurethane, as the water in them causes rust.

In Victorian Britain, the hallmarks of a grand home included walls and ceilings of carved wood, stamped metal, tooled leather, and ornamental plaster. Even then, these labor-intensive embellishments were expensive, and homeowners enthusiastically used affordable substitutes.

Embossed Papers

Lincrusta was an embossed covering with a base of linseed oil, like traditional linoleum. **Anaglypta** looked somewhat the same, but was made from cotton pulp and weighed less. Both products are still in production, although homeowners don't frequently install them.

You can buy vinyl embossed papers that are both inexpensive and easy to put up. The ceiling or wall is primed, and the paper is applied in the conventional way, although care must be taken to avoid flattening the embossing by rolling seams. The surface then can be painted by brush or roller; or you can use a washing technique (see "Color Wash," page 72) to emphasize the contours of the design. These papers are useful in covering walls with cracks and other flaws that would be obvious through a conventional wallpaper.

Installing a Tin Ceiling   199

Faux Plaster Rosettes and Crown Molding

Older stately homes were given lavish molding details in every possible location. Ceiling rosettes—round decorative plaques traditionally molded of plaster—were mounted in the center of ceilings surrounding light fixtures. Popular again, ceiling rosettes accent almost any room decor, making an ordinary light fixture exceptional or an elegant chandelier grand.

Ceiling rosettes are available in traditional plaster, but they are heavy and difficult to mount—especially to drywall ceilings. Lightweight rosettes made from gypsum or polyurethane are comparatively easy to install. Sizes range from 9 inches to 36 inches diameter.

Polyurethane also is used for linear moldings, such as chair rail and crown moldings, and has several advantages over wood. Polyurethane is stable. The moldings are formed in a mold, so they are straight and uniform without the possible warps or flaws of wood. It cuts, drills, and handles just like wood, but is lighter in weight and easier to install. And polyurethane molds into highly decorative profiles at less cost than wood moldings that require hand or laser carving for the same details.

The rosette and the molding above both look like plaster, but modern materials let you install these items with a minimum of tools to gain maximum effect.

Ceilings

Installing Faux Plaster Rosettes

STUFF YOU'LL NEED

✔ Polyurethane rosette
✔ Polyurethane crown molding
✔ Latex adhesive caulk
✔ Electronic stud finder
✔ 2¹⁄₂-inch trim-head screws
✔ Electric drill and driver
✔ Hand saw or power miter saw
✔ Adjustable combination square
✔ Framing square

Wisdom of the Aisles

"It seems like new products come on the molding market everyday. Companies are making everything from selection to installation easier for homeowners. It's worth taking a look at what's available before you decide whether a project is more than you can handle. You might be surprised at what you find."

— *Erica Barrett*
  Downers Grove, IL

Prep Work

Before you install a polyurethane rosette, turn off the power to the light fixture, disconnect the wiring, and remove the old fixture. Depending on the thickness of the fixture and the type of electrical box in the ceiling, you may have to use longer screws or a longer threaded tube to accommodate the ceiling rosette. After the rosette is in place, reinstall the fixture and turn on the power.

1 **Trace rosette on ceiling, and locate the joists.** With the fixture out of the way, center the rosette over the ceiling box. Lightly trace a pencil line on the ceiling around the perimeter of the rosette. Remove the rosette and use an electronic stud finder to locate the ceiling joists that pass above the rosette. Mark joist locations along the perimeter line of the rosette. Reposition the rosette and mark screw hole locations on the rosette where they will meet the joists. Select an area of the rosette where a transition between details will conceal the screw holes. Predrill holes through the rosette for the screws.

2 **Apply adhesive to the ceiling.** Apply a bead of construction adhesive or latex adhesive caulk to the area within the rosette outline. Keep the adhesive an inch or so away from the edge of the outline to minimize squeeze-out.

3 **Attach the rosette to the ceiling.** Position the rosette to align the screw holes with the joist marks, and press the rosette into the adhesive. Drive screws into the joists, and tighten gently to avoid crushing the rosette. Wipe off excess adhesive immediately. Remove the pencil marks at the joists with warm water and a cloth. Patch the screw holes with latex caulk or putty; then paint the installed rosette.

Ceilings

Installing Faux Plaster Crown Molding

Installing polyurethane crown molding is similar to installing wood crown molding. (See "Installing Crown Molding," beginning on page 141.) The difference is in the corners: Polyurethane crown has corner blocks for both inside and outside corners, eliminating the need for compound miter cuts or cope cuts at the corners. Outside corner blocks also can be used as finished returns to end a run of molding at high windows or doors.

1 **Install the corner blocks following the manufacturer's instructions.**
Position the corner blocks before installing them. Inside corner blocks self-register against the two walls and the ceiling. Outside corner blocks are likely to be

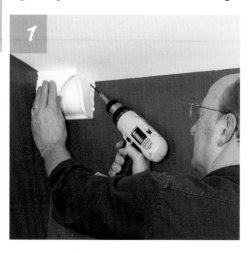

out of square. Hold an outside corner block in position, as close to square as you can judge. Lightly mark a pencil line on the ceiling around the outside edges of the block. Remove the block, hold a framing square against one of the walls, and check to see if the line is square. If necessary, draw new layout lines slightly darker using the framing square. Apply adhesive latex caulk to the surfaces of the corner blocks that contact the walls and ceiling. Align and screw them in place with trim-head screws.

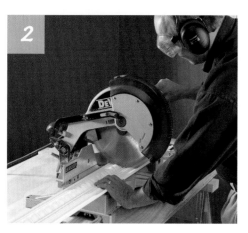

2 **Cross-cut the molding to length.** Measure the distance between corner blocks. Mark the straight moldings across the face with a pencil and adjustable combination square. Cut the molding on a power miter saw or by hand in a miter box.

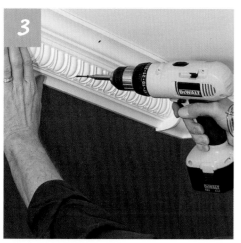

3 **Install the molding.** Apply a bead of latex adhesive caulk to the edges of the molding that will contact the ceiling and wall. Once in place, snug it into position to equally contact the wall and ceiling. Then drive trim-head screws through the molding and into the wall studs and ceiling joists. Wipe away excess caulk. Fill gaps along the wall and ceiling with latex caulk, fill the screw holes, and paint the molding.

Carpenter's Secret

The trim-head screws used to hold these moldings in place leave smaller holes than drywall screws. The holes are large enough, however, that they should be filled. The usual solution is joint compound or plaster patch. Use glazing putty to shape to the molding profile. Roll up some in a ball and pack it into the hole. Run your thumb along the molding and over the putty for a patch that follows the molding shape. Paint over it almost immediately—see the manufacturer's directions on the back of the can for specifics.

Wisdom of the Aisles

"It's improtant to keep perspective when you're doing any kind of home improvement work around your house. You've got to be as careful and as accurate as you can be but little mistakes can be hidden with all kinds of tricks. Caulking cornice seams to hide gaps is a good example. When the room is finished and all put back together nobody will notice."

— *John Rimar*
Old Bridge, NJ

Painting a Ceiling

Painting a ceiling is different from painting a wall.

The right equipment makes the job more enjoyable. Get a roller extension—a long handle that screws into the handle of a roller—so you can stand on the floor and paint. Wear a painter's cap to keep paint out of your hair.

1 **Mask the walls.** Professional painters can get away without masking tape, but they've been at it for years. To keep the brush or roller from painting the wall at the same time you paint the edge of the ceiling, mask off the top of the wall around the entire room.

2 **Cut in the edges.** A paint roller won't reach into the edge of the ceiling. Paint the strip around the edge of the room with a brush—a job painters call cutting in. Cut in only a few feet at a time so that the paint is wet when you roll the area next to it.

3 **Roll on the paint.** After you cut in about 5 feet of ceiling, put down the brush and pick up the roller. Roll paint into the brushed in area, removing as many of the brush marks as you can. Pros will tell you two things about this part of the job. Always roll into a wet area—you can't remove brush marks once they dry; and apply the paint up with a wet—but not dripping—roller. Once it's up, spread it out with a dryer roller.

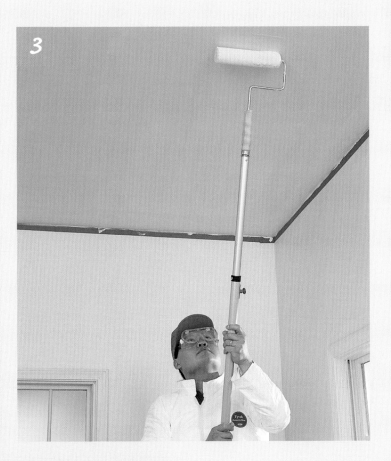

The Prime Directive

Ceilings, like other surfaces, need to be primed before you paint them. If you paint faux plaster ornamental moldings, however, they won't need priming except for any putty you use to fill the nail or screw holes.

Ceiling Lighting

Ceiling lighting is first about function—the quality and nature of the light a fixture imparts to the room. After function comes form because ceiling fixtures do as much to define style and look as other elements in the room.

There are many options of ceiling fixtures available. Home centers and lighting showrooms are well-stocked, and lighting specialists bring a high level of sophistication to the process of matching lights to a particular room. As you shop for light fixtures, be aware of the size, style, and wattage that will best fit your room.

Lighting reflects style. Recessed lights disappear discreetly into the ceiling, while surface-mounted track lighting protrudes into the room. Each can be fitted with a wide variety of bulb types to achieve the correct quality of light. Chandeliers and lighted ceiling fans hang down into the room and become a center of focus, more than a light source. Fluorescent lights are cool and functional but no longer exclusively for the kitchen and office. Finally, don't rule out finding or restoring a one-of-a-kind antique light fixture to give a room a unique source of light.

We've come a long way from bare lightbulbs in the center of the room. You can customize your lighting scheme to get exactly the look and feel you want.

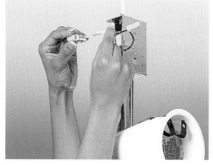

Running Wire For a New Ceiling Fixture

Installing a ceiling fixture where there is none may seem like a challenge, especially if you're not comfortable working with electricity. Should you try it yourself or should you call an electrician? If you do it yourself, check local codes and make sure you comply. The main challenge is running new wire through hidden wall spaces. This will likely involve cutting access holes in drywall, which will later have to be patched and repainted. An electrician may be stuck with the same scenario, but an experienced pro also may have a solution that minimizes cutting and patching the drywall. Before cutting into the wall or ceiling, make sure the wires cannot be routed through accessible spaces, such as the basement ceiling or an attic space above where the fixture will be installed.

Consult local building codes to determine which methods are approved for your area. Some general rules that apply to installing new wiring:

The easiest way to get power for your new ceiling fixture involves tapping into an existing outlet and cutting holes in the wall so you can run the cable.

• Make sure the circuit you add to can handle the additional load. To find out, check the amperage of the new fixture, and add it to the amperage of fixtures on the same circuit. They should total no more than 80 percent of the circuit breaker rating. Note that you can have no more than eight devices—fans, lights, stereos, etc.—on a 20-amp circuit.

• Use the same gauge wire that's already used on the circuit, typically 12- or 14-gauge.

• **Turn off the power at the circuit box** before working on wiring.

To route the wire through the wall and ceiling, assess the most likely route the new wiring will take. For a new ceiling light, install a wall switch. Run wire from the new fixture to the switch and then to a power source—typically an existing outlet in the room.

Running Wire for a New Ceiling Fixture

Cut the new switch box opening. Switches are typically located next to doors and at elbow height—48 to 52 inches from the floor to the center of the box. Pick the location, put the box against the wall, make sure the sides are plumb, and trace around it. Cut out along the lines with a keyhole saw and install the box. A variety of boxes can be installed into the drywall without having to be anchored to a stud. Ask for one that best fits your needs. Plastic boxes simplify the wiring, require less hardware, and meet code, so they're good for remodeling projects.

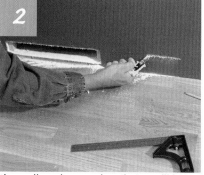

Cut an opening in the wall across the studs. If you put the new switch directly above an outlet, it will be easy to run wire between the two. It's more likely, however, that while the new switch will be next to the door, the nearest outlet will be in the middle of the wall. If so, open up the wall along the path between the two, and drill holes through the studs for the new wires. The opening can be located at any height in the wall, and remember that you'll have to patch it. Close to the floor is least conspicuous; behind the baseboard is even better, if that is an option.

Start the job by finding the stud next to the switch opening and the stud next to the outlet—the ones that fall between the new switch and the outlet. Mark the location on the walls. You can locate the studs with a stud finder, but a simple and more exact method is to drive nails through the wall until you hit a stud. Do this, of course, in the area you'll be cutting out.

Using a level as a straightedge, lay out the top and bottom of a rectangle 3 or 4 inches wide that runs between the two studs. Then lay out the sides of the rectangle so that they run up and down at the center of the marked studs. Cut the drywall with a utility knife or keyhole saw, and remove the drywall or plaster and lath.

In some cases, the new fixture won't be aligned above the outlet. You'll have to run the wire past the outlet and farther along the wall before feeding it up the wall. Continue the rectangular cutout in the drywall as necessary.

Drill holes in studs for wire. Slip a drill into the cutout, and drill 1-inch diameter holes through the center of the exposed studs.

Ceilings

3

STUFF YOU'LL NEED

✔ Switch box
✔ Switch
✔ 12-2 cable with ground
✔ Ceiling box and mounting hardware
✔ Black electrical tape
✔ Wire caps
✔ Stud finder
✔ Keyhole saw
✔ Utility knife
✔ Level
✔ Electric drill
✔ ¾" or 1" drill bit
✔ Fish tape
✔ Screwdriver
✔ Needle-nose pliers
✔ Wire strippers

Electrician's Secret

Attaching Wires to Screws

Use needle-nose pliers to make a loop in the end of all wires that will be attached to a screw. According to code, the loop must go clockwise around the screw so that tightening the screw will also tighten the loop.

Code also is strict about how many wires can be attached to a screw: One, and only one. If you have two wires that need to go under one screw, twist them together with a third wire, and run it to the screw. Twist a wire nut over the exposed ends where the three wires meet.

Choosing a Chandelier

Good lighting is as important as adequate and safe wiring. Insufficient or too-bright lighting frustrates homeowners as much as no lighting. Choose wisely.

Chandeliers don't have to be large to cast the right amount of light. As a rule, purchase a chandelier that is an inch long for every foot of room length. A room 12-feet long, for example, is well-lit by a 12-inch chandelier. For dining rooms, select chandeliers that are smaller than the table below them.

Avoid mounting the chandelier too high. In dining rooms with 8-foot ceilings, chandeliers should be 25 to 30 inches above the table. Because much of the light that reaches the table reflects off the ceiling, make adjustments for higher ceilings. Put the chandelier 3 inches higher for each foot higher than 8 feet.

In choosing bulbs for general use, plan for 2 watts of incandescent light per square foot. Higher chandeliers need more wattage. Experiment, and err on the large side, since two 50-watt bulbs don't produce the light of a single 100-watt bulb. For dining, use the light produced by a single 100-watt bulb. For fixtures with more than one bulb, use about 120 watts. No matter how many bulbs you use, install a dimmer switch instead of an off-on toggle switch. (Installation is the same for both switches.) You'll be able to control the light so that you can set it at levels to suit the uses of the room.

In the dining room, a chandelier provides both general light and task lighting to help you see your food.

This large room requires a good-size chandelier. Make sure the chandelier hangs high enough to prevent guests from bumping their heads when they get up from the table.

Keep general lighting in bedrooms softer than lighting in kitchens, dining rooms, or foyers. Bedside lamps provide additional light.

To light this room well, the chandelier needs a high-powered bulb. Mirrors help to spread the light and reduce shadow, and large windows provide extra illumination during the day.

Ceilings

Choosing a Chandelier   207

Running Wire for a New Ceiling Fixture

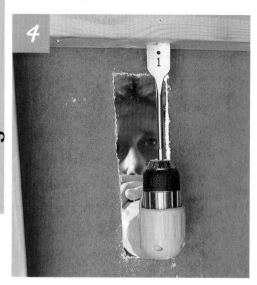

4 Cut an access hole near the ceiling. At this stage, you should be able to run wire to and from the switch, past the outlet (if necessary), and up between the studs toward the ceiling. At the top of the wall, however, the framing will block the path to the ceiling space. To drill a hole through the top plate of the wall, cut an access hole in either the wall or the ceiling where the two meet.

Make the hole big enough to put a drill into the opening and to drill through the top plate of the wall.

If the ceiling joists run parallel to the wall you're working on, cut an opening in the ceiling that runs from the wall out to the fixture opening and then drill through each joist—just as you did to run the wire through the wall studs. If the joists run perpendicular to the wall, run the wire within a joist cavity.

5 Cut the fixture hole, and fish the wires. Use a stud finder to find a spot for the fixture that's at least a few inches away from the nearest stud. Lay out a hole for the fixture box at this point by placing it against the ceiling and tracing around it. Cut out the plaster or drywall. Run electrician's fish tape into the hole in the wall, up through the hole in the top plate, and across the ceiling to the fixture hole. Tape the wire to the end of the fish tape and pull it down through the top plate and the access hole. Feed it through the wall to the floor, then past the receptacle to the switch box. Then feed another length of cable from the receptacle opening over to the new switch box opening.

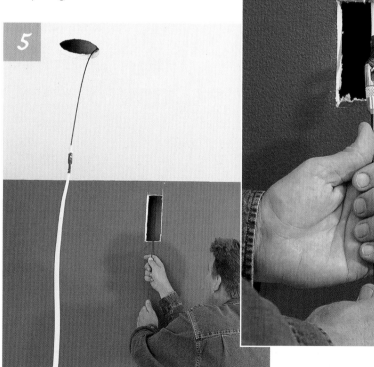

TOOL TIP

Fishing Wire With a Fish Tape

Getting new wiring from one place to another behind walls or above ceilings is like working while wearing a blindfold. To make matters worse, the wire often gets held up on framing, especially when turning corners. The solution is fish tape, a strong length of wire that will snake around corners without crimping or bending the way a length of electrical wire might. Feed the fish tape from one point to the other, hook the bare cable ends of the wire onto the fish tape, wrap the assembly with electrical tape, and pull it back through.

Electrician's Secret

Metal Boxes

Wiring a metal box is more involved than wiring a plastic box, only because the box must be wired into a grounding system. The rest of the wiring is the same; but if you have a metal box, there must be a connection between it, the grounding wires in any cables that enter it, and the body of the switch or receptacle, or fixture. Most of this is a matter of twisting the wires together, adding the necessary pigtail, and connecting the pigtail to the box. Newer boxes will have a tapped hole in them for a green grounding screw that you buy separately. If the box doesn't have space for a grounding screw, ask the home center for a "grounding clip" that slides onto the box.

6 **Mount the ceiling box.**
Use a ceiling box with an expandable mounting bar. The device has two feet that stand on the drywall while you turn the bar. Turning the bar drives the pointed ends into the joists. If the box is metal, first make an opening in it for the cable by punching out a knockout with a screwdriver and then adding a cable clamp. If the box is plastic, you won't need a cable clamp, and the opening is usually there. Pass the mounting bar up through the opening; tighten the bar so it extends and locks into the two joists. Next, position the U-bolts on the mounting bar, feed the cable into the box, and attach the box to the U-bolts from below. (Note in the inset photo that some boxes require separate wires that pass individually through small holes in the box.)

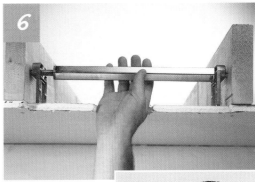

7 **Connect the wires to the outlet.** The number of cables entering the box varies, depending on where the outlet falls in the circuit. Regardless of the number, twist all the black wires, plus a black pigtail, together under a wire cap. Wrap tape around the cap and the wires, holding them together. Do the same with all the white wires. Run the pigtail from the black wires to the brass color screw on the outlet. Run the pigtail from the white wires to the silver color screw on the outlet. Connect all the bare grounding wires (they are occasionally coated in green vinyl) to a pigtail, cap and tape them, and run the pigtail to the green screw on the outlet.

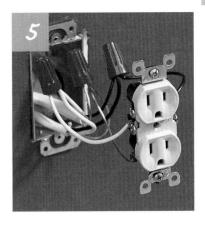

8 **Connect wires at the switch.** In Step 5, two cables fed into the switch box, one from the receptacle, and one from the light. Strip about ½ inch off the ends of the two white wires, twist them together with a pair of pliers, and cover them with a wire cap. Repeat for the green wires or bare wires. Strip the black wires, and put a loop in the end with a pair of needle-nose pliers. Attach either black wire to either of the screws on the switch, and attach the other black wire to the other side, positioning the loop so it runs clockwise around the screw. Wrap tape around the caps and the wires. Fold the cable into the box, and screw the switch to the box.

Follow the installation directions provided with the fixture. Generally, match the color of the wire in the cable with the color of the wire in the fixture and connect them with a wire cap. The green wire connects to a green grounding screw in either the fixture or the junction box.

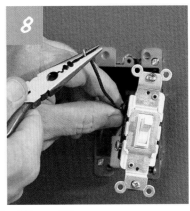

Running Wire for a New Ceiling Fixture 209

Ceilings

Installing a Chandelier

Lighting fixtures impact the ambience of a room. Besides the quality of light they produce, there's also the appearance of the fixtures. This is especially true of chandeliers because they are prominent room features.

Although "chandelier" may bring to mind ornate lights with sparkling crystals, for practical purposes it includes any ceiling-mounted fixture that hangs from a chain or wire. This includes an incredibly wide range of hanging fixtures that complement any style of decor, from early-American candle types to stained-glass Arts-and-Crafts designs.

Despite the variety to choose from, installation of ceiling-mounted fixtures is similar to one another, regardless of the style. The biggest issue is determining whether the electric box that houses the wiring connections in the ceiling is adequate to support the weight of the chandelier. If you replace a hanging fixture with a fixture about the same weight, the existing box is probably fine. If the new fixture is heavier than the old one, you may need to replace the ceiling box with one rated to hold more weight. If you put in a new box, make sure it's rated for a heavy fixture. (See "Installing a Ceiling Fan," pages 214-217) for more on choosing the right ceiling box for heavy fixtures.

Some form of chandelier illuminates most dining tables. Plan the placement of one as carefully as you would plan a good meal. To give off a pleasing light, a chandelier should be centered over the table and about 30 inches above it. If there is one socket, use a single 100-watt bulb. For two sockets, use two 60-watts bulbs. For three or more sockets, use 40-watt bulbs.

Installing a Chandelier

STUFF YOU'LL NEED

✔ Chandelier
✔ Appropriate ceiling electrical box
✔ Ladder and support platform
✔ Screwdriver
✔ Wire strippers
✔ Wire nuts
✔ Electrical tape

Smart & Safe

Once you've connected the wires with wire caps, wrap electrical tape around the wire and the cap. It's not always necessary, but it will help keep the wire from popping free and charging the metal parts of the chandelier with electricity.

Electrician's Secret

Need parts? Break something while you were working on the chandelier? Many—but not all—parts of a chandelier or lamp are interchangeable. Take the broken part to an electrical department or a lighting store and show them what you need. Brass globes, threaded fittings, and brass stems almost always can be replaced with new parts.

1 **Assemble the canopy and hanging hardware.** Remove any components that can be installed after the fixture is hanging (globes, glass panels, light bulbs, etc.). Follow the specific instructions provided with the fixture. Remember to slide any necessary parts over the wiring and hanging chain.

Support the fixture close to the ceiling by screwing a platform to the top of a stepladder with a few drywall screws. This provides a good work surface, and should put the chandelier close enough to the ceiling to allow you to do the wiring without having to hold the chandelier in midair. Having a second person on a second ladder may also work, but can be difficult with a heavy fixture.

Fixtures usually come with a new mounting strap—a strip of metal that screws into the junction box in the ceiling. You can often use the existing strap, but if not, unscrew the old strap, and screw the new strap in place.

2 **Connect the wiring.** Check the supply wires for fraying or damage. If necessary, cut the wires and strip off about ¾ inch of insulation. On older fixtures, like this one, the wires aren't color coded. Connect one fixture wire to the black supply wire and the other fixture wire to the white supply wire. Newer fixtures have a black and white wire. Twist the bare end of the black supply wire together with the bare end of the black fixture wire, and twist on a wire nut. Repeat with the white wires. Carefully tuck the wires into the junction box. Put a bulb in the fixture and check that connections work before finishing.

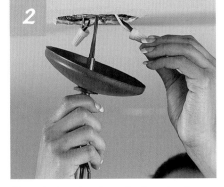

3 **Hang the fixture.** Thread the fixture's mounting stem into the mounting strap on the ceiling box. The fixture is now securely hanging from the ceiling, but the box and mounting hardware are still visible. Slide the canopy up against the ceiling to cover the mounting hardware, and tighten the lock nut against the canopy.

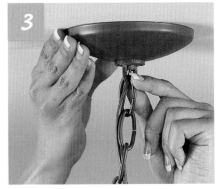

Ceilings

Restoring a Light Fixture

Desk lamps, table lamps, and chandeliers are often reproductions of familiar designs. They are valued not only for lighting, but also for warm reminders of older rooms and associations. As good as reproductions are, they only imitate the heft and patina of authentic fixtures. With this in mind, reconsider current ceiling fixtures that may be worth saving. If they aren't, check out broken lamps that may be gathering dust in an attic or basement. Mechanical repairs are quite simple and restoration of sconces and table lamps is similar to ceiling fixtures.

Repairing lamps requires confidence. Your work will be tested when the lamp is plugged into a 120-volt circuit. If you haven't worked with electrical repair before, have an electrician or a knowledgeable friend check your work to make sure the lamp is back together and in safe working order before plugging it in.

Before assuming a fixture is broken, make sure the lightbulb is good. Rest assured that most of the odd little parts—nipples, hickeys, harps, and sockets—are still available. If you don't find what you need in hardware stores or home center lighting departments, take the broken piece to the service desk of a lighting fixture store.

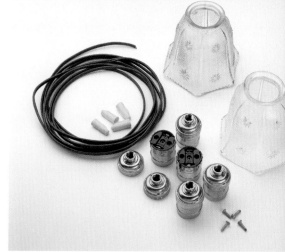

Restoring a dusty old light fixture to its original state can add a touch of authenticity to a period room. If you compare the price of reproductions, you'll probably find that rebuilding an antique saves money. You might have to search for parts, but most are available through specialty lighting stores and catalogs.

Restoring a Light Fixture

1 **Take apart the fixture.** Turn off the power at the breaker box, and check by flipping the switch in the room once or twice. Remove the fixture. Put it on a worktable, and take it apart. Make a sketch of the fixture and of the wiring to help with reassembly. The brass used in many fixtures is relatively soft, so be careful to avoid scratching or deforming parts as you work. Most parts, except for the socket, screw together. To remove the socket body from the base, you typically press the sides of the body, and pull apart the pieces.

Once the fixture is apart, remove the wires. If they are held in the socket by two individual lines knotted together, tie the new wire the same way. If there is more than one socket, label the wires with masking tape to know which wire goes where.

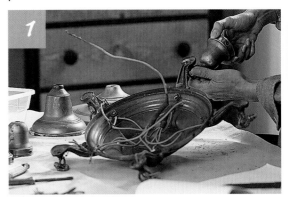

2 **Shop for missing or broken parts.** Inspect the fixture and note which items need to be replaced. Put new wiring on the list. You'll want 18-gauge stranded wire for most wall, table, or ceiling fixtures. It's sold as 18/2 wire, meaning 18-gauge wire with two conductors. To make sure you get the right wire, take a length of the old wire with you to the store and ask a salesperson to help you pick the replacement. If the socket is damaged or if the switch doesn't work, replace the socket. If you fix a table lamp, remember to buy a plug.

3 **Put the lamp back together.** Strip the ends of the new wire with a pair of wire strippers. Attach the wires securely to the screws in the socket. Code requires that a hook be put in the end of the wire with needle-nose pliers, wrapping the hook clockwise around the screw. (Tightening the screw tightens the hook.) Make sure that the insulating cardboard sleeve is in place over the socket; then reassemble the socket. Rewire, following the sketch, twisting the wires together and then twisting a wire cap over the bare wires. Wrap the cap and wire in electrical tape.

If you're fixing a table lamp, place felt pads on the base to protect the table. Put in a bulb, turn on the power, and test your work. If the bulb flickers or doesn't light, have an electrician look at it.

STUFF YOU'LL NEED

- ✔ Screwdrivers (slot and phillips head)
- ✔ Needle-nose pliers
- ✔ Brass polish
- ✔ Spray-on clear lacquer
- ✔ Replacement wire that matches the original
- ✔ Replacement parts as necessary
- ✔ Wire strippers
- ✔ Wire caps
- ✔ Electrical tape

Smart & Safe

Older fixtures don't have labels stating maximum bulb wattage. Be safe; use nothing brighter (or hotter) than a 40-watt bulb in a table lamp, and nothing brighter than 60 watts in a ceiling fixture. The heat created by larger bulbs could damage the fixtures.

Installing a Ceiling Fan

A light breeze gently relieves the swelter of a hot summer day, but Mother Nature just doesn't always oblige. Ceiling fans, which have been around in one form or another for hundreds of years, provide relief with the flip of a switch. Combine a fan with a light fixture for relatively low-energy consumption that does double duty. Unlike window fans and air conditioners, which have to be lugged in and out for the season, ceiling fans become a permanent part of the room.

When selecting a ceiling fan, make sure there will be adequate clearance for the fan blades. Height clearance to the blades should be no less than 7 feet from the floor. Certain models are designed to fit close to the ceiling to maximize clearance in rooms with lower ceilings, and other models have adjustable shafts so they can be hung lower from high ceilings. Additionally, the blades should swing no closer than 18 inches to the nearest wall.

Hanging a ceiling fan is not mechanically difficult, and most fans come with good installation instructions; however, they are fairly heavy, so a helper is recommended.

Just as important, ceiling fans need to be properly anchored to an electric ceiling box that's designed to hold a heavy fixture. Not only will it hold the wiring, but it will also support the full weight of the fan. If you replace a simple light fixture, the box will likely have to be replaced with one rated for a ceiling fan

A fan—or a fan with a light—helps cools the house and adds a decorative touch.

STUFF YOU'LL NEED

✔ Ceiling fan
✔ Ceiling fan fixture box (if the existing one is not correct for mounting fan)
✔ 10×1½-inch wood screws
✔ Wire nuts
✔ 64″ drill bit
✔ Screwdriver
✔ Electric drill

Smart & Safe

Ceiling fans are relatively heavy and awkward to handle, so have a helper available to watch the ladder and lend a hand when you need it.

Prep Work

Safety First: Turn off the power at the breaker box and remove the old fixture. For extra security, tape a "DO NOT TOUCH" note on the box to avoid any accidents. If necessary, install a new junction box capable of supporting a fan.

1 **Remove the old fixture.** Turn off the power at the panel and check to make sure it is off by flipping the wall switch. Remove glass domes as well as the bulbs from the old fixture to avoid breaking them. Some fixtures have a metal canopy that covers the wiring—remove it by unscrewing the flat locknut. Other fixtures are attached with a mounting plate or base directly to the electric box within the ceiling—simply remove the screws. Unscrew the wire nuts connecting the fixture wires to the supply wires, and disconnect the ground wire.

2 **Screw the fan mounting plate to the outlet box.** Make sure the ceiling box is suitable for supporting the weight of the fan. (See "Mounting an Electrical Box for a Ceiling Fan," on page 216.) With the box securely in place (inset photo), thread the supply wire through the fan mounting plate and attach it to the box with threaded screws. If you've replaced the box, you may need longer screws than the ones provided. Make sure that the screws match the female threads on the box and that they thread into the box at least ½ inch.

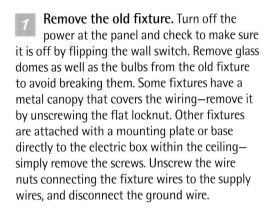

3 **Connect the fan wires.** With the fan motor and canopy in place but hanging loose from the mounting plate, twist the end of the white supply wire with the end of the white fan wire, and screw on the wire nut (which is usually supplied). Repeat, twisting the black wires together. (If the fan includes a light, there will be an additional wire that should be twisted together with the other black wires.) Attach the ground wire to the green screw in the box. If there's no green screw, tighten the wire underneath the head of one of the mounting screws.

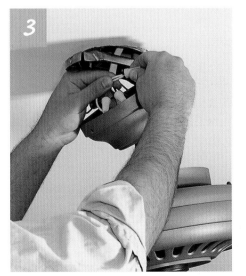

Installing a Ceiling Fan   215

Mounting an Electrical Box for a Ceiling Fan

Unless you replace one ceiling fan with another, the existing ceiling box probably won't support the weight of the fan. It's a good idea to replace the box before installation.

All fans are designed to be attached with threaded screws to a ceiling box, so if your box doesn't accept two threaded mounting screws, replace it with one that does. Many sizes and shapes of boxes will do the job. The box must be attached securely to the ceiling joists and must be rated to hold the weight of the fan. (The weight capacity is printed on the box.) Here are three mounting options:

1 **Mount box directly to joist.** If the existing box is screwed directly onto the edge of a joist (common in older plaster and lath ceilings), install the new one the same way. Remove the screw or screws holding the box to the joist and take it down. Select a box of the right depth—it should be flush or nearly flush with the ceiling surface. Punch out the knockout in the back of the box, and if the box is metal, install a cable clamp. Pull the wire through the knockout hole or clamp. Position the box so the two mounting holes are centered on the joist. (Some boxes have a self-stick patch on the back that makes positioning the box easier.) Predrill $7/64$-inch-diameter holes for a 10×1$1/2$-inch wood screw, which may be supplied with the box. Then drive the screws through the back of the box into the joists.

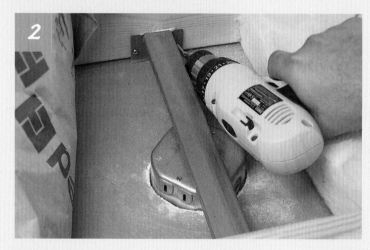

2 **Use a bar hanger installed from above.** If you can access and work in the space above the ceiling, this is the way to go. The box hangs from a sturdy expandable bar; the ends of the bar are screwed to the joists. The photo shows a typical setup. Position the bar with the box in the opening. After the ends of the bar are screwed to the joists, tighten the box to the bar from below.

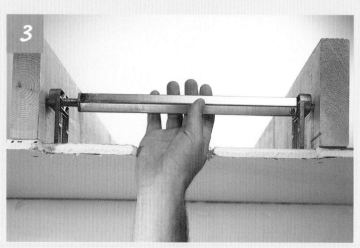

3 **Use a bar hanger installed from below.** If you don't have access to the space above the ceiling, this adjustable bar hanger works perfectly. First, adjust the length of the bar to about 1 inch shorter than the span between the joists. Then pass the bar through the opening for the old box and position it perpendicular to the joists. Finally, reach up through the opening and turn the bar counterclockwise to expand its length until the end feet press tightly into the joists.

4 **Hang the fan and tighten the canopy.** The fan assembly will vary depending on the style and model used. There are usually two mounting options with most fans: tight to the ceiling for a low-profile look or hung from an extension pipe that drops the fan farther from the ceiling. Regardless of the style you choose, attach the motor and housing to the ceiling mounting plate. The fan blades are always attached after the motor housing is in place. Be sure to thread the supply wires through the fan assembly in the sequence shown in the fan installation instructions. With the fan hung, slide the canopy up against the ceiling and tighten the locking screws.

5 **Complete the fan assembly.** Assemble the fan blades to the brackets—do this on a table or the floor. Then screw each bracket to the motor.

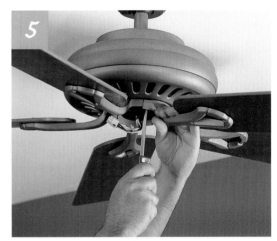

6 **Assemble the light fixture.** Connect the wires from the fan to the light assembly, which is usually a separate piece. Slide the light base over the mounting rim and tighten the mounting screws. Install a bulb, and attach the light globe.

Installing a Ceiling Fan **217**

Ceilings

Installing Track Lighting

Track lighting offers a way to get directable light from a single ceiling fixture. The track works with a narrow-focus bulb to spotlight a piece of artwork, a wide-focus "wall washer" to bathe a wall with light, or a general-purpose bulb to light a kitchen counter or reading chair. Halogen bulbs provide a wide range of focusing options; incandescent systems are generally less expensive and generate less heat. Keep in mind that you can have more than a single track. Some systems allow you to link tracks for long straight runs or 90-degree turns.

While installing plug-in track systems involves only a screwdriver and perhaps a drill, this project shows how to hard-wire a track directly to an existing switched outlet. If you aren't confident with working on home wiring, shop for a system and then have an electrician put it up. The procedure given here is for commonly available systems; read the manufacturer's directions for specifics on installation.

Once used primarily for commercial applications, track lighting fixtures offer an excellent way for homeowners to distribute light.

Installing Track Lighting

1 **Attach the mounting plate and live-end connector.** A floating live-end connector can be placed at any point along the track. Follow the manufacturer's directions to attach it and the mounting plate to the track at the spot where you pick up power from the existing ceiling outlet box. Pass the connector wires through the plate for attaching to the box wiring.

2 **Lay out the track.** Tracks are either fastened directly to the ceiling or snapped into clips that are first attached to the ceiling. If the manufacturer doesn't provide mounting hardware, use toggle bolts. Typically the track is installed parallel to a wall of the room. Measure the distance from the wall to the box; then make marks on the ceiling at this distance on both sides of the box to lay out the track. With a straightedge, draw a line connecting these two marks.

3 **Drill pilot holes for mounting.** To install mounting clips, drill pilot holes along the line you've drawn and attach the clips. Snap the track into the clips. To attach the track directly to the ceiling, hold the track in place over the line and make marks for pilot holes through the mounting holes, as shown. Drill pilot holes the diameter given by the manufacturer (see inset). Use mounting hardware provided by the manufacturer, or use toggle bolts.

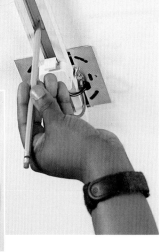

4 **Mount the track.** Attach either the track-mounting clips or the track directly to the ceiling.

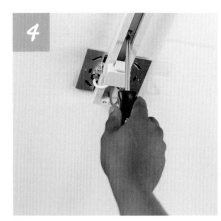

Good idea! → **If you can't buy the right size track, use a hacksaw to cut it to length.** Remove the dead-end cover, guide the cut with a miter box, and remove sharp burrs with a fine-tooth file. Replace the cover.

STUFF YOU'LL NEED

✔ Stepladder
✔ Tape measure
✔ Straightedge
✔ Screwdriver
✔ Electric drill
✔ Track and individual light

Toggle Bolts

When you have a heavy object to hang and nothing to nail or screw it into, toggle bolts are the solution. The nut folds to slip through a hole drilled in the wall or ceiling. It pops open once it's through the wall or ceiling, creating a nut that provides support for the bolt that passes through it.

Prep Work

Before removing the existing fixture, turn off the power to the circuit at the service panel. Disconnect the fixture by twisting off the wire nuts attaching its wiring to the circuit.

Installing Track Lighting

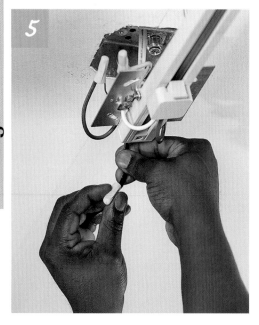

5

Connect the wiring. Make sure the power is turned off. Connect the white and black wires of the fitting to the same-color wires from the circuit. Connect the green or bare grounding wires of both the fixture and the circuit with the grounding terminal or wire on the box. Push the wires inside the box, using care to avoid undoing any connections.

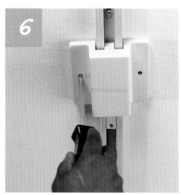

6 **Install the power supply canopy.** Attach the canopy to the mounting plate with the screws provided.

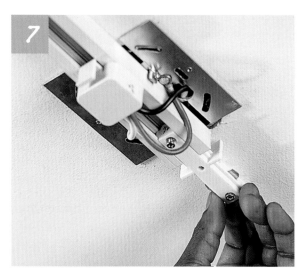

7 **Add connectors to extend track.** If you wish to add tracks, use live-end connectors, either for a straight run or a 90-degree turn. Install additional sections and cap the end of the final run with a dead-end cover.

8 **Install the individual lights.** Place the lights in the track and twist to lock them in position. Screw bulbs into them, restore power to the circuit, and adjust the beams.

Wiring Pointers

It's neither safe nor legal to put two wires under the same screw. If two wires need to go to the same screw, twist them together with a third wire, cap them, and run the third wire to the screw.

Use needle-nose pliers to make a hook in the end of a wire before fastening it to a screw terminal. Position the hook so it runs clockwise around the screw. Tighten the screw to make the hook tighter.

Although not always necessary, it's good practice to tape a wiring cap to the wires that run into it. Wrap the tape around the cap and then around the wires to prevent accidental shorting if the cap comes loose.

Most ceiling boxes have only one cable coming in. If the box you're working on has more than one cable, connect the wires for the new fixture to the same wires that served the old fixture.

All new fixtures will have ground wire, which is either bare or green. If there's no ground wire in the existing cable, hook the fixture's ground wire to a screw in the ceiling box.

Installing Recessed Lighting

Recessed lights shining on the wall provide accent lighting, intended for effect as well as light. Those shining on the table provide general lighting for the room and task lighting for dining.

Recessed lights fill a wide range of needs and work out of sight. They discreetly become part of the ceiling while contributing a major and necessary element to the room. The simple, functional elegance makes recessed ceiling lighting a popular choice.

Before you select lights, decide the part they will play in the room. General lighting provides diffused light to a broad area of a room. Task lighting is directed at an area where defined tasks are performed—cooking, reading, or using a computer, for example. Accent lighting is focused on a specific object, such as artwork or a bookcase. "Wall washers" do what you'd expect—they wash the wall with light. They're usually grouped and arranged to create patterns on the wall.

Once you determine the part each light will play, read the light boxes to see what kind of trim piece the light has. The trim piece helps determine the type of light provided by the fixture. Trim options include baffle (minimizes glare), reflector (maximizes output), and eyeball (directs light toward specific point).

When purchasing lights, note that there are two distinct types: new construction (when you have access to the open ceiling), and remodeling (when you have to install the fixtures through a finished ceiling). Both types come in 4-, 5-, and 6-inch diameters and can be installed in suspended ceilings as well as drywall ceilings.

Installing Recessed Lighting

1 **Lay out a spot between ceiling joists.** All recessed ceiling lights are designed to fit between the ceiling joists, so the exact location of the fixtures is determined by the joists. Find the joists in the general area by using a stud finder, or

by tapping firmly on the ceiling with your knuckle or a rubber mallet. The sound will be higher pitched at a joist. Check by driving a nail through the ceiling at that point. If you're nailing into solid wood, it's a joist. Mark the joists with a light pencil line or a piece of masking tape. Then use the template supplied with the fixture to lay out a hole for the light.

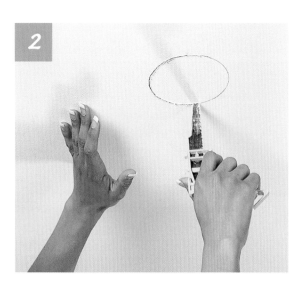

2 **Cut the hole.** Plunge a keyhole saw through the drywall and cut the hole. If necessary, feed a cable to supply the light through the hole and fish it toward a power source. **Make sure the power is turned off before making connections to any existing wiring.** Leave about a foot of extra cable hanging through the ceiling hole.

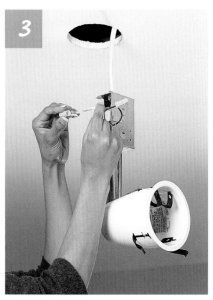

3 **Wire the new fixture.** The fixture comes in two pieces—a housing and a light canister. Remove the canister from the housing, and wire the housing following the instructions provided with the fixture. When connecting wires, twist them together first, then twist on a wire nut. Though not strictly necessary, most electricians wrap electrical tape around the wire nut and wire to provide extra security.

STUFF YOU'LL NEED

✔ Stud/joist finder
✔ Masking tape
✔ Keyhole/drywall saw
✔ Wire nuts
✔ Pliers
✔ Electrical tape
✔ Recessed light fixture
✔ Stepladder

Electrician's Secret

If you're concerned about leaving enough room between the fixture and a joist, here's a test. Tap a small hole with a screwdriver at the center of the proposed hole for the fixture. Bend a piece of coat hanger to an L-shape, with the bent end one-half the diameter of the fixture hole, plus an inch. Slip the bent end of the hanger into the hole so it lays on the top side of the ceiling, and rotate it in a circle. If the wire rotates freely, you have enough clearance for the fixture.

Ceilings

4 **Push the housing up into the ceiling.** Depending on the design, the fixture will either be approved or not approved for contact with insulation. If the fixture is not rated for contact with insulation, cut the insulation away from the hole so it doesn't touch the housing. Loose-fill insulation requires a barrier—usually a piece of 2x6—to hold back the insulation. This can be difficult to install without damaging the ceiling. If you think you'll run into loose fill, get a contact-rated fixture. Once the opening is clear of insulation and other obstructions, feed the housing into the ceiling.

Power Up

Getting power to a fixture in an existing ceiling can be challenging. The easiest (though perhaps least likely) scenario is replacing an existing light with a recessed light. If you're comfortable making basic electrical connections, this type of installation is straightforward. Installing a light in a new location means you have to tap into an existing electrical circuit—a wall outlet, for example—run a line, and put in a switch. (See "Running Wire for a New Ceiling Fixture," page 205, for more on new electrical wiring.)

5 **Install the light canister into the mounting frame.** Most housings have a leveling system that pulls the housing tightly against the ceiling. Level the frame, and then plug the light canister into the housing.

6 **Install the light canister.** The canister shown snaps into the housing. Some canisters have trim pieces that snap into the housing or that is held in place by springs. Other fixtures have trim that is built into the canister. Put the light canister in the housing, following the directions provided with the unit. Install trim pieces as necessary.

Ceilings

Ceilings

Installing Fluorescent Lighting

Fluorescent lights flaunt their efficiency in electricity consumption and bulb life. Because of the broad cast of light, a single fixture is often enough for an entire room. Fluorescent light is cooler than incandescent bulbs, although incandescent bulbs that provide softer or warmer light are available.

Fluorescent fixtures come in a wide range of sizes and styles, from slim under-counter models with a single 1-foot-long bulb, to large ceiling fixtures with a small army of 4-foot-long bulbs.

In most cases, fluorescent fixtures are used to replace less efficient light—in kitchens, bathrooms, recreation rooms, home offices, workshops, or utility rooms. If you're replacing it's just a matter of removing the old light and putting up the new one in it's place. If you put the light in a spot that requires new wires, however, the job may be more complicated. (See "Running Wire for a New Ceiling Fixture," page 205.)

A fluorescent light casts a whiter, brighter light than an incandescent bulb using the same power. It's perfect for use in kitchens, home offices, or laundry rooms. The basic white fixture above matches the appliances. If you want more style, solid wood frames with shoji screen diffusers are available.

Installing Fluorescent Lighting

STUFF YOU'LL NEED

✔ Stud finder
✔ Keyhole saw
✔ Wire-fishing tool (if new fixture location)
✔ Mounting screws
✔ Drill or driver

1 **Locate ceiling joints.** A heavy fluorescent fixture needs to be screwed securely to the ceiling joists. Locate the studs with a stud finder and mark the locations on the ceiling with a pencil. If you mount the fixture perpendicular to the joists, you're bound to catch a couple of joists, but the light's mounting holes aren't

likely to align with them. If this happens, drill new mounting holes in the light, using a drill bit slightly smaller than the screw you will use.

If the fixture runs parallel to the joists, slightly adjust the location of the light under at least one joist. When you hang the fixture, use toggle bolts to attach the side that isn't under a joist.

Toggle Bolts

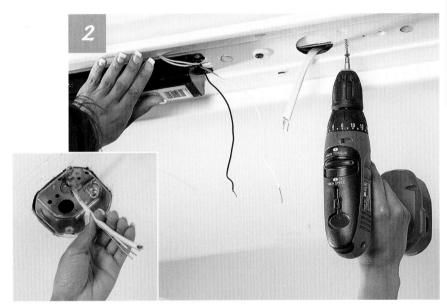

When you have something heavy to hang, but can't find anything to nail or screw into, a toggle bolt is a great solution. The nut folds up so you can slip it through a hole you drill in the wall or ceiling. It pops open once it's gone through the ceiling, creating a nut that provides support for the bolt that passes through it.

2 **Mount fixture to ceiling.** Turn off the power at the box and take out the old fixture by removing the screws or threaded ornaments that hold it in place. Disassemble the new fixture, if necessary, to expose the mounting holes and the wiring. Pull the supply wire from the existing junction box through the fixture. Screw the fixture to the joists with the mounting screws. With large ceiling fixtures, you'll need a second pair of hands.

3 **Connect the wiring.** Follow the wiring instructions provided with the fixture to connect the wires. Generally, the black wire from the supply line connects with the black wire from the fixture. The white wire from the supply line connects with the white fixture wire. Connect the ground wire from the supply line, which is either bare or green, with the bare or green wire from the fixture. Install the wiring cover plate and put in the bulbs. Turn on the power and check that the light works before installing the light cover.

Ceilings

Section 4
Windows

Windows are the product of centuries of experimentation on how to enjoy a view without getting frostbite. As a result, they're intricate pieces of work. Movable frames, complex joinery, and the physics of letting in light while keeping out the cold and bugs are complicated. Windows present technical challenges (they're tricky to paint). They also offer design challenges to decorators, including decisions about color, form, and the elements that embellish them. Thoughtful use of blinds, shades, curtains, or shutters is key in capturing style and theme for features that open your home to the light and views of the great outdoors.

Windows

Windows

Painting and Staining Windows

Framing the views from your home with good-looking windows becomes an essential part of room design. Painting or staining windows should fit into your overall decorating plan.

Getting the look and finish you want requires planning and preparation. Wooden windows take a beating from ultraviolet rays, temperature changes, and moisture. Additionally, angles and crevices challenge even the best painters.

Regular window maintenance pays off in long service. Painting or varnishing the windows before they show wear makes the work easier and ensures an investment in your home's appearance.

A good sash brush is a necessary purchase. All of those ledges and right-angle turns demand a bit of finesse, which becomes much easier and more professional looking with a quality brush.

Protect your investment. Keep your windows in good repair to enjoy the inside and outside views.

Window Painting Basics

Basic to the appearance of a window is the quality of its finish, the casing, the ledge, and the sashes with delicate mullions (vertical wooden strips that separate the lights, or panes of glass). This adds up to a lot of surfaces and edges to cover with a brush, as well as panes to avoid brushing. To make the job of painting or varnishing still more demanding, windows take a beating from sun, rain, and condensation, from potted plants, and from being opened and closed.

Prep work is essential before painting windows. Scuff and sand the existing finish so that the new fiinsih will adhere well; chips and blistering are common with windows, requiring use of a scraper and sandpaper. Take time to mask off both glass and the surrounding wall to save time cleaning up afterward.

Finally, reduce frustration and enjoy this somewhat finicky job by purchasing a good angled sash brush. Windows deserve high quality, smooth, and durable finishes.

A scraper, sandpaper, elbow grease, and some quality paint make this old window look like it was built yesterday.

Windows

Window Painting Basics

1 **Scrape and sand the window.**
If either of the sashes is painted shut, free it with a sash saw. Slip the blade through the paint holding the window shut, and work the blade back and forth to break the bond. Wash greasy or dirty areas with TSP or phosphate-free cleaner. Remove loose paint with a scraper. Sand the wood, both to blend in scraped areas and to remove the sheen from glossy paints. Be careful to avoid scratching the glass when scraping and sanding. Go over the wood with a tack cloth to remove the dust.

2 **Fill holes and caulk the gaps.**
Use wood putty to fill in flaws in the wood. If gaps have opened between the wall and window frame, fill them with paintable caulk. Level the wood putty with a putty knife. Smooth the caulk with your finger.

3 **Remove the sashes.** If possible, remove the sashes from the frame and paint them on sawhorses; it's easier to contain runs. On many newer windows, the sashes pop out with little trouble. To remove those on older windows, carefully pry off the side trim. Use a wide, stiff putty knife before graduating to a pry bar. Some sashes just won't come out and you'll have to paint them in place.

STUFF YOU'LL NEED

- ✔ Paint
- ✔ Primer
- ✔ Paintable caulk and caulk gun
- ✔ Wood putty and putty knife
- ✔ TSP or phosphate-free equivalent
- ✔ Sash saw
- ✔ Paint scraper
- ✔ Sandpaper
- ✔ Tack cloth
- ✔ Wide putty knife or pry bar (for removing trim)
- ✔ Low-tack painter's masking tape
- ✔ 2-inch sash brush
- ✔ Utility knife
- ✔ Bucket
- ✔ Sponge

Wisdom of the Aisles

"To pick up any remaining fine dust, just go over the wood with the palm of your hand. That's the best tack cloth there is."

— *Wilfrid Feteau
Evanston, IL*

Prep Work

The most controversial aspect of painting is which kind of paint to use—latex, oil, or both. Some pros recommend oil for the primer, saying it holds up best. They follow up with either oil or latex paint, which, despite what you may have heard, works well over an oil primer. Most homeowners use latex because its relatively innocuous smell and easy cleanup outweigh the compromise in durability.

*Designer's Tip

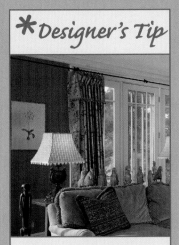

Use bold colors on the walls and neutral colors to paint the trim. You won't have to redo the trim if you change the color of the room or the fabric in the curtains.

Painter's Secret

Have your paint supplier tint the primer to match the paint. It will be lighter than the final coat because it will only take about half as much tint. It will cover well enough, however, that you might not need a second top coat.

4 **Mask panes and the surrounding wall.** If the sash won't come out, as shown here, use low-tack masking tape to avoid getting finish on the glass and wall. Some are made for wallpaper, others for walls, still others for either long- or short-term use.

Good idea! **Apply the masking tape over the glass so that it doesn't quite touch the wood.** This allows the paint to make a weathertight seal with the glass. Moisture will be less likely to enter the wood, extending the life of the finish.

5 **Apply primer with a sash brush.** If the window has snap-out muntin grids, remove them for easier painting. If it has actual muntins, paint them first. Then paint the horizontal parts of the sash, followed by the verticals. Paint the sill last. If you work in this order, each step removes excess paint, splashes, and drips from the step before.

To keep the sashes from sticking, do not paint the sides of the windows or the track in which they travel. If you paint the sashes in place, lower the upper one and raise the lower one to get to any surfaces that are inaccessible when the window is closed. Move the sashes a few times as the paint dries to keep them from sticking.

Good idea! **To use an old painter's pun, mullions are a pain.** If you can't remove the sash and lay it flat before painting, do the verticals first—it's easier to catch running paint.

6 **Apply one or more finish coats.** Again using the sash brush, apply paint the same way you applied primer. If you used a tinted primer, one top coat may be enough. If the primer peaks through or an edge didn't get painted, apply a second top coat.

Windows

Window Painting Basics   231

Window Painting Basics

7 Remove the masking tape or scrape the windows. Remove the masking tape from the glass as soon as the paint skins over to prevent pulling up dried paint when you remove it. If you haven't taped off the glass (or if your masking technique isn't perfect), draw a sharp utility knife along the edges of each pane, leaving a narrow margin of paint on the glass; then push a window scraper toward this cut line to remove the paint.

Painter's Secret

Liquid glass maskers can be an alternative for masking tape on window panes. The compound is applied directly to the glass and allowed to dry. After painting, remove maskers with the scraper included in the kit.

Keeping Windows in Good Repair

Windows may be the most difficult feature in your house to keep in good repair.

The paint is in direct sunlight. One side of the window gets coated in rain, sleet, snow, and ice. The other side is dry and heated, or in summer it's dry and cool if air conditioning is used. Condensation builds on the inside during the winter. Windows have twice as many moving parts as doors. All in all, windows are troublesome and require regular maintenance.

Keep on top of the situation to minimize problems:

- During the winter, water builds up on the inside of the window when moist air hits cold glass. Dripping condensation is one of the biggest causes of paint failure. To avoid it, put in storm windows. Storms have small drainage holes along the bottom; moisture that builds up between the windows escapes through the holes. Make sure the holes are open.

- It's tempting to coat everything in sight when you pull the windows out to paint them. Don't. The sides of the sash are purposely left unpainted so that they don't stick to the running tracks. If you got paint on the sides of the sash, sand it slightly if the windows are sticking. If they aren't sticking, leave well enough alone.

- Crazing is a sign of paint failure, usually caused by very old oil paint. The oil has completely dried and turned powdery. Finish on top of it cracks and crazes; and no matter what caused the crazing, the only thing that fixes it is removing it. The best solution is to take the window to a dip-and-strip shop to remove the paint.

- Sometimes paint buildup on the face of the window causes it to stick. If that's the case, you'll see a thin line of paint wearing away where the sash meets the trim. Have the window stripped, or remove the window and sand it—being aware that aggressive sanding will leave a window that rattles in its track.

- Maintain the glazing compound. This is the white putty around each pane on the outside of the window. It eventually dries out and breaks away from the wood. Water that works its way between the putty and wood causes both paint failure and wood rot. If the window putty/glazing is cracked, gently remove as much putty as you can. If the new putty won't stick to the wood, seal the wood with a thinned coat of latex paint.

Windows With Natural Finishes

A window takes a beating. Even if you remember to close it before every rainstorm and almost never overwater the plants parked on the sill, a window's finish degrades over time. Eventually, the effects of sunlight and moisture make it necessary to sand and strip the window.

Before the 1950s, most windows with clear finishes were shellacked. Lacquers followed, and now polyurethane is standard for homeowners who refinish their windows. Fortunately, it's not necessary to know what's on your windows—polyurethane does a good job of covering it. Either oil- or water-based poly works well. (Water-based is easier to clean up.) Be scrupulous with the prep work. If you won't be stripping the old finish, sand carefully to ensure that the new coats adhere well.

What about stripping a painted window and finishing it clear? You face the challenge of coaxing paint out from the crevices of the trim, the window frame, and perhaps the muntins (moldings that hold individual panes). It can be done, but it's difficult to do well. Take a good look at the job and all the nooks and crannies to assess how much work you have ahead of you. Maybe you'll want to send the woodwork out to a dip-and-strip shop.

Natural finishes allow the grain and color of the wood to make a decorating statement.

Windows with Natural Finishes

1 Sand or strip the existing finish. Examine the window. If it is in reasonably good condition, sand it to smooth the finish and dull the sheen. Begin with 120-grit sandpaper, and once it's done most of the work, sand with 180-grit for a smoother surface.

If the finish is badly damaged or unattractively built up, remove the finish. Remove the sashes and place them on sawhorses. On many newer windows, the sashes pop out easily. To remove sashes on older windows, you may have to carefully pry off trim pieces. Brush paint and varnish remover onto the window sashes, following the manufacturer's directions. (Provide good ventilation and wear gloves.) Scrape off the finish with a putty knife. Rinse with the recommended solvent for the remover.

2 Fill holes. Use wood putty to fill flaws. Spot-sand these areas when the putty dries. Go over the window with a tack cloth (if you'll be using an oil-based finish) or damp paper towel (before using a water-based finish).

Unfortunately, no putty matches the wood exactly. If you stain the wood, a stainable putty absorbs the stain and comes close to a match, but it won't be perfect. Experiment with different brands to see which works best with your stain.

If you're not going to stain, make your own putty. Gather a few pinches of fine sawdust from the type of wood you'll be patching, mix with five-minute epoxy, and fill in any holes. After the epoxy dries, trim off any bumps with a utility knife or sharp chisel, and then sand.

3 Mask panes and the surrounding wall. Use masking tape to keep from getting finish on the glass and wall. The new, low-tack tapes are easy to remove and leave less residue. They'll work well when you mask off trim, too. Use white or blue rolls instead of brown—they stick better. There are several types of low-tack tape, so read the label carefully and choose the one that best meets your needs.

Make sure you mask the two side edges of the sash. They're traditionally left unfinished so that the finish won't stick when you open the window.

STUFF YOU'LL NEED

- ✔ Paint and varnish remover
- ✔ Stain (optional)
- ✔ Clear finish
- ✔ 120- and 180-grit sandpaper
- ✔ Rubber gloves
- ✔ Putty knife
- ✔ Wood putty
- ✔ Tack cloth or paper towel
- ✔ Low-tack painter's masking tape
- ✔ 2-inch sash brush
- ✔ Utility knife
- ✔ Window scraper
- ✔ Inexpensive brush
- ✔ Drop cloth
- ✔ Steel wool

Prep Work

The more complicated the paint job, the more important it is that the surface beneath it is smooth and defect free. Paint doesn't hide irregularities—they show through, interrupting the pattern you're creating. Patch, prime and sand before putting on two coats of the base color.

Windows

4

234 Windows

Painter's Secret

Scraping away paint remover is a messy job. If you strip a large surface, such as a door, let the remover do its work, and—wearing rubber gloves—rub handfuls of sawdust or bedding chips into the goo. The sawdust will absorb the remover and you can finish up easily with a scraper. Throw out the sawdust when it is thoroughly dry.

4 **Stain the wood.** If you have stripped the window and want to darken or warm its color, stain it now. Note that stain will only take evenly if you've been thorough in removing the old finish. If the window is made of soft wood—such as pine—you'll have an additional problem staining it. The wood absorbs the stain unevenly, giving it a blotchy look. Avoid this by applying a gel stain, which won't blotch because it doesn't soak deeply into the wood.

Wisdom of the Aisles

"You can't go by the names of stains—one manufacturer's walnut stain is another manufacturer's cherry stain. To match a stain in your home, pry off a piece of trim, take it into the store, and match it with samples on display."

— *Mel Sanders*
Totowa, NJ

5 **Apply the finish.** Brush on the finish the same way you brush on paint. (See "Window Painting Basics," page 229.) Apply at least two coats for greater durability; sills take the greatest beating and benefit from three coats. Sand lightly between coats, wiping up the dust with either a tack cloth or damp paper towel.

6 **Remove the masking tape or scrape the windows.** Remove the tape from the glass as soon as the finish begins to dry to prevent adhesive residue. If you haven't taped off the glass (or if your masking job wasn't quite as good as you thought), draw a sharp utility knife along the edges of each pane, leaving a narrow margin of finish on the glass. Push a window scraper toward this cut line to remove the finish.

Troubled by sticking sashes? Spray silicone along the channels in which the windows travel. Mask off the surrounding wood because silicone will repel finish the next time the window needs refinishing.

Good idea!

Windows with Natural Finishes

Blinds, Shades, and Shutters

Sometimes we need to block the view—in, or out of, the house—and draperies aren't always the answer. Traditional fabric treatments don't suit every decor. Blinds and shutters are simple solutions to the problem of modifying the flow of light into a room. They filter the outside world much the way a dimmer switch controls the lighting in a room.

Installation is straightforward. Usually all you need is a tape measure and a few basic tools. If you like the comfort of draperies, combine them for a look that blends the softness of fabric with the solid security of built-in blinds and shutters.

Technology and style of blinds have evolved dramatically. If it's been a while since you checked a window treatment department in a home center or paged through a mail-order catalog, treat yourself to a look. You'll find a wide array of ready-made choices and endless custom options.

The simple look and appeal of cellular shades is that they keep out harsh light. They also make complex and dramatic statements about decor and design. The choice is yours.

Installing Shutters

In an era before screens and blinds, interior shutters graced many homes. A practical window treatment, they conserve heat in winter and allow both ventilation and privacy in summer. Shutters provide architectural elegance and a sense of structure different from the flounce and flow of draperies, curtains, and other fabric treatments.

Shutters can be installed in several configurations: full-height, double-hung (shown left), as separate shutters for the bottom and top halves of the window, and café-style with shutters at the bottom half of the window. Typically, interior shutters have operable louvers connected with a tilt bar to moderate light, but they also are available with fixed louvers. A version that's suited for Country, Traditional, and Victorian styles is the solid frame-and-panel style.

Multipurpose louvered shutters control the level of light, provide ventilation, and offer privacy in a room.

Installing Shutters

1 **Measure the window opening.** If the installation will be outside the opening, measure so that the shutters will slightly overlap the jamb. If the shutters are to be placed inside the window opening, measure the width and height of this space at several places; use the narrowest width and use the smallest figure for the height. Inside-mounted shutters should have a margin, top and bottom, of at least ⅛ inch and no more than ¼ inch.

2 **Trim the shutters if necessary.** If a shutter is too large, plane or saw equal amounts from the outside edges of both stiles (the vertical frame members) or both rails (the horizontal members), as

needed. Do not remove so much stock to compromise the appearance or the strength of the shutters. Test the fit by wedging the shutters in the opening, considering whether you will recess the hinges in mortises. Plane or cut again if necessary. If the shutters aren't already finished, paint or stain before putting them up.

Good idea! → **Measure all the windows in the room before** you order shutters. It's tough news to learn that some of your made-to-order shutters don't quite fit.

3 **Lay out the hinges on the jambs.** Hinges are usually placed 1½ inches from the top and bottom of the shutter; if the shutter is over 3 feet tall or especially heavy, add a third hinge midway. Note that shutters fit more closely to the sides of the window opening when the hinges are set into mortises, both on wood window trim and on the shutters. Before cutting the hinge mortises, mount the hinges temporarily on the jambs, then use a utility knife to outline them. Drill pilot holes for the screws, if necessary.

4 **Chisel out the jamb mortises.** If the directions for the shutters direct you to mortise the jambs for the hinges, use a chisel and hammer to remove the wood, working to a depth that makes the leaves of the hinges flush with the surface. Place each hinge in its mortise, mark for pilot holes, drill, and temporarily install with just one screw for each hinge.

If wood shutters will be used in a *Good idea!* high-humidity area—over the kitchen sink or in the bathroom—prime and paint ← every surface, or condition, stain, and finish with a coat of polyurethane.

STUFF YOU'LL NEED

✔ Shutters with installation hardware
✔ Tape measure
✔ Utility knife (if hinges are mortised)
✔ Wood chisel (if hinges are mortised)
✔ Hammer (if hinges are mortised)
✔ Electric drill
✔ Screwdrivers

Mounting Interior Shutters

Interior shutters are installed either outside or inside the window jamb. Decide which way before measuring and ordering them.

Outside mount is the most common mounting method. If there is no trim, attach the hang strip to the wall and hang the shutter from it. If there is trim on the wall around the opening, the hang strip can be mounted to it.

Inside mounts are tricky because mismeasured shutters or an out-of-square window opening may leave light gaps around the perimeter. Also, you need two, three, or more inches of jamb depth for the shutters to operate without interfering with the operation of the window.

Two types of inside mount:

• If the window opening is surrounded by a wood jamb, use a direct mount, with one-half of the hinge attached to the jamb and the other to the shutter.

• If the window jamb is drywall, use an indirect mount, with one-half of the hinge attached to a hang strip and the other to the shutter. This installation method is also used to deal with an opening that is out of square because the strip position can be adapted to allow the shutter to operate properly.

Refinisher's Secret

Why are interior shutters so often stained? It could be just for the dark handsome look, but convenience also may have something to do with it. Painting louvered shutters is like an SAT exam for brush skills. But stain can be wiped on quickly using a rag.

5 Lay out and chisel the shutter mortises. Temporarily wedge the shutters in place with cardboard or tapered cedar shims, and check for proper clearance all around. Make sure they open the right way and operate freely; then trace the hinge outlines on the shutter stiles. So that the hinge mortises will have crisp, true edges, go over the pencil lines with a razor knife held against a straightedge.

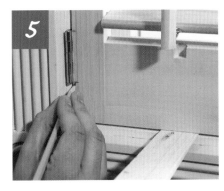

6 Finish installing the shutters. Remove the shutters, and mortise them for the hinges if directed to do so. Drill pilot holes and install the shutters. Adjust the jamb hinges, if necessary; then drive the remaining screws.

Combining Shutters and Draperies

When draperies are used to frame a window rather than to close it off, interior shutters are a good partner. Whether the shutters are full height or halfway, they can be closed to provide privacy and to dim the room. Use shutters with these window treatments:

• **Swags** sweep dramatically from the top of the window and aren't operable. Couple a swag with a side jabot, joining the two with a rosette. Make sure that the shutters clear the swags, or just shutter the bottom half of the windows.

• **Valances** balance the tops of windows that are covered with café shutters on the lower half.

• **Curtains** duplicate the area covered by shutters. They allow flexibility in moderating light, privacy, and appearance of the room.

*Designer's Tip

Shutters aren't just for windows. Use tall shutters as freestanding room dividers and smaller shutters as cabinet doors.

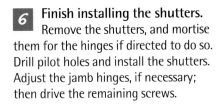

Installing Vertical Blinds

Although horizontal and vertical blinds both create atmosphere and control light, they have different personalities. Horizontals can look businesslike or create a cozy, comfortable feeling. Vertical blinds are at home in almost any contemporary setting and do an excellent job of masking floor-to-ceiling windows or sliding glass doors.

Some vertical models have vanes that take color inserts to match the decor of a room. Although verticals can combine with swags and other soft window treatments, they are decorative enough to stand alone.

For inside mounts—inside the window openings—precise measurements are required for the blinds to fit well. The window inset needs to be at least as deep as required by the manufacturer. An outside mount—one that hangs over the window—increases privacy and does a better job of excluding light. There is no maximum width for outside-mounted blinds, and they can be installed oversize to make windows appear larger.

Gracious vertical blinds rise to the full height of the room and also sweep the floor.

Installing Vertical Blinds

STUFF YOU'LL NEED

✔ Blinds
✔ Screws, and anchors, if necessary
✔ Tape measure
✔ Level
✔ Drill and bits
✔ Screwdriver

Wisdom of the Aisles

"If you have a window with a view you love, use blinds instead of curtains. It can be difficult to pull curtains back to take full advantage of the scenery. Just make sure the stack (when the blinds are pulled all the way up) doesn't get in the way either."

— *Kelly Banducci*
San Leandro, CA

Smart & Safe

To prevent young children from becoming entangled in control cords, install cord cleats to keep the cords out of reach. Or shorten the cords by sliding up the knob, retying the knot that secures the knob, and cutting off the excess. Look for blinds that use wands instead of cording for opening and closing.

1 Measure all the window openings and number them before you go to the store. Decide whether to mount the blinds inside the window or outside it. **For an inside mount**, measure the width of the opening at the top. Measure the height in the middle of the opening and along both sides. Use the shortest of the three heights. (Don't deduct for inside clearance unless instructed by the manufacturer.) Finally, check the opening for square—measure from the top left to lower right of the window opening, and from the top right to lower left. If measurements differ by more than $1/2$ inch, use an outside mount.

For an outside mount, add at least 5 inches—2 or 3 inches above the window for mounting hardware, and at least 3 inches below the opening. If you have an obstruction on the bottom, such as a large threshold, include that in your measurements. You may have to install the mounting hardware higher up the wall.

You have more choices for width. Either allow an overlap of at least $3^1/2$ inches on each side or have the blinds align with the outer edge of the window frame. More width, however, adds a sense of formality, ensures privacy, and minimizes light leaks from the sides.

2 Attach the brackets. Hold the end brackets (and central bracket, if included) in place and mark the screw holes on the wall and ceiling. Check to make sure sets of holes are level with each other. Make necessary adjustments and drill the holes. If you drill into wood trim or framing, drill holes slightly smaller than the screws you'll use. Otherwise, use wall anchors, toggle bolts, or other hardware, and follow the hardware manufacturer's directions.

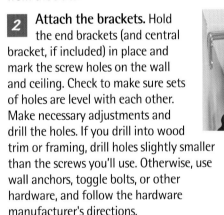

3 Install the head rail. Place the head rail into the brackets and lock it in place, as directed by the manufacturer.

4 Attach the valance and vanes. If the blinds have a decorative valance, attach it as instructed. Also attach any hardware for adjusting the vanes. Attach the vanes into clips in the head rail.

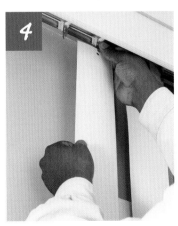

Good idea!

 Vanes can break, and although you can order new ones, the color might not match. Order a few extra vanes at the time you purchase the blinds and set them aside. If a vane breaks, you're assured a perfect match.

Installing Horizontal Blinds

Horizontal blinds with variable-pitch slats regulate light levels, ranging from gentle filtering to darkness.

Slats are made of aluminum, vinyl, PVC, or wood and come in many widths. Micro blinds average just ½ inch, minis are about 1 inch, and standard-width slats are 2 inches wide. Aluminum blinds fold into compact stacking height—just 3 inches or so for a 6-foot blind. Wood blinds have a handsome, substantial look and provide a warm glow as outdoor light passes through them. But 6-foot wood blinds have a stacking height of 8 inches to more than a foot, potentially blocking some of the view. (Manufacturers have charts that show stacking heights.) The longer blinds are, the heavier they get and the more difficult to raise and lower. Consider installing several narrower blinds rather than one large one.

Blinds are installed two basic ways: mounted either inside or outside (over) the window opening. An outside mount makes the windows look large because the stack goes above the window. A valance mounted on the wall can conceal the raised slats. Inside-mounted blinds look trim, and if recessed, they allow access to plants or knickknacks on broad windowsills when lowered. Because they don't overlap the window opening, they admit more light around the edges. Careful measurement is important to ensure that they'll fit the available space.

Wooden blinds are attractive; however, they don't necessarily close tightly. Other styles are more suited to privacy and to block light.

Adjust the horizontal movable slats to control light levels, to filter, and to direct the light.

Installing Horizontal Blinds

~~~~~~~~~~~~~~~~~~~~~~~~~~~~

STUFF YOU'LL NEED

✔ Blinds
✔ Screws, and anchors, if necessary
✔ Tape measure
✔ Level
✔ Drill and bits
✔ Screwdriver

* Designer's Tip

Choosing between an inside and outside mount is usually a matter of depth and style, but if your windows are out of square, your best bet is an outside mount. To check for square, measure the window diagonally—top left to lower right of the window opening, and from the top right to lower left. If measurements differ by more than ¹/₂ inch, go with an outside mount.

Smart & Safe

Being Kid-Safe

• **If you plan to hang aluminum blinds in the nursery,** make sure the paint on them is certified lead-free by the manufacturer.

• **To prevent young children from becoming entangled in control cords,** install cleats to keep the cords out of reach. Or shorten the cords by sliding up the knob, retying the knot that secures the knob, and cutting off the excess. Choose blinds that use wands instead of rope to open and close.

1 **Measure all windows for the blinds.** Decide whether to mount inside or outside the window opening.

Ⓐ For an inside mount, measure the width at the top, middle, and bottom, and use the smallest figure. Unless specified by the manufacturer, do not measure for clearance. That will be accounted for when the blinds are cut to size. Measure the height at the left and right sides and center, and use the largest figure.

Ⓑ For an outside mount, measure the overall width and add at least 8 inches to allow a generous overlap on either side to block light. Measure the height, adding at the top to account for the mounting brackets and enough at the bottom for a satisfactory overlap.

2 **Install the brackets.** Note that on some units, the same brackets are used for both inside and outside mounting. Hold the end brackets (and central bracket, if included) in place and mark for pilot screw holes. Use a level to make sure each set of holes is level with the others. Drill the holes for the screws and install the brackets. In wood or wood framing, drill the hole slightly smaller than the screw you'll use. If you aren't going into wood trim or wood framing, use wall anchors, toggle bolts, or other hardware, and follow the directions supplied.

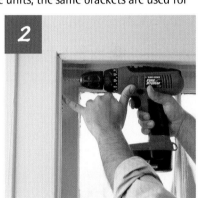

Good idea! →

Annoyed when blinds blow about in the wind? Some manufacturers offer hold-down brackets to keep lowered blinds from swaying. A pin in each bracket fits into a hole in the bottom rail. Request this feature when ordering.

3 **Install the head rail.** Place the head rail into the brackets and lock it in place. Note that the brackets on some units are adaptable for either inside or outside mounting; on others there are two types of brackets. If blinds hang long, check the directions for removing some of the slats from the bottom.

4 **Attach the valance.** If the blinds have a decorative valance, attach it as instructed. Also attach the wand for adjusting the vanes.

Windows

Gallery of Blinds

Blinds and shades filter, direct, diffuse, and even quietly tint the light. Blinds and shades are crisply attractive in their simplicity and efficiency.

Even if blinds alone don't suit your plush traditional living room, you can combine them with traversing draperies or a swag and tails to soften the practicality with yards of fabric.

Many blinds and shades don't need to be buffered by other window treatments. The photographs in this gallery present rooms that rely on the simple mechanics of blinds and shades to treat the windows.

Restful adaptations, such as a Japanese shoji screen, tame the harshness of sunlight with shadowless glow and keep the outside world at bay.

Wooden blinds especially suit a room that features natural color. Slats add subtle warmth to the daylight filtering through.

Roller shades have evolved remarkably over the years. With subtly scalloped trim, these diaphanous shades look anything but utilitarian.

Vertical blinds become part of the room, especially if they pick up color from the trim or walls.

If you want shades and fabric too, consider soft, generous folds of Roman blinds.

Horizontal blinds come in a range of colors.

Install roller shades at midpoint or higher on windows. A cornice conceals mechanics.

Lots of Options

Shopping for blinds and shades requires time and research. Home centers and decorator showrooms carry huge displays showcasing hundreds of colors and styles. New technology in the operating mechanisms makes blinds and shades easy to install. Innovations in design and new materials offer choices for privacy and light diffusion throughout the room. Perforations in plastic and metal blinds allow more light without sacrificing privacy. Cellular shades and honeycomb shades are soft variations of blinds, with horizontal tubes of fabric that are barely visible when raised. When lowered, they provide soft, diffused light with little insulation. Double- and triple-cell shades increase the R-value. Shades operate in several ways—from the top down, bottom up, or both. And the top can be sheer while the bottom is opaque. Wallpaper and fabric inserts change the personality of vertical vanes—handy if you repaint the room.

Pleated shades are trim, simple, and easy on the checkbook.

Honeycomb shades soften sunlight because there are two layers of translucent fabric.

Window Treatments

After the rest of the room is in shape, you can hang the curtains. Choosing the right treatments for your windows is a challenging design decision. You may want to seek advice from a professional. Designers and window treatment specialists will share basic knowledge of fabrics, hanging methods, and accessories to help you select a style that best suits your room.

Choose from three options for purchase: custom, semi-custom, and off-the-shelf.

For unusual or complex window treatments, seek out a home center with a design staff or a custom drapery or decorating store to design and, if you wish, manufacture draperies to your specifications.

Decorating stores and design centers also carry a wide assortment of semi-custom draperies. Basic designs in several different fabrics and lengths range from simple to high fashion.

Other home furnishings and accessories stores have basic options on the shelves. For do-it-yourself window treatments, you also can find no-sew techniques, such as heat sensitive adhesives that let you iron in hems, rod pockets, and tabs. They also carry curtain rods and other hangers to match almost any room decor.

With the abundance of beautiful fabrics and accessories available, you can get exactly what you want in window treatment design.

Traversing Draperies

The grandest and most practical way to cover windows is to draw fabric along a mechanical track. The pull of a cord can dramatically change both the light level and the appearance of a room. If desired, a decorative cornice or valance can conceal the rings, pleats, and hooks behind this operation.

For a plush, luxurious look, combine traversing drapes with stationary panels. Or use double tracks with heavier draperies to block light and add color and pattern to the room paired with sheers close to the window to diffuse light.

Outside-mounted draperies block light best, make the window appear larger, and can run from ceiling to floor.

Send draperies whispering across the window and wall with a pull on the cord of a traverse rod system.

Traversing Draperies   247

Traversing Draperies

1 **Measure the width.** To mount draperies outside the frame, measure the distance between the outer edges of the window moldings. Extend this measurement 4 to 5 inches beyond the moldings to ensure that side hems won't be seen from the outside. If you want full clearance to reveal the entire window, consult your drapery professional for the correct measurement.

∩∩∩∩∩∩∩∩∩∩∩∩∩∩∩∩∩∩∩∩∩∩∩

STUFF YOU'LL NEED

✔ Draperies
✔ Traverse rod set
✔ Stepladder
✔ Tape measure
✔ Electric drill
✔ Screwdriver

Use a metal tape to accurately measure for window treatments. Cloth tapes stretch when drawn taut, which may distort the measurements.

Good idea!

2 **Measure the height.** For inset draperies, measure the distance between the bottom of the molding above the window and the windowsill. The draperies should not drag when operated. For outside-mount draperies, measure the distance from the top of the molding above the window to the bottom edge of the molding below the sill; extend this distance as you wish to extend the draperies to the floor (as shown) or to the ceiling.

A Gallery of Holdbacks

Holdbacks draw draperies back from the edge of the window, making the most of available light and a good view. The fabric can be arranged to create a swagged effect above the holdbacks. When mounted at the top corners of the window frame, this hardware is used to create a scarf swag.

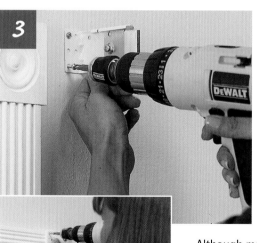

3 **Install the brackets on the molding.** Mount the brackets far enough out from the wall or window to allow the draperies to travel freely; some brackets are adjustable. If you anchor the ends of the rod in wood molding, drill pilot holes and use wood screws. To install the brackets on drywall, use toggle bolts or screws in plastic anchors, or drive wood screws through the drywall into studs.

Although mounting brackets on decorative molding is not recommended, there may be occasions where there is no other choice. Mount the brackets with wood screws.

4 **Install the traverse rod.** Attach the traverse rod to the mounting brackets as directed in the hardware manufacturer's instructions.

5 **Install a double traverse rod.** A double rod supports two rows of draperies, each operable separately. This two-layer treatment allows you to moderate light, change the mood of the room, and insulate windows in cold weather.

Good idea! →

In your eagerness to hang draperies, you might consider removing shipping wrinkles with an iron. Don't. You may damage the draperies beyond repair. Send them to be professionally pressed at a dry cleaning shop, or allow the wrinkles to fall out over time.

6 **Hang the draperies.** Slip curtain hooks into the pleats, and place each hook in a carrier along the track of the traverse rod.

*Designer's Tip

Weather or Not:

To play down the effects of fading in a sun-drenched window, use subtly colored solids rather than brightly colored patterns.

Lined draperies provide insulation from the cold and heat. Use lined draperies to conserve heat, and to block drafts or sunlight.

Selecting a Traverse Rod

Determine which traverse rod will work best. A center-close rod (top) brings two panels together at the middle of the window. If a window isn't very wide, you might prefer a single panel operated from either side; choose between one-way right (center) and one-way left (bottom) rods. A single rod will block light only on one side.

Windows

Traversing Draperies   249

Roman Shades

Windows

Roman shades provide a softer, more sophisticated look than standard roller shades. As the shade is raised, it stacks in loose, graceful folds. You get drapery fullness along with the easy operation that contributes to the popularity of Roman shades.

Roman shades can use heavier fabric than standard roller shades, allowing the selection of substantial materials (and linings) to block light and to provide insulation. Home centers and decorative showrooms make custom Roman shades, or you can special order from the manufacturers. Or buy kits, choose the fabric and lining of your choice, and make the shade yourself.

Roman shades offer a soft and luxurious alternative to roller shades. The alternative at right allows light into the room while maintaining a feeling of privacy.

Roman Shades

STUFF YOU'LL NEED

✔ Stepladder
✔ Tape measure
✔ Electric drill
✔ Screwdriver

1 Measure for the shade. Roman shades typically are mounted inside the opening. Find the narrowest width and greatest height of the window opening, measuring in several places. If you live in an older house, measure the two diagonals across the window opening to check it for square—an out-of-square window may not allow the shade to unroll fully. For out-of-square windows, mount the shade outside the opening, adding enough to the height measurement to allow mounting above the window.

Good idea!

Top-Down Shades

To admit light without sacrificing privacy, install a shade that folds down from the top.

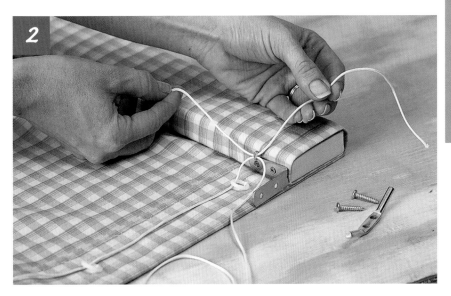

2 Assemble shade. Attach the mounting brackets to the head rail, positioning them as shown for an inside mount, and under the rail for an outside mount. Thread the cord used to operate the shade. Attach the cleat for securing the cord, placing it in a convenient place on the window molding.

3 Hang the shade. Install the shade by driving wood screws through the mounting bracket and into the window molding.

*Designer's Tip

Roman Poufs

Unlike flat Roman shades, a soft version builds up fullness as it is raised.

Windows

Roman Shades   251

Tab-Top Panels

Informal tab-top panels are charming and practical. Place the loops at the top of the panels over a rod or pole, or clip the rings along the top. For café curtains, use half-length panels to cover just the lower sash of the windows.

Tab-top panels are straightforward treatments that can be dressed up with attention-getting finials at the ends of the pole or rod. Fancy and whimsical tabs are available. Use button tabs or ties, or replace the tabs with those of a fabric used elsewhere in the room.

Decide whether to mount the curtains inside or outside the window opening. If you choose outside, mount the rod high enough so the tabs do not hang in front of the window glass. The visible gaps between the tabs are a possible drawback to inside mounting because the curtains won't completely cover the top of the windowpanes.

The crisp, simple look of these tab curtains is underscored by the sheer fabric, as well as by the white pole and mounting brackets.

Tab-Top Panels

STUFF YOU'LL NEED

- ✔ Tab curtains
- ✔ Pole or rod with mounting brackets
- ✔ Stepladder
- ✔ Tape measure
- ✔ Electric drill
- ✔ Screwdriver

1 **Measure the width and height.** For inset curtains, measure the distance between the inside surfaces of the window molding. For outside-mounted curtains, measure between the outer edges of the window molding, or extend this distance beyond the molding to make a narrow window look wider.

Measure for the desired height of the curtains. Tab treatments can end at or just below the bottom of a window frame, but they usually extend to the floor.

2 **Install the mounting hardware.** Attach the brackets that support the pole or rod, driving screws, toggle bolts, plastic anchors, or speciality mounting systems (such as the one shown) into the window molding or studs. The keyhole-shape holes in the back of this bracket slip over the heads of screws anchored in the wall.

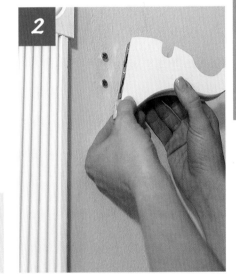

Good idea! → **If you expect to open and close panels frequently,** hang them from rings rather than tabs for smoother operation.

* Designer's Tip

Tabs can be tricky on wide windows that require a center bracket. The tabs won't clear as the curtain opens. Purchase extra curtains if you want them to open fully.

* Designer's Tip

Try This Top Treatment

Tabs and rings aren't anything to hide; nevertheless, you might want to have a valance across the top of the curtains.

Windows

Tab-Top Panels

Windows

3 Install the rod or pole. Slip the tabs over the pole or rod before resting the rod on its brackets.

Wisdom of the Aisles

"Fabrics for window treatments are rated for how well they stand up to the UV component of sunlight. If the fabric you like would be vulnerable in a sunny window, use a substantial lining to protect it."

— Edna Adkins
Willow Grove, PA

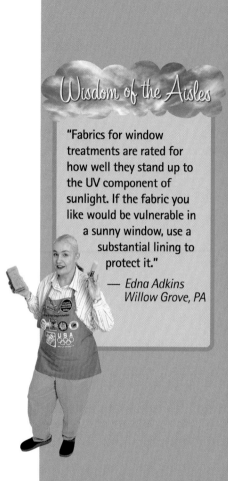

Choosing a Fabric

Sheer and Not-So-Sheer

When selecting translucent curtain fabric, consider how much incoming light you want to filter and the degree of privacy you want. Three samples are shown on one window, each with differing levels of opacity.

A Gallery of Finials

Finials are fun. Choose from an astounding array of finials for metal rods and wooden poles. Styles are made to complement the decor or to add a bit of whimsy.

Scarf Swags

Make a valance from a single length of fabric? It sounds too simple to be possible, and yet a scarf treatment looks very sophisticated. The scarf is suspended above the window by draping it along a pole or passing it through a pair of bracketlike sconces, as shown. The tails can end just below the sill of the window or fall to the floor. For a finished look, make or order scarves that taper at the ends.

Arrange the fabric so that it looks natural—an easy trick compared to more elaborate window treatments. Just tweak and pluck, then stand back to judge the effect. Adjust the fabric until you get the look you want.

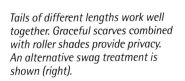

Tails of different lengths work well together. Graceful scarves combined with roller shades provide privacy. An alternative swag treatment is shown (right).

Scarf Swags

1 **Determine the length of the scarf.** Drape the fabric the way you want it suspended to determine how much fabric you will need. To hold the scarf in place, have a helper on hand or use thumbtacks to hold the fabric.

Good idea!

Self-lining scarves don't have a side to conceal. Self-lined scarves are two pieces of fabric sewn together back-to-back. It's a good trick to use when the back of the fabric is markedly different from the front.

2 **Install the sconces.** Attach the sconces to the wall on both sides of the window, using the hardware provided. The keyhole-shape holes in the back of these sconces slip over the heads of screws driven into the wall.

3 **Arrange the scarf.** Pass the scarf through the sconces, creating a gracefully swooping length of fabric between them.

STUFF YOU'LL NEED

- ✔ Fabric for scarf swag
- ✔ Thumbtacks
- ✔ Pair of sconces
- ✔ Stepladder
- ✔ Tape measure
- ✔ Electric drill
- ✔ Screwdriver

Wisdom of the Aisles

"If you want a room to look more formal and reserved, consider long window treatments that sweep the floor, or full treatments that use a lot of fabric."

— *Josephine Jackson Bronx, NY*

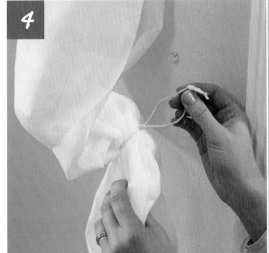

*Designer's Tip

Take Home Swatches

If you aren't absolutely sure about which fabric to use for a window treatment, take home swatches of your favorites. Look at them next to upholstered furniture and paint samples in the room you're decorating, ideally under both daytime and nighttime lighting conditions.

4 **Make bishop sleeves.** Add interest to this treatment by bunching the tails into bishop sleeves. Use string to gather each swag, then suspend a loop of the string from a thumbtack or cup hook in the window molding or wall. The gathered fabric conceals the string.

If one bishop sleeve looks good, you may wish to try two or more down the length of each tail, repeating the step above. Bishop sleeves requires more fabric than straight falls.

5 **Arrange the tails.** Tails can be the same or differing lengths on the sides of the window. Options for the long side include having the fabric just touch the floor, or leaving the fabric a little long to create a puddling effect.

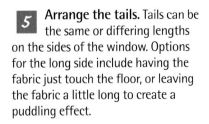

Scarf Swags   257

Roller Shades

Remember the old roller shades that played bit parts in old slapstick movies? They snapped up sharply with a will of their own and they came in one color—inky green.

Today's models operate smoothly. Home centers and decorative showrooms also make custom roller shades, and you can special order from the manufacturers. You also can buy kits and use the fabric of your choice. Shades can be lined for greater opacity.

Roller-shade kits are available at window-treatment specialty shops and home centers, as well as by mail order. Instead of sewing the hems, fuse them with tape activated by the heat of an ordinary clothes iron. Typically, the shade is attached to the roller with a staple gun. That's about all there is to it.

There are grander window treatments, but there's nothing quite so cheery and practical as a roller shade.

Roller Shades

STUFF YOU'LL NEED

✔ Roller-shade kit
✔ Fabric
✔ Scissors
✔ Clothes iron
✔ Staple gun
✔ Stepladder
✔ Tape measure
✔ Electric drill
✔ Screwdriver

1 **Measure for the shade.** Roller shades typically are mounted inside the opening. Find the narrowest width and the greatest height of the window opening, measuring in several places. If you live in an older house, measure the two diagonals across the window opening to check for square—an out-of-square window may not allow the shade to unroll fully. If so, mount the shade outside the opening, adding enough to the height measurement to allow mounting above the window.

2 **Cut the interfacing and fabric.** The shade is sized to allow for hems along the sides, and long enough for both a slat pocket at the bottom and a few rolls at the top. Cut the interfacing (if you choose to use it) and fabric to size as directed by the shade manufacturer's instructions.

3 **Fuse the interfacing and fabric.** Center the interfacing adhesive side down on the back side of the fabric. With the iron on the setting stated in the instructions, fuse the two layers together.

Prep Work

A word of caution in planning for tall windows. As the shade is raised, heavier fabrics may bunch up around the roller, preventing the shade from operating smoothly. Check with your salesperson for details.

✱ Designer's Tip

The Inside Story on Light

An inside-mounted shade may admit an annoying amount of light around the perimeter of a sunny window. Test for penetrating light by inserting a sheet of cardboard in the window opening, allowing the necessary gap all around ($1/2$" to $3/4$") for smooth operation, and judging the effect of the gap.

To block as much light as possible, use an outside mount and avoid scalloped shades.

Windows

Roller Shades

4 **Hem the shade and attach the bottom slat.** Hem the sides of the shade with hem tape and an iron. The slat gives rigidity to the bottom of the shade and helps keep it from flapping; make a pocket for the slat by using hem tape. Attach a pull to the bottom of the shade, if you wish.

5 **Staple the shade to the roller.** Use a staple gun to attach the shade securely to the roller. You may be able to substitute high-tack two-sided tape if you don't have a staple gun.

6 **Mount the shade.** Use screws to anchor the mounting brackets to the window molding or through drywall and into studs. Slip the roller into the brackets.

✳ Designer's Tip

Pick a Pull

Operate a roller shade with a simple tug. These ornamental pulls take window treatments beyond utilitarian.

Padded Cornices

A wood window cornice is often used to incorporate a window treatment with the architecture of the room. In our project, the cornice is upholstered and fabric is applied over padding. The cornice piece is foam that cuts easily and assembles with glue. As a result, the cornice is lightweight and easy to install.

A cornice conveniently hides the ends of traversing drapes, blinds, and roller shades installed outside of the window opening. Buy a kit with everything included or purchase lightweight materials to construct the cornice.

Although they look substantial, padded cornices are made of lightweight materials such as foam. The fabric and padding are glued or stapled to the basic form.

Padded Cornices

1 **Measure the width of the window frame.** Use a tape measure to determine the width of the window frame, measuring between the outer edges of the molding to both sides of the window.

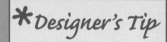

STUFF YOU'LL NEED

✔ Stepladder
✔ Tape measure
✔ Padded cornice kit
✔ Fabric to cover cornice
✔ Razor knife
✔ Electric drill
✔ Metal straightedge
✔ Screwdriver

2 **Cut the foam to size.** Lay out the pieces of the cornice on sheets of foam, using a metal straightedge to guide you. With the foam on a work surface, cut the sheets with a razor knife.

✱ Designer's Tip

To make a narrow window look wider, build an extra-wide cornice. To make the window look taller, place the cornice higher above the window.

3 **Glue the cornice together.** Using the adhesive that comes with the kit, assemble the cornice. Brace the pieces with books or other heavy objects until the glue has dried.

✱ Designer's Tip

Custom Cornices

Custom-made cornices can be purchased at drapery showrooms and home centers. They can be expensive, but in relation to other custom over-the-window treatments, they're one of the least expensive. The advantages are that you can get exactly what you want and somebody else will do it for you.

If the cornice installation is more complex than you can handle because of the weight, have professionals install them.

4 **Attach the cotton batting.** Cut the cotton batting to size. Attach it to the glued-up cornice, using the adhesive as you wrap the batting over the edges

5 **Attach the fabric.** Cut the fabric to size. Apply it to the padded cornice, folding over edges and securing them with ordinary pins.

6 **Mount the cornice.** Position and attach L-brackets to the wall above the window frame so that the cornice will be at the desired height when rested upon them. Use wood screws into wood framing in the wall. For drywall that isn't backed up by framing, drive screws into plastic anchors or use toggle bolts. Rest the cornice on the brackets.

Windows

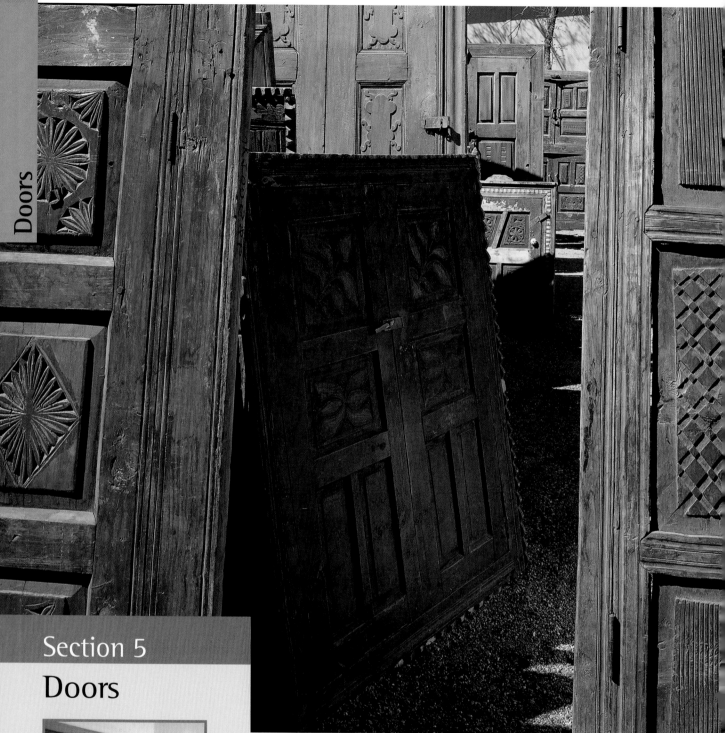

Section 5

Doors

Doors are the first and the last part of a room you see. Like the first and last lines of a well-executed speech, they should make a good impression.

There are three ways to change doors. Repair and paint them, attach new hardware, or replace them. Paint is the least expensive, quickest, and in many cases, the best solution. New hardware offers a solid old door a new lease on life, assuming the shape and style are pleasing and fit in your overall plan. However, if you have a home with flat, hollow-core doors trimmed with clamshell molding, paint and expensive hardware will not give them a Southwestern, Colonial, or Victorian look. Doors that fit the style of your home help to unify the total look, while creating pleasing transitions from room to room.

Doors

Doors

Painting Doors, Trim, and Woodwork

Doors are the valves by which we regulate the flow of our daily lives. They also are the ultimate symbol of protection, safety, and security. It takes a good door to do the job well.

What is a good door? A good door has heft to it for security and to block the passage of sound. It should have character as well.

Traditional doors were either frame-and-panel constructions with or without lights (panes of glass), or they were a less sophisticated row of boards held together by horizontal bracing, cross bracing, or both. Whatever the style or method of construction, they all require a good finish to survive and do a good job.

Braced doors look best in single colors. Frame-and-panel doors with concentric rectangles are perfect for two- and three-color paint schemes. Refer to Section One to choose colors that work together and to experiment with combinations. Discover clues for the doors and trim in the color scheme of the room. If a door is kept open most of the time, the side that shows should relate to the room from which it is most often seen.

A door in its natural state, awaiting artistic touches.

Painting a Door

Six-panel doors are an American classic, but stain and natural finishes are a relatively new look.

If you want a professional-looking job, follow the advice of professional painters. These pointers will help you to keep drips and runs to a minimum, to get enough paint on the door, and to cover up your mistakes.

Here are a few general principles:

- Prep work is the most important part of painting. On a door, it may take 80 to 90 percent of your time.

- Use a primer. It's designed to seal any stains in the surface below it and to make the surface above it stick better to the door.

- Always paint the edges first. Extra paint will roll up onto a wider, flat surface, where it's easy to work it into the rest of the door.

- Apply enough paint on the door. Painters think of it as a two-step process. Apply the paint with a loaded brush; then "lay it off" with a drier brush.

- Paint the shorter pieces, then the long ones they run into. Any brush marks will end at the joints between them.

Doors

Doors

Painting a Door

1 **Prep and prime the door.** If the door is new, sand it with 120-grit paper. Round over the edges slightly to keep them from peeking through the primer.

If the door is already in use, wash it with TSP, following the package directions. Scrape off any chipped paint with a paint scraper and sand the door with 80-grit paper.

After you've sanded, prime the wood. On a previously painted door, you usually can just prime the areas of bare wood. On a new door, prime the entire surface with primer designed for bare wood.

Good idea! →

We used white primer here to enable you to see which coat is primer and which is top coat. When you buy paint, have the primer tinted the color of the top coat. The primer will be lighter than the final coat because it can only hold about half as much tint, but it helps the top coat to cover better. If you tint the primer, you're more likely to need only one top coat.

2 **Sand to create a smooth surface.** Once the primer has dried, sand the entire door with 120-grit sandpaper. Sand lightly to remove fuzzies, not to sand through the paint.

Look carefully at the door. If there are any gaps in the joints or between panels, fill them with paintable caulk. Choose a 40-year caulk to avoid filling the same gaps when you paint the door 10 years later. Ask the home center which caulk works best—some caulks can't be painted. Caulk the gaps and use your finger to force the caulk into the gaps and to smooth over the surface.

STUFF YOU'LL NEED

- ✔ Paint
- ✔ Primer
- ✔ Trisodium phosphate (TSP)
- ✔ 80-grit sandpaper
- ✔ 120-grit sandpaper
- ✔ Brush
- ✔ 40-year paintable caulk

Painting Metal Doors

Metal doors expand and contract more than wooden doors. If you prime and paint them with an acrylic latex, the movement is less likely to crack the paint.

Use a dense foam roller instead of a brush. Although it takes more coats, the finish will be much smoother.

Prep Work

Professionals usually paint doors while they are on the hinges. It's faster, there's less bending, and they can paint one side without having to wait for the other to dry. The easiest way for homeowners, however, is to remove the door and paint it on sawhorses. It's a little slower, but gravity slows dripping. Save time by driving two long screws into both the top and bottom edges of the door to suspend the door on the sawhorses. Paint the surface of one side and flip the door to paint the remaining side without damaging the fresh paint.

Painter's Secrets

Overpainting Makes for Sticky Situations

A new coat of paint gives a door a fresh look, but too many coats will make the door bind. Take off the hinges instead of painting them; and as long as the hinges are off, clean them. Dip them briefly in stripper and wait a few minutes. Take off the paint with a putty knife, and polish the hinges with 0000 (called "four-aught") steel wool.

While you're at it, scrape excess paint from the door jambs and stops, as well as the edges of the door itself—they are often the culprits when doors don't shut tightly.

Wisdom of the Aisles

Make it easy on yourself. "Doors are large, heavy, awkward objects. Ask someone to help you remove the door, place it on sawhorses, and remove all the hardware."

— *Greg Korczak*
Lodi, NJ

Painting a Door

3 Apply a top coat to the door edges and panels.

Paint the edges of the door first. Then apply paint to the panels, one panel at a time. Start with the sloped part of the panel, called the bevel. Paint all four of the panel bevels, working paint into the molded edge of the frame as you go. Once you paint all four bevels, paint the flat part of the panel.

A good paint job requires a fair amount of paint, so when you start on the flat part, make a diagonal swipe across the surface just to get some paint in the area. Then get a little more paint on your brush—tap off the excess against the side of the can—and paint with the grain to work the paint into the panel.

4 Paint the short pieces.

Painters paint the short pieces first so that the brush strokes on the finished door always end where one piece runs into another. Start by making a pass with a loaded brush to get paint on one of the short pieces of the frame that makes up the door. Don't worry if some of the strokes go onto the longer pieces—you'll brush them out later.

5 Paint the long pieces. Put some paint on the pieces with a loaded brush. Then work the paint in with a drier brush. Work the brush in long, diagonal strokes. Continue each stroke right past the edge of the door, so that the brush doesn't leave marks.

Look at the door carefully when you finish. If you see the old color or bare wood peaking through, or if the paint looks thin, it needs a second top coat. Wait for the first coat to dry, and then apply the second coat the same way as the first.

Doors

Painting Woodwork and Trim

Whether you paint door trim, window trim, or crown molding, the technique is the same. If you have the sure hand of a professional painter, pick up a brush and go to work. If you're less sure of your skills, mask the walls thoroughly. Masking goes quickly and lets you concentrate on the job at hand—getting a smooth coat on the trim. Whichever way you do it, painting woodwork and trim is a two-step process: Apply the paint with a wet brush. Smooth out the coat by going over it when most of the paint is out of the brush.

Painting trim in this Traditional style hallway and staircase takes patience and preparation to establish the professional look.

Painting Woodwork and Trim

STUFF YOU'LL NEED

✔ Paint
✔ Primer or stain sealer
✔ 120- and 180-grit sandpaper
✔ Denatured alcohol and clean rag
✔ Wood putty
✔ Paintable caulk and caulking gun
✔ Low-tack tape
✔ Window glazing putty
✔ Sash, trim, or oval brush

TOOL T P

Choose from these three styles of brushes for painting trim.

An angled sash brush, shown in Step 3, is designed for painting window sashes. It lays down a fine, thin edge. Brush in the direction of the short bristles to avoid splattering paint everywhere. It's the easiest of the three brushes to use.

A trim brush has a square edge, and you can work in both directions when painting on edge. It's a little more difficult to use when you're trying to put down a fine line of paint along the edge of molding.

An oval brush has a round handle. Look at the fibers from the end—you'll see it has an oval shape. Professionals like these because they turn the brush to get any profile they want against the wood. They're the most difficult to use.

If you purchase only one brush, choose a sash brush. If you're painting something, such as a fireplace surround, use a sash brush where the wood meets the wall and a trim brush on broader expanses.

1 **Sand the trim.** Sand the trim to smooth out any chips or drips. Then sand the entire surface to smooth it and to remove any gloss that might prevent the new paint from sticking. When you're done, clean up with a damp cloth dipped in denatured alcohol.

2 **Repair the surface.** Fill gouges, dings, and dents with wood putty. Caulk to fill gaps between different surfaces—between the wall and molding, the wall and ceiling, or two pieces of molding, for example. Use a long-life paintable caulk; cut the tip of the tube to leave about a 1/8-inch opening. After you apply the caulk, smooth it out by running a finger along it. If there are nail holes, fill them with a dab of window glazing. It's easier to apply than wood putty and just as durable. Sand any repairs when they're dry, and wipe the immediate area with a rag dampened in denatured alcohol.

Good idea! → **To paint window trim,** paint the edge of the trim the same color as the wall. It's easier and it looks better.

3 **Mask and paint.** Tape off areas to avoid getting paint on them. Ask at the home center for a low-tack tape that prevents damaging the wall when it is removed.

Seal bare wood with an oil-based stain sealer. (Oil-based seals better than most water-based primers and latex can be applied over it.) If the wood has been painted before, prime it with primer tinted the color of the top coat. When the primer or sealer has dried, sand and wipe down with a rag dipped in denatured alcohol. Apply the paint with a wet brush; then smooth it out in the direction of the grain, using a slightly drier brush. A single top coat applied over primer or sealer is often enough. If you see bare spots, apply a second top coat.

Remove the masking tape while the paint is still wet so that any paint you got on the tape won't pull off neighboring trim paint.

Doors

Natural Finishes for Woodwork

Compare the labels on a can of stain and a can of varnish—they're completely different products. Stain is full of dyes and pigments that change the color of the wood. Varnish is full of resins that protect it. Neither does both jobs. Although varnish can stand on its own, stain can't. You have to apply varnish over stain to give it shine and to protect it from grime. If you don't, the stain will look flat and grime will eventually work its way into the pores where you won't be able to get it out. If you stain the wood, also apply varnish.

It doesn't matter whether it's a door or trim underneath the finish. The application technique is the same. The condition of the door or trim does matter, however. Stain will never look any better than what's underneath. If you put up new molding, make sure it's stain grade. Paint grade is made of short lengths glued together. Using stain on paint grade will emphasize the joints and the different shades of wood.

If you redo a varnished surface, apply new product directly over the existing finish. Modern varnishes adhere well to whatever is underneath. Clean the finish well by wiping it with denatured alcohol. Sand carefully with 180-grit paper, and wipe off the dust with a rag dampened in alcohol. Let it dry thoroughly before applying the finish.

If you have a painted surface to stain and varnish, you have a larger challenge. Even a thorough dipping in stripper almost never removes all the paint. Whatever paint remains will show through. Plan to spend quality time with more stripper and a stout brush before you stain and varnish.

Natural finishes on the doors and trim in this Victorian dining room and hallway set a warm and inviting tone. The finish was chosen to complement the rich, natural floor finish and the decorative inlay.

Natural Finishes for Woodwork

STUFF YOU'LL NEED

✔ Varnish, either water- or oil-base

✔ Stain, water- or oil-base, to match varnish

✔ Denatured alcohol

✔ Stainable wood putty

✔ Wood conditioner, unless using gel stain

✔ Paintbrush, natural bristle for oil-based finish; synthetic bristle for water-based finishes

✔ Brush or sponge (optional)

✔ Sandpaper

✔ Putty knife

Testing Stain

Stain can look a lot different on your door than it does in the sample brochure. Test it first on the edges, top, and bottom of the door. On trim, use the back of the molding or a scrap. A clean cotton T-shirt is the best applicator. Dip the shirt in the stain, wipe it on, and then wipe away the excess.

Prep Work

Sand and stain new trim before installing it. The sanding is easier, and you won't get stain on the wall near the molding.

1 Sand the trim and clean it with alcohol. Sand to remove dings, dents, and imperfections. Then sand all the trim, starting with 120-grit sandpaper to create a smooth surface. Follow up with 180-grit to remove the marks left by the 120-grit; follow the 180-grit with 220-grit.

Wipe up the dust with a rag dampened with denatured alcohol. Tack cloths, popular with painters, leave a residue that may interfere with the finish, especially if it's a water-based finish.

2 Repair anything you can't sand away. Although patches will never match the rest of the wood perfectly, damaged wood looks far worse. Fill dents and gouges with stainable putty. Level them off with a putty knife or your thumb. Let the patches dry, and if any of them shrink while drying, patch again. Sand smooth and wipe with a rag dipped in denatured alcohol.

3 Apply a conditioner. Softwoods, such as pine, look blotchy when stained. Prevent this by brushing on a thinned finish, sold as "wood conditioner." The directions usually advise to let dry 15 minutes to 2 hours. Many painters admit they have better luck if they wait only 10 minutes, and most agree that you should not wait longer than 2 hours. At that point, the resins in the conditioner have dried out, and you can barely stain the wood. If this happens, sand the surface, and reapply the conditioner.

You can avoid the need for conditioner entirely by using gel stains, which don't penetrate deeply and, therefore, don't blotch.

Because the density of pine varies throughout a board, pine stains unevenly, as shown on the left side of this board. If you don't like the look, treat the wood with a conditioner or stain the wood with a gel stain to get the even look shown on the right side of the board.

Good idea!

Doors

Natural Finishes for Woodwork

4 Brush on stain. Brush on the stain, let it soak in a bit, and then wipe it off, following the directions on the can. Old T-shirts are excellent for wiping. If the color of the wood isn't dark enough, wait the recommended time on the product and apply a second coat of stain the same as you applied the first. If you use a gel stain, apply it with a sponge. Take it off using a brush instead of a rag.

5 Apply the varnish. Brush the varnish onto a short section of trim. Go back over it quickly and lightly to brush out imperfections. Overbrushing leaves brush marks.

Let the varnish dry according to the recommended time. Sand it with 220-grit sandpaper to smooth it and to remove any dust that settled in the finish. If the paper clogs with little spots of finish, let the varnish dry longer. Once you sand, wipe down with a rag dipped in denatured alcohol, and apply another coat of varnish. Repeat as necessary to create a finish at least three coats thick.

Stripping Trim

How you strip a finish depends on what you're stripping and why. Ninety percent of all clear finishes will come off with an off-the-shelf liquid stripper. Follow the directions on the can and sand when the wood is dry. If the wood is stained, you may need to apply a new coat of stain to even out what the stripper leaves behind. If you're stripping off paint—particularly if you suspect it's lead paint—use a peel and strip paste, which removes the paint without fumes or chipping. Trowel on the paste, cover with the plastic sheet that comes with it, and a few hours later, the paint and paste peel off like strips of putty. In the worst case—a project with lots of paint that probably contains lead—gently remove the trim, and have it stripped at a dip-and-strip store. Apply the new finish before reattaching the trim.

Wisdom of the Aisles

"Decide whether you want to use oil- or water-based varnish. Oil has a brown or yellow sheen that warms up the wood. Oil-based varnish cleans up with mineral spirits. Water-based dries almost, but not quite, clear and cleans up with water. Make a choice and get the same kind of stain: water-based stain under water-based varnish, and oil-based stain under oil-based varnish."

— *Romeo Julian*
Chicago, IL

Pressed Hardboard Doors

Many new six-panel doors are actually molded hardboard, similar to Masonite. To apply a wood-like finish, first prime the door and paint it with tan-color paint. Rub on a gel stain, and brush it out with a paintbrush while the gel is still wet. Brown stain looks most like wood, but you can use any color.

Refinisher's Secret

Varnish settles in the can while sitting on the shelf. You'll often see a layer of goo at the bottom of the can, which is a "flatting agent" that is designed to control the sheen. Mix the settling into the varnish before starting. Stir varnish, do not shake it. Shaking creates and traps bubbles that show up in the finish.

The Stylish Door

Doors reflect a room's style and the world they came from. The Colonial six-panel door was made by hand; six small panels were easier to make than three or four larger ones. The flat, four-panel Country door was a wonder of the machine age. Massive wood and beefy wrought iron were the height of the Southwestern woodworker's skill during the Spanish Colonial era. Arts-and-Crafts designers favored oak and strong lines that mimick the size and shape of room details. The Traditional door might have lots of small glass, a reminder of the days when large panes were difficult to make. Doors, like the rest of a room, are part appearance and part history. The two work together to create style.

A thumb latch completes the statement of this Country door.

These Southwestern doors mirror the rest of the construction, including the furniture.

The flat, simple lines of this door lay the foundation for the Modern style.

Palladian windows over French doors create a refined, Traditional style.

This door's oak and horizontal lines are classic Arts-and-Crafts style.

Hanging and Trimming Doors

When it comes to replacing interior doors, you have two choices: Fit a new door (or an old salvaged one) to the existing frame, or remove the door and frame and replace them with a prehung door. Look at the pros and cons of each approach before making your purchase.

Prehung Doors

A prehung door is a door and hinges prehung in a factory-made frame. Most new homes have prehung doors: Carpenters build rough door openings as they construct the walls. When the drywall is up, they slide the prehung door and frame into the opening and nail it to the rough frame. Because the door and frame have been matched at the factory, the hinges fit perfectly, the door is square and plumb in its frame with even gaps all around, and the holes and mortises for a lockset are precisely drilled and cut. Even the trim has been attached to one face of the door frame. With prehung doors, most of the work has already been completed.

To install a new prehung door, remove the entire door frame and the trim around it. This is one disadvantage of a prehung door. However, you generally can reuse the existing trim. (You also can take the opportunity to upgrade the door trim.) Setting the new unit in the frame is not difficult, but it does have to be done carefully. Otherwise, you may force the frame out of square and the door may not open and close smoothly, or the lock may not work properly.

Slab Doors

The building industry calls any door that isn't prehung a slab door—no matter how nice or unslablike it may be. Fitting a freestanding slab door to an existing frame allows you to leave the trim intact. It seems like it would be easier than installing a prehung unit, but before choosing this approach, carefully check the existing door frame for problems.

Examine Your Door

Examine the existing door. Does it swing freely? Are the gaps around the sides and top fairly consistent? Does the latch catch? Next, remove the existing door from its hinges and examine the frame, as shown below.

If the old door swings just fine and the frame is plumb and square, then installing a new slab door is a viable option. If the frame is twisted, out of square, or cracked, installing a prehung door is a better approach.

Before committing to the job, measure the existing door. New doors range from 24 to 32 inches wide, in 2-inch increments; they're always 80 inches tall. If the job requires it, you can trim off up to $\frac{1}{2}$ inch from the bottom of a door, $\frac{1}{4}$ inch off each side, but none off the top. Cut off more than that and you'll see the ugly inner workings of the door—dowel joints, chipboard, and worse. If the existing door is more than $\frac{1}{2}$ inch narrower or taller than a standard size, get a prehung door and, if necessary, change the size of the rough opening.

What's the Problem?

Hanging a door successfully depends as much on the opening as it does on the door. If the opening isn't level, plumb, square, and parallel, there's no way to hang a plumb, square, level door in it. Don't assume that because the existing door works well, a new door also will fit the opening. A door and its opening grow old together—the warps in one often compensate for the winds in the other. Check the opening carefully, as shown. Anything out of square, plumb, or level may mean trouble, as does any binding or rubbing. Ask a carpenter or a home center or lumberyard salesperson for advice. It may be better to install a prehung door, or it may be better to refinish and repair the existing door.

● Look for gaps to see if the door fits its frame.

● Check the top corners of the opening to see if they're square.

● Check the header to see if it's level.

● Check both jambs with a level to see if they're plumb. Measure from jamb to jamb at the top, middle, and bottom of the door to see if the opening is consistent.

● Check the wall with a level to the left and right of the door to see if both sides are plumb.

● Check to see if the door swings freely.

Hanging and Trimming Doors   277

Replacing a Door

When you hang a new door in an old opening, much of the work revolves around hardware. The hinges, for example, are mortised (inset) into both the door and the door frame. The hinges on the door need to be positioned to match the existing mortises in the frame.

The same situaiton applies to the door latch, or lockset. Some doors are sold with the mortises for the lockset precut. But it is unlikely that the precut latch will align perfectly with the existing latch hole in the frame. Use doors that will allow you to drill your own mortises for the lockset so you can be sure everything will match up. If you are using a door with a precut latch you may want to get someone with experience to help you.

Measure carefully before purchasing a new door. Doors have hidden joinery and cores that are hidden by the edge of the door. You can cut off up to $1/2$ inch from the bottom of a door without revealing its inner workings, up to a $1/4$ inch from each side, but none from the top.

Dress up a wall with a handsome door. If your home is older and has old hollow doors, investigate the variety of new doors available at lumberyards and home improvement centers.

STUFF YOU'LL NEED

- ✔ Door
- ✔ Hinges and screws
- ✔ Lockset
- ✔ Hammer
- ✔ Screwdriver
- ✔ Tape measure
- ✔ Plywood and screws for jig
- ✔ Clamps
- ✔ Circular saw
- ✔ Shims
- ✔ Utility knife
- ✔ Hand plane, 10 to 15 inches long
- ✔ Drill
- ✔ Drill bits slightly smaller in diameter than hinge and lock screws
- ✔ Hole saws, as specified by lockset manufacturer
- ✔ Chisel
- ✔ Combination square

Wisdom of the Aisles

"If you're replacing an old door that fits well in its opening, use it as a template to cut the new door to size and shape. Center the old door on the new one, trace around it, and then cut along the layout lines. After you trim the door, put the old one back on top of it, and align the hinge sides of the doors. Mark the new door lightly with a utility knife to show the location of the old hinge mortises, and then lay them out with a knife, guided by a combination square."

— *Debi Peoples*
Rancho
Cucamonga, CA

1 **Remove the old door from its hinges.** Remove the hinge pins. Have someone hold the door as you work from the bottom hinge pin to the top. Once the pins are out, and the door is out of its frame, unscrew the hinges from both the door and the frame.

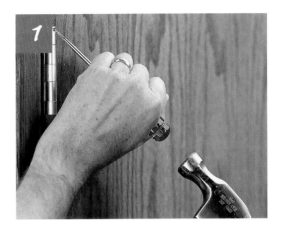

2 **Trim the new door.**
Check the dimensions of the old door and transfer them to the new door. Trim small amounts with a block plane. Trim amounts larger than $1/8$-inch with a circular saw.

Guide the saw against a jig such as the one shown. Make the jig by screwing a piece of 3- or 4-inch-wide plywood to a wider piece. Before you trim the door, trim the jig: Guide the saw against the narrow piece of plywood to cut off the wider piece. When you're ready to cut the door—or any other piece of stock—align the cut edge of the jig with your layout line, clamp the jig to the door, and make the cut.

3 **Lay out the hinge mortises.**
The hinges sit in recesses called hinge mortises in both the door and the frame. In this project, the frame is already mortised and the door is mortised to match.

Put the door in the opening, and shim it so that the hinge edge is tight against the hinge jamb. Shim the bottom of the door until you have a uniform gap of about $1/8$ inch at the top of the door. Mark the door with a utility knife at the location of the existing mortises.

Tape a nickel near each edge on the top of the door and use it as a spacer when shimming the door. When the nickels are tight against the door frame, the gap is right.

Good idea!

Doors

Replacing a Door

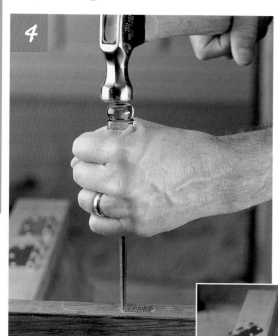

4 Lay out and cut the hinge mortises on the door. Put the hinges between the utility-knife marks made in Step 3 on the door edge and trace around them with the utility knife.

With a sharp chisel or utility knife, make a series of shallow cuts across the width (short direction) of each mortise. Then come in from the face of the door to pare out the bottom of each mortise, as shown in the inset.

High Anxiety

If a hinge won't sit flush in its mortise, there's a high spot somewhere in the mortise itself. To find it, rub the back of the hinge with lipstick, put the hinge in the mortise, and tap it gently. When you remove the hinge, the high spots will be highlighted in red.

5 **Bevel the latch edge.** Unless the latch edge of the door is bevelled, it will rub against the jamb when the door is opened. To bevel the edge, clamp the door

upright against a bench or saw horse with the latch edge facing up, as shown in the inset. Make sure to bevel the door in the right direction—taking most of the wood from the corner diagonally opposite the hinge barrel. Draw a line along the face of the door 1/8 inch from this edge, and plane down to the line to create the bevel.

For the smoothest bevel, begin with a few passes about 1/2 inch wide along the edge that gets trimmed the most. Gradually widen the cut, moving toward the opposite edge but not planing it. When the bevel reaches the pencil line, make a final pass with the plane flat against the entire bevel.

TOOL TIP

The front of the chisel has a bevel on it, and the edge it leaves slopes as a result. When you want a nice, crisp chiseled edge, cut it with the back of the chisel. The bevel causes the chisel to move slightly backward when you strike it. To keep this from pushing the chisel beyond the layout line, sneak up on the line with a series of cuts, rather than putting the chisel directly where you want the cut to be.

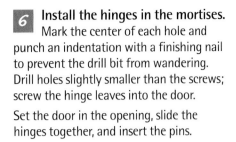

Carpenter's Secret

If you put a door into an existing frame, chances are that one of the hinge holes has worn so much that it won't hold the screw. If the hinge will take one, put in a larger screw. If not, fill the hole with epoxy and wooden matchsticks from which you've removed the flammable head. When the epoxy dries, trim the opening flush with a chisel, and drill a new hole, making it smaller than the screw.

Wisdom of the Aisles

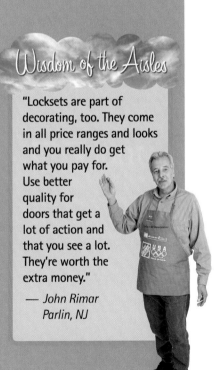

"Locksets are part of decorating, too. They come in all price ranges and looks and you really do get what you pay for. Use better quality for doors that get a lot of action and that you see a lot. They're worth the extra money."

— *John Rimar*
Parlin, NJ

6 **Install the hinges in the mortises.** Mark the center of each hole and punch an indentation with a finishing nail to prevent the drill bit from wandering. Drill holes slightly smaller than the screws; screw the hinge leaves into the door.

Set the door in the opening, slide the hinges together, and insert the pins.

7 **Lay out the lockset.** Many slab doors come with the lockset hole already drilled. This is a real timesaver—if it's at the right height and if you don't have to trim the latch edge of the door. Otherwise, save the cost and drill for the lockset yourself.

When you drill for the lockset, locate the lock so it lines up with the existing latch plate in the frame. Strike a center line, as shown, from the center of the latch hole in the frame onto the door. Use the line as your center line for positioning the template supplied with the lockset.

8 **Mark the hole centers on the door face and edge.** Fold the supplied template over the door edge and align it with the mark made in Step 7. Follow the lines on the template, and mark the center of the lockset hole on the face of the door and the center of the bolt hole on the edge of the door. Many templates have a set of marks for different models made by the same manufacturer. Be sure to use the set that matches the lockset you install. Mark the center of each hole with an awl.

9 **Drill the main lockset hole.** First drill a $\frac{1}{8}$-inch pilot hole at the center mark that goes all the way through the face of the door. It's easy to accidentally drill at an angle, so use a square to guide the drill perpendicular to the face of the door. Then use a hole saw (typically $2\frac{1}{8}$-inch diameter, but check the instructions that come with your lock) to drill the main hole. Drill halfway through from each face to avoid splitting the wood.

Doors

Replacing a Door   281

Replacing a Door

10 **Drill the hole for the lock bolt.** The hole for the lock bolt (typically 1 inch in diameter, but always check the instructions) is drilled into the edge of the door. A spade bit works fine in a softwood door, but a hole saw may be needed to get through hardwood. Whichever you use, drill a ⅛-inch pilot hole first to guide the larger hole. Then drill into the edge of the door with the larger bit until the bolt hole intersects the main hole.

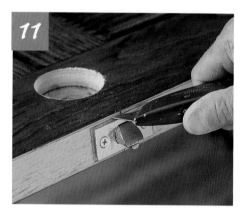

11 **Lay out the mortise for the bolt plate.** For the bolt plate to be flush with the edge of the door, cut a recess, or mortise, for it. Place the bolt assembly into the bolt hole, make sure it's squared up, predrill for the mounting holes, and screw it in place. Trace around the bolt plate with an awl or knife to mark its location on the door.

12 **Mortise for the bolt plate.** Remove the bolt assembly. Using a 1-inch-wide chisel, make a series of crosscuts within the layout lines to make it easier to remove the wood. Chisel out the waste. Reinstall the bolt assembly, and don't tighten the screws all the way.

13 **Install the lockset in the door.** The handle assembly comes in halves, one for each side. Fit each half through the bolt assembly; then insert the screws that hold the halves together. Hang the door and check that the lock operates smoothly. Make any necessary adjustments, and then tighten all the screws.

Carpenter's Secret

Chiseling Tips

The way you hold a chisel determines how it acts. If you make a cut with the bevel up, as shown on page 280, you can take off a lot of wood quickly. If you lay it flat with the bevel up, you can pare off thin shavings of wood. If you work with the bevel side down, the bevel will help prevent cutting too deeply. Some carpenters do this job bevel up, others work bevel down, still others flip the chisel back and forth. Experiment to find the right technique for you.

TOOL TIP

Lock Installation Kits

People often avoid projects they could do easily because they don't have all the tools. Manufacturers are making it hard to say no to DIY by assembling kits that put everything in one package.

Door lock installation kits come with hole saws, edge bore bits, countersinks, and punches. All you need is some hand tools, a drill, and a door. When you're done, you have a new look and some new tools for your tool box.

Old Doors, New Places

The line between old and new doors is a thin one. Specialty millwork houses often have huge stocks of old doors that can be copied to your specifications. Salvage houses, packed with every imaginable size and shape of door, take advantage of the tendency to tear down the old and build new. Before the wrecking ball hits, they buy the contents—doors, windows, fireplace surrounds, sometimes even the floors. They are great sources of high-quality, solid-wood doors, some of which are available for only a few dollars. Ask about vintage hardware as well.

If you want a period decor, but also want crisp edges, dent-free surfaces, and a sparkling finish, go to an architectural millwork house. They make many door styles—whether to match an old door or to create a door that exists only in your imagination.

These doors, left and above, from a New Mexico salvage shop, date back to Spanish Colonial days.

The old entry door, below left, is just one of the surprises to find in salvage shops. The Traditional-style cabinet doors, below right, are newly built in a modern millwork shop.

Doors

Installing a Prehung Interior Door

Installing a prehung door is easier and faster than starting from scratch because most of the difficult operations have already been completed. All that's left is to pop off the trim from the existing opening and remove the jambs. This may sound and look like major work, but all it takes is time and muscle. Once the jamb is out, putting in the new door is a matter of shims and a few finishing nails.

Doors

STUFF YOU'LL NEED

✔ Prehung door
✔ Putty knife
✔ Small pry bar
✔ Large pry bar or crowbar
✔ Shims
✔ Level
✔ #8 and #6 finish nails
✔ Hammer
✔ Nail set
✔ 2¼ inch screws

1 **Remove the door trim from both sides of the doorway.** Installing a prehung door means you'll have to remove the existing trim and frame. Slip a stiff, wide putty knife under the trim, and pry to loosen it. Put a small pry bar in the opening created by the knife, and slip a piece of wood between the wall and the pry bar. Pry against the block, reposition it, and pry again. Continue along the entire length of the trim until you remove it.

2 **Remove the old door frame.** Start with the two side pieces, (the side jambs) and pry them away from the studs with a heavy pry bar or crowbar. Once you pry the side jambs away from the studs, pry down the head jamb. The head and side jambs are usually nailed together, and it's easier to remove them from the opening at the same time.

Carpenter's Secret

Don't assume the door and frame are square. The frame, especially, can move around during shipping. Once you put the assembly in the opening, check it for square. Framing squares aren't always reliable, and the surest way to check is with a level. If the head jamb is level, and both the side jambs are plumb, the opening is square. Check by measuring the diagonals of the opening. If they're equal, the opening is square.

3 **Slide a new prehung door unit into the rough opening.** Put the door in the opening and push against it until the trim is tight against the wall. Make sure that the door opens in the direction you want, and into the room you want it to swing into. Remove and reposition, if necessary.

Good idea!

Paint can get between the door trim and the walls and cause the drywall to tear as you pull away the trim. Run a utility knife between the trim and the wall before removal.

Budget Busters?

A prehung door costs **30–40 percent more** than the same door without a frame. If you factor in the price of the frame, the trim, and the hinges, the price difference may be negligible.

Installing a Prehung Interior Door

Carpenter's Secret

One side of the door will either have a strip of wood nailed diagonally across the opening, or it will have the corners reinforced with plywood. Reinforcements keep the door square until you get it nailed in place. Remove them only after you're satisfied with the fit and position of the door and ready to test how the door swings on its hinges.

Stuff You Won't Need

A prehung door has packing on it that you should remove before you put up the door. Wrappers and plastic banding are obvious; but there also may be a plastic plug that fits in the lock mortise to keep the door from swinging open during shipping. The strip of wood across the bottom of the opening isn't a threshold—it's there to keep the legs from coming loose during shipping. Pull it off before you hang the door.

4 **Shim the frame plumb, level, and straight.** The door frame is slightly smaller than the opening it fits in. This allows you to shim under and behind the frame to get it level, plumb, and straight. Slip shims under the side jamb until the head jamb is level. Then shim between the sides of the frame and the studs to fill in the spaces between them. On the hinge side, start with the bottom and top of the frame. Then shim between the hinges and the studs, positioning the shims so that about half the shim is above the hinge. (This will help you later when nailing.) Make sure the jambs are plumb. On the latch side, shim at roughly the same places and at latch level.

Check, check, and double-check to make sure that the head jamb is level and that the edges and face of the side jambs are plumb. Shim as necessary to correct any problems. Make sure that the trim is tight against the wall. Put a level on the face of the door jamb to make sure it is straight and the shims haven't created any bumps or dips. Add or remove shims, as necessary.

5 **Nail the door frame to the studs.** Drive #8 finish nails through the frame, through the shims, and into the studs. Drive two nails through each shim, spacing them about an inch from each edge of the jamb, with one about 1/2 inch above the other. Don't drive any of the nails home until you open and close the door. If you're happy with the way it works, drive and set the nails. If there are problems, remove the nails, correct the problems, and reinstall the door.

Good idea!

Replace at least two of the screws in each hinge with 2¼-inch screws. The screws will go through the frame and into the studs to provide extra support for the door.

6 **Nail the preattached trim to the studs.** Drive #6 finish nails through the trim and into the studs behind the wall, spacing the nails about 16 inches apart. Trim any exposed shims by scoring with a knife, and then breaking them along the line. Cut and install trim on the second side of the door. (See "Installing Door Trim and Molding," page 286, for more on installing trim.)

Doors

Installing Door Trim and Molding

Door trim, door molding, and door casing all refer to the same material—they are the wood that goes around the door. There are several styles of door trim and a couple of techniques for installing it. The most common method, shown here, is also the oldest. The trim pieces are mitered where they meet. A more decorative approach is to install blocks at the base and at the top of the door trim with a straight stretch of molding running between. This was a Victorian solution that, although simple to install, used more wood. As the cost of wood went up, miters again became fashionable. You can still get Victorian-style trim, and you can see how it's installed in "No Miter/No Cope Baseboard," page 127.

Matching or getting a good substitute for old-fashioned molding may be easier than you think. The wood-molding industry long ago standardized molding profiles. You should be able to match a standard molding in your home with one in the lumberyard, even if the molding is decades old. Be prepared for slight variations—the profile actually changes as the cutters wear down. If you have difficulty finding what you want, contact architectural millwork houses that make moldings and other trims. They can reproduce molding or create a profile just for you.

Door trim makes a statement about your decorating scheme. Plain moldings are Contemporary; corner blocks are Victorian. It's all in the details.

Installing Door Trim and Molding

STUFF YOU'LL NEED

✔ Molding
✔ #6 and #8 finish nails
✔ Combination square
✔ Miter box
✔ Hammer
✔ Nail set
✔ Glazing putty or wax stick for filling nail holes

Carpenter's Secret

Which came first?

When installing door trim, some carpenters begin with the vertical pieces (called legs); others prefer to hang the top trim first. Installing the top first has the advantage of offering precise control over the most finicky part of the installation—the miters. Once the top trim is up, install the legs one at a time, positioning each so that the miter is perfect. If you do the legs first, you'll have to fit the top trim on both miters simultaneously. Unless both miters are perfect and the legs perfectly parallel, you're bound to get gaps you can't close.

1 **Lay out the reveal.** The door trim is never flush with the edge of the jamb; typically it sits back from the edge by about ⅛ inch. The space, or reveal, leaves enough room for the hinge barrel and provides a margin of error if the jamb dips. The frame on a prehung door is likely to have a layout line on it that marks the edge of the reveal. If you work on a door frame that isn't already marked, set a combination square to ⅛ inch, and guide it and a pencil along the frame. Mark the reveal on both sides and above the door.

2 **Measure and miter the top trim.** First cut a 45-degree miter on one end of the top trim piece; hold it in place to mark the inside point of the second miter cut. Lay out the cut with a combination square, and cut it with a miter box.

3 **Nail the top trim in place.** To help position the trim, miter a short piece of molding, and clamp it in place along the sides of the door frame. Put the top trim in place, and adjust as necessary to get a tight miter. When you're satisfied with the fit, nail the trim into the jamb with #6 finish nails; drive #8 finish nails through the trim and into the studs. Don't drive the nails all the way yet. Leave at least ⅛ inch exposed in case you need to remove them.

Doors

Installing Door Trim and Molding

4 Miter the legs. Mitering a piece to fit can be tricky. Make it easy on yourself by mitering the legs before you square them off. Then place the legs against the frame so they're upside down. This leaves the miter on the floor and the full length of the trim extending toward the ceiling. Mark where the top trim touches the leg, and cut the leg square at the mark.

5 Nail the legs to the door frame. Start at the top, holding the leg so the miter closes tightly, and drive a #6 finish nail through it and into the jamb. Work down the leg, flexing it if necessary so that it aligns with the line that marks the reveal. When you're satisfied, drive #8 finish nails into the framing behind the wall. Repeat on the opposite leg, and then set all the nails.

To keep the corners tight, predrill and drive a #6 finish nail at an angle up through the edge of the leg, through the miter, and into the header molding.

Carpenter's Secret

Hide nails by driving them into one of the grooves in the molding. After you set the nail, fill the hole with glazing putty if you paint. If you stain, stain and varnish before you putting up the molding, as shown. After the trim is up, fill the nail holes with colored wax sticks sold in paint departments. Pick a stick that matches the stain and rub it across the nail hole until it is filled.

TOOL TIP

Lipstick makes quick work of measuring.

On a door trim, rub lipstick against the point of the miter. When you put the leg against the miter, it makes a bright mark where you need to make the cut.

Use the same technique to install drywall. To lay out the hole for a switch or outlet, rub lipstick on the junction box. Put the drywall in place and push gently in the general area of the box. You'll get a bright mark on the back of the drywall showing the location of the box.

The Victorian Approach

Victorian molding took a more decorative—and simpler to install—approach toward doors. Plinth blocks were installed at the bottom trim and rosette blocks at the top corners. Molding was then cut to fit between the blocks.

An advantage of this approach is that there are no miter joints to cut; another is that it adds Victorian style.

Plinth blocks, rosettes, and reversible pilaster trim are available in packaged kits. Install the blocks first with construction adhesive; then crosscut lengths of trim to fit between them.

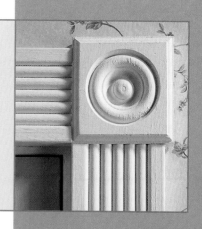

Dressing a Door

There's more to a door than the door. Half the beauty is derived from the hardware. Brass knobs and plates say Victorian. Hand-wrought nickel copper or nickel silver indicate Arts and Crafts. Wrought iron points to Colonial.

Exterior doors are part of interior decorating. In many cases, you'll see hardware for an exterior door from inside the house better than you will from the outside. If you want an old look and won't settle for an old, flimsy door lock, look for reproduction locks. Many combine the look of the original with the security of a modern lock.

Hinges reveal the character of a door, also. Brass hinges with decorative finials are formal. Patterns cast on the leaves provide an old-fashioned look. Consider unusual doors that hinges can create—swinging doors, Dutch doors, or pocket doors that slide into the wall. The right choice makes your house unique and functional.

Doors

Section 6
Floors

Your home's floor treatment makes one of the largest statements in your overall decorating scheme. Flooring choices are both aesthetic and practical—raising questions about look, durability, style, color, and texture. The basic selections include wood, ceramic tile, laminate flooring, and carpet. Combine the basics, and the choices become more complex. Wood choices range from wide planks to narrow strips; decorative inlay or intricate medallions may enhance them. Tile is available in a large variety of shapes and colors. Laminate flooring imitates both wood and stone. Carpet covers whole floors or areas and can be mixed and matched in single pieces or different rooms. A hand-painted canvas floorcloth can serve as a striking carpet. Choose your flooring with your eyes, ears, and sense of touch. Your goal is a floor that is useful and beautiful, and one that puts your decorating ideas on solid ground.

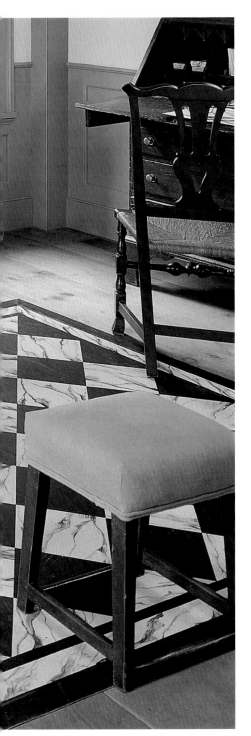

Floors

Floor Refinishing

Hardwood floors typically last for the life of a home. Of course, they become worn over time and occasionally need refurbishing or complete refinishing.

If your floors are simply dirty from years of use but aren't worn through to bare wood, you can probably clean and recoat them instead of entirely refinishing them. Clean floors with household detergent and elbow grease, or rent a floor-buffing machine and use it with an abrasive pad. Remove all the dirt, waxes, and old chewing gum from the floor but not the finish itself. Once you've cleaned the floor, apply a new finish coat right over the old.

On the other hand, if your floors are deeply stained, discolored, or damaged from wall-to-wall carpeting or laminate flooring, you can refinish them, which involves sanding back the finish, or even the wood, before applying a new finish coat. It's work, and some of it makes a mess, but as you take away the dirt, you remove years from the floor. When you're done sanding, you'll see the wood as the original owner did—clean, solid, and ready to take your choice of finish.

Refinishing a floor restores its beauty. On heavy-duty jobs, sand right down to the wood—first with a drum sander, above right, then with an edge sander, above left. Apply stain with a rag and apply finish with a lamb's wool applicator.

Floors (side tab)

Sanding and Refinishing

Before you sand the floor, study it carefully. Solid-wood strip floors can be sanded and refinished several times. Some wood strip floors, however, are made from laminated wood products—a thin surface layer of wood glued to plywood that can be sanded only once and with great care. Examine an edge of the floor—under a threshold, for example—to determine the floor's thickness. If the floor is laminated wood, leave the job to professionals.

If the floor is solid wood, refinishing it begins with a choice: If only the finish is damaged, sand it with a user-friendly vibrating sander. If the floor has worn through in spots to bare wood or if it has suffered from previous refinishing attempts that have left gouges, consider sanding off the entire finish more aggressively with a drum sander.

Let's take the best case first: The floor is reasonably flat and free of old dips and gouges. All you need to do is remove the finish with a vibrating

It isn't the floor that ages—it's the finish. With careful sanding, staining and finishing, even the oldest floor relives its youth.

sander. Vibrating sanders work on the same principle as handheld finishing sanders—a flat pad or plate with sandpaper on it vibrates and oscillates to remove the old finish. Floor models are bigger and heavier, of course, but work gently enough that they are easy to control.

Second case: You think the floor needs sanding. The vibrating sander probably isn't aggressive enough; you need a drum sander. Using a drum sander requires more skill than most people realize—some rental companies require customers to demonstrate their ability on a sheet of plywood before they'll rent the equipment. When you get it home, go slowly. Practice with fine grit paper and work your way to heavier grit as you gain experience. A note of caution: Floor sanders are aggressive machines and can cause more damage than they fix unless you are careful. If you're not comfortable running the machine, call a professional to do the sanding; then do the finishing and staining yourself.

Sanding and Refinishing

Floors

1 **Remove the base molding.** A floor sander may bang against base molding, so remove it. Usually all it requires is removing the shoe molding—the quarter-round piece that runs along the floor. Pry it off as shown, protecting the baseboard with a piece of scrap wood. If there is no shoe molding, either remove the base molding or take care not to damage it with the sanders.

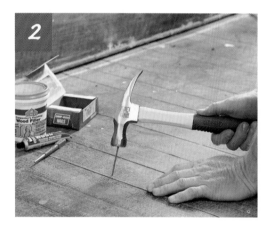

2 **Check for squeaks, and nail loose floorboards.** This is a good time to nail down that pesky squeak in the floor and secure any boards that may be loose. The best approach is to nail into a floor joist—not just the subfloor—with #8 finish nails. Set the nails and fill the holes with latex wood putty. Set protruding nails that would tear the sandpaper.

3 **Contain the dust.** To prevent dust from sifting throughout the house, close off doorways with plastic sheeting. Stick strips of masking tape around the edges of closet doors. If possible, pull the dust toward a window or door with a box fan. Wear a dust mask when sanding.

STUFF YOU'LL NEED

- ✔ Wood stain
- ✔ Varnish
- ✔ Lamb's wool applicator pads for varnish
- ✔ Clean rags
- ✔ Paintbrush or foam brush
- ✔ Wood putty
- ✔ #8 finish nails
- ✔ Plastic sheeting
- ✔ Masking tape
- ✔ Pry bar
- ✔ Hammer
- ✔ Nail set
- ✔ Putty knife
- ✔ Drum sander and sandpaper
- ✔ Vibrating sander and sandpaper
- ✔ Edge sander or portable hand sander and sandpaper
- ✔ Dust mask
- ✔ Broom
- ✔ Shop vacuum
- ✔ Paint tray

TOOL TIP

A sander drum is usually rubber wedged between two discs held in place by a nut. To lock a roll of sandpaper in place, tighten the nut, squeezing the sides of the drum together. This increases the diameter just enough to prevent the sandpaper from slipping off. Loosen the nut to remove the sandpaper.

Wisdom of the Aisles

"Wondering whether the floor is too thin to sand? Pull up the floor vents and take off the threshold or the baseboard. Removing any of them reveals the edge of a floorboard, and you'll get to see exactly how thick the floor is."

— Ed Czyr
Lansdale, PA

Smart & Safe

The heat from dry, oily rags can set the rags on fire, especially if the rags are bunched together. Hang the rags outside, away from any structures, and let them dry thoroughly before throwing them out.

4 **Rough-sand with drum or vibrating sander.** If the floor itself (as opposed to just the finish) is in bad shape, start with a drum sander. If the floor is good, and needs refinishing, use a vibrating sander (Step 6) instead. If in doubt, talk with the rental company to see what they recommend. When drum-sanding, start with the coarsest sandpaper grit—typically 36- or 40-grit—then switch to 60-grit. Finish with 80- or 100-grit. Move the sander so it travels along the length of the boards with the grain of the wood. Work the drum sander forward and back over 3- to 4-foot lengths of floor, overlapping the strokes.

Good idea! → **Drum sanders are very difficult to maneuver at first.** Many rental companies offer a training demonstration, and then you're on your own. To minimize potential damage to your floor, start by using fine sandpaper on a small area to become familiar with machine. Later switch to coarse paper and start the real sanding.

5 **Sweep and vacuum between sanding grits.** The sanding dust eventually gets in the way of the sanding process and has to be swept and vacuumed. Always sweep and vacuum before starting with the next grit of sandpaper. It not only makes the floor cleaner, but it also picks up any grit that may have been left by the sandpaper—grit that would scratch the job of finer grit paper.

6 **Fine-sand with vibrating sander (optional).** These sanders level minor unevenness left by drum sanders. If you use both tools, use the drum sander for the two coarse grits (36 and 60), and then use the vibrating sander for the medium and fine grits (80 and 100). If you use only the vibrating sander, start with 60-grit, then sand with 80-, and finally with 100-grit.

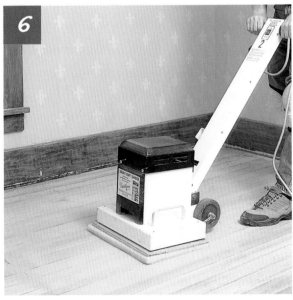

Floors

Sanding and Refinishing 295

Sanding and Refinishing

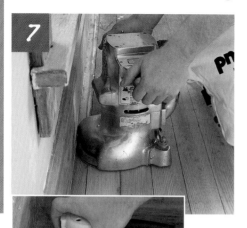

7 Sand corners and edges with a hand sander. Use a portable sander with 80-grit paper to reach areas that the large sanders cannot reach: corners, under radiators, small closets, etc. Rental companies rent edge sanders similar to the one shown that work well, but that can be hard to control. A random orbital sander (see inset) is less aggressive, less likely to gouge, and does an excellent, but slower, job.

8 Apply a wood stain (optional). When the sanding is done, clean up all the dust with a vacuum and tack cloth. Apply wood stain with a foam applicator pad. Work one manageable area at a time—4 square feet, for example. Follow the directions on the can when applying stain. Most wipe on, then the excess is wiped off after a few minutes. Use clean cotton cloths or paper towels to remove the excess stain. Do the job with far less bending by wiping the floor with a cloth wrapped around a dry applicator pad. Always stain in the direction of the grain.

9 Apply a clear finish. Allow the stain to dry as recommended before applying the first coat of varnish. Polyurethane, either oil-based or water-based, is a reliable finish for floors. Apply the finish with a lamb's wool applicator.
Sand the floor lightly with 220-grit paper, vacuum up the dust, and apply a second coat of varnish. Repeat for a third coat, if desired.

Which is for you?

Oil-Based vs. Water-Based Polyurethane

Oil-based polyurethane is reliable and has been around for years. It imparts warmth to most wood colors, darkening them slightly. Use a brand that is recommended for flooring and has a warranty. Some brands are slow drying, requiring a full day between coats. Others are fast drying (4 hours is about the minimum), which allows you to get two, even three, coats on in a single day. Good ventilation is a must and you should consider wearing a ventilating respirator.

Water-based polyurethanes dry quickly and are nearly odorless. They're also virtually clear when dry—an advantage if you don't want the finish to darken the wood. Many professionals use commercial water-based polyurethane that holds up well; but reports are mixed on the water-based varnish available to consumers. Quality seems to vary from brand to brand. Check warranties and discuss your choice with knowledgeable floor finish experts.

Refinisher's Secret

To keep a lamb's wool applicator from drying out overnight, wrap it in a tightly sealed plastic bag. Unwrap it when it's time for the next coat, and you're ready to go.

Decorative Wood Floors

Wood is one of the oldest materials used for floors. No wonder—even rough-hewn wood is resilient, flexible, and insulating against the cold earth. Carefully selected and machine milled, modern wood flooring is a feast for the eyes. Wood floors are warm, inviting, natural, colorful, and long-lasting.

The options for wood flooring range from the classic narrow-strip floor with a contrasting border to the wide-plank floors reminiscent of Colonial homes. Additionally, wood floors form ideal canvases for specialty stains and finishes, including paint and stencils.

All wood floors require a stable subfloor. Three-quarter-inch plywood or tongue-and-groove common pine are typical good quality subfloors. Particleboard is adequate but not as strong as plywood. Ideally, floorboards should be installed perpendicular to the floor joists. Installing them parallel to the joists is acceptable if the subfloor is sturdy, but weight may cause more deflection or spring in the floor, and possibly more squeaks.

Floors

Installing a Strip Wood Floor

The classic wood floor consists of solid strips of wood, typically ¹/₂-inch thick, with tongue-and-groove joints along the edges. The tongue-and-groove joints keep the surface of each board flush with the next board. They also provide a method for concealing nails—the nail is driven through the tongue and covered when the groove of the next board slips over it.

Oak strip flooring is available as a stock item in most home centers. For slightly higher cost, choose from many wood species at flooring suppliers or as special orders through home centers. Maple, walnut, cherry, hickory, and other hardwoods make distinctive floors. Each wood species has its own personality. All hardwood strip floors wear exceedingly well, take sanding and refinishing several times, and usually last for the life of a home.

You can buy strip flooring in 2¹/₄-inch or 3¹/₄-inch widths, sold in bundles of approximately 22 square feet. It's also sold in random widths to create less formal floors. Buy it either unfinished or prefinished with a durable commercial finish. The higher cost of prefinished strip flooring is worth considering because you'll avoid the most onerous part of the job—sanding the floor. Prefinished strip flooring has a small V-groove along all the joints that conceals slight unevenness, since the boards can't be sanded flush like unfinished flooring.

Hardwood floors mean quality. Top-notch flooring is readily available, and most existing subfloors are adequate to support hardwood floors. A few rental tools put installation within the homeowner's reach.

STUFF YOU'LL NEED

✔ Wood flooring
✔ Building paper
✔ Floor finish
✔ #6 finish nails
✔ Pry bar
✔ Stapler
✔ Tape measure
✔ Chalk line
✔ Hammer
✔ Nail set
✔ Drill
✔ 3/32-inch drill bit
✔ Floor nailer
✔ Miter saw
✔ Saber saw
✔ Table saw (optional)

*Designer's Tip

In general, strips of flooring running in the longer direction of the room make the space look bigger; strips running in the shorter direction make it look smaller.

Installing Wood Over Concrete

If you plan to lay wood flooring over concrete, put down a moisture barrier and a plywood floor, supported by wooden strips. Cover the floor with strips of plastic sheeting. Place 2×2 strips on the sheeting along the wall, and 16 inches on center in between. Every 4 feet, put in a 2×2 cross bar that connects the strips. Glue the strips and cross bars to the plastic with construction adhesive, and nail the plywood on top. For a firmer, insulated floor, cut foam insulation to fit between the 2×2s.

Installing a Strip Wood Floor

1 Remove shoe molding or base molding. If the room has a shoe molding (a small quarter-round molding right against the floor along the base molding), remove it. After the new floor is installed, re-install it, concealing the gap around the perimeter of the room. If the room has a small one-piece base molding, use a pry bar to carefully remove it.

2 Tack down building paper. Professional floor installers are divided on the value of building paper. Some suggest that it reduces squeaks and sound transmission to rooms below the floor. Others don't bother. It can't hurt, it adds a vapor barrier, and it's not expensive or difficult to install. Just roll it out and staple it every 8 or 10 inches. Overlap the strips about 3 inches.

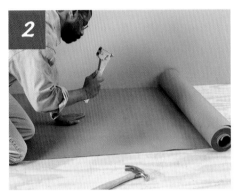

3 Determine the width of the starter strip. Calculate how many strips it will take to complete the width of the floor. Unless you're lucky, it won't be a whole number of strips, and you'll have to cut the first and last strips to fit. The first strip and last strip should be relatively equal in width—don't end at the opposite side of the room with a very narrow strip of floor. If the room is not too large, assemble enough short pieces to span the whole room and determine the correct width for the first and last pieces. Otherwise, use a calculator and divide the room width by the width of an individual strip of flooring. Allow a 1/4-inch gap for expansion along both walls; the base molding will cover the gap. (Continued on page 301.)

Floors

Installing a Decorative Border

Insert a contrasting wood strip around the perimeter of the room for an elegant classic look.

A decorative border frames the room and defines its shape. It can be a lavish assembly of inlaid wood (available from specialty suppliers) or a simple contrasting band of wood.

An easy way to make a decorative border is to buy a small amount of flooring in a different wood species from the same manufacturer as the rest of the floor. This works whether you use finished or unfinished strip flooring. For example, if you use natural oak for the floor, use walnut for the border.

A border creates two distinct spaces—the perimeter area outside the border, and the main floor field inside the border. The floor strips outside the border as well as the border itself are either mitered at the corners or lapped one over the next for a "log cabin" effect. Either approach creates the framed look that visually distinguishes the border and perimeter from the floor field.

The space inside the border is treated the same as a regular strip floor installation, except that the end joints that meet the border have to be cut to fit precisely. To include a wood border, install it first, then proceed with the perimeter area, and finally the main body of the floor.

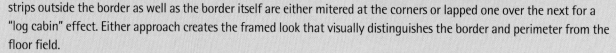

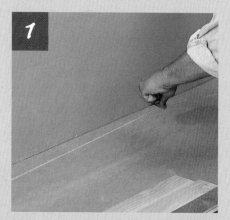

1 Determine the location of the border. A border can be located a few inches to a foot from the wall, depending on the size of the room and how the room will be used. Locating the border farther in from the walls makes the floor look smaller. You may want to frame a smaller area, such as the space around a dining table, for example. Take time to lay out short lengths of the flooring across the whole width of the floor. Measure carefully, and then lay out a field composed entirely of full-width strips. Strike chalk lines to mark the inside edge of the inlay.

2 Cut the inlay and nail to the floor. If you use a piece of standard flooring for the inlay material, first cut off the tongue edge on a table saw. Rip the inlay piece to a narrower width at the same time. Miter the inlay at the corners using a miter box and handsaw or a power miter saw. Predrill holes through the inlay and nail it to the subfloor with #6 finish nails. With a framing square, check that the inlay is square in the corners. Countersink the nails and fill the holes with a matching latex wood putty.

3 Install the perimeter flooring. Cut and fit mitered pieces of the regular flooring at the corners. Because they are close to the wall, you won't be able to use a flooring nailer. Face-nail them instead. You may be able to use the tongue-and-groove joint for the perimeter pieces, but you will have to cut off the tongue to fit the last piece against the wall. Install the field as if the borders were walls surrounding a standard strip floor.

Installer's Secret

The first row is made up of several lengths of flooring joined end to end. Even with a straight chalk line, it's easy to have the starting row get off a little. If the starting edge is not straight, it becomes progressively harder to form tight joints as you install the floor. To help keep the starting edge straight, use the factory edge from an 8-foot strip of plywood as a guide. The straighter the starting edge, the more easily the rest of the floor will go down.

TOOL TIP

Predrilling for Nails

Nails may be meant to be driven through wood, but for finish carpentry, it pays to drill a hole in the visible surface. It keeps the wood from splitting and helps prevent the nail from bending over and marring the wood. A $3/32$-inch drill bit is about right for #6 finish nails, but the best drill bit is an extra nail. Clip off the head, pop it in your drill, and use it as you would a standard drill bit.

4 **Rip-cut the starter-row strips.** Use a table saw with a sharp rip blade to cut the starter strips of flooring. Because the tongue edge of the first strip must face into the room, you will cut off the groove edge. Most home centers that sell flooring will make this cut for you in the millwork department. Take in enough stock for the starter row length. If the end row needs to be cut, take that in also.

5 **Snap a chalk line for the starter row.** Determine the width of the starter strip and snap a chalk line to show where the edge of the tongue will fall. It's important that this line be straight because the straightness of the starter row affects the entire installation. Don't use the wall as a guide—it may not be perfectly straight.

6 **Face-nail the first strips.** A flooring nailer can't be positioned to nail the first one or two strips; these strips have to be face-nailed. Align the first piece with the tongue edge on the chalk line. Predrill holes every 12 inches along the length of the strip, drive #6 finish nails through the holes, and set the heads. Note the expansion gap between the first floor board and the wall.

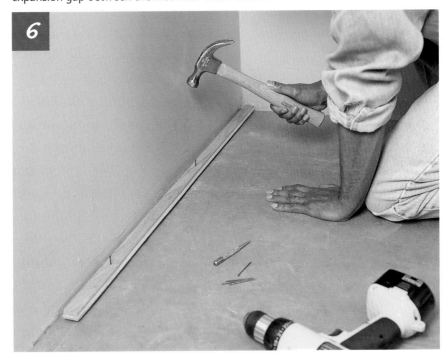

Floors

Installing a Strip Wood Floor

7 **Nail subsequent strips with nailer.** Flooring nailers are stock items at tool rental centers and well worth the rental cost. You can, of course, manually nail all the boards, but a nailer does a better job. Position the nailer on the tongue edge of the board, and whack the plunger head with the heavy rubber mallet that's supplied with the nailer. After the first few nails, you'll realize how easy it is to do.

Good idea!

For a balanced look, avoid bunching seams together in the same area, and stagger the end joints at least a foot apart.

8 **Crosscut end pieces.** At the end of each row, the last piece needs to be crosscut to fit. You can allow a small gap here, not so much for expansion but to make getting the piece in place easier. Avoid using an end piece that's less than a foot long; instead use two medium length pieces to end the row. Mark a pencil line across the piece with a square. Crosscut the piece in a miter box, or cut it freehand.

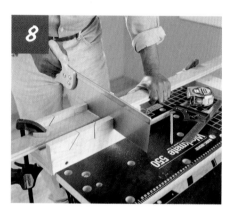

9 **Tighten seams.** Even the best milled flooring will have pieces that are not perfectly straight. Set these aside initially; and if you have enough extra, you may not have to use them. If you do have to use a piece that's bowed along the edge, screw a piece of scrap to the floor about an inch from the strip and tap a wood wedge into the gap, as shown. Another approach is to coax the joint tight by slightly wedging a chisel edge into the subfloor and then prying against the edge of the bowed strip.

Wisdom of the Aisles

"Shuffle the Deck: As you unbundle the flooring, you'll see that all wood is not alike. Some boards will be dark; some will be light. Some will be highly figured; others won't. Professional floor installers don't try to group similar boards. Instead, they shuffle the boards, mixing them for a random looking floor."

— *Terry Sanders*
Geneva, IL

Installer's Secret

Acclimate the Flooring

Wood expands and contracts with changes in moisture, and even kiln-dried boards will warp. To acclimate the wood to the moisture content of your house, put the bundle in the room where they'll be installed. Unpackage them, cut any binding, and leave the flooring for a week or so. The wood will gradually come to the same moisture content as the room, minimizing problems that might occur after installation.

Carpenter's Secret

Installing Shoe Molding

Shoe molding is the quarter-round molding that is nailed to the bottom of the baseboard to protect it from shoe scuffs. Protect the flooring while nailing the molding in place. Use a small piece of cardboard placed below the nail you're driving into the quarter-round. Stray hammer blows will bounce off the cardboard instead of the floor. Drive a nail, then slide the cardboard along the floor to the next.

10 Fit pieces around obstacles. Where the flooring meets a jog in the wall or other obstructions, cut the pieces to fit. Position the piece of flooring as close to its destination as possible, and transfer the measurements for the cuts directly from the wall or obstruction to the flooring. Remember to allow the gap along the length of pieces that meet the wall.

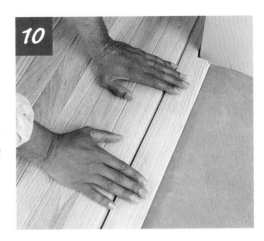

11 Cut and fit the last row. The last row, like the first, may have to be ripped to width. It also will have to be face nailed. To tighten the joint between the final two pieces, use a pry bar between the wall and the edge of the last strip, with a scrap block of wood protecting the wall.

12 Apply base and shoe molding. If you use unfinished flooring, sand and apply the finish before installing the base molding. (See "Sanding and Refinishing," page 293.) Once the floor is completely finished, cut and fit the base molding. (See Chapter 4, "Molding and Trim," beginning on page 126, for molding options.)

Floors

Installing a Strip Wood Floor 303

Installing a Decorative Wood Inlay

Make a beautiful floor spectacular uisng decorative inlays. Decorative inlays were once the domain of highly skilled flooring installers. Now, preassembled inlays are available through many flooring products manufacturers. An inlay becomes the focal point in an entryway, at the base of a stairway, or in front of a fireplace.

Inlays are available in several thicknesses, as well as finished or unfinished, to match existing flooring materials. Inlays match most off-the-shelf flooring from home centers, though they may have to be special ordered. The installation procedure for an inlay depends on the manufacturer. Some provide a template with each inlay that requires a router to cut the recess into the surrounding floor. The special router bit is included in the installation kit. This approach, shown opposite, is nearly foolproof. It's also ideal if you want to install an inlay in an existing floor. The inlay will have to match the thickness of the existing floor. To measure, remove a threshold or baseboard to expose an edge of the floor.

Inlaid borders are made by installing contrasting floor boards. This medallion is purchased preassembled; templates and router bits come with it to simplify installation.

Installing a Decorative Wood Inlay

STUFF YOU'LL NEED

✔ Medallion
✔ Template
✔ Glue
✔ Construction adhesive
✔ #4 finish nails
✔ Drywall screws
✔ Router
✔ Flush-trim bit
✔ Notched trowel
✔ Corner chisel

DOs and DON'Ts

DO - Double check to make sure the medallion and the floor are the same thickness. Sanding down one or the other more than a little is virtually impossible without damaging both.

DON'T - Get stuck. Use construction adhesive to hold down the medallion, and use glue to put the covers over the screws. Whatever you use is bound to squeeze out—and glue is easier to clean up than adhesive.

Prep Work

Some installers put tarpaper over the subfloor. It's optional, but it helps to deaden the sound made by walking over the floor.

1 Locate inlay on the floor.
Take time to position the inlay. Position the inlay on the floor with straight edges parallel to floor strips to prevent awkward seams. When you have it where you want it, use a pencil to trace around the perimeter of the inlay onto the floor.

2 Nail the template to the floor. Lay the template on the floor so the inside edges line up with the pencil lines traced from the inlay. Nail each corner of the template to the floor with #4 finish nails.

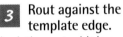

3 Rout against the template edge.
Lock the router bit in a router and adjust the router to make a ⅛-inch-deep cut into the excess flooring. (The first cut should be deep enough to skim across the top of the tongues on the boards.) Start the bit into the flooring about an inch away from the template to avoid damaging the template. Guide the router clockwise around the template. Blow out the dust and examine the cut; look for exposed nail holes where the cut passes over a tongue edge, and set any exposed nails all the way down through the boards. Lower the bit ⅛ inch and repeat the process until you've cut all the way through the floor strips—three passes is recommended in ⅜-inch thick flooring. Remove the floor strips within the inlay area. Use the chisel that came with the kit to knock out the corners, then check the fit of the inlay.

Floors

Installing a Decorative Wood Inlay

4 **Apply adhesive to the floor.** Use high-quality construction adhesive available in caulk tube form. Evenly spread the adhesive with a small notched trowel (the kind sold for applying base cove molding adhesive) around the entire surface of the inlay area.

5 **Attach inlay to floor.** Drop inlay into the recess and press it into the adhesive. Use a rubber mallet if it gets hung up on a corner. Then walk all around on the inlay to set it firmly into the adhesive. Drive 1⅝-inch drywall screws into the predrilled holes to secure the inlay to the subfloor.

6 **Glue in screw covers.** Apply yellow or white glue to the back of the loose pieces of the inlay that cover the screws. Set the pieces into the recesses and tap them down with a block of wood and hammer. Let the glue set for at least an hour before sanding the inlay.

Flooring With a Personality: Options for Inlay

Classical Motif

Starburst

Mixed Inlay

Floral Centerpiece

Installing a Wide-Plank Floor

Wide-plank flooring, with its Old World charm and solid craftsmanship, graces many homes built in the 19th century. Though floor manufacturers consider planks wider than 4 inches "wide" planks, 150 years ago boards were routinely milled to a full 12 inches. Most of the large old trees that yielded wide planks are long gone. The depletion of old-growth forests led to the harvesting of smaller trees, which yield narrow boards for flooring.

Wide-plank floors are again finding favor among homeowners. The raw material for this type of flooring—big, old trees—has renewed itself over the years and is being harvested with more environmental foresight. Additionally, an entire industry is devoted to salvaging wide-plank flooring from old homes and industrial buildings that fall under the wrecking ball. Sources for both new and salvaged wide-plank flooring are many, though a large percentage specialize in this product area, so you may have to look beyond your supplier of regular wood flooring.

Installing wide-plank flooring has notable differences from installing regular wood flooring. (See pages 298-303.) Compared to regular strip flooring, you'll use from one-half to one-third as many pieces of wide-plank

This simple pine wide-plank flooring reflects simplicity and solid craftsmanship, as does hardwood wide-plank flooring with simulated pegs.

floor, which means the installation will go more quickly. (Wide-plank floorboards are typically supplied in longer lengths than standard flooring as well.) Though the edges in wide-plank floors are sometimes tongue-and-groove jointed, the end joints are not. Finally, wide-plank floorboards are face-nailed across the wide widths into the joists. Square-head cut nails are recommended because they hold well and mimic the look of older floors.

Be aware of one potentially negative characteristic of wide-plank floors. Wide boards expand and contract more than narrow boards, resulting in wider gaps or cracks along the seams, especially during heating season.

Installing a Wide-Plank Floor

1 **Mark the floor joists.** Wide boards are more resistant to lay flat, and they also expand and contract more than narrow boards. Therefore, nail them through the subfloor and into the floor joists. On plywood subfloors, the nailing pattern should reveal the joist locations. On a tongue-and-groove subfloor, the nailheads

won't be visible, so find the first joist by trial and error. Drive nails through the subfloor until you hit the solid underneath—it's a joist. Typical spacing from center to center of joists is 16 inches, so after you find one joist, move over and drive more nails to find the next joist. Snap a chalk line to show the joist location.

2 **Nail down the boards.** If the boards are tongue-and-groove, use a power edge nailer to start the nailing process. Don't stop there: Face-nailing is necessary on wide boards. Cut nails, with rectangular heads, hold well and look similar to those used on old floors when cut nails were the norm. Use two nails across

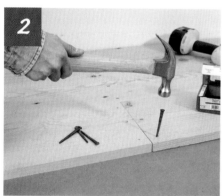

the width of boards up to six or seven inches wide, and three nails on wider boards. Keep the outer nails at least $^3/_4$ inch in from the edge of the board to prevent splitting. Orient the nailheads so the long side is parallel to the length of the board. Predrilling is not necessary in pine but is required in harder woods. However, predrill holes for the nails closest to the end cuts to keep the ends of the boards from splitting.

3 **Screw down the planks.** Pegging is an alternate look in wide-plank floors, based on the antiquated practice of drilling holes and inserting pegs into the floor beams below. This was more common in hardwoods such as oak than in pine. The modern facsimile of this approach is to screw down the planks using

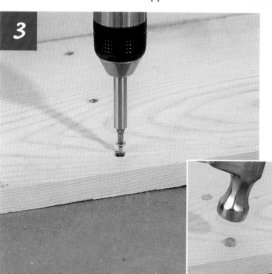

counterbored holes; then plug the holes with wooden dowel plugs. Some planks come predrilled; if they don't, use a counterbore bit to drill a stepped hole—part of it is wide enough for the screw, and part of it is wide enough for the plug. Get a counterbore bit designed to match a specific matching wood plug. After the screws are in place, apply glue to the hole and tap in the plugs.

STUFF YOU'LL NEED

See page 299 for a list of tools and materials needed for a typical strip floor installation. These additional items are specific to wide-plank floor installations.

- ✔ Wide-plank flooring
- ✔ Circular saw
- ✔ Quick square
- ✔ Hammer
- ✔ Cut nails

TOOL TIP

Most power miter saws (sliding miter saws are the exception) can't cut boards wider than about 5 inches. Wider stock should be cut with a circular saw. Use a fine blade and cut with the face side down to get a clean cut on the face. Use a speed square to guide the saw across the boards.

Installer's Secret

To drill holes for screws in plank flooring, make a jig that will help to keep them aligned. Drill two holes at the desired spacing in a scrap piece of flooring. Position them so that they are the right distance apart and the desired distance from the end of the board. When you're ready to drill the holes in the floor, align the edges and end of the scrap with the edges and end of the floorboard. Feed the drill down through the holes, and drill into the floor to the desired depth.

Pickling Floors

Pickling refers to the whitewashed look that is achieved in a number of ways on just about any wood floor. Though once based on the reaction between the wood and an acid such as vinegar, pickling today is done with either a stain or a thinned paint that's brushed on and wiped off. Because it is now done with paint or stain, pickling works with light or pastel shades, not just white.

Stain manufacturers sell products specifically designed to get the pickled look. Since there's no difference between pickling and staining, however, you may want to experiment with leftover paint to get an idea how the process works. When it's time to make a choice between paint and stain, let the color choice guide your decision.

Woods with open pores—oak, ash, and walnut—show a pickling effect best because the color lodges more heavily in the pores and contrasts with the smoother parts of the wood surface. Closed-pore woods, such as pine and maple, take an even coat of stain or paint, which looks more like a color wash than typical pickling. The grain remains visible, rather than changing to the color of the pickling pigment. Experiment to determine what effect the different paints or stains have on your floor.

Pickling softens the color of the wood, giving it a whitewashed effect.

Pickling Floors

1 **Prepare the floor.** Use an oscillating floor sander to remove the finish on an old floor. (See page 293 for details on floor sanding.) This type of sander is less aggressive than a drum sander and won't gouge the floor. Remove all the old finish. When you have, the wood requires only a light sanding. Thoroughly vacuum all the dust.

STUFF YOU'LL NEED

- ✔ Pickling stain or paint
- ✔ Sanding sealer
- ✔ Vibrating floor sander
- ✔ Vacuum
- ✔ Polyurethane top coat
- ✔ Paint rollers
- ✔ Clean rags or sponge mop
- ✔ Lamb's-wool or similar floor-varnish applicator
- ✔ 180-grit sandpaper

2 **Apply a sealer.** A coat of sealer limits the pickling effect somewhat and makes the effect more consistent across the floor. Apply a commercial sanding sealer with a low-nap roller. When the sealer dries, sand the floor lightly with the sander and 180-grit paper; then vacuum all the dust.

3 **Apply the pickling medium.** Thin paint with about 25 percent thinner—water for latex, or paint thinner for oil-based. Apply pickling stain as it comes from the can. Use a wide foam brush or a medium-nap roller to apply the stain or paint. Work one 3×3 foot area at a time. To get color into the wood grain as well as into the seams between boards, first work the paint across the boards, and then along them.

Smart & Safe

Dispose of varnish soaked rags and applicators safely. Varnish gives off heat as it dries—enough heat to set rags on fire. Hang all rags outdoors, away from any structures, and let them dry thoroughly before placing them in the trash.

Let's Make This Perfectly Clear

The varnish you choose depends on what you have applied under it.

Apply a water-based varnish over a water-based (latex) pickling agent. Apply an oil-based varnish over an oil-based pickling agent.

Any varnish you put over a finish will change its appearance somewhat. For a warm glow, choose an oil-based finish (and pickling agent). For a clearer finish, apply a water-based pickling agent and varnish.

4 **Remove the excess.** While the pickling medium is still wet, wipe off the excess with clean rags, leaving a consistent amount of color. On open-grain woods, such as oak, much of the color will be in the pores, and you can remove most or all of the material from the surface. On closed-pore woods, such as pine or maple, leave a thin layer on the surface of the wood. With a latex paint or stain, use a slightly dampened sponge mop to remove the excess. Advance along the length of the floor in a 3-foot swath until you reach the other end of the room, then go back and start the adjacent section, slightly overlapping sections.

5 **Apply a clear top coat.** Lock in the pickling effect with a clear finish, such as polyurethane. Low-luster satin looks better over pickled wood than semi- or high-gloss. Apply two coats of polyurethane with a lamb's-wool applicator. (See page 296 for details on applying polyurethane to floors.)

Good idea!

Because it dries relatively fast, using latex paint for pickling requires quick work to remove the excess paint before it dries. Slower-drying oil-based paints allow you more time and make it easier to blend one section to the next. Use them only with adequate ventilation, because they typically have more odor.

Painting Floors

Decorative floor painting offers design possibilities that don't exist in flooring inventory. Painting is particularly effective in creating Country or Colonial looks, but it's also a way to create any design you want in any colors your imagination desires.

Modern paints are plenty durable for floors, and a top coat of clear polyurethane will protect the painted design from wear. You can paint a floor a single color or lay out a geometric pattern. You can even use paint to simulate wood, stone, ceramic tile, or an Oriental rug. Artists traveling through the West in the 19th century painted portraits on the floors of homes and businesses.

Painting a decorative pattern on a floor is an especially good choice for floors that are not good candidates for refinishing but are in otherwise good shape. Good preparation is the key to great-looking results.

This floor is painted a traditional three-dimensional 18th-century Colonial pattern. Stencil the floor, paint it to look like a checkerboard, or apply a color wash.

Painting Floors

STUFF YOU'LL NEED

- ✔ Paint
- ✔ Low-tack masking tape
- ✔ Paint rollers with 3/8-inch nap
- ✔ Paintbrushes
- ✔ Paint tray
- ✔ Clear satin polyurethane and applicator pad
- ✔ Architect's scale
- ✔ Latex wood putty and putty knife
- ✔ Hammer and nail set
- ✔ Portable sander (or vibrating floor sander)
- ✔ Shop vacuum
- ✔ Chalk line
- ✔ Tape measure

TOOL TIP

Lay out the pattern by making a scale drawing. Use an architects scale rule, sold at art supply and office stores, to make your drawing. The tool has a triangular end and several rulers—each drawn to a different scale. On one of them, each inch represents 1 foot. Use it to lay out an 8×10-foot room. Each 1×1-foot square equals 1 inch. Combined with graph paper, an architects scale allows you to draw a precise scale drawing that you can use to lay out your design.

1 Prepare and sand the floor.
Carefully look for any protruding nails and drive them below the surface with a nail set and hammer. Fill cracks wider than 1/8 inch with latex wood filler. Then sand the entire floor to remove any surface dirt and wax that

prevent a good paint bond. You won't have to remove the existing finish. For most floors, manual sanding is sufficient; wrap a piece of scrap wood (or a sponge mop) with a full sheet of sandpaper and sand the floor. You can also use an electric pad sander, as shown here. For large floors, or floors that have a lot of uneven edges, rent a large vibrating floor sander.

2 Vacuum and wipe the floor.
Sweep and pick up the dust as thoroughly as possible; then use a vacuum cleaner to remove all remaining dust, especially from cracks between floorboards. Wipe the floor with a rag dampened with paint thinner, and then allow it to dry thoroughly.

3 Prime the floor. Apply a primer to ensure the new paint adheres to the floor surface. Mask off the base molding (unless you plan to repaint it after you paint the floor). Tint the primer to the main background color of the floor to help the top coat cover more easily and to provide a preview of the top coat color. (Tinted primer will be slightly lighter than the same color top coat, however, because primer doesn't absorb as much pigment.)

Floors

Painting Floors

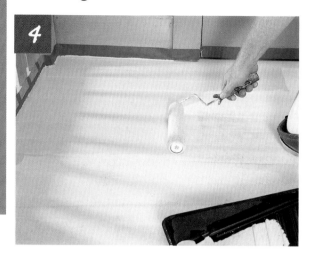

4 Paint the background color. Once the primer is dry, apply background-color paint with a paint roller that has a ³/₈-inch nap. Apply paint over a fast-drying primer, either latex or shellac-based, after only an hour or two of drying time.

5 Lay out the design on the floor. Draw the design on the floor using a chalk line to strike the main lines of the pattern. Start with the border, and make sure it's square by measuring the diagonals—they'll be equal if the border is square. Adjust the perimeter lines if necessary; then lay out the other elements in the design with a pencil and straightedge.

6 Mask off and paint the second color. Apply low-tack masking tape to areas that don't receive the second paint color. The key is to get a continuous bond along the edge of the tape, so press it down firmly with your thumb along the entire edge. Then apply the second paint color. A brush is easier to control than a roller for painting against masked off areas. Brush out the paint so it doesn't pool against the tape. Remove the masking tape as soon possible after the paint is dry to the touch. If you leave it longer, pulling up the tape may also pull up the edges of the fresh paint.

Painter's Secret

Low-tack masking tape works better than standard masking tape for floor painting. Available in widths up to 6 inches, it allows you to cover large swaths of the floor quickly. Only the edge of the tape sticks to the floor, making it easier to remove than standard masking tape.

TOOL TIP

You'll probably spend more time with a paintbrush on this project than on any other project in this book. If you don't have a good brush, invest in one. Choose a stainless steel or copper ferrule that holds the fibers because they don't rust. When you look at the brush from the side, the bristles should come to a blunt point—a chisel edge—making it easy to apply the paint. Look from the front, select a brush that's straight from side to side. Angled brushes are good for tight spots, but tough to control when you brush back and forth. Give the bristles a tug to make sure they're firmly anchored. Get natural bristles for alkyd (oil) based paints, and synthetic for latex paints.

7 Paint additional colors and the border treatment. If your design has a third color (see photo on page 312), repeat the masking off and painting steps. When the field area is painted and the paint is dry, mask it off and paint a border.

8 Simulate wear for an antiqued look. After you've painted the floor, wrap a wood block with 120-grit sandpaper and scuff through the top coat in parts of the floor to reveal the color underneath. Work randomly over most of the floor area, and sand more at areas that would receive high wear—in front of a window or the path between two doors, for example.

9 Apply a clear finish. To protect your painted floor design from scuffs and scratches, apply two coats of clear satin polyurethane, sanding lightly between coats. The clear coat will lock in the color and add vibrancy to the floor.

Floors

Painting Floors   315

Stenciling a Floor

Stencils offer a foolproof method for applying uniform decorative patterns. Spice up a floor with decorative border stencils to define space and highlight architectural features, such as doorways, a fireplace, or built-in furniture. The traditional way to achieve this effect is with costly inlaid borders, which is not practical for an installed floor. Border stencils work on any wood floor, from classic oak with a natural or stained finish to yellow painted pine floor. Combining stenciling with faux-finishing techniques described in Chapter 18 simulates wood inlays, adding another level of decorative accent to your floors.

Add color to an existing floor with stencils. This Southwestern pattern, originally designed for walls, proves that imagination and inspiration is what decorating is about.

Same Technique, Different Surface

Although wall stenciling is a common decorative application, stenciling a pattern on the floor is also a classic decortating technique. In many ways it's also easier to do. You won't be running up and down a ladder or working above your head, the paint won't run down the wall, and laying out the design is less difficult. Floor stencils work well with almost any decorating style, but the technique really shines as part of a Southwestern, Colonial, Country, or Victorian scheme. Though kits are made especially for floors, wall border kits can be used on the floor as well. And, of course, you can make your own.

Stenciling a Floor

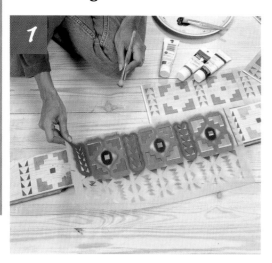

1 **Make a sample stencil.** Make a sample stencil to get a preview of both the pattern and the colors. If you have an extra piece of matching flooring, use that. Otherwise, use a piece of plywood or cardboard. Tape the stencil to the sample material, and paint the sequence of colors.

STUFF YOU'LL NEED

✔ Stencils
✔ Stencil paint
✔ Stencil brush
✔ 180-grit sandpaper
✔ Shop vacuum
✔ Measuring tape, ruler
✔ Masking tape
✔ Paper plate palette
✔ Single-edge razor blade
✔ Rubber sanding block
✔ Clear polyurethane
✔ Lamb's-wool varnish applicator for floors

2 **Sand the floor.** Slightly abrade the surface with 180-grit sandpaper for the stencil paints to adhere. Make a quick pass with either an electric orbital sander

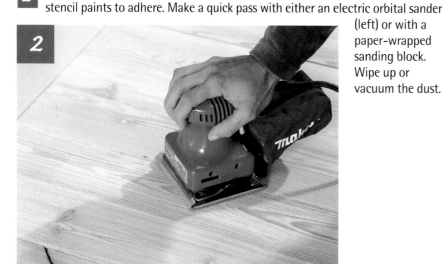

(left) or with a paper-wrapped sanding block. Wipe up or vacuum the dust.

3 **Measure and mark layout line.** While you can lay a stencil against the wall or baseboard, a border generally looks better away from the wall. Measure and

mark several spots along the wall, and then connect the marks with a band of painter's tape for a stencil guide. The tape is easier to remove than either a pencil line or chalk line.

Make Your Own Stencils

Wall stencils work equally well for floors.

Make your own stencils at the copy center. Find a pattern you like—a leaf, a wallpaper detail, or a pattern from a book. Photocopy it onto transparency film—the sheets of clear plastic sold at office supply stores for overhead projectors. Take home the photocopy and cut out the pattern with a mat knife to make the stencil. Tape the stencil in place, and begin. Most photocopiers enlarge or shrink images, allowing infinite control over the size of your pattern.

4 Plan the stencil layout. The hardest part of stenciling is making the pattern turn corners cleanly. It's easy with some patterns (flowing floral patterns, for example), but difficult with others (such as the rigid geometric pattern used at right). Start at the most visible corner of the room and work out. Inevitably one or more of the corners will end up with an incomplete pattern, but they'll be less conspicuous corners. Map out exactly how  the pattern will fall in the corners by making several photocopies of the stencil, cutting them out, and laying them along the wall. Find the best starting and ending point for your particular room.

5 Position the stencil on the floor in the first position. When you decide on the best starting point, position the stencil on the layout line and tape it to the floor. Use masking tape or painter's tape to cover the parts of the stencil that don't receive the first color.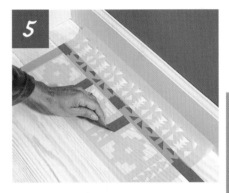

6 Paint the first color. Pour paint onto a paper plate. Lightly dip the stenciling brush into the paint and apply it to the floor. Use either stippling or swirling to apply stencil paint. Stippling maintains the stencil outline more crisply, and swirling looks more fluid and may allow some paint to bleed under the edges of the stencil. Experiment with the paint and the brush to decide which looks best; maintain that approach throughout your project.

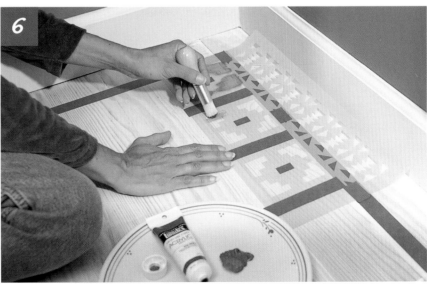

Floors

Stenciling a Floor

7 **Paint additional colors.** Remove the tape covering the stencil parts that receive the second color, and tape over the portion that received the first color. Use blue painter's masking tape, available in many widths with adhesive along only one edge, for this step. It covers a wide area and is easy to remove.

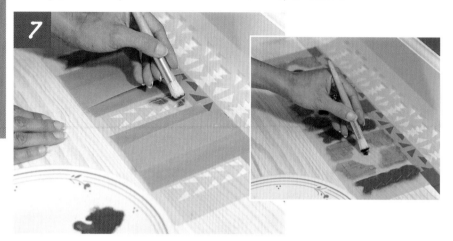

8 **Remove the stencil.** After all the stencil colors have been applied, remove the tape and carefully lift the stencil from the floor. If some paint has bled under the stencil, allow the paint to dry thoroughly, and scrape off the excess paint with a single-edge razor blade. Do not blot the paint while the paint is still damp.

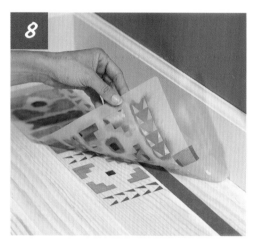

9 **Reposition the stencil.** Move the stencil to the next position. Align the registration marks that ensure regular spacing of the pattern (the solid line on the left side of the stencil), as well as the marks that align with the layout line (the broken line running lengthwise through the stencil).

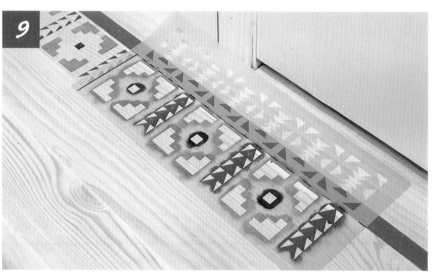

✱ Designer's Tip

Whole-House Stenciling

Pick an easy pattern that requires only one color. Randomly stencil the entire floor, providing accents by changing the color from time to time. When the floor is dry, sponge-paint the space between the stencils, as described in "Sponging On," page 62. For a different effect, color wash the floor first (page 72) and then stencil over it.

When you reach a corner that ends with less than a full stencil pattern, use an even increment within the pattern. (In this stencil there are three repeats of the pattern.) When that doesn't work, fudge the spacing a little, as shown.

10 **Continue the pattern around corners.** Restart the stencil pattern when turning corners. Depending on the pattern, you may have to turn the stencil face down in order to match the pattern. If so, be sure to completely clean the painted side.

11 **Sand lightly.** Let the paint dry thoroughly for a day or two; then sand it lightly. If you want to impart a slightly aged look to the stenciling, sand a little heavier in some areas to simulate wear.

12 **Apply a clear finish coat.** To lock in the crisp colors in the stencil and to prevent the paint from wearing off, apply a coat of clear polyurethane. If you apply the polyurethane to only the stenciled area rather than the entire floor, match the sheen that's on the rest of the floor.

Floors

Stenciling a Floor   321

Wooden Flooring Options

Wooden floors can be bold and colorful as well as subtle and warm. Solid wood flooring adds beauty and excitement to the surface of your home. Whatever your flooring choice, interesting design details reveal your personality and your choice of style, while complementing your home's finest features. Flooring design ideas are limited only by your imagination.

The photographs on these two pages show just a few of the options available for making a wooden floor part of your decorating plan. The basics:

- *Paint can go a long way toward dressing up a floor—whether it's a solid bold color or a Country checkerboard.*

- *Solid expanses of hardwood decorated with rugs do double duty, providing rich areas of comfort and durable surfaces.*

- *Contrasting woods turn a floor into a color composition—without introducing additional elements.*

Painted Floor Pattern—Victorian

Inlaid Border—Arts and Crafts

Strip Flooring—Traditional

Painted Floor—Country

Wide-Plank—Colonial

Floorcloth—Colonial

Flooring plays an
important role in
your decorating plan.

Striped Inlay—Victorian

Wide-Plank—Country

Floors

Floor Coverings

Floor coverings anchor a room in obvious and in subtle ways. Floor color becomes a foundation for selecting other elements in the room—paint colors, wallpaper, and furniture. When doing a complete room makeover, decide on the floor material while you are making other major choices. Less obvious, but equally important, are the textural characteristics of floors and how they affect the overall ambiance of the space.

Floor coverings are either hard or soft. Carpet and floorcloths are soft, while tile and laminate floors are hard. Wood floors fall somewhere in between. Soft floor coverings absorb sound and tend to be warm, while hard ones reflect and amplify sound and tend to be cool. Combine both surfaces with an area carpet over a tile or wood floor.

Floor coverings range from practical to whimsical. Both make strong design statements if they work with the rest of the room.

Another way to categorize floor coverings is formal or informal. This may be a little more complicated because most flooring materials can be either. Wide-plank wood floors are informal, but add an Oriental rug and you've changed the equation. Inlay strip flooring is unquestionably formal. The same carpet can look formal in one room setting and informal in another. Imagine the floor and the room together. Do they make the same statement about the activities that take place there?

As you narrow your choices, think about maintenance and life span. Most floor coverings require maintenance, and with proper care they will last for years. Ask your supplier the hard questions when you're narrowing down your choices. Will the grout in the tile need constant cleaning? How do I prevent water stains on my marble tiles? Will gaps open between wide-plank floorboards? What kinds of carpet are best for growing families? In general, you'd like what's on the floor to hold up longer than the paint, and perhaps longer than the decorating scheme itself. Think long-term when selecting floor coverings.

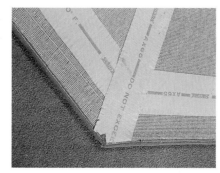

Painting a Checkerboard Floorcloth

Before vinyl flooring there was linoleum, and before linoleum there was the painted floorcloth. In fact, floorcloths have been used as long as woven rugs, but they are humbler and easier to make.

Custom-made floorcloths offer an alternative to purchased or ready-made floor coverings because you can customize designs to perfectly fit your decorating needs. Painted floorcloths have several advantages over area rugs: Floorcloths are easily washable, they don't harbor dust and other allergens, and they can be sized exactly to fit the space where you want to use them.

Like exquisite handmade rugs, floorcloths can mimic fine works of art; yet you don't need to be an artist to make your own. You can base designs on whimsical shapes or geometric patterns, as well as artistic representations. Find design patterns for floorcloths in magazines or books, or make your own. Make a scale drawing of the design on a standard sheet of paper, and color in the design elements to help you choose the colors. Use the scale drawing as a guide when laying out the pattern on the floorcloth.

Purchase floorcloth canvas already primed and ready to paint. For less cost, buy standard art canvas and prime it yourself with an acrylic or oil-based primer.

The design used above includes a stenciled border. Omit that for a basic checkerboard floorcloth, or use any of the other special painting techniques described in this book. For more designs, see page 330.

When you paint a floorcloth, you're reviving a tradition and creating a customized product. Here, shades of gold match the wall, and shades of blue complement the wall.

Painting a Checkerboard Floorcloth

1 Prime the canvas and paint the background color. If the floorcloth material is not preprimed, paint the surface with a latex primer. When dry, paint the cloth with the background color. Depending on the pattern, this coat may be one of the pattern colors. For example, on a checkerboard pattern that covers the entire cloth, choose one of the colors as the background, and roll it on. Apply the other color over it later. The cloth shown is more complicated. The white background is visible in the frame around the checkerboard. The border itself is made of two colors painted on separately.

2 Lay out and draw the design. With the scale drawing as a guide, use a yardstick and framing square to measure and lay out the design on the canvas. For larger floorcloths, a longer straightedge is helpful; use a straight piece of molding or a strip of thin plywood or paneling.

3 Mask off the pattern for the first color. Mask off the border if applicable. Mask off one set of alternating blocks using 2-inch-wide painter's masking tape. To cut corners square, hold a drywall taping knife where you want the cut and pull the excess tape against the edge of the knife.

STUFF YOU'LL NEED

- ✔ One piece of preprimed canvas, available at art supply stores
- ✔ Latex paints and foam brush
- ✔ Yardstick, measuring tape
- ✔ Framing square or right-angle drafting triangle
- ✔ 1½- or 2-inch wide double-side carpet tape
- ✔ Scissors
- ✔ Masking tape
- ✔ Layout pencil or pen
- ✔ Stencils and stenciling paints (optional)
- ✔ Water-based polyurethane
- ✔ Butcher's wax

TOOL TIP

The best place to work on a floor cloth is on a table—if you can find one big enough. If you can't, you'll have to work on the floor, as shown here. You can make it easier on your knees, and give yourself a smoother-working surface, if you line the floor with corrugated cardboard before you start. Cut up old cardboard boxes, and then tape them together to provide a continuous surface that will stay in one piece as you work.

Preparing Your Own Canvas

You can buy floorcloth canvas ready for painting that is primed and has crisp edges that won't fray. There also are alternatives if you can't find it preprimed, if your room is an unusual size, or if you're looking for a bargain.

Standard artist's canvas from an art supply store will work for a floorcloth. This material will need to be hemmed if you want a finished edge, and then primed with either an acrylic latex or oil-based primer.

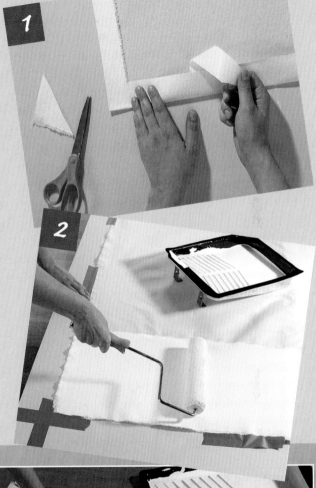

To hem a piece of canvas for a floorcloth:

1 **Cut the canvas to the finished size of the floorcloth, plus two inches in each dimension.** Fold under one inch around the perimeter and make a hard crease along each edge by pressing against the edge with a wood block. At each corner cut off a 45-degree triangle from each of the flaps to form a miter joint. Cut out one triangle, as shown right; then fold both hems into place, with the uncut hem underneath the one just cut. Trace the cut hem to lay out the diagonal on the uncut hem.

2 **When you finish cutting the corners, cut strips of double-side carpet tape** and press them onto the body of the floorcloth inside the crease. Remove the layer of protective paper from the second side of the tape, and press the flaps down onto the tape to create a perfect hem around all four sides of the floorcloth. Apply a coat of primer to the floor-cloth after it's hemmed.

No Hem, No Problem

To avoid hemming, paint the floor cloth directly onto thin, flexible, and durable vinyl flooring. The back surface is smooth and perfect for painting. Use an old piece of flooring or buy a bargain remnant. If the piece has been rolled up, roll it in the opposite direction until it is flat on the floor. There's no need to hem the cut edges of the vinyl. Make the cuts with scissors or a utility knife and then apply primer.

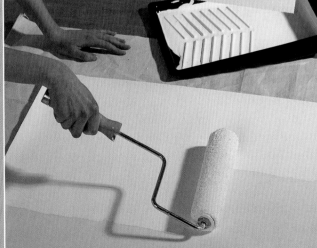

Painting a Checkerboard Floorcloth

4 **Apply the colors one at a time.** Work from the middle toward the edges so that you walk (or crawl) over your fresh work as little as possible. In this project, start with the checkerboard, first applying one color, retaping, and then painting the next color. A foam brush or small foam roller leaves a more even coat than a brush, and doesn't leave brush marks.

Remove the tape before the first color dries completely to avoid pulling up the edges of fresh paint. Let the paint dry thoroughly before applying the masking tape for the second color. (Blowing a fan across the paint speeds drying time.) Mask off the painted blocks, exposing only the unpainted blocks. Make sure the tape is applied firmly; then paint the squares with the second color. Remove the tape before the paint dries completely.

Floor Cloth Facts

• There are several grades of canvas used for making floorcloths, most of which are available at art supply stores. A number 10 duck—the second lightest grade available—is what most people use. It's light enough to work with; it's flexible; and if you decide to sew the seam instead of taping it, you'll be able to feed it through the machine.

• Art stores, and some crafts stores, also sell preprimed canvas like the one used in this project. One side has a single coat of primer and goes against the floor. The other side has two coats of primer to provide a good surface for your paint. It's a thinner canvas, but well up to the job.

• Cleaning a floorcloth is comparable to cleaning a vinyl floor. Sweep or vacumm the dirt, then wipe the cloth with a mop and soapy water. Rinse off the soapy water and then go over it with a damp mop to dry the surface. Don't use abrasive cleaners, ammonia, alcohol, or oil-based cleansers. Periodically wax the floor cloth the same way you would a vinyl floor, using a non-yellowing paste wax.

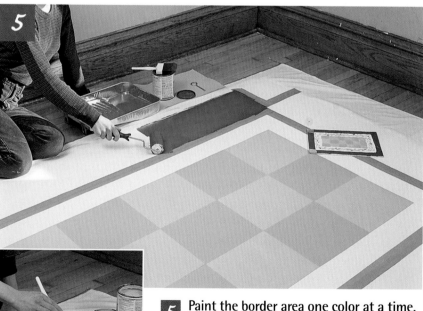

5 **Paint the border area one color at a time.** When the middle of the cloth is done, move to the edges. Apply masking tape, if necessary, to define an outside border area. Then paint the border area with a roller. This design has contrasting corner blocks; mask them off and paint them after the main border area has dried.

6 **Add stencils to the border.** Stencils add a distinctive touch to a floorcloth and are easy to apply. The size and shape of the border on this floorcloth was designed with a specific stencil in mind. Choose a stencil pattern first, and design the border to match.

Apply the first stencil color to the stencil area, as shown in **A**.

Tape over the parts of the stencil used for the first color and apply the second color, as shown in **B**.

You may select a single element of the stencil and apply it randomly, as shown in **C**.

7 **Apply a top coat of varnish or polyurethane.** To seal and protect the colors in your new floorcloth, apply two coats of a clear finish, such as polyurethane. Water-based polyurethane is white, while oil-based polyurethane may darken the colors and yellow slightly as the floorcloth ages. When the varnish has dried, protect it further by applying a coat of floor wax, if you desire.

*Designer's Tip

To prevent your new floorcloth from slipping around on a hard floor, place an antislip mat under it. It is made of thin mesh rubber and can be easily cut to the size of your floorcloth. A mat will cushion the floorcloth and also reduce wear. An alternative is to use carpet tape along the edge to fix the floorcloth to the floor.

Floors

Painting a Checkerboard Floorcloth   **329**

Floors

Floorcloth Ideas

There are infinite possibilities when it comes to floorcloths. Find patterns you like, design your own, or use these as inspiration.

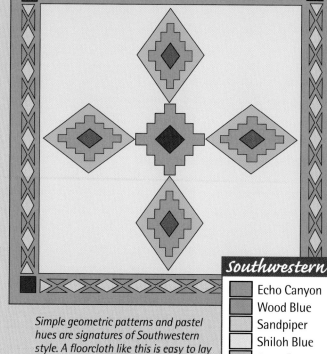

Simple geometric patterns and pastel hues are signatures of Southwestern style. A floorcloth like this is easy to lay out on a grid, and execution is simple.

Southwestern
- Echo Canyon
- Wood Blue
- Sandpiper
- Shiloh Blue
- Aqua Foam
- Stallion
- Choctaw

The tree of life is a common theme in 18th-century floor coverings. This oval shape and leafy border complement a Colonial dining room.

Colonial
- Barbizon
- Ruby Amber
- Golden Straw
- Wild Cattail
- Talisman Blue
- White Silence

The Arts-and-Crafts movement made use of softly rendered geometric patterns taken from nature. The floorcloth above has an almost Oriental feeling.

Arts and Crafts
- Rice Cake
- Saddle Soap
- Briny
- Mauve Nougat
- Chartreuse

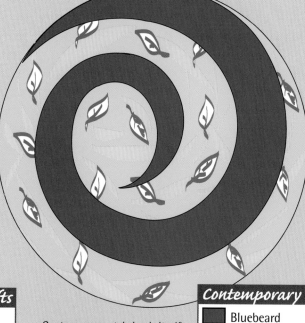

Contemporary style lends itself beautifully to abstract design. No rules apply—except pleasing yourself and deciding on a color scheme that works in the room.

Contemporary
- Bluebeard
- Vivid Lime
- Radiant Daisy
- Green Court
- UltraPure White

Carpet

Wall-to-wall carpet offers great choices for many living situations. In bedrooms, carpet is warm and comfortable under bare feet. In halls and on stairways, carpet quiets the noise of walking or pounding feet. In basement rooms with concrete floors, carpet is one of the easiest floor coverings to install because no structural subfloor is needed. (Install basement carpeting only if the concrete stays dry throughout the year.) For any room in the house where a plush feel and a calming effect are part of the objective, carpet fits the bill.

Choosing Carpet and Padding

Carpet retailers carry a wide range of carpet grades, styles, and textures, as well as a choice of pad materials. The broader the selection available, the more likely you are to choose the best carpet for the location and conditions in your home.

There are two classes of carpet fiber: natural and synthetic. Wool is the primary natural fiber used in carpet. It's generally more expensive and wears less well than synthetic fibers. Wool is commonly used in fine area rugs, generically referred to as Oriental rugs. (Authentic Oriental rugs are area rugs handmade from wool or silk and are quite expensive.) Wool is not common in wall-to-wall carpet.

Choosing a carpet is a matter of color, texture, and style. Once you've made your selection, have the installer make exact measurements.

Synthetic fibers include nylon, polyester, and olefin. Each has unique characteristics employed for different types of carpet. Nylon, the best-selling carpet fiber, combines superior durability, resilience, appearance, and stain resistance. Polyester is softer to the touch but less resilient and less stain resistant. Olefin is best suited for indoor/outdoor carpet and commercial carpets. Certain carpet styles combine more than one of these fibers. Berber carpets, for example, often combine olefin and nylon.

Choosing the right padding for your carpet is as important as choosing the right carpet. Again, a reputable retailer is your best guide in this decision. Carpet padding increases the durability of the carpet. The best pad is neither the thickest nor the most cushioned. In fact, thin and dense is generally better because it provides the best combination of firmness, support, and cushioning. Carpet padding is made from a variety of materials, including urethane foam, rubber, and felt, which have replaced the once-common horsehair padding.

Specific carpets require padding with a specific weight, density, and thickness—features that are stipulated by the carpet manufacturer. Using an appropriate padding is typically a condition for any warranty claim, so follow the information provided by the carpet manufacturer carefully.

Carpet Textures

Carpet comes in a variety of patterns and textures. Though you'll hear talk of saxony, plush, cut loop, and multilevel loop—to name a few—there are two basic types of carpet: loop pile and cut pile. In loop pile carpet, the surface of yarn passes through the backing, is looped over, and then passes back through the backing. Cut-pile carpet has the tops of the loops trimmed off to create a plusher-feeling carpet. Berber, which salesmen often refer to as a third style, is really a looped carpet made with thicker yarns.

Although durability, stain resistance, and resilience are determined primarily by the type of fiber you choose, texture plays a role, too.

Cut Pile

Cut pile includes two styles—saxony and plush. Saxony is dense and has twisted fibers that make it firmer. Plush has longer fibers, but they're not as dense as saxony, giving the carpet a softer, luxurious feel. Because of the open fibers and cut ends, cut-pile carpets get dirty more quickly.

Loop Pile

The loops on a level-loop pile carpet are all the same height, creating a smooth, dense surface that cleans easily. It's wear resistant and good for high-traffic areas. Multilevel loop has both long and short loops, creating a random, textured pattern. It tends to retain dirt because of the texture, and it wears slightly less well than level loop. Cut loop has patterns created by clipping off the top of some of the loops. It's slightly less durable than multilevel loop.

Berber

Berbers were originally a level-loop, light-colored wool rug made from thick yarn. Modern berbers are available in wool, synthetics, or a blend of the two. Berbers tend to have a rugged appearance, with the loops readily visible. Because of its texture, it can be harder to clean than other carpets and isn't recommended for high-traffic areas.

Installation: To DIY or Not

Most carpet retailers have subcontractors that install carpet, and the installation is generally between 15 and 30 percent of the entire cost, depending on the cost of the carpet. That's enough to get cost-conscious homeowners to consider installing the carpet themselves. Installing wall-to-wall carpet may seem easy, but there are several reasons to go with a pro.

Some carpet manufacturers balk at any warranty claim if you install the carpet yourself—even if your installation wasn't the cause of the problem. Second, there's the size and weight of a roll of carpet, which comes in standard 12-foot-wide rolls. It takes at least two strong people to lift even a short roll for a 10×12-foot room. Third, to install carpet properly requires several special tools you won't likely have in your toolbox. Carpeting a room with a single piece of carpet (no seams) requires a kicker and a power stretcher. If there are seams in the carpet, you also need a carpet iron. If you don't get the seam right the first time, it's hard to correct the problem; and a bad seam effectively ruins a carpet. Also, making a good seam in patterned carpet is more difficult to do than in standard carpet.

The most commonly used installation involves nailing tack strips around the perimeter of the room, stapling down the pad material, then stretching the carpet and pushing it down on the tack strips.

Another approach—and a less difficult one—is to glue down the pad and carpet using special carpet glues. First the pad is glued to the subfloor (any solid flooring surface: wood, plywood, concrete, glued-down vinyl); then the carpet is glued to the pad. With this approach, you don't have to stretch the carpet because the glue keeps it from moving.

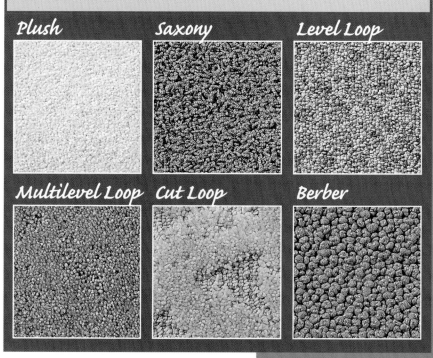

Plush · Saxony · Level Loop · Multilevel Loop · Cut Loop · Berber

Carpet retailers can sew pieces together to create almost any custom carpet design you can imagine. Area rugs come in a variety of patterns, too, although they're generally available only in specific patterns.

Custom Carpet Designs

One of the criticisms of wall-to-wall carpet is that it's so uniform it can become bland. This may be especially true in a large room.

Break up a huge span of wall-to-wall carpet by combining two or more colors into a custom design. A common approach is to choose a carpet and then create a border of contrasting color. This can make the room appear smaller and more intimate. There are really no limits to the design possibilities—geometric patterns, abstract shapes, a profile of your prized poodle—whatever your artistic palette desires.

Producing a custom design involves careful cutting and seaming together of the carpet, left. The process is typically done in a carpet workshop with specialized tools. Some carpet retailers provide this kind of service and others do not. If you're interested, shop by phone before setting out. Then, take along a carefully measured drawing of the floor and the design you'd like.

Another less expensive option exists. Some suppliers of area carpets offer a selection of premade custom area rugs. Design selections are limited, but you usually can find typical carpet colors in the designs. The sizes offered are also limited, from 4×6 feet up to 9×12 feet. If you like one of these designs and are willing to settle for an area carpet, it can be just as effective and less expensive than a custom-designed wall-to-wall carpet.

Installing a Laminate Floor

Laminate flooring is one of the most popular flooring materials available to homeowners. Designed to resemble wood, stone, or tile, laminate flooring installs easily and can even be applied over most subfloors or existing floors. It's ideal for do-it-yourself remodelers.

Laminate flooring is composed of three elements: a plastic laminate wear surface that includes the design pattern, a core stock made of fiberboard or particleboard, and a backing layer of moisture-resistant laminate. The edges and ends are milled with tongue-and-groove joints, much like traditional hardwood flooring. Unlike authentic wood strip flooring, laminate flooring is a precisely manufactured product and is extremely stable; it doesn't warp, twist, or bow like a piece of real wood can.

Laminate flooring is installed over a thin layer of foam by gluing the planks (typically measuring $3/8 \times 6 \times 48$ inches) one to the next. It can be installed over a variety of surfaces, including wood, vinyl and ceramic tile, linoleum, and concrete. It requires a modicum of care to get the joints tight and to clean off the excess glue, but is otherwise an easy job. The end result becomes a single mass of "floating floor," so called because it's not anchored to the subfloor and because the foam provides a cushioning effect to the floor.

It looks like marble, but it's laminate. There's no need for nailing—just snap the pieces together to install.

Some manufacturers use a snap-together joint system that requires no gluing. Pieces snap together like building blocks, and the floor can be taken up and reinstalled in other spaces several times before the precision of the edge joints degrades.

The practicality of laminate floors is best conveyed by comparison to the other familiar plastic laminate product—kitchen countertops. Laminate floors withstand normal use without any sign of deterioration for many years unless the floor is unusually abused. Everyday dirt wipes up with water and a mild detergent.

Installing a Laminate Floor

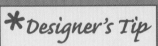

STUFF YOU'LL NEED

- ✔ Laminate flooring
- ✔ Transition strips
- ✔ Base molding (optional)
- ✔ Underlayment
- ✔ Masking tape
- ✔ Glue
- ✔ Installation kit (depending on the manufacturer, it may include some of the items listed below)
- ✔ Pry bar
- ✔ Tape measure
- ✔ Woodworking clamps
- ✔ Circular saw
- ✔ Saber saw
- ✔ Handsaw
- ✔ Straightedge
- ✔ Square
- ✔ Spacers
- ✔ Hammer
- ✔ Tapping block
- ✔ Floor clamp
- ✔ Plastic putty knife
- ✔ Glue solvent

1 **Remove base molding.** If your room has traditional base molding with a quarter-round shoe molding, removing the quarter-round is sufficient. If you have a one-piece base molding, remove the entire molding. Work the molding away from the wall a little at a time so it doesn't break; then reinstall the molding when the floor is done. Label the back side of the molding to identify its location.

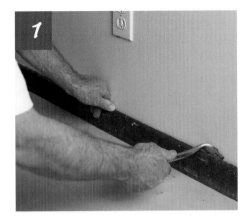

2 **Roll out the underlayment.** Most laminate flooring manufacturers sell a variety of underlayments; some include a vapor barrier, others include extra sound-dampening features. Check the manufacturer's recommendations for your floor conditions. Standard underlayment can be laid one width at a time as you lay the floor, with the edges of the underlayment sheets butting together. Short strips of masking tape can be applied to keep joints flush. Some special-feature underlayments are overlapped at the seams, so check the instructions on the material you use. Also note which side of the underlayment faces up—it's commonly printed on the material.

3 **Cut the first three rows of planks.** For a strong floor and balanced look, the end joint in one row shouldn't be too close to the end joint in the next row. For best results, start the first row with a full-length plank and start the second row with a plank two-thirds the length. Start the third row with the ⅓ cutoff from the second row. Measure and mark a plank for cutting. Clamp the plank upside down on a work surface, and make the cut with a circular saw guided by a straightedge.

*Designer's Tip

For an attractive floor, lay the plank parallel to incoming sources of light. A raking light tends to emphasize irregularities. If you install laminate in a hallway, run the planks the length of the hall.

Good idea! →

Most wood products expand and contract with changes in humidity, laminate flooring included. To acclimate the laminate floor and to minimize problems before installation, store it at least two days in the room where it will be installed.

Installing a Laminate Floor

4 **Dry-fit the first three rows.** The first three rows of a laminate floor are usually clamped together to start the installation process. To minimize the time it takes to spread the glue and get the clamps in place, first lay out and fit together (without glue) all the pieces for the first three rows. Working from the left side of a room, the edge tongue should face left and the end tongue should face right. Label the partial planks on both ends of the rows so you can put them back in the same position to apply the glue. (A small tab of masking tape makes an easily removable label.)

5 **Insert perimeter spacers.** As you dry-fit the first three rows, insert spacers between the wall and the flooring planks. This perimeter space is necessary to allow for expansion and contraction caused by humidity. The floor could actually buckle if installed too tight to the walls. You can usually buy spacers as part of an installation kit, or you can make your own by cutting strips of 1/4-inch plywood into small spacer blocks.

6 **Apply glue to the edges of the planks.** Manufacturer's instructions may vary slightly, but typically the groove should be completely filled with glue. You

should get a thin bead of glue squeezing out when the planks are clamped together, but not so much that the glue prevents the planks from coming together tightly. It may take the first couple planks to get a feel for just the right amount. With that in mind, spread glue onto the first few plank edges, assembling them as you go to gauge the squeeze-out.

Wisdom of the Aisles

"If you plan to put laminate flooring in a basement, make sure you have the right kind. Some laminate floors can be installed in a basement and others can't. Put down a vapor barrier first over a concrete floor to keep moisture from damaging the laminate. Don't use a vapor barrier over a wood subfloor; it may cause the floor to rot."

— *Romeo Julian*
Chicago, IL

Applying Glue

Where you put the glue depends on the product you buy. Some manufacturers call for glue on the tongue of the flooring; others advise putting it in both tongue and groove. Make sure you use enough glue. The minute the job starts looking neat and tidy, you know you're not putting on enough glue. If you have enough glue in the joint, some of it will squeeze out as you apply the floor.

Cleaning up the squeeze-out is usually a matter of wiping it with a wet rag. If the glue is stubborn, wipe it with 1/2-cup ammonia mixed with a gallon of water.

Applying Laminate over Crawl Spaces or Concrete

Moisture can be a problem if you install laminate over either a concrete floor or a crawl space. If the floor will go over a crawl space, make sure the space is ventilated enough to keep it dry.

Manufacturers specify so many square feet of vent space per so many square feet of crawl space. Check that your area meets or exceeds the requirement. Some manufacturers also require a vapor barrier over the ground of the crawl space. Even if it isn't required, it's a good idea. Install one before you install your floor.

If you install laminate over a concrete floor, make sure you have the right kind of laminate. Most can be installed over concrete; some can be installed in a basement. Some can't. Level out any dips in the concrete with a floor leveling compound before you start. Once it's dried, put down a moisture barrier. Put underlayment on top of the moisture barrier, and install the rest of the floor normally.

TOOL TIP

No matter how careful you are, sometimes even clamping won't close part of a joint. It may be that the glue started to set up before you got the clamps in place. Insert a pair of wedges against a wood block that's been screwed to the floor adjacent to the open joint. Another trick is to tap the surface of the plank near the open joint with a hammer and scrap block of wood to break the premature bond.

7 **Press and tap the planks together.** Continue gluing and assembling all the planks that form the first three rows. Use the tapping block (supplied with the flooring) and a hammer to press the planks together. Use the pull bar (see Step 8) to tighten the end joints. Work all three rows at the same time, gluing both the end and edge of each plank.

8 **Use a pull bar to tighten the last piece in a row.** When measuring for the last piece in a row, allow for the quarter-inch expansion gap. Use the pull bar (included in most installation kits) to tighten the end seam. You also can use the pull bar as a lever on the last piece by pressing it at an angle against the wall.

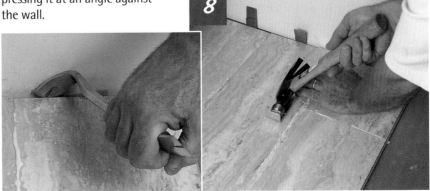

9 **Clamp the first three rows together.** No matter how carefully you assemble the planks or how quickly you work, clamp the first three rows to get all the joints tight. Rent specially designed laminate floor clamps where flooring is sold. The first three glued rows should be left to dry for at least an hour before removing the clamps and continuing the installation.

Installing a Laminate Floor **337**

Installing a Laminate Floor

10 Clean off squeezed-out glue. Clean off the glue before it completely dries. Allow the glue bead to dry partially (from 5 to 15 minutes) so it has a dry shell around it. Scrape along the seams with a plastic putty knife to remove both the dried shell and the wet glue inside. (A metal putty knife might scratch the floor.) Clean any remaining glue with a sponge dampened in warm water, and wipe the area dry with clean rags or paper towels. (An abrasive pad, such as Scotchbrite, also can be used to remove dried glue. Do not use steel wool, which will scratch the floor.) Don't saturate the floor or let water stand on it because water will get into the seams before the glue can dry.

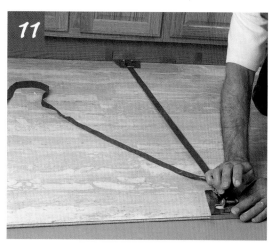

11 Install additional rows. After the first three rows have dried, continue to install rows of planks in the same manner. Stagger the joints between rows—the end joint in any given row should be at least 8 inches from the end joint in neighboring rows. Some manufacturers advise clamping each row (or two or three at a time) to the already-glued portion of the floor, and they rent strap clamps designed for that. You may be able to assemble the rest of the job without clamps, depending on the manufacturer's instructions and how easily the joints slide together with glue.

12 Undercut door trim. When you reach door openings with casing (wood trim), cut the bottom of the casing to allow the laminate flooring to slide under it. Hold a scrap piece of the flooring flat on the subfloor and against the casing. Rest a handsaw flat against the flooring scrap to guide the saw and cut.

The Right Stuff

Don't save a couple bucks on glue by buying an off-brand. Use the exact glue the manufacturer recommends. The bond between the joints is crucial, and the manufacturer's recommendation has been blended to work best. Manufacturers feel so strongly about it that using the wrong glue often voids the warranty on the whole floor.

*Designer's Tip

If you have a heater vent that comes through the floor, replace it with a real wood vent. They're available in a range of species and finishes that will match any floor.

TOOL TIP

Sometimes you'll have to trim around obstructions or bumps in the wall. Using a small square of ⅝-inch plywood is a great way to lay out the cut. Drill a hole in the plywood big enough to hold a pencil, and then cut the plywood as big as needed to get the layout line in the right place. Push the pencil through the hole, and guide the plywood along the wall to lay out the cut. Make the cut with a laminate blade in a saber saw.

*Designer's Tip

Stairs are no barrier for laminate flooring. Separate stair nosing pieces are made to match most styles of laminate flooring, and the same floor planks can be used to cover the treads and risers. Look for specific instructions for stair installations where you purchase laminate flooring.

13 **Cut and fit around obstacles.** At doorways and closets, cut planks to match the layout of the room. Mark the plank to be cut by holding it in position against the obstacle. Be sure to maintain the ¼-inch expansion gap. Draw lines on the back of the plank, and cut it with a saber saw.

14 **Fit the last row.** Saw the last row of planks to a narrower width. Measure several places along the wall in the remaining space for the last row, and cut each plank for a specific place along the wall. Be sure to allow a ¼-inch space along the wall. Clamp the plank face down to a bench top with the cut line extending over the edge of the bench. Also clamp a straightedge to the plank to guide the saw. The last row (in fact, the last several rows) can be tightened by using the pull bar as a lever, as shown in Step 8.

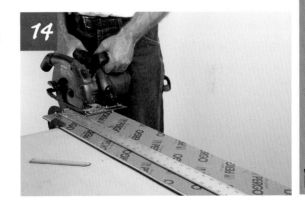

15 **Install transition strips.** Where the new laminate floor meets different floor material in adjacent rooms, install transition strips. These are supplied in the same finish as the floor for transitioning to carpet, tile, or resilient flooring. (You also can buy baseboard that matches flooring.) Cut the transition strip to length and nail it in place with #6 finish nails. Replace the base molding or shoe molding to finish the installation.

Floors

Installing a Ceramic Tile Floor

Versatility and durability stand out as the strengths of ceramic tile. Most tile suppliers carry a wide selection to mix and match tiles to suit your design. Although hard-surfaced, tile comes in textures that look soft and inviting. Cost per square foot is comparable with or less than many other high-quality flooring materials, especially if you install it yourself.

Installing ceramic floor tile is challenging. There are more steps to follow and more materials involved than with other flooring choices, but the process itself remains uncomplicated.

It is important to start with a flat, stable subfloor. A floor that gives will result in cracked tiles. Lay down backerboard, the cement version of drywall, to ensure a permanent bond between the floor and tiles.

The tiles shown are hexagonal. As with many small tiles, they are held together in mesh sheets and are approximately 1 foot square. Apply each sheet as if it were a single, solid tile.

Tile is tough, durable, and water resistant—perfect for the bath, the kitchen, and high-traffic areas.

Installing a Ceramic Tile Floor

STUFF YOU'LL NEED

✔ Tile
✔ Latex-portland cement mortar
✔ Unsanded grout
✔ #10 finish nails or 2½-inch finish screws
✔ Cement backerboard
✔ Backerboard scoring tool
✔ Backerboard screws
✔ Tile spacers
✔ Floor leveling compound
✔ Medium grit sandpaper
✔ ½-inch drill and screwdriver bit
✔ Mixing paddle for drill
✔ Notched trowel
✔ Tape measure
✔ Chalkline
✔ Tile saw, tile cutter
✔ Nippers
✔ Grout float
✔ Sponge
✔ Bucket

Installer's Secret

Applying mortar to the subfloor

Backerboard is set in a bed of mortar that is troweled onto the existing floor. The mortar fills any voids between the floor and the backerboard—voids that could allow the backerboard to flex and cause the tile to crack. Apply the mortar with a notched trowel, the same way you apply it when setting the tile.

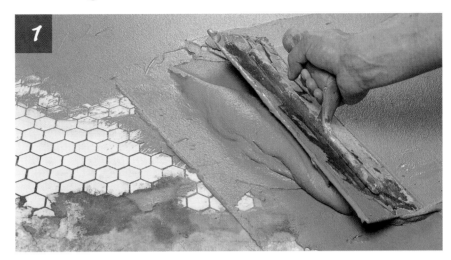

1 **Prepare the subfloor.** Laying new flooring presents the opportunity to check the existing floor or subfloor for problems, such as loose joints, raised nails, and squeaks. Drive #10 finish nails (or 2½-inch finish screws) through the floor and into joists to secure loose areas. Check for nails that have popped, and drive them below the surface with a nail set.

Most existing floors need to be covered with cement backerboard. Ask your dealer to tell you about any special prep work. Be sure to check the existing floor material for loose areas, and nail or glue them down with the appropriate adhesive.

If you have an existing tile floor, you can tile directly over it. Use floor-leveling compound to patch dips or broken areas.

2 **Install the backerboard.** Cement backerboard is the recommended underlayment for ceramic tile. Cut the panels to fit by scoring one face with a utility knife, snapping the panel along the cut line, and then cutting the back face to complete the cut. Trowel dryset mortar onto the floor, and screw the backerboard to the subfloor with hardened screws sold for use with the backerboard. Leave a ⅛-inch gap between the edges of each sheet.

3 **Fill backerboard joints.** To complete the backerboard installation, apply a coat of thinset adhesive to all the joints and feather it out evenly over an 8-inch swath. Thinset adhesive is a mortar designed to be used with backerboard. (Some installers reinforce the seam by taping it with fiberglass tape before applying adhesive. Taping is optional on floors.)

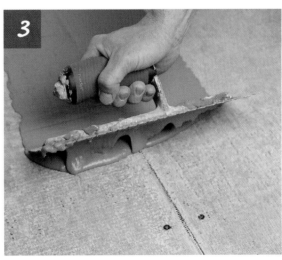

Installing a Ceramic Tile Floor

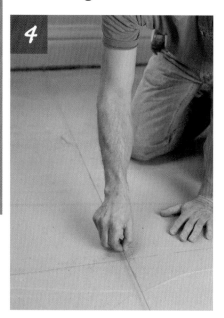

4 Strike layout lines for the starter courses. In order to center the pattern and avoid problems caused by out-of-square rooms, tile is laid from the center of the room out. To find the center of the room: Measure along each wall and mark the center point; then snap lines connecting the marks. Check to make sure the lines are perpendicular; snap a new line if they aren't.

Checking for Square

To make sure layout lines are perpendicular, use the 3-4-5 triangle method. Make a mark 3 feet from the room's center point along one line, and a mark 4 feet from the center along the other line. If the lines are perpendicular, the distance between the marks will be 5 feet. If it's not, adjust one or both of the center lines until they are perpendicular.

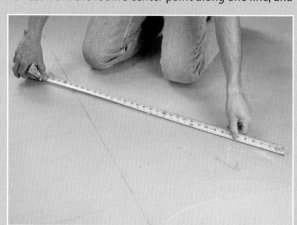

5 Lay out the tiles. From the center point, lay out tiles along both center lines to check the size of the tiles that meet the wall. (In the installation shown, there will be a row of border tiles, so they are temporarily set in place.) If the tiles against opposite walls (or border) aren't the same size or if either is less than half a tile wide, shift the pattern to solve the problem. If the perimeter tiles are very small, use partial tiles only along two adjoining walls and full tiles along the other two walls. Although this method reduces the number of tiles to cut, its success depends on tile pattern and shape of the room.

Moisture Barriers

Tile — Waterproof membrane — Thinset adhesive — Cement backerboard — Subfloor

If you install tile in an area that's going to get soaking wet, you need a moisture barrier to protect the floor and framing below the tile. Moisture barriers include polyethylene plastic, tar paper, and proprietary products made specifically for use with tile. Installation varies. Follow the manufacturer's recommendations precisely to ensure that your floor is protected.

Installer's Secret

Nail a ledger strip along the start line. Use this optional step that pros use to guarantee straight tiles in the first row. Use a 1×6 or 1×8, if you can find a straight one. If not, use a 8- to 10-inch wide and 8-foot long plywood strip, making sure one edge is the original straight factory edge. Tack the plywood along the starting line and butt the first row of tiles against it.

6 **Mix thinset mortar adhesive.** Follow the manufacturer's instructions for mixing the tile adhesive. For large jobs, a mixer attachment on an electric drill works better, but you can mix it with a trowel. When you mix a batch of adhesive, it has a "working time" within which it must be used; mix only enough for one portion of the job at a time. You'll know the working time has run out when the mixture starts to set up in the bucket, getting thick and pasty. Discard the adhesive, and mix a fresh batch.

7 **Trowel mortar adhesive onto the floor.** Spread the adhesive onto the floor with a notched trowel—the adhesive package should have instructions for the size of the notch depending on the size of the tile. The key to spreading the adhesive is evenness, not neatness. Hold the trowel hard against the floor at a 45-degree angle, and pull it through the adhesive. If you let the floor guide the trowel and maintain the angle (more or less), the bed of adhesive will be a uniform thickness.

8 **Lay the first tiles.** Lay the first group of tiles into the adhesive. Press down firmly with your hands. (Some professionals advocate slightly twisting each tile to bite into the adhesive.) Align the edges with the starting line. If you lay a standard tile floor you will have to insert plastic spacers, available in tile departments, to keep the tiles even. (See "Tiling a Countertop," beginning on page 400.)

Floors

Installing a Ceramic Tile Floor   343

Installing a Ceramic Tile Floor

9 **Set and level the tiles.** Press the tiles into the adhesive and level them with the surrounding tiles by tapping them with a 2-foot long 2×4 covered with a scrap of carpet. Lay the carpet-covered board across the tiles and tap firmly (not hard) with a rubber mallet.

10 **Mark the perimeter tiles.** Set the perimeter tiles in place along the wall—or along the border tiles, in this case—and mark them for cutting. If the wall joint will be exposed, allow enough gap for the grout seam to match the rest of the job. If the wall joint will be covered by base molding, you don't have to be as careful—just leave about a $1/4$-inch gap between the tiles and the wall.

11 **Cut the perimeter tiles.** There are two practical options for cutting tiles: a tile saw or a tile score-and-snap type cutter. Tile saws are available for a few hundred dollars—a lot to pay for one job. A good scoring tile cutter costs a fraction of that; quality models can be purchased for less than $50 or rented for as little as $15 a day. To use a score-and-snap tile cutter, position the tile under the scoring wheel, and slide the scoring wheel firmly over the tile with even pressure and in one continuous motion. Score the tile, flip down the pressure pad onto the tile (around the middle of the cut), and press down to snap the tile.

All About Grout

Grout is available either sanded or unsanded. If the spaces between tiles are $1/8$ inch or less, an unsanded grout sits better in the spaces. Unsanded grout is also better to use on highly glazed tiles, which might get scratched by sand. For larger space between tiles, use the more durable sanded grout.

Glaze is also available in several colors. Mixing the colors yourself can be tricky, so opt for a premixed colored. Look at a sample brochure and find one that complements your tile.

TOOL TIP

If you don't want to cut the tiles, you can still install a ceramic tile floor.

Mark all the perimeter tiles for cutting and take them to the supplier for a small charge. They will usually have a tile saw to do the job.

Dryset vs. Thinset

Confused about the difference between thinset and dryset mortar?

They're actually different names for the same mixture of cement, sand, and lime. Dryset—the technical term—is a mortar for installing tile in a bed about ⅛ inch thick. As a result, it's sometimes called thinset. Latex-portland cement (also called thinset) is a mortar with a latex additive. This latex thinset is stronger and more water resistant; however, either of the thinset mortars may be used for this floor.

Grout Sealers

Grout—especially grout that's on a floor—will quickly get stained unless you seal it. Let the grout dry thoroughly, following the manufacturer's directions. When the floor is dry, apply the sealer to the grout—not the tile. (You can brush it on, or use a special applicator.) Wipe off any smears within the first five minutes or so of application. Let the sealer dry for 24 hours—longer if recommended by the manufacturer—before you wash it.

12 **Fit tiles around obstacles.** Some tiles need to be fitted around obstacles, such as pipes, vanities, or toilet fixtures. Mark the tiles by making a cardboard template. Get the fit right before tracing it onto the tile, then nip away at the waste area with a pair of tile nippers. Be patient and take small nips; biting off too much at a time causes the tile to crack. Let the mortar set for at least 8 hours, or as recommended by the manufacturer, before setting the grout.

13 **Grout the tile.** Grout protects the edges of the tiles and prevents moisture from penetrating under the tiles, where it would damage the adhesive bond. Because the spaces between the tiles are so narrow, mosaic tiles require unsanded grout. Mix the grout according to the manufacturer's instructions. With a rubber float, spread grout to small areas at a time, working at a diagonal to the tile joints. Press the grout all the way down into the joints.

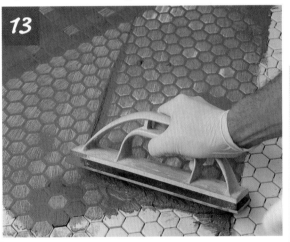

14 **Wipe away excess grout.** Use a clean sponge and clean cold water to remove excess grout. Rinse the sponge often. Remove all the grout from the surface of the tiles while removing only a minute amount from the grout joints. Wipe and rinse each area several times to remove all the excess grout. When you finish, grout lines should be slightly below the tile surface, and the tile surface should be free of grout. Continue grouting and cleaning adjacent tile areas until the entire floor is grouted and clean.

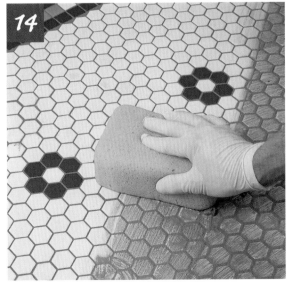

Floors

Installing a Ceramic Tile Floor 345

Floor Tiles

Tile is an extermely versatile flooring material with options to fit nearly any room in a variety of colors, textures, and patterns. Because tile is permanent, choose it for long-term use. Begin your research at a well-stocked home center to become familiar with the choices. Then visit a tile specialty supplier; you'll be amazed at the variety of custom tiles available.

Ceramic tiles include glazed and unglazed tiles for floors and walls. Surfaces are either smooth and flat or undulate with the natural texture of the clay from which they are made. Stone tiles are made from marble and granite, which is typically polished, or slate, which is more textured. Other manufactured tiles use cement and related materials.

Floors

Varied sizes of the same tile are combined to create the textured mosaic above.

Tile and wood, as shown below, work well together. Framing each marble tile with a band of hardwood transforms this floor into a work of art.

A combination of durable custom and stock tiles creates this elegant tile countertop that beautifully complements the tile floor.

Tumbled marble accent tiles repeat in a diagonal treatment.

Fashion underfoot. The rich terra-cotta ceramic tile floor was the starting point for this room scheme. A nubby sisal rug and a polished wood side table set at an angle to the tile layout highlight the geometric pattern.

Two shades of the same tile form an eye-catching harlequin design.

DIY vs. Professional Installation

You'll save money if you install your own tile, but be sure to meet manufacturer's specifications for materials and carefully follow the manufacturer's installation directions. To determine whether to do the job yourself or hire a pro, balance the expense against your time and skill, and the difficulty of the job. Your home center can help you qualify yourself in terms of skill level.

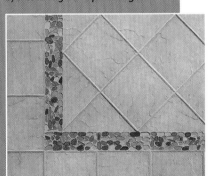

A frame of tumbled marble rock strips adds drama to this flooring.

Classy and elegant, tile is also durable, making it an excellent choice for high-traffic areas such as the bathroom, above, or the kitchen, below.

Floors

Floor Tiles 347

Section 7

Furniture Finishing

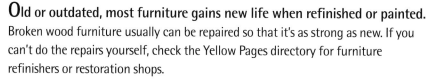

Old or outdated, most furniture gains new life when refinished or painted. Broken wood furniture usually can be repaired so that it's as strong as new. If you can't do the repairs yourself, check the Yellow Pages directory for furniture refinishers or restoration shops.

Scouting for furniture to refinish or paint is fun, as well. Antiques shops are an obvious source, though they tend to charge premium prices for even run-of-the-mill furniture. Genuine bargains are found at tag sales and secondhand stores. And don't overlook the stuff you're already living with.

Furniture Finishing

Furniture Finishing

Prepping Furniture

Before you refinish or paint a piece of furniture, prepare the surface. Surface prep can make or break a refinishing job. Expect to spend as much or more time preparing the piece for paint or finish as you do applying the new finish. Prep work includes minor repairs, filling gashes or dents, and sanding the wood.

Minor Repairs

Before refinishing a piece of furniture, check the structural integrity. If joints are loose, separate the parts as much as possible, squeeze yellow or white wood glue into the joint, and clamp the parts together. Look for loose veneer (a thin layer of premium wood applied to a lesser wood or plywood substrate), especially around surface edges, and glue it securely. To clamp the furniture piece, place waxed paper on top of the repair, and place a heavy book on top of that. Where splits have developed, clean out the gap, insert glue, and clamp it together. (If the split reappears, it's either a flaw in construction or a defect in the wood. Consider it part of the charm of the piece.) On pieces to paint, fill dents and gashes with latex wood putty. On pieces to varnish, use a matching wood-toned filler.

Furniture doesn't always age gracefully. Combine patience, care, and muscle to make almost any piece as good as new.

Stripping Furniture

Stripping furniture to the bare wood is necessary only when applying a new wood finish. Paint will cover most surfaces if they are properly scraped, cleaned, and sanded before application. (See page 354.) Although stripping away the old finish is a messy process, it's a necessary for a professional result.

Many furniture stripping products contain caustic chemicals. Use them cautiously in a well ventilated space (outdoors, if possible, or near an open door or window). Wear protective gloves and safety glasses, and use a fan to draw the fumes out of the room.

Strippers are divided into paste and liquid types. Paste strippers are thick and gooey and cling to vertical surfaces, as well as nooks and crannies on carved or turned parts of furniture. Paste strippers are all purpose—they strip thick layers of paint and thin layers of finish equally. More difficult to apply evenly, liquid strippers work well to remove thin finishes as well as small parts that can be dipped. After using a paste stripper to remove most of the finish, use a liquid stripper to remove remaining finish in hard to reach spots .

Products labeled "furniture refinishers" and "restorers" are designed to remove finishes along with steel wool. They are weak strippers that allow you to carefully remove finish without heavy scraping and without the risk of gouging the wood. They require more elbow grease and they work well on finishes that are not heavily built up.

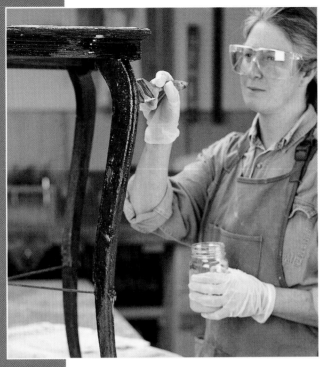

Work Smarter

Heat Guns
Heat guns strip paint off houses—not furniture. They're so hot that they'll scorch the wood, leaving burn marks that are nearly impossible to sand out. They also can cause veneers, inlay, or delicate marquetry to peel off, ruining the look and value of the piece.

Furniture Finishing

Stripping Furniture   351

Stripping Furniture

1 **Apply the stripper.** Read the label carefully before you begin so you understand the directions and safety instructions. Place the furniture on newspapers over a canvas drop cloth. Wear rubber gloves and safety glasses. Brush on the stripper, working from the top of the piece down—top, then aprons, then legs, etc. With liquid strippers, it's important to apply it and leave it alone—don't rebrush it to even out the paste. Liquid stripper tends to splatter and spray off the brush when you're applying it to irregular surfaces. Brush it on carefully and if the stripper gets on your skin flush it off immediately with clean water.

STUFF YOU'LL NEED

- ✔ Liquid stripper
- ✔ Newspapers and canvas drop cloth
- ✔ Rubber gloves
- ✔ Safety glasses
- ✔ 3-inch-wide paintbrush
- ✔ 3-inch-wide putty knife (metal or plastic)
- ✔ #00, #000, and #0000 steel wool
- ✔ Wire brush or toothbrush
- ✔ Clean rags
- ✔ Mineral spirits

2 **Allow the stripper to do its work.** You don't want to rush this part of the process. Wait as long as directed on the label, and then scrape off the old finish and stripper with a wide-bladed putty knife. Slightly round the sharp corners of a metal knife with a file to prevent gouging the wood. Plastic putty knives are a good and inexpensive alternative if you don't want to alter a metal knife.

Wisdom of the Aisles

"Stripper is easy to put on, but hard to get off. Although a putty knife is your best bet for flat surfaces, get some sawdust (or hamster bedding) for stripping carvings, turnings, frame-and-panel doors, or any other uneven surface. Let the stripper do its work as directed on the label. Put on a pair of heavy rubber gloves, pick up a handful of sawdust, and rub down the uneven surfaces. The sawdust picks up the stripper and residual finish. When it becomes saturated, grab another handful, and keep going."

— *Romeo Julian Chicago, IL*

3 **Use steel wool on irregular surfaces such as turned legs or carved moldings.** Start with a coarse grade of steel wool (#00, double aught) to remove most of the stripper and finish. Go back over the surfaces with very fine steel wool #000 (triple aught) or #0000 (four aught). You also can use synthetic steel wool for this—it doesn't break apart like steel wool does.

Refinisher's Secret

Don't be alarmed if your furniture is dried out and looks bleached after using a commercial stripper. The dryness is a result of a chemical process. Sanding will remove most of the chemical residue, and the new finish will restore the wood to its natural beauty.

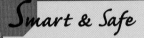

Smart & Safe

Open the windows and turn on the fans before using chemical strippers. It takes potent chemicals to remove finishes—chemicals you should not breathe. If you get dizzy, get into fresh air immediately. If possible, strip furniture outside—and never strip it in the basement. A respirator—with fresh cartridges—will protect you from the fumes. A regular dust mask won't do the job.

4 Use a wire brush or old toothbrush for carved surfaces and turned parts. Table legs and bedposts often have recessed details that need special attention. Carvings are even harder to remove finish from. After the surrounding areas have been stripped, brush fresh stripper into the recessed areas and let the stripper work. Remove the stripper and old finish with a soft, brass-wire brush or toothbrush.

5 Wash off the residue with mineral spirits. If you don't remove all the stripper, the new finish won't adhere well. Wash down the piece with a rag and plenty of mineral spirits (paint thinner). Once you clean off the piece, you'll probably find areas where some of the old finish is still intact. Reapply stripper to the area, remove it after the recommended time, and rinse again with mineral spirits.

The Dip 'N' Strip Approach

Stripping furniture is messy; and the chemicals, fumes, and all the muck it generates can be exasperating and potentially dangerous.

You may choose to take your furniture to a commercial stripping operation and avoid the mess entirely. Commercial strippers dip furniture into large vats of finish-dissolving chemicals until bare wood remains. Be aware that this approach can weaken joints and lift veneer if the chemicals affect the glue that holds the furniture together. They also leave the wood rough compared to hand stripping, so you need to sand more. If the piece you want to strip is solid wood, it should survive a dip stripping well. If it is veneered or if it's an especially valuable piece of furniture, find a shop that will do the stripping by hand.

Furniture Finishing

Sanding

Sanding smooths wood surfaces and it makes paint and finish adhere to the wood properly. With a stain or clear wood finish, the degree of sanding determines how the finishes will look. Poorly sanded surfaces will look uneven, blotchy, or scratched. Although paint is generally more forgiving than stained or clear wood finishes, deep scratches, especially those that run across the grain, will still be visible.

Use these three keys to good sanding. First, sand all the wood thoroughly. Second, work from a coarse or medium-grit sandpaper up to a fine grit. Third, sand in the direction of the grain. For most furniture projects, use two or three grits. (The lower the number assigned to the grit, the coarser it is.) For example, you start with 120-grit

sandpaper and finish with 180-grit; or start with 100-grit, then switch to 150-grit, and finish with 220-grit. (You might need to start with 80-grit on new wood, especially hardwoods such as cherry, maple, or oak.)

Sanding with the grain ensures that the scratches left by the sandpaper are concealed within the grain pattern of the wood. Sanding across the grain leaves visible scratches that are magnified after the finish goes on—especially if you stain.

Stains (especially water-based stains) can raise the grain of the wood as they dry. This leaves a rough surface that has to be sanded. Unfortunately, sanding can scratch through the stain and make a mess. To avoid this problem, raise the grain before the final sanding (and staining) by wiping the surface with a cloth dampened with water or paint thinner. The final sanding knocks down the whiskers of grain, so that when you apply the stain, the wood stays smooth.

To avoid leaving scratches in the wood, always sand in the direction of the grain. When you finish sanding with one grit paper, remove the dust before switching to the next finer grit.

Sand flat surfaces with an electric sander or with a sanding block. Make your own sanding block by cutting a piece of 1×4 or 2×4 to about 4 inches long. Tear a standard sheet of sandpaper into quarters and wrap the paper around the block.

Sand curved surfaces by hand. Hold the sandpaper in the palm of your hand, allowing it to conform to the shape of the wood.

Electric Sanders

Electric sanders make a tedious job bearable. They get the work done faster and more consistently than most of us can do by hand. There are three types of electric sanders to consider—orbital, random orbit, and belt.

Orbital sanders (A) are primarily finishing sanders. They vibrate in an orbital pattern and remove small amounts of wood at a time. They are excellent for refinishing projects where the wood has been sanded thoroughly and all you have to do is sand lightly. However, they tend to leave telltale swirl marks that show up when the finish is applied. To counter this, sand by hand for a final pass.

Random orbit sanders (B) are similar to orbital sanders but are more aggressive. While the sanding pad vibrates in an orbital pattern, the entire pad spins in a random pattern. Random orbit sanders are less likely to leave swirl marks on the wood. These sanders offer the best combination of power and finesse and will conquer almost any sanding task.

Belt sanders (C) are the brutes of the family. Unless you have a great deal of skill, don't invite them to the party. They often sand wood more quickly than you want; and it's easy to ruin a project, especially a veneered one, with a belt sander. They're more suited to carpentry than to refinishing work.

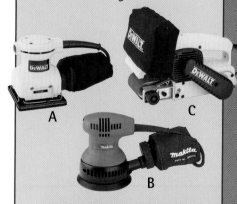

Chapter 17

Applying Furniture Finishes

Applying stain and a clear finish is a classic approach to finishing furniture.

To Stain or Not to Stain?

While paint covers the wood, a clear finish draws attention to the beauty of the wood. Staining changes the color of the wood, while leaving the character of the material intact. Many contemporary furniture designs don't use stain at all, but let the natural beauty and color of the wood shine through a clear finish.

To help decide which approach is best for the piece you plan to finish, examine the entire piece carefully. If it was previously stained, the remaining stain is likely to be uneven. Furthermore, old furniture was often made with two or more species of wood, all of them stained the same color. Either of these conditions suggests restaining the piece.

If you consider staining a piece that wasn't originally stained, study the surface carefully. Stain will highlight dents and dings that even a thorough sanding beforehand isn't likely to solve; the damage is usually too deep. If the piece is old, the dents and dings may add to its character. If the piece is new, they may detract—it's better to apply a clear finish.

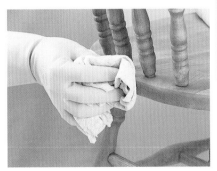

Furniture Finishing

Applying Wood Stains

Wood stains change the color of wood, making lighter woods look darker. Darker woods tend to look richer, more refined. People have stained wood as long as they've made furniture. With a wood stain, inexpensive or plain-looking woods, such as pine, poplar, or maple, can be made to look like walnut, mahogany, or ebony. Most wood can be made to look more even in color and consistent in grain with a wood stain.

Basically there are two types of wood stain: those that use a pigment and those that use a dye. Dye stains are typically more powerful because they penetrate more deeply into the wood. Most stains available to consumers, however, are pigment stains. They are easily distinguished because some of the pigment settles to the bottom of the can and needs to be stirred well before using.

Recently, water-based stains have come onto the market. Their advantages include easy water cleanup, lower odors, and faster drying times. However, they are more expensive, less widely available, and offered in fewer colors. Because they raise the grain more than oil-based stains, to use a water-based stain effectively you should raise the grain first (see "Sanding," page 354), then do a final sanding before applying the stain.

Water-based stains are available in pure, bright colors—red, green, and orange, for example. They work well for accenting details along with other wood stains. There are also several products that combine a stain and polyurethane in one can. These are meant to be brushed on like a varnish, not rubbed in like a stain, because the color sits on the surface rather than penetrating into the wood.

Water-based or oil-based, stain provides wood color that isn't there. Woods such as pine or maple can be the color of walnut or cherry. Wood that varies in hue can be made the same homogenous color.

Applying wood stain is easy. Simply wipe or brush it on, let it soak in for several minutes, then wipe away the excess with a clean cloth. If the color is not dark enough, apply more stain. Let the stain dry thoroughly before applying a clear top coat of finish. Stains seal the wood, but aren't a complete finish—follow up with one of the clear finishes suggested on the following pages.

Some woods stain more evenly than others. Softwoods with inconsistent density, such as pine, tend to get blotchy. For better results, first apply a stain controller or wood conditioner. (The name varies from manufacturer to manufacturer.) These products seal the wood slightly and limit the amount of stain that gets into the wood, evening out the differences in density.

Gel stain, a thick-bodied form of pigment stain, is perhaps the quickest and easiest solution to the blotching problem. It reduces blotching because it penetrates less than regular pigment stains. Gel stain is readily available.

Applying Wood Stains

STUFF YOU'LL NEED

✔ Wood stain
✔ Sandpaper
✔ Tack cloth
✔ Paintbrush
✔ Clean cotton cloths

Refinisher's Secret

Always sand in the direction of the grain. Sanding across the grain leaves scratches, like these, that show up when stain is applied.

1 **Sand thoroughly.**
Whether you work with refinished wood or new wood, sanding is essential. Sand with the grain, starting with 120-grit on refinished pieces. (Start with 80-grit on new wood, and then treat the wood as if you're refinishing it.) When you have removed imperfections and sanded the entire surface thoroughly, wipe off the dust and all loose sandpaper grit. Sand with 180-grit until you've removed all the marks left by the 120-grit. Brush clean.

2 **Wet the wood to raise the grain.** If you don't raise the grain now, the stain will raise it later. Resanding to get the wood smooth again removes much of the stain. To avoid this vicious cycle, wipe down the piece with a wet rag before staining, let it dry, and sand with 180- or 220-grit paper. Remove dust with a tack cloth.

Dealing with Dents

Even minor, barely visible dents are painfully obvious after finishing, especially if you stain. Most dents can be steamed away with a hot iron and a wet rag. Set the temperature on the iron to high and dampen a clean cloth with water. Lay the cloth flat on the dent and apply the iron for several seconds. The steam raises the dented wood fibers back to the surface of the wood. Sand the area after the wood has dried.

Furniture Finishing

Applying Wood Stains 357

Applying Wood Stains

3 **Apply conditioner and stain.** Some woods, such as cherry and pine, turn blotchy when stained. Others, such as oak, maple, and walnut, don't. If you work with cherry or pine—and aren't using a gel stain—apply a commercially available stain conditioner. It seals the wood, preventing the uneven absorption that causes blotching. If you use a gel stain, you can apply it without applying a conditioner. Whatever wood you work with, it's less important how you get the stain onto the wood—cross grain or with the grain—just get on plenty.

4 **Wipe away excess stain.** Wipe off the stain with a cotton cloth—old T-shirts work well. Again, it doesn't matter how you wipe off most of the stain, but do wipe the last strokes with the grain.

If the stain has dried too much, it will be difficult to remove. Loosen it by applying more stain and rubbing vigorously. If it dries hard, paint thinner will loosen it.

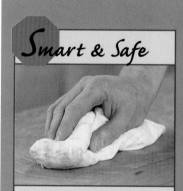

Smart & Safe

Get rid of those rags. Oil-based stains and finishes turn rags into a fire hazard. As the rags dry, the oil generates heat. In a very short time, it generates enough heat to set the rag and any remaining finish on fire. Do not throw finishing rags into trash cans. Instead, soak the rags in a bucket of water, then let them dry outdoors, draped over the edge of an empty bucket, a sawhorse, or the clothesline. After they are completely dry, throw them out.

Applying Varnish

Varnish, a mixture of oil and resin, dries to a warm and long-lasting luster. Varnishes are flexible as well as water resistant and alcohol resistant, making them versatile for use on almost any furniture project. Heavy-duty, "marine" varnishes are formulated for use on outdoor furniture and woodwork.

Although traditional varnishes are available, polyurethane is the varnish of choice. It's less expensive, easy to apply, and faster drying than its predecessors. Polyurethane is a varnish that is also available in a water-based form, which is clearer and easier to clean up.

Varnishes are brushed on and left to dry; the brushing technique and the quality of the brush are both important. Several light coats are better than one or two heavier coats. Always brush in the direction of the grain. Use a high-quality, natural-bristle brush designated for oil-based varnish.

For small projects or those with many surfaces, such as chairs, consider polyurethane in an aerosol can. It's easier to apply and there's no brush to clean up. With a spray, apply several light coats rather than one or two heavy coats. If the spray runs or sags, go over the area with a disposable foam brush to pick up and to even out the finish.

Varnish ranks as the most durable furniture finish. It protects the wood with a hard surface that brings out the color and figure of the wood.

Because it dries slowly, varnish picks up dust from the air. To minimize this, work in a clean room and refrain from stirring up any dust while your project dries. Allow the recommended drying time, and then sand the surface lightly with fine sandpaper (280- or 320-grit). This will knock off much of the dust and flatten the varnish for the next coat.

After the last coat of varnish dries, polish the surface with paste wax and a clean rag. Buff to a satiny smooth finish with a little wax and #0000 steel wool.

Applying Varnish

STUFF YOU'LL NEED

✔ Varnish or polyurethane
✔ China bristle brush
✔ Sandpaper and sanding block
✔ Paste wax
✔ Soft cloth
✔ #0000 steel wool

1 **Varnish the horizontal surfaces.** Brush on the varnish, working in the direction of the grain and applying a thin coat. After it dries, apply two more coats. Several light coats look better than one heavy coat.

2 **Even out the coat.** When you work on a broad, flat surface—such as a table—apply the varnish, and then go over the entire surface with long, light strokes to even the coat. Work quickly with water-based polyurethane so that it doesn't dry as you brush. Remember to work in the direction of the grain.

Smart & Safe

Polyurethane: Water-Based or Oil?

Due primarily to environmental concerns and worker safety issues, manufacturers have developed water-based polyurethanes as an alternative to oil-based versions. Water-based polys dry more quickly and can be recoated sooner than oil-based ones. Water-based polys emit fewer odors and the brushes clean up in water.

There are disadvantages, however. Because water-based versions dry more quickly, it is more difficult to evenly brush on a large surface. Also water-based polys have a reputation for less durability.

One last point: Oil-based polys make the wood look darker or yellow over time. Water-based coats are clear.

3 **Varnish the vertical surfaces.** To prevent runs and sags, it's especially important to apply a light coat to vertical surfaces. Work from top to bottom in order to clean up drips as you brush. Check a few minutes later to brush away sags that may have developed.

Sandpaper grits range from 60 to 2000. The coarsest you are likely to use is 80-grit, which is used on raw wood. Follow up with 120, 180, and perhaps 220. On finishes, start with 220 and follow up with 280, 320, and perhaps 400. Some pros say there's no point sanding past 280; others like to sand to 400. Experiment to see which sandpaper you prefer.

4 **Sand the first coat and apply a second coat.** When the varnish is dry, sand the surfaces lightly with 220 or finer grit paper; then apply another coat of varnish. Let it dry, and sand the surface. If the surface has picked up dust, sand with 220-grit paper. If it's smooth, use 320- or 400-grit paper.

5 **Apply a third and final coat.** Brush on the third coat as you did the first and second coats. After it dries, apply paste wax with a rag and polish to protect it. For a smooth, silky feel, buff out the finish with #0000 steel wool and wax.

Applying Shellac

Shellac is an organic finish processed from a resin secreted by a particular species of Asian insect. It's available in ready-to-use cans or in flakes that are mixed with denatured alcohol. Natural or "amber" shellac gives the wood an orange tone, while blonde, white, or clear shellac is nearly colorless. Ready-mixed shellac is widely available in paint stores and home centers and is well-suited for homeowner use. Shellac flakes are not widely used these days except by very particular refinishers. (If there's a difference, it's very slight and why mix when you can buy ready-made?) They can be found in specialty paint stores or at woodworking supply companies.

Shellac is a brushed-on finish that dries more quickly than varnishes. This makes it useful for applying several coats in a short time. It's relatively low in odor, both wet and while curing, which makes it good for sealed in areas such as inside cabinets. Shellac is not resistant to alcohol, so it is not a good choice for tabletops and counters.

Brush on the shellac in the direction of the grain. Because it gets tacky quickly, move briskly over an area. After coating a broad, flat surface, go over the entire surface with long, light strokes to even the coat. When dry, sand lightly with 220 or finer grit paper, then recoat.

Furniture Finishing

Applying an Oil Finish

Varnishes and oil finishes are mixtures of oil and resin, except oil finishes are mostly oil. The practical difference is that varnish creates a film on the surface of the wood, while oil finishes penetrate the surface of the wood. Even after several applications of oil finish, the surface film is negligible.

Although varnishes are more durable and resistant to general wear and tear, oil finishes are easier to apply and bring out more of the natural beauty of wood. Additionally, oil finishes are easier to repair or refurbish by simply applying another coat and buffing the wood dry.

Linseed oil and tung oil are the two oils commonly used for finishes. "Boiled" linseed oil (not raw linseed oil) is the type used for furniture finishes. It's not actually boiled (and don't try boiling your own, as it's extremely flammable). "Boiled" refers to the dryers that have been added in order to speed the curing time from several days to 24 hours. Tung oil takes slightly longer to cure than boiled linseed oil and also may be more protective.

In addition to these oils in their pure forms, many finishes claim to be tung-oil or linseed-oil finishes but actually are souped-up oil finishes. Read labels to determine which one to purchase. If the finish contains ingredients such as thinners, which affect the ease of application, and resins, which affect the ability to build up a film, it's been souped-up. It may or may not be better than the pure stuff—the only way to find out is by trial and error.

Whether you choose an oil finish in its pure form, the application is the same: Rub or brush it on, let it soak in, and wipe away the excess.

Oil finishes soak into the wood, leaving a thin protective coat that creates less sheen than varnish. They're a traditional finish that is convenient to apply, especially in dusty furniture shops. Spruce up the finish years later by applying a new coat.

ꟿꟿꟿꟿꟿꟿꟿꟿꟿꟿꟿꟿꟿꟿꟿꟿꟿꟿꟿꟿ

STUFF YOU'LL NEED

✔ Oil finish
✔ Brush
✔ Rags

Smart & Safe

Oil-soaked rags are a serious fire hazard. The oil generates heat as it dries—enough heat to set fire to the rag and whatever finish remains on it. To dispose of oil-soaked rags, soak them in a bucket of water; then hang them over a bucket or outdoor line until they dry. After they are completely dry, throw them out with the trash.

1 **Apply the finish.** It doesn't matter how you get an oil finish on the wood—wipe it on with a rag, brush it on, even pour it on and spread it around with a spatula. Don't be stingy; get the wood really wet. The first application will soak in quickly, and dry spots may appear in a few minutes. Wipe more finish over the bare spots as part of this first application. Keep the wood wet with oil for 10 to 15 minutes.

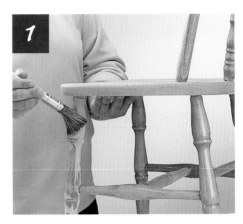

2 **Wipe off the excess.** Let the finish get a bit tacky, and then wipe off all the excess with soft cloths or paper towels. It's essential to get all the finish off and leave the surface dry. Any remaining finish will take too long to dry and will get sticky and dusty as it dries.

Vigorously buff dry the surface, wiping in the direction of the grain and removing any residue. Sometimes the wood pores will emit some of the finish back onto the surface of the wood after it has been wiped dry, so wipe it down a second time 10 to 20 minutes after the first wipe-off.

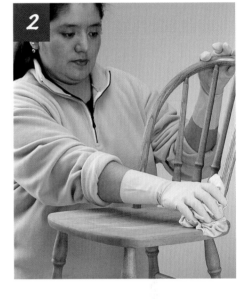

3 **Apply a second, and then a third coat.** Apply and rub out each coat the same as you applied the first coat. Sanding between coats is not necessary with a wipe-on finish, primarily because it doesn't pick up dust as it dries.

Making Your Own Oil Finish

Homemade wipe-on oil finishes have been around a long time. Recipes have been passed down and guarded jealously by furniture refinishers. There's no secret to mixing your own oil finish, however. In addition to one of the oils (boiled linseed or tung) add a thinner (turpentine or paint thinner) and a resin (polyurethane or varnish), to create your own oil-based finish. The proportions are not critical. Start out with equal parts of each ingredient; increasing the amount of thinner makes it easier to wipe off the finish and less likely to build up a film. Increasing the varnish or polyurethane makes it thicker and harder to wipe off, and builds a film more quickly. This basic finish is sold commercially under several names, including wiping varnish and wipe-on polyurethane.

Furniture Finishing

Two-Coat Faux Finishes

Painted furniture finish has a complicated history. Originally, painted finishes were put on common woods, such as pine, poplar, or maple. The grain and pattern in these woods weren't considered particularly attractive, and paint provided good protection, an easy-to-clean surface, and color. Before electricity allowed homeowners to balance the light levels, furniture color created a cheery and comfortable atmosphere.

The two-coat finishes in this chapter build, in part, on this tradition. They create the look of furniture that was painted, repainted, weathered, and worn. The finishes here also build on a tradition that grew alongside the utilitarian tradition—painting plain woods to resemble other woods or materials. The technique was prevalent where traditional cabinetmakers worked in utilitarian woods. With paint, their products took on the appearance of more expensive woods, and even of tortoise shell. Faux finishes were popular in the city, too, where simple woods made up much of the furniture for the working class. For society, the illusion could be even more complete—leaf-thin sheets of gold were applied over wood carvings and moldings for opulence and to project a sense of wealth.

The color palette for the furniture painter is as vast as the palette of the artist who works on canvas. The furniture painter who copies the grains and patterns in different species of wood works in the colors of nature.

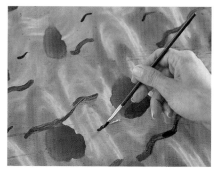

Two-Coat Paint Finishes

Refinish antiques or make new pieces look like antiques with the many techniques and materials available. Sponging, antiquing, and crackling are effective treatments for unfinished pine and other furniture. Invest a few dollars and a little time to create a look to match your style.

Each of these finishes is a two-coat process; each coat is a different color. After the base coat dries, a second (and sometimes a third) color is applied over it.

Like most painting techniques, sponging, antiquing, and crackling began as specialty oil or lacquer finishes. Glazes and crackle mediums are available for easily applied latex-based paints. The finish begins with sanding, cleaning, and applying a base color.

• **Sponging** is the process of painting over the base coat by dabbing on paint with a sea sponge. It creates a multicolor finish without the difficulty of graining or marbling.

• **Antiquing** is the process of applying layers of paint and then hand sanding through parts of the layers to reveal colors beneath.

• **Crackling** is the process of applying a base coat and covering it with a crackle medium. When you paint on a top coat, the medium causes it to crackle like a coat of old paint, revealing the color below.

Two-coat paint finishes offer versatile decorating options. Similar pieces of furniture take on three distinct looks depending on the painting technique used. From top to bottom: sponging, antiquing, and crackling.

Preparing for Two-Coat Paint Finishes
Common Steps for Antiquing, Sponging, and Crackling

1 **Sand the surface.** Do not expect paint to hide dents, scratches, or machine marks left from planing at the lumber mill. Unless you want the flaws, and you might (see "Antiquing," page 367), take the time to get the surface exactly how you want it before painting. Start with 80-grit sandpaper and move to 120-grit. Round

over the edges and corners—paint won't stick to sharp edges. The edges should feel smooth to your hand. Finish with 180-grit paper.

Use the primer to help build up the color. Have the paint store tint the primer when they tint the paint. By putting about half as much tint in the primer, you can see what has been painted when you apply the top coat. Brush on the primer, let it dry; then sand with 120-grit paper.

Good idea! **Apply a stain-sealing primer.** The primer provides a solid base for coats to follow. The stain sealers in the primer lock the resins in the wood to prevent them from bleeding through the paint and ruining your work. (Latex-based sealers sometimes allow the resins around knots to bleed through. Get an oil-based primer; finish coats can be latex.)

2 **Apply the base color.** The base color is the coat of paint that peeks through subsequent colors to create the desired effect. Choose a traditional color scheme from the color palette, right, or experiment with your own combinations. Buy the paints for the entire color scheme from the same manufacturer.

3 **Before painting, wipe off all dust with a damp rag.** Brush on the base color. If the color looks good when it dries, you may not need to apply a second coat of the base. If primer shows through or if the color isn't as dark as it should be, however, sand the surface with 180-grit sandpaper and apply a second layer of base color. Once it dries, apply the finish of your choice.

STUFF YOU'LL NEED

✔ Stain-sealing oil-based primer
✔ Latex paint in chosen base color
✔ Natural-bristle brush for oil
✔ Synthetic-bristle brush for latex
✔ 80-, 120-, 180-grit sandpaper
✔ Tack cloth

Colors That Work Together

Night Sea over **Sashay Red**

Pine Song over **Sashay Red**

Pine Song over **Vermouth**

Chaste over **Sashay Red**

Moondrop over **Vermouth** over **Night Sea**

Ink Black over **Sashay Red** over **Gaucho**

Antiquing

In the 19th century, most, if not all, furniture sported a coat of bright paint to bring color into the home. When its age began to show, the piece would be repainted—often in another color. Paint was the major redecorating tool of the time, just as it is today. Continued use caused the original color to wear through in exposed places, and that's what we simulate when we "antique" a piece of furniture. It's easy to do—apply two (or three) coats of paint, distress, and sand the piece to simulate everyday wear and tear. **Choose your color scheme,** then sand, prime, and apply the base color following the instructions on page 366. Then you're ready to begin antiquing. Dings and chips are common on the surfaces of old furniture, so begin by distressing the surface.

1 **Distress the surface.** Put a combination of old and new keys on a large key ring. The variations will help to vary the texture. Holding the keys by the ring, randomly bounce them against the surface to simulate wear. Make a few scratches with a coin or a nail; scrape off some paint by dragging the edge of a knife across a couple of spots. Once the piece is properly distressed, resand to simulate more wear.

Distressing imitates the effects of real-life wear and tear. Tabletops are scuffed and scratched by knives, silverware, plates, dishes, and pans; table and chair legs are bumped together, causing scratches; paint on chair seats and backs are worn away with use. Sand sparingly to imitate wear; sand through paint to the wood in spots that typically receive the heaviest wear, such as edges, corners, and knob and handle areas.

Good idea! ←

2 **Apply, then distress the top coat.** The color of the top coat contrasts with the base coat. Brush on the top coat, let it dry, and then distress this coat, using the techniques used previously. In occasional spots that would have received a lot of wear, sand through to the first coat, and then sand through part of the first coat to reveal the wood. Elsewhere, sand through the paint just enough to reveal the first coat. Repeat, if desired, with a third color and distress it, also.

STUFF YOU'LL NEED

✔ Latex paint for base color and top coat
✔ Synthetic-fiber brush
✔ 80-, 120-, 180-grit sandpaper
✔ Several keys attached to a large key ring

✱ Designer's Tip

Go easy when you distress wooden furniture. Working slowly allows you to see and re-create the effects of time and hard use. You can always intensify or add a dent or a scrape. No matter how much fun it may seem at the time of distressing, it takes time and effort to sand out the results of aggressive thumping and banging.

Finisher's Secret

Many people discover scratches in a furniture piece after they've painted it. They have usually done a good job of sanding, but did not sand in the direction of the grain. Sanding against the grain scratches the wood, and paint magnifies every little mistake. Once that happens, you can either learn to like the scratches, or strip the piece and resand with the grain.

Furniture Finishing

Antiquing **367**

Milk Painting

Before Country was a decorating style—when it was a place where people lived, worked, and farmed—there was milk paint. An ancient paint formula made with real milk, it was commonly made and used in country settings—"down on the farm," where milk was plentiful. Milk paint is made by mixing milk with lime, clay, and earth pigments, such as ochre, umber, and iron oxide. Proteins in the milk make the paint bind well to most surfaces.

Now that Country is a style, milk paint has made a comeback, and you no longer have to make your own. Milk paint powder is available from several mail-order companies. Just add water and get out the paintbrush. You can smell the nontoxic and environmentally friendly milk in the mixture. It contains no hydrocarbons, petroleum derivatives, or other potentially harmful ingredients.

Sold in a broad range of colors, which are easily mixed to create custom colors, milk paint does not resemble latex or oil paint. It has a flat sheen and soaks right into the wood surface, similar to wood stain. The first coat is a primer coat that's sanded lightly before applying the second coat to get a solid color. Milk paint can take on an aged look by applying linseed oil and rubbing it down with steel wool. (Use commercially made boiled linseed oil; do not attempt to boil it yourself.)

Milk paint doesn't chip like normal paint but wears gradually through to the wood. Because you mix milk paint yourself, you can mix it as a thin wash coat or as a thicker solid color coat.

1 **To mix milk paint, put equal parts powder and water in separate containers.** Pour the powder into the liquid to avoid lumps. Mix the paint for 2 to 3 minutes with a paint stirrer (or an old eggbeater). Let the paint stand for another 10 to 15 minutes, while the bubbles escape and the paint thickens.

2 **Apply milk paint with a synthetic-bristle brush.** Because it soaks into the wood, work quickly to achieve even coverage. The first coat may look blotchy, much like a coat of primer looks. The second coat conceals the primer. If you mix more than you need for the first coat, put it in a sealed jar and store it overnight in the refrigerator. After more than one night in the fridge, or if left unrefrigerated, the milk paint goes bad—the same as fresh milk turns sour.

3 **Milk paint dries quickly, and usually can be recoated in an hour.** Sand the first coat very lightly with 220-grit sandpaper. Look for blotches of powdered paint—where too much paint settles—and sand them away. Remove the dust, and apply the second coat.

Depending on how the piece will be used, you may want to seal in the milk paint with a clear top coat. Spills will leave a mark on a milk-painted surface, so anything subject to spills—tables, kitchen cabinets, dresser tops—should receive a clear top coat. A coat of polyurethane or shellac works well.

Sponging

Sponge painting, a technique for applying color over a base coat, achieves a multitone finish. A sponge-painted surface has a subtle and natural character that is more interesting than a plain-painted surface. It's not used to imitate a particular effect but suggests fabric, stone, leaves, or a cloud-filled patch of sky. Commonly used on walls, sponging also works well on furniture—especially to differentiate one surface from another.

Though you can sponge on a finish with plain paint, it works better when a glazing liquid is mixed with the paint. The glazing liquid has more body than paint and gives the sponged surface more depth and texture. It also makes the mixture workable for a longer period of time than plain paint. Follow the manufacturer's instructions for mixing the glazing liquid and paint.

A natural sea sponge works best to apply the glaze mix, although a synthetic sponge also can be used. Choose one that fits comfortably in your hand.

1 Mix the paint and glaze. Glaze may be white or translucent—mix four parts glaze to one part paint to achieve the color you want. To keep the color constant, mix enough to do the entire job. The directions on the label will give you an idea how much you need for a specific area. Once you mix the glaze, pour into a flat container.

2 Sponge on the glaze. Dampen a sponge in water to help it absorb the glaze. Dip the sponge in the glaze and paint mixture, and then dab it on a paper plate or paper towel to remove the excess. If the paint drips when you apply it, dab more onto the plate. Apply the paint with a light touch. Work in random patterns or in rows, and rotate the sponge so that the pattern constantly changes. Cover a 4×4-foot section, and do the edges last so that they're wet and blend easily into the next section. After you finish each section, stand back to look at your work. If you see lines or patterns, blot on a little more glaze to break them up. Apply the next section, working from the wet edge.

3 Add a second color. If you apply a second color, wait at least 48 hours for the first coat of glaze to dry thoroughly. Sponge on the second color the same as you applied the first.

STUFF YOU'LL NEED

✔ Choice of paint colors
✔ Glaze
✔ Mixing bucket
✔ Synthetic-bristle brush
✔ Sea sponge
✔ Paper plate or paper towel

Wisdom of the Aisles

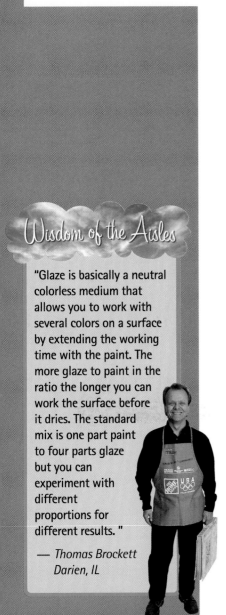

"Glaze is basically a neutral colorless medium that allows you to work with several colors on a surface by extending the working time with the paint. The more glaze to paint in the ratio the longer you can work the surface before it dries. The standard mix is one part paint to four parts glaze but you can experiment with different proportions for different results. "

— *Thomas Brockett*
  Darien, IL

Crackle Finishing

Often the top coat of paint on an old piece of furniture crackles with age and allows the previous layer of paint to peek through. Reproduce this look by painting a "crackle medium" over a base coat, letting it dry, and then applying a top coat. This effect, once used only by professional finishers, is now simple to recreate using latex-based crackle medium. Buy the same brand paint and crackle medium because the two usually are formulated to work together. Begin by applying a base coat and letting it dry.

STUFF YOU'LL NEED

✔ Choice of latex paints
✔ Crackle medium
✔ Water-based polyurethane varnish (optional)
✔ 80-, 120-, 180-grit sandpaper
✔ Synthetic-bristle brush

1 **Apply the crackle medium.** Once the base coat has dried, paint on the crackle medium with a brush, pad, or roller. Let it dry as recommended, usually 1 to 4 hours.

Finisher's Secret

Alter the effect of the crackle finish by wiping an artist's oil, colored wax, or wood stain into the cracks. Be sure to wipe away all the excess and let it dry thoroughly before sealing with a clear topcoat.

2 **Apply the top coat.** Use a matte or satin paint—gloss paints usually don't crackle well. The more paint you apply, the larger the cracks. Control this by the way you apply the paint. Sponging it on tends to apply less paint and results in smaller cracks. Brushing applies more paint, resulting in larger cracks. Whichever method you choose, avoid going over the same area twice; it will either fill the cracks or cause the top coat to lift altogether.

3 **Apply a clear sealer coat.** A crackle finish may need as much as a month of curing time before it can be subjected to normal use. If the surface will receive frequent use, especially if it is exposed to spills, protect it with a coat of clear shellac or water-based polyurethane. (See "Applying Varnish," beginning on page 359.)

Prep Work

As with all painted finishes, thoroughly clean and sand the surface before applying primer and a base coat of paint.

Two-Coat Graining Finishes

Faux painting common lumber to simulate expensive woods and other materials is an ancient practice. Homeowners have employed artists for centuries to duplicate delicate wood grains and shell patterns on furniture and molding. Faux graining and painting are enjoying renewed interest and respectability because of the beauty and uniqueness of the process as well as the protection of dwindling supplies of exotic woods. Additionally, faux treatments are used where authentic wood does not stand up as well to everyday use. Look closely at elegant entry doors on older homes in cities such as Philadelphia and Boston—the rich mahogany finish you see may actually be faux graining.

Creating faux wood finishes follows basic steps: Prime the surface, apply a base paint, apply contrasting color glaze, and then manipulate the glaze for the desired effect. The surprise is that no special tools are required and the artistry comes from lots of practice.

The maple, burl oak, and tortoise shell headboards, above, are faux finishes created on simple pine headboards. Create finishes similar to these with only brushes, paint, and a little practice.

Basic Faux Maple and Oak

Throughout history, oak has been the dominant lumber choice for furnituremakers. Strong and hard, its bold, open grain allows stain to contrast dark and light tones. Maple, also a dense hardwood, has a flat, subtle grain and understated character. Faux maple has a flatter and less dramatic grain than faux oak and is somewhat simpler to create. The large flat surfaces of furniture, such as tabletops and cabinet sides, are made up of individual boards glued edge to edge. Duplicate this effect by masking off board-like sections and painting them with slightly varying patterns.

STUFF YOU'LL NEED

✔ Primer
✔ Latex glaze
✔ Light or medium tan latex paint for initial glaze coat
✔ Medium brown latex paint for glaze top coat
✔ Masking tape
✔ Sandpaper
✔ Graining tool
✔ Check roller or fine-tip artist's brush

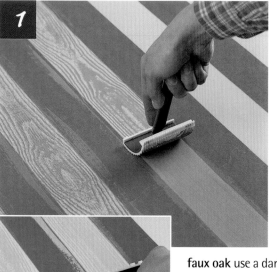

1 **Create the faux grain.** After the base coat is dry, section the furniture and grain one section at a time. On a table, for example, mark off three sections: legs, aprons, and top. On large surfaces, such as a tabletop, simulate individual boards by masking off lengthwise sections. Mix glaze and paint for the appropriate color glaze. Apply the glaze to the surface and run a graining tool through it. For **faux oak** use a darker tan glaze. Make varied grain patterns by rocking the graining tool back and forth more as you drag it through the glaze. For **faux maple** (see inset) use light tan glaze to keep the grain fairly flat and subdued. Drag the graining tool through the glaze; rock it slightly to create a flat grain pattern.

2 **Add texture for faux oak.** Add texture to the grain for a faux oak effect. Authentic oak has short grain lines running through the major grain pattern, which gives oak its distinctive appearance. Apply the short lines with a check roller, available at art supply stores. The lines also can be applied with a fine tip paint brush, which requires time and patience. Using either method, the lines should run predominantly in the direction of the primary grain pattern.

Prep Work

Sand with 80-, 120-, and 180-grit paper, consecutively. Apply primer; after it dries, apply a base coat of light or medium tan paint. Use light tan for faux maple; use medium tan for faux oak.

Burl Oak

Burl oak (also called burr oak) is obtained from "burls"—growths that develop on the sides of tree trunks. The wood has a distinctive pattern of swirls and knots completely unlike traditional oak. Burls form in many tree species, including ash, maple, walnut, and oak. Burl woods are dramatic and richly colored.

Applied primarily in veneers, burl woods are used on fine furniture. Transform a simple piece of furniture into a visual gem by applying a faux burl oak treatment.

1 **Apply a yellow-brown glaze coat.** Apply the primer and base coat. After the base coat is dry, mix paint and glaze to create a yellow-brown glaze mix. Paint the entire piece with a 2-inch brush. Form the mottled, haphazard background of the burl pattern with the base coat. After covering the surface, dash the brush every which way to get the effect shown.

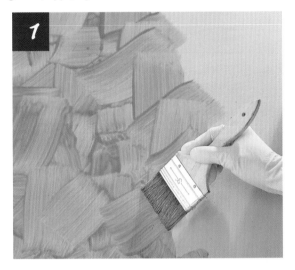

2 **Add wide veining.** While the background glaze is wet, paint broad medium to dark brown squiggles, using a 3/4-inch brush. As you paint, think of the path of a bumper car or the mark left in sand by a snake, and duplicate those effects.

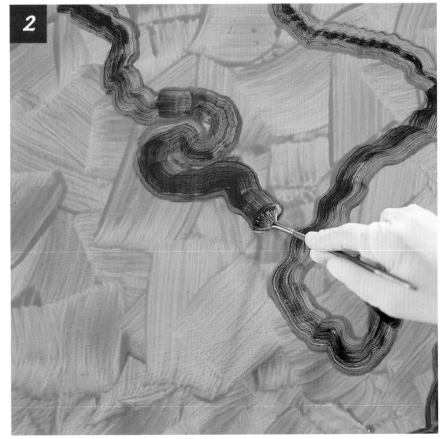

STUFF YOU'LL NEED

✔ Primer
✔ Tan latex paint for base coat
✔ Latex glaze
✔ Yellow latex paint for glaze
✔ Medium brown (burnt umber or raw sienna) acrylic paint for glaze
✔ Paintbrushes (2", 3/4", and a fine-tip artist's brush)
✔ Small piece of sea sponge

TOOL TIP

A graining tool, like the one shown in Step 1, (page 372) simplifies faux wood graining. Essentially, the tool is a stamp with a wood grain pattern. The stamp is curved to create different effects. Roll the stamp as you move it along the board to create different patterns. Rolling it slowly along the board, for example, makes widely spaced grain lines similar to those found in maple or pine. Moving it slowly as it is rolled mimics a tighter grained wood, such as oak. Rolling the pattern back and forth creates circular grain patterns that resemble knots.

Prep Work

Sand with 80-, 120-, and 180-grit paper. Apply primer; after it dries, apply a base coat of tan latex paint.

Furniture Finishing

Burl Oak   373

Burl Oak

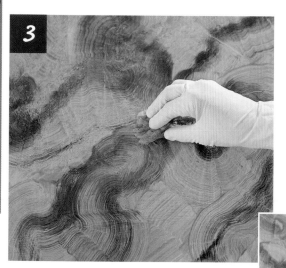

3 **Blend the veining into the background.** Use the sea sponge to swirl along the vein lines, blending them into the background pattern. Use a light touch, just enough to soften the veining and anchor it into the background glaze. Repeat the light swirling motion with a 2- or 3-inch brush.

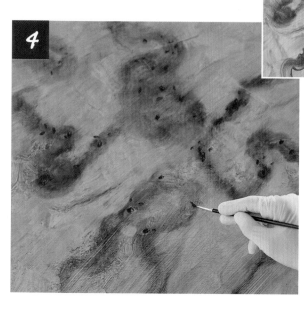

4 **Add small knot clusters.** With a fine-point brush, paint random oval or irregular shape clusters of small dark brown knots. Knot clusters are typically found in and around the veins in bunches of six or eight. Don't get carried away—a cluster or two every square foot is adequate.

5 **Blend and soften with a dry brush.** Use a clean, dry nylon bristle brush to lightly blend the veining and knot clusters into the background glaze. Follow the vein lines to pull background glaze into swirl patterns around the veins.

Wisdom of the Aisles

"A lot of people ask us why they can see scratches in a piece after they paint it. They've usually done a good job of sanding, but they usually haven't sanded in the general direction of the grain. Sanding across the grain scratches the wood, and paint magnifies every little mistake. Once that happens, you can either learn to like the scratches or strip the piece, and resand with the grain."

— *Joseph Palinsky*
South Plainfield, NJ

*Designer's Tip

The Look of Burl

Burl wood is derived from irregular tree growths. The naturally varied character of the wood means that you don't have to achieve a specific look. Use your imagination to contribute to the desired effect.

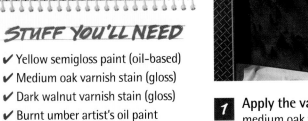

STUFF YOU'LL NEED

- ✔ Yellow semigloss paint (oil-based)
- ✔ Medium oak varnish stain (gloss)
- ✔ Dark walnut varnish stain (gloss)
- ✔ Burnt umber artist's oil paint
- ✔ Two 3-inch wide paintbrushes
- ✔ Fine point (⅛" and ¼") paintbrushes
- ✔ Dry rags

Prep Work

Paint the surface medium yellow using oil-base semigloss paint. When it dries, sand the surface with 220-grit sandpaper.

Faux Tortoise Shell

Tortoise shell is easily simulated and creates a warm, dense look. Once used for finely made decorative objects, such as combs and brushes, tortoise shell is characterized by mottled shades of yellow, amber, and brown.

1 **Apply the varnish stain.** Use a 3-inch brush to cover the surface with medium oak varnish stain (not dark walnut). Work quickly, ignoring bubbles and brush strokes in the varnish. Cover the surface with a heavy, even coat.

2 **Brush varnish in diagonal zigzags.** Use the same 3-inch brush to work the varnish stain into a series of zigzagging columns running diagonally across the surface. Don't be precise; but keep the columns parallel because subsequent steps follow the diagonals.

Faux Tortoise Shell   375

Faux Tortoise Shell

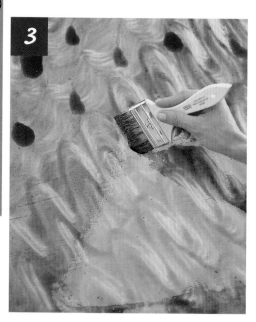

3 **Add dark walnut dabs.** Use the corner of the 3-inch brush or choose a smaller one. Using the diagonal zigzag columns as a guide, apply circular dabs of dark walnut varnish stain about 3 inches apart. Make the dabs thick enough to drag out the varnish after the next step.

4 **Paint squiggles.** Using a ¼-inch artist's brush and the burnt umber oil paint, paint a series of evenly spaced dark squiggles in between the circular dabs. Add small dabs in the remaining spaces (see inset). There should be three sizes of dark wet dabs on the surface.

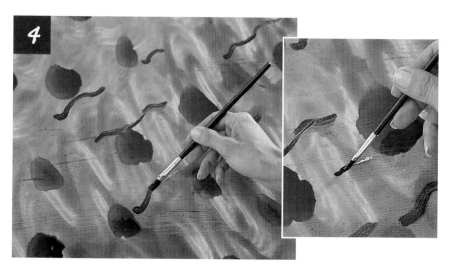

Finisher's Secret

Varnish stain dries quickly. Work quickly to get the tortoise-shell effect because after the varnish sets up, you can't rework it. This may be challenging when working on large surfaces. Work around this challenge by masking off small sections. Complete one section, let it dry overnight, remove the masking tape, and complete adjacent sections.

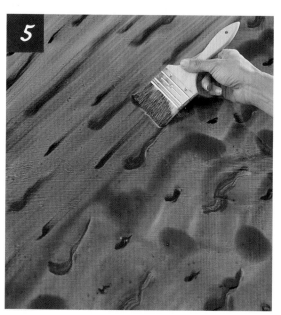

5 **Blend the design.** Following the diagonal direction of the design, drag a dry 3-inch brush across the surface. Start lightly, then add more pressure to the strokes to pull the paint and elongate the dark dabs and squiggles. Periodically unload excess varnish from the brush onto a rag to keep the brush dry.

Dealing with Drying Varnish

Good idea! ←

If you're near the final steps in the tortoise shell process and the varnish sets up too quickly, dip the brush in paint thinner and then dab it almost dry onto a rag. The paint thinner will loosen the setting varnish.

Stamping and Stenciling

Stenciling and stamping, two traditional methods of decorating furniture, are easy to master. Crafts stores carry many stencil patterns and stamps to decorate furniture, walls, and accessories. Layout is important with both techniques, so plan carefully before applying the paint. Use fast-drying acrylic paints, and seal stencil and stamped surfaces with polyurethane. See page 98 for more on wall stenciling.

6 **Dry-brush in the opposite direction.** Repeat the dry-brushing process, this time brushing across the pattern—perpendicular to the previous brush strokes. Use a very light brush stroke to add the representative iridescent quality to the dark design features without pulling them apart. Unload excess varnish onto a rag as needed to keep the brush dry.

7 **Make the final pass.** Go back and gently pull the varnish into the original diagonal direction by removing the crossing brush strokes. Don't undo the effect of the previous step. Make the brush strokes recede into the background by having them go in the same directions as the original pattern.

Furniture Finishing

Applying Gold Leaf

Applying gold and other precious metals to wood imitates the work of an alchemist's workshop. Although it is a delicate process, it's neither magical nor mysterious.

Gold leafing is ideal for special objects—picture frames or decorative trays—that aren't handled regularly, or use it to highlight small features on a larger piece, such as bedpost finials.

The metal is supplied in tissue-thin leaves that are packaged in a small book. Each leaf is separated by a piece of tissue paper to protect the fragile metal, which will crumble more easily than tissue paper or a dried leaf.

Genuine gold and silver leaf are very expensive, but composite gold leaf and aluminum leaf serve as affordable substitutes. Pure copper leaf is also available. All the metals are applied the same way: small pieces are laid onto a coat of sizing varnish and pressed smooth with a firm brush.

Golf leaf, easily applied, adds classical glamor to an old picture frame and a flea market find.

Applying Gold Leaf

STUFF YOU'LL NEED

✔ Gold leaf
✔ Sizing varnish
✔ Small brush
✔ Scissors
✔ Spray finish

Prep Work

Gold leafing requires an especially smooth surface for good adhesion. Fill any small dents or cracks with a latex wood filler. Sand the surfaces with 180-, then 220-grit paper.

Because gold leaf is slightly translucent, the base coat underneath affects the look. A red or brown paint will impart a warmer tone, white provides a cooler cast. After the base coat dries, sand it smooth with 320- or 400-grit wet/dry sandpaper.

1 Apply the gold leaf. Brush on the sizing varnish, applying no more than a few square inches at a time. Remove a gold leaf from the booklet, including the tissue paper on both sides. Position the sheet, then slip the backing tissue paper from behind before applying any pressure. Avoid grasping the metal leaf directly with your fingertips. Cut the gold leaf into smaller pieces as needed.

2 Smooth the gold leaf. The gold leaf will inevitably crinkle as you lay it down. Use a firm-bristled brush to smooth out the wrinkles in each sheet as it's laid. Add more sheets, overlapping them approximately ¼ inch with the applied sheets. (See inset below.) Brush the sheet smooth which makes the overlap virtually invisible. Continue applying strips around the frame.

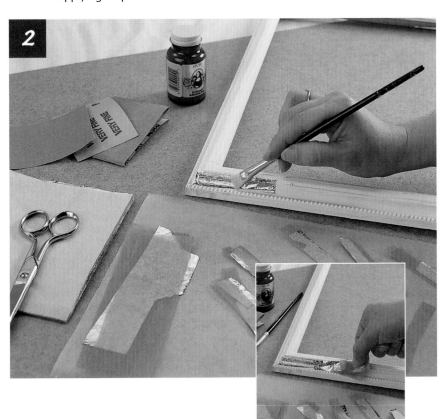

3 Apply a sealer coat. A clear top coat will protect the gold leaf from scratches. Spray finish is ideal for small gold-leafed objects. Spray two or three light coats of clear lacquer, and buff the final dry coat with a soft cotton cloth.

Furniture Finishing

Section 8

And Finally...

Accents bring focus, personality, and style to a room. Delightful embellishments that reveal taste and style, accents range from decorative faucets to wall color to polished brass lamps to roughly woven throws that cover chairs and sofas. Perfect accents also include understatements, such as the choice of unusual or handmade knobs and pulls for kitchen and bathroom cabinetry. Sometimes accents make a large statement—a new tile countertop, a stained-glass window, a reproduction of a vintage stove, or a salvaged and refinished fireplace mantel. Accents such as towel bars and shaving mirrors accessorize the kitchen and bathroom. Creatively chosen and thoughtfully used, accents provide insight into your personal style and taste while their presence completes the room.

And Finally...

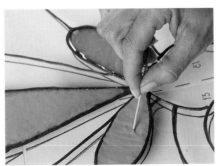

Finishing Touches

If you've attempted home remodeling, you may have noticed that one improvement makes the elements surrounding the improvement show its age. If you do something nice for a room—replace the sink, for example—you may also decide it's time for a new faucet, a new countertop, or new cabinet knobs. The same type of list applies to the kitchen and goes on and on through every room of your home.

Faucets are easy to install; knobs are easily replaced. There are many small touches that improve the room. Larger improvements—new appliances and fixtures, countertops, reproduction clawfoot tubs, antique stoves, period lighting, and specialized accessories for every room—are becoming easier to find and install. If you're interested in more than reproductions, antiques shops and salvage warehouses stock time-tested and interesting objects as well.

Little touches equal big improvements in the look and feel of a room. Some elbow grease may be all that's necessary to provide a new lease on life to a dusty, old accessory.

Replacing a Bathroom Faucet

Liven up a utilitarian bathroom sink with a new faucet. Contemporary fixtures have many styles. Especially consider reproduction faucet sets for older model sinks. The next time you face the job of fixing a dripping faucet, replace the whole unit. While you're at it, add shutoff valves to the supply lines, if they're missing. These valves are useful to turn off the water when changing out faucets.

The most difficult part of replacing faucets is working in the tight quarters under the sink. Wall-mounted and pedestal sinks make the job easier. Innovative quick-connect faucets are sold that make installation easy.

Sinks have specific hole sizes and arrangements to accommodate faucets. If you are unsure about the holes in the sink, remove the old faucet and take it in with you to shop for a new one. Standard spreads are 4 and 8 inches.

Before replacing an older sink, consider giving the fixture a facelift with a new faucet set.

And Finally...

Replacing a Bathroom Faucet

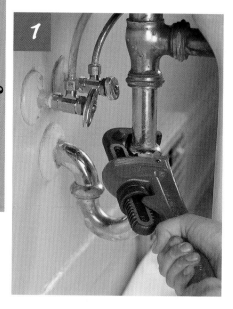

1 **Shut off the water and loosen the drain line.** If the drain is metal, use a pipe wrench to disconnect it. Work carefully to avoid marring the chrome finish. If the pipe is plastic, it probably was hand tightened. If it won't loosen, use a pair of water pump pliers.

Good idea!

The toothed jaws of a pipe wrench can damage the finish on pipes. Protect the vulnerable plating by cushioning the jaws with a rag.

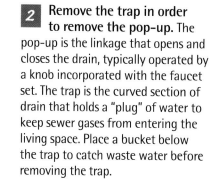

2 **Remove the trap in order to remove the pop-up.** The pop-up is the linkage that opens and closes the drain, typically operated by a knob incorporated with the faucet set. The trap is the curved section of drain that holds a "plug" of water to keep sewer gases from entering the living space. Place a bucket below the trap to catch waste water before removing the trap.

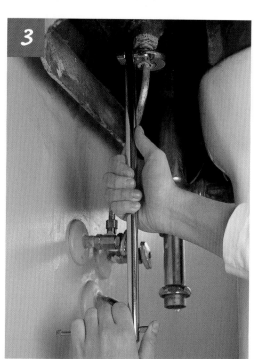

3 **Remove the old faucet.** Use a basin wrench to loosen the nuts attaching the supply lines to the sink. This wrench has a long extension to make these hard-to-access connections easier to reach. Lift the old faucet from the sink, and thoroughly clean the surface where the new faucet set will be installed.

STUFF YOU'LL NEED

✔ New faucet
✔ Pipe wrench (if necessary)
✔ Water pump pliers
✔ Basin wrench
✔ Crescent wrench
✔ Bucket
✔ Screwdriver
✔ Plumber's putty
✔ Teflon tape
✔ Rags
✔ Supply lines (optional)
✔ Shutoff valves (optional)

Prep Work

Turn off the water that supplies the sink either at the shutoff valves or elsewhere. Relieve the pressure by opening the valves on the faucet you remove. If you shut off water somewhere other than at the sink shut-off valves, open a faucet somewhere lower in the house to enable water to flow out of the pipes.

Plumber's Secret

Look at the fittings on the supply tubes to determine whether any of them are compression fittings. You'll recognize them by the little metal bead around the tubing just under the nut. Tightening the nut squeezes the bead into any seam that might leak—an act that unfortunately can't be repeated. Cut off enough of the tube to remove the bead, take it to the plumbing department, and get a same-size replacement. The fittings are cheap—get an extra one in case you have to remove the faucet sooner than expected.

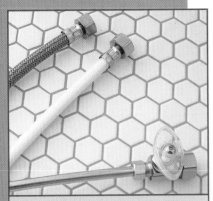

Supply Lines with Flex

Traditional supply lines are rigid metal pipes (shown above, third from the top). They often have to be cut to length and bent to accommodate particular sinks and sites. The two flexible lines shown at the top are easier to work with.

Replace the supply lines and shutoff valves when you replace a faucet. They're inexpensive, and you'll be reassured that water won't drip when you finish the project.

TOOL T|P

If you drill into tile, you'll need a masonry bit that has a carbide tip for cutting through tile. Scratch a dimple into tile with a nail to keep the bit from skating around when you begin to drill.

Just So You Know

Not all manufacturers suggest plumber's putty as a sealer. Check the instructions provided with the unit or ask a home center or plumbing supply associate for advice.

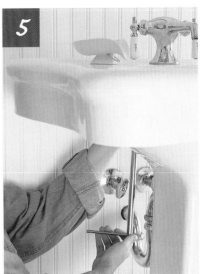

4 **Apply plumber's putty.** Work a small amount of plumber's putty in your hands until it is pliable; then roll it into a coil roughly as big around as a drinking straw. Place a ring of putty around the base of the new faucet.

5 **Attach the new faucet.** Again use the basin wrench to tighten the nuts and secure the new faucet. This will compress the putty and make a good seal with the sink.

6 **Attach the supply lines.** Before connecting rigid metal supply pipes to the new fixture, consider replacing them with up-to-date flexible lines.

7 **Install the pop-up.** Following the manufacturer's directions, attach the pop-up between the new faucet set and the drain. The linkage allows you to adjust the action so that the pop-up works efficiently. Reconnect the drain and restore the water supply.

Good idea! **If the faucet has an aerator,** unscrew the assembly and run water through it to flush out debris that has accumulated in the fixture or lines during installation.

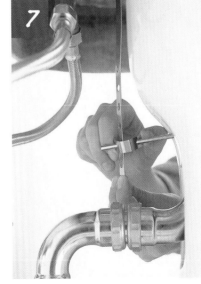

And Finally...

Installing Bathroom Accessories

Updating the bathroom is often thought of as an all-or-nothing situation. Tear out everything and start from scratch or get a new rug and leave it alone.

Many improvements can take place without getting into heavy construction and great expense. Changing or adding wall accessories, while leaving everything else intact, can make a bathroom look and feel new.

Think from the faucet out into the rest of the bathroom when you choose accessories. It's the center of the room, and the accessories should coordinate with it.

When choosing towel bars, towel rings, and soap and toothbrush holders, look for fixtures with mounting plates the same size or larger than those on the old fixtures in order to cover old mounting screw holes and wall discoloration.

Although some accessories are mounted with exposed screws, most have concealed mounting plates. In either case the process is similar—mark the mounting holes on the wall, make sure they are level, choose a wall anchor, drill the holes, and mount the accessory. Many manufacturers include mounting templates with their products.

Towel racks, towel rings, mirrors, and toothbrush and soap holders make the bathroom more functional and attractive. Big or small, accessories install similarly. Screw them into solid background and cover the screws with accessory trim.

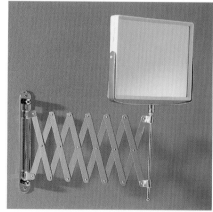

Installing a Towel Bar

STUFF YOU'LL NEED

✔ Towel bar
✔ Wall anchors and screws
✔ Level
✔ Drill
✔ Drill bit, sized to match wall anchors
✔ Screwdriver

TOOL TIP

If you drill into tile, you'll need a masonry bit that has a carbide tip for cutting through tile. Scratch a dimple into the tile with a nail to keep the bit from skating around when you begin drilling.

1 **Mark centerlines for the mounting plates.** Position the towel bar and make a light pencil mark at the center of each mounting plate to mark its location on the wall. Level the bar and trace lightly around the bottom of the mounting plates to mark the towel bar height.

2 **Mark holes for mounting plate.** Remove the mounting plates from the towel bar and align one of the plates with its pencil line. Trace around the holes in the plates to mark the location of the screw holes. Repeat with the other plate, drill for the screws or anchors, and install the plate.

3 **Install the rack.** Once the mounting plates are on the wall, place the towel rack over them, and attach the rack to the plates—usually with a small screw at the bottom of the rack.

Wall Anchors

Don't nail or screw directly into drywall or plaster. Use anchors to secure the hanging fixture and follow the manufacturer's advice to choose the right anchor.

When you hang fixtures, shelving—or anything else—the first task typically is to locate something solid to screw into, usually the studs behind the wall. If you're lucky, the studs will be in the right place; it's more likely that you'll have to use at least one wall anchor—hardware designed to grip tightly in drywall or plaster—because the studs aren't where you want to hang the object. If you're not sure, assume you need wall anchors. If you don't need the anchors, keep them for another job.

There are four common types of wall anchors. Each requires a predrilled hole in the wall. Read the package label or ask a salesperson to find the proper size.

To use **plastic inserts (A)**, drill a snug hole in the wall, tap the insert into the hole, and drive the screw. The screw spreads the back end of the insert apart to grip the drywall or plaster. Plastic inserts are inexpensive and simple to use.

Molly bolts (B) also expand when a screw is driven into them. The screw is part of the insert and the expanding action of the device is stronger than plastic inserts. Get molly bolts designed for the combined thickness of the wall and whatever is attached to it.

Aluminum inserts (C) are self-tapping and can be driven into drywall without drilling a hole. A specific size screw then fits securely into the threaded interior of the insert. These don't work well in plaster walls.

Toggle bolts (D) rely on spring-loaded wings that expand when pushed through a hole in the wall. They are strong, but the required hole can be large, which often means using a washer under the head of the bolt.

(A) Plastic inserts

(B) Molly bolts

(C) Aluminum inserts

(D) Toggle bolts

And Finally...

The Joys of Salvage

The special details of craftsmanship builders and homeowners once took for granted have become part of our history. Major factors in the decline have been expense, lack of skilled craftspeople, and changing tastes. As a result, tons of beautiful examples of style and craftsmanship ended up in landfills. With increased interest in architectural past, salvage shops have made a business of saving fixtures and accessories from the wrecker's ball. As appreciation for old homes has grown, so has the supply of salvaged material grown.

Small shops and huge warehouses specialize in lighting fixtures, old stoves, doors, fireplace mantels, and plumbing supplies. It would be no surprise to discover a complete Victorian dining room. Some shops carry anything they can get their hands on—from old gargoyles to stained glass. Prices vary from astronomical to bargain basement, especially if you're willing to put some energy and time into restoration.

If you're looking for objects that blend in with the local style, the first place you should look—obviously—is locally. If you live in Ohio, however, and are attempting to create a Southwestern look, finding the right salvage shop requires research. Check online, look at ads in home and shelter magazines, and contact local contractors and architects.

Part of the fun in discovering salvage pieces is searching the countryside for out-of-the-way places. Genuine articles are almost always better than reproductions—even if they require some restoration. The stories you can tell about how something old and wonderful became part of your home makes the hunt even more pleasurable.

You'll Never Know What You'll Find Until You Look

Salvage shops and warehouses are full of great period details that can make a big difference in any decorating plan.

And Finally...

Replacing a Medicine Cabinet

Most homeowners who remodel are familiar with the "one thing leads to another" phenomenon. It begins with a simple plan to replace or upgrade the kitchen sink, for example. As the project progresses, one thing leads to another, and soon the countertop, backsplash, cabinets, and who knows what else need replacing.

Projects that snowball prevent many do-it-yourselfers from completing small upgrades in bathrooms, where down time is the most inconvenient. Homeowners live with what they have until they can't stand it anymore, and then they tear out the whole room. It doesn't have to be that way. Of all the fixtures in the bathroom, the medicine cabinet is one that can be replaced without one thing leading to another. A simple change can invigorate a tired, dreary bathroom.

The conventional medicine cabinet was a tiny recessed shell with a mirrored door. Today a wider range of sizes and styles is available to choose from—many with light fixtures incorporated into the design. Installing a new medicine cabinet requires removing the old one and carefully measuring the opening in the wall, not the cabinet itself, to make sure the replacement will fit. It's imperative to note the depth of the opening as well as the height and width.

If your old bathroom needs a new medicine cabinet, it's usually just a matter of turning a few screws. Replacements come in a variety of standard sizes, one of which is likely to match the existing opening. They also come in a variety of styles, one of which is bound to suit your taste.

Replacing a Medicine Cabinet

STUFF YOU'LL NEED

✔ Medicine cabinet
✔ Electric drill
✔ Screwgun or screwdriver
✔ Level

1 **Remove the old cabinet.** If the old medicine cabinet has an attached light, turn off the power at the circuit box before removing the cabinet. Take out the mounting screws, typically in the sides of the cabinet. Slide the cabinet out of the wall. If there are wires for lighting, tilt the cabinet out at the top until the wires are accessible before disconnecting them.

Electrician's Secret

For more light in the bathroom, select a medicine cabinet with lights. You may have to run new cable from a ceiling fan or light; but after you pull out the old cabinet and expose the framing, the installation is relatively simple.

2 **Position the new medicine cabinet.** Slide the new cabinet into the opening and check the fit. The overlapping face of the cabinet should be tight against the wall. Level the cabinet.

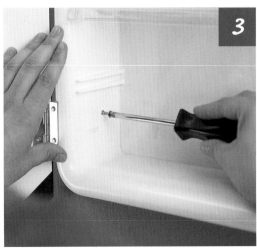

✱ Designer's Tip

For a new cabinet larger than the one you have, buy a surface-mount cabinet. They screw directly to the wall, rather than in a recess, and are available in a range of styles and sizes.

3 **Attach the cabinet to the wall.** Drive the mounting screws through the holes in the sides of the cabinet into the studs. Don't overtighten the screws. There may be space between the cabinet and the stud; do not to bend the sides of the cabinet.

And Finally...

Resurfacing a Tub or Sink

Heavy-duty enameled iron or steel tubs and sinks are designed to last a lifetime. The brittle finish, however, is vulnerable to chipping; and over the years, chemicals and minerals in the water supply stain the enamel. Before ripping out the existing fixture and installing a replacement, consider resurfacing the old clunker. Resurfacing kits use a durable epoxy resin and the project is comparable to a detailed paint job.

Resurfacing works for tubs and bathroom sinks. It is not suitable for toilets because of standing water, or for kitchen sinks because of wear and tear. Resurfacing does not restore fixture to like-new condition; the process is cosmetic and worthwhile if you don't want to replace an old bathroom sink or tub. You don't have to do the work yourself: Check the Yellow Pages under "Bathtubs and Sinks—Repairing and Remodeling" for a resurfacing firm. The bid may seem high, and you might be able to buy and install a new fixture for about the same cost. If you love your old tub, however, resurfacing adds years to its life.

Patience and an alternate means of bathing is required while you complete the project. It may not take long to prep and paint, but adhere strictly to manufacturer's recommended drying times. If the materials don't cure properly between coats, your hard work is in vain.

Working with small amounts of epoxy is not dangerous, but the amount required to resurface a tub requires that you carefully read all warnings, and wear safety glasses and a quality respirator.

Although some battle-scarred tubs benefit from a sponge and cleanser, this older tub received a relatively inexpensive facelift with epoxy enamel.

STUFF YOU'LL NEED

✔ Heavy-duty rubber gloves
✔ Safety glasses
✔ Respirator
✔ Patching compound
✔ TSP or phosphate-free equivalent
✔ Muriatic acid
✔ Fine-grit (400-600) wet-dry sandpaper
✔ Tack cloth
✔ Low-tack masking tape
✔ Resurfacing kit
✔ Universal colorant (optional)
✔ Drop cloth
✔ Trim paintbrush
✔ Lacquer thinner

Smart & Safe

Muriatic acid, another name for hydrochloric acid, is an extremely strong and dangerous chemical. Heed safety warnings on the label.

Dust-Free Environment: Use a quality respirator because the windows and doors need to be closed while you apply the paint and while it cures. Even the smallest amount of dust will mar the surface.

Prep Work

Before buying a resurfacing product, make sure the tub or sink really needs it. The first steps involve cleaning the fixture, and you may find that the sink or tub looks good after expending all that effort.

Resurfacing a Tub or Sink

1 **Repair chips and cracks.** Surfaces should be as smooth as possible because the paint does not fill in cavities. Repair cracks and chipped finish with metallic patching compound or a special-purpose tub-patching product.

2 **Clean the fixture.** Wear gloves and provide good ventilation while you're working. Clean the tub thoroughly with TSP or a similar product. Follow with a solution of muriatic acid, using it according to the label directions. Rinse well with water.

Good idea! →

If you have a fiberglass tub or shower stall that needs a beauty makeover, there are special products available to restore them, too.

3 **Sand and rinse the fixture.** To help the new finish adhere, sand enameled surfaces with wet-dry sandpaper. Rinse the fixture and allow it to dry completely.

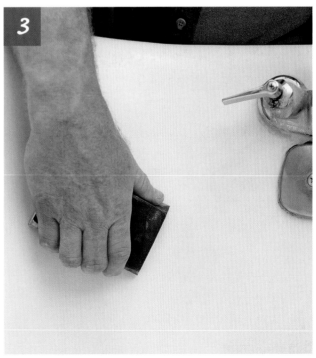

Resurfacing a Tub or Sink

4 **Pick up dust with a tack cloth.** Before applying the paint, go over the dry fixture with a tack cloth. Check that the surfaces are dust-free by running the palm of your clean hand over them.

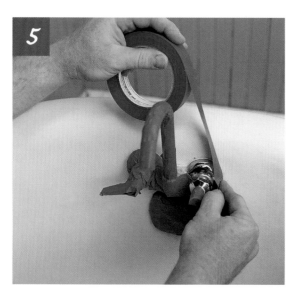

5 **Tape off faucets, taps, and drains.** Use low-tack masking tape to protect metal hardware from the new finish. (If you plan to replace the faucets, remove them before refinishing—new fixtures may may vary in size from the old and reveal unresurfaced sections of the tub after they've been installed.)

6 **Mix the epoxy.** Check the manufacturer's coverage chart to make sure you have enough product for the number of coats you plan to apply. Shake both cans and mix as directed. Depending on the brand, the mixture may have to stand a specific length of time before applying it. If you wish to tint basic white paint a pastel shade, add a small amount of universal colorant sold in paint departments. (See inset.) Generally speaking, dark shades can not be created; the epoxy absorbs only a limited amount of colorant.

To DIY or Not to DIY

Calling In a Pro

Doing it yourself is only one way to refinish your tub. Professional refinishers also will do the job, and they have more tools at their disposal. They use an acrylic finish, which is more durable than the product purchased off the shelf. It dries faster and because it's sprayed on, there are no brush marks.

Some companies put a 1/4-inch acrylic liner in the tub. The liner is made at a factory from a mold made similar to your tub. The edges of the liner are wider and longer than needed, and the installer trims them for a perfect fit against the wall. Once it's trimmed, the liner is glued in place and caulked with silicone to match the color. An added bonus: Acrylic holds heat better than cast iron, and the bath will stay warm longer.

7 Apply the first coat. Protect the floor with a drop cloth. Brush on the initial coat as directed by the manufacturer, and allow it to dry fully. To prevent dust from marring the wet paint, seal off the room during the drying period. Remember, however, to provide good ventilation while working.

Good idea! → One of the most important personal qualities for a tub resurfacing job is patience. Allow plenty of time for prep, and follow the manufacturer's directions for drying times to the letter.

8 Sand and tack the first coat. When the paint has dried completely, use wet-dry sandpaper to lightly abrade it for a second coat. Rinse the fixture and allow to dry.

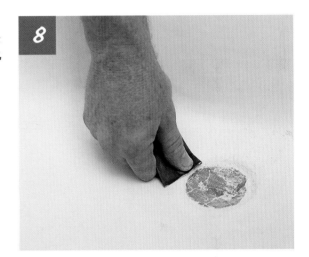

9 Apply subsequent coats. Repeat the above prep and painting procedure for one or two additional coats. Clean with lacquer thinner. Allow the new finish to dry as directed before using the tub or sink.

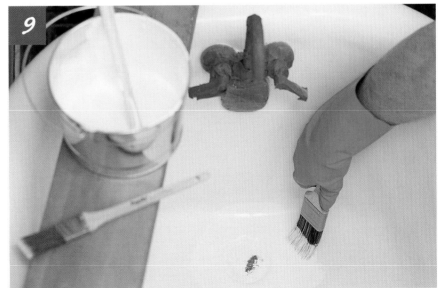

DOs and DON'Ts

Avoid abrasive cleansers in order to get more use from the new coating. In the resurfaced tub or sink, avoid using hair dye or colorful bubble bath, which may leave behind a tint.

Have some leftover paint? Stretch its storage life by placing well-sealed containers in a freezer.

And Finally...

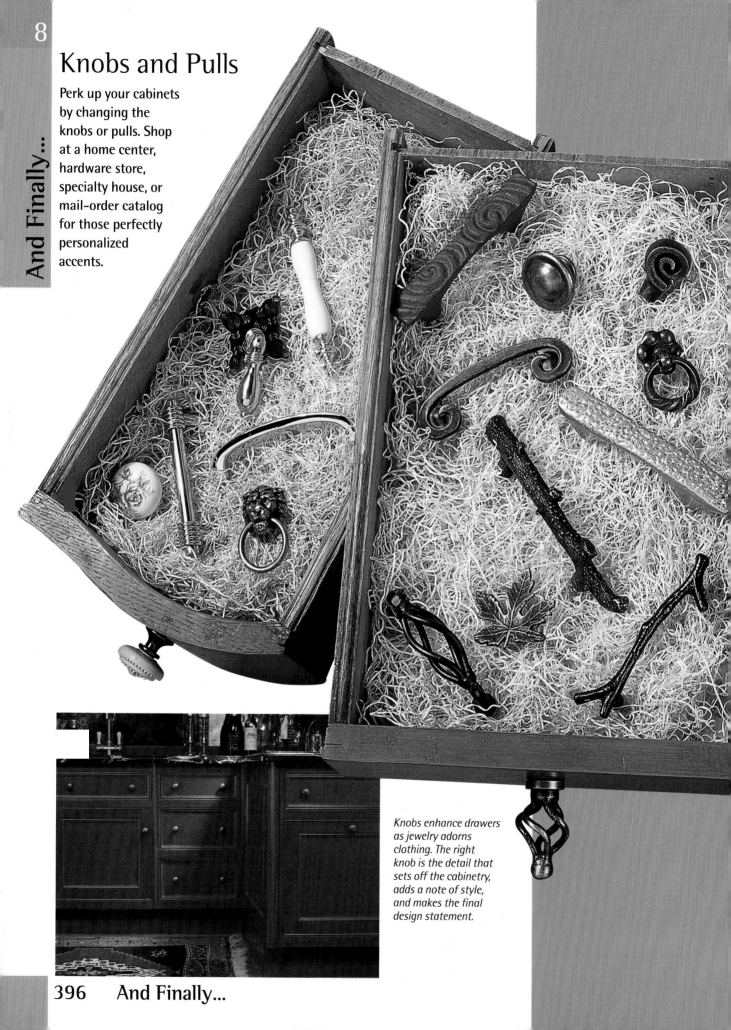

Knobs and Pulls

Perk up your cabinets by changing the knobs or pulls. Shop at a home center, hardware store, specialty house, or mail-order catalog for those perfectly personalized accents.

Knobs enhance drawers as jewelry adorns clothing. The right knob is the detail that sets off the cabinetry, adds a note of style, and makes the final design statement.

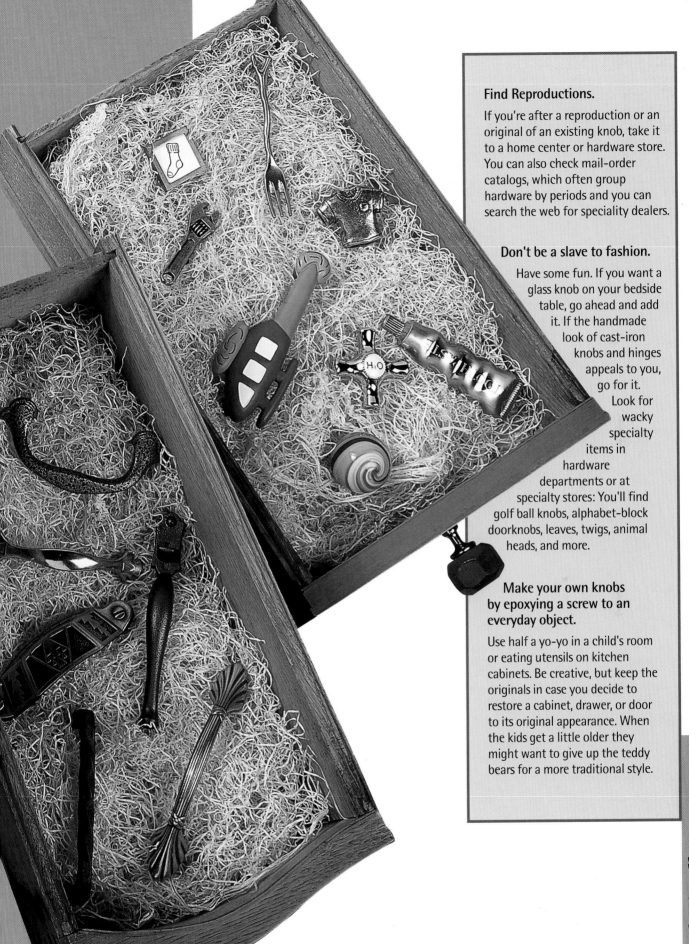

Find Reproductions.

If you're after a reproduction or an original of an existing knob, take it to a home center or hardware store. You can also check mail-order catalogs, which often group hardware by periods and you can search the web for speciality dealers.

Don't be a slave to fashion.

Have some fun. If you want a glass knob on your bedside table, go ahead and add it. If the handmade look of cast-iron knobs and hinges appeals to you, go for it.

Look for wacky specialty items in hardware departments or at specialty stores: You'll find golf ball knobs, alphabet-block doorknobs, leaves, twigs, animal heads, and more.

Make your own knobs by epoxying a screw to an everyday object.

Use half a yo-yo in a child's room or eating utensils on kitchen cabinets. Be creative, but keep the originals in case you decide to restore a cabinet, drawer, or door to its original appearance. When the kids get a little older they might want to give up the teddy bears for a more traditional style.

Vintage and Reproduction Stoves and Tubs

Even in this age of microwave meals, home cooking requires a good-quality stove. With renewed interest in large old-fashioned, nickel plated, lustrous black ranges, refurbished antiques and new reproductions are becoming the centerpiece of the kitchen. They may even change your eating habits—encouraging you to bake bread, cook stovetop corn muffins in a cast-iron skillet, or make long-simmering stews on a back burner.

Old stoves burned coal, wood, or both fuels. Later, gas-wood hybrids came along. Reproductions use electricity, natural gas, or propane, with gas, electric, or electric convection ovens. Sources for reproductions include appliance stores, the Internet, and magazines.

Coal and wood models have limited applications because of safety concerns. They also require patience. Slow to fully ignite, they continue to burn after meals are prepared, doubling as space heaters, which is welcome bonus in winter and a liability in summer.

Restored stoves can be found through the Internet and antiques shops that carry large heavy-duty items. Tracking down an old stove is only part of the challenge. Stoves in original condition have to be restored to work safely and be properly installed. A wood or coal stove dealer or the gas utility company provide the best sources for help.

Reproduction cookstoves have the heft and polish of antiques, while allowing you the modern luxury of efficient gas or electric cooking and baking.

The oven window with it's half moon shape lends a hint of Art Deco to this modern stove.

Tubs for Every Taste

When's the last time you soaked in a big bathtub?
You can buy reproduction clawfoot tubs that are deep enough to submerge in, and old clawfoot tubs are ready and waiting at architectural salvage yards throughout the country.

Before buying a clawfoot, new or old, make sure you have enough clearance to get it into the bathroom. As a test, measure the tub and make a corrugated cardboard box of that exact size, using cartons and duct tape. Carry this box along the path that the tub would follow—around corners, up stairs, through doorways. Once you're sure everything fits, the next hurdle is enlisting strong friends to get the tub to the bathroom. All tubs are heavy and awkward; older tubs are among the heaviest. (If you can't negotiate the obstacles, consider resurfacing your old tub; see pages 392–395.)

Replacement tub hardware is easy to find and install—check home centers and plumbing supply houses. Unless you already have a clawfoot in place, however, or the new tub is exactly the same size, the existing pipes in the bath are going to be in the wrong place. Moving them is potentially major work—add plumbing expenses to the cost of the job.

In early plumbing, form followed function. Pipes were exposed, as was the space beneath sinks and tubs. Sleek modern designs are more practical but less charming.

The shower stall, right, with its coordinated tile and curtains echoes the shape of the tub beneath it. Oversized clawfoot tubs such as the one on the far right with fixtures mounted in the center for easy access make for luxurious and relaxing soaks.

And Finally...

Vintage and Reproduction Stoves and Tubs 399

Tiling a Countertop

The kitchen is once again the center of social activity and interaction in the home, and the kitchen countertop is a major part of the equation. Not surprisingly, people often lavish more attention on the countertop than other elements of the kitchen. Sure, plastic laminate is functional, but it's not very distinctive. Installing a ceramic-tile countertop calls attention to the counter and creates a long-lasting, functional work surface.

Tiling countertops takes more time and effort than installing laminate countertops. Like floor tile, countertop tile is permanently installed using mortar adhesive and grout. (At least you don't have to work on your hands and knees to tile a counter.) Use any tile as countertop material—glazed, quarry, mosaic, even stone tiles such as slate or granite. You have your choice of many sizes and shapes of tile, though different sizes affect the finished appearance. Smaller tiles require more grout lines that may stain or degrade with use. Larger tiles are more appropriate for floors. Midsize tiles (4 to 6 inches) are a safe bet for countertops.

The surface below the countertop tile may be more important than the surface beneath a tiled floor. Carefully follow the steps involved in preparing the substrate (the surface below the tile) to avoid problems.

Beautiful, strong, and durable, a tile countertop is a job you can do yourself.

Tiling a Countertop

STUFF YOU'LL NEED

✔ Ceramic tiles
✔ Edge tiles or edge bead
✔ Latex-portland cement mortar
✔ Grout
✔ Grout sealer and applicator or foam brush
✔ $3/4$-inch exterior grade plywood
✔ 4-mil plastic sheeting
✔ Cement backerboard and mounting screws
✔ $1 1/4$-inch drywall screws
✔ 3-inch fiberglass tape
✔ Tile spacers
✔ Grout
✔ Drill with phillips screwdriver bit
✔ $1/8$-inch masonry bit
✔ Utility knife
✔ Notched trowel
✔ 4-inch drywall tape knife
✔ Tile cutter
✔ Tile nippers
✔ 2- or 3-foot scrap of 2x4
✔ 2-foot level
✔ Grout float
✔ Burlap

Prep Work

Conventional cement backerboard is a dark gray material encased in fiberglass mesh. It's tough to work with (heavy, rough on the hands, hard to cut and drill) but is right for the job. Use $1/2$-inch thick material.

A newer generation of backer board is typically light gray and composed of denser cement materials. It's lighter in weight and easier to work with than the conventional backerboard.

1 **Install plywood substrate.** If you work with completely new installation, the base cabinets will form the structural support for your new tiled counter. Install $3/4$-inch-thick exterior grade plywood over the assembled cabinets. Cut the plywood to fit, allowing an overhang around the exposed sides of cabinets and factoring in a tile or wood edge treatment. Screw the plywood to the cabinets with $1 1/4$-inch drywall screws. Use a straightedge to check that the plywood surface is flat, and add shims if needed.

2 **Cut out plywood for sink.** The sink cutout should be made through the plywood substrate, and then the backerboard and tile can be fit around the sink opening. New sinks are supplied with a template or measurements for the cutout. (If you are reusing your old sink, measure the old opening after you remove the sink and use that to create a template.) Position the template for the sink. Check to make sure the faucet you plan to use will clear the wall behind the counter. Mark the cutout using the template. Drill a $3/8$-inch starter hole inside the cutout near one of the corners; then cut the plywood with a saber saw.

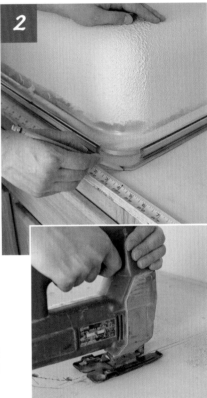

3 **Install cement backerboard.** Cut backerboard to fit by scoring one face with a utility knife, snapping the piece back along the score line, and cutting the back side with the utility knife. To cut curves around the sink, score freehand on both faces, then chip the material away with pliers. Leave a $1/8$-inch gap between pieces of backerboard, which will be filled in the next step. Predrill holes for screws every 6 to 8 inches.

The backerboard isn't applied directly to the plywood; remove the cut pieces, and staple 4-mil plastic sheeting to the plywood to protect it from moisture. Apply mortar on top of the plastic, combing it out with a $1/4$-inch notch trowel. Reposition the backerboard and screw it to the plywood with screws sold for the purpose.

And Finally...

Tiling a Countertop

4 **Tape and fill seams in backerboard.** Reinforce exposed edges of the backerboard with three layers of fiberglass tape. Then apply a 3-inch-wide layer of latex-portland cement mortar to fill the gaps between sheets of backerboard. Lay a strip of fiberglass mesh tape across the gap. Press the tape firmly into the mortar with a 4-inch drywall taping knife.

5 **Apply an edge bead.** Special edge tiles (V-cap trim) are designed to wrap around the front edge of the counter. They're rounded for a soft touch and add a professional look to the job. If you use edge tiles, dry fit them first, and cut the corner edge tiles with a miter joint. An alternative approach for the counter edge is to use a stainless steel decorative bead, as shown. Metal bead usually can be bent around corners. Nail the bead to the backerboard with galvanized nails.

6 **Cut tiles to size.** Use a standard score-and-snap-type tile cutter to make straight cuts in the tile. (If you don't want to buy one, rent one for the day at a tool rental company.) Mark the tile with a felt-tip pen and position it against the

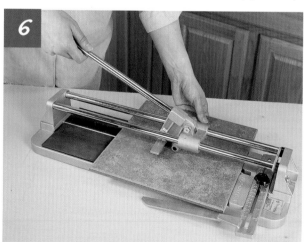

fence on the tile cutter. Hold the tile firmly and slide the scoring wheel across the tile in one continuous motion. Reposition the tool with the pressure plate flat against the face of the tile, and press down to snap the tile.

Know Your Materials

Mortar is a mixture of sand and portland cement.

Dry-set mortar is a specially formulated mixture for application over backerboard.

Latex-portland cement mortar has a latex additive, which makes the mortar more flexible, and is best suited for countertops. There are two types—one is a powder, to which a liquid latex additive is added; the other is a powder containing dry latex resin to which water is added. Both do the job equally well.

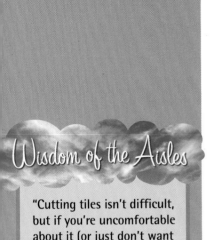
Wisdom of the Aisles

"Cutting tiles isn't difficult, but if you're uncomfortable about it (or just don't want to spend money on a one-time use of a tool) mark all the tiles that need to be cut and take them to a tile supply company or a home center with a good tile department. They usually have a tile cutter on hand and will make the cuts—for a fee. Be sure to mark the tiles carefully with the location in the layout."

— *Dale Solomon*
San Diego, CA

7 **Dry-fit tiles.** Rather than discover after laying half of the countertop tile that the tiles don't fit the way you anticipated, lay out the entire countertop before putting down the mortar. This allows you to make all the cuts in advance and to be sure every tile fits correctly. In countertops with a sink, adjust the layout to ensure the tiles are fairly even on the sides of the sink. On an L-shape countertop, start with a full tile at the inside corner to avoid having a cut tile there. Lay out all the full tiles using tile spacers to maintain even spacing. Then cut and fit all the partial tiles. Leave a 1/8-inch gap between perimeter tiles and the wall. Mark the cut tiles to remember where they go.

8 **Cut tiles around sink.** Cutting curves or notches is more challenging than straight cuts. Mark the cut with a felt-tip pen. Gradually nip off small pieces of tile with tile-nipping pliers to reach the mark.

9 **Spread the mortar.** Mix the mortar according to the label directions. Spread an even coat of mortar with a notched trowel. The mortar instructions will specify the appropriate notch size, which is determined by the size of the tile. Hold the trowel at a consistent angle (about 45 degrees) and drag it against the backerboard surface.

Good idea! → **Mixing good mortar is trial and error.** You can tell if it's the right consistency by scooping up some with your trowel and holding the trowel upside down. If the mortar runs, it's too thin. Add more powder and mix thoroughly If it's too thick, add small amounts of water until it's right.

And Finally...

Tiling a Countertop

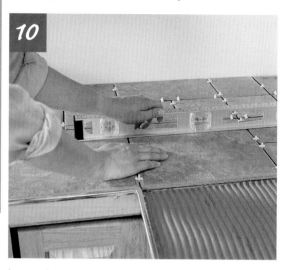

10 **Lay the tiles in the mortar.** Start laying the full tiles at the more critical areas of the layout—around the sink or at an inside corner of an L-shape counter. Work from front to back, placing as many of the full tiles as possible, then adding the partial tiles around perimeter areas. Press each tile into the mortar with a slight twisting motion. Use tile spacers to keep the tiles aligned. Level the set tiles by tapping gently on a straight piece of 2×4 set on its edge across the tile. Check for flatness with a 2-foot level.

11 **Lay partial tiles at the perimeter and around the sink.** When all the full tiles are in place, set the partial tiles and any tiles cut to fit around the sink. Use the spacers between cut tiles and full tiles and let discrepancies in spacing end at the wall.

12 **Tile the backsplash.** A tiled backsplash naturally complements a tiled countertop. A single row of 4- or 6-inch tiles is a common backsplash width. Or tile all the way up to the wall cabinets. Finish the counter first, taking the back row of tile to within 1/8-inch of the wall. Install the backsplash tiles using the same thinset mortar used on the countertop. If there are electrical outlets in the backsplash wall, cut tiles around them and add spacers (available at an electrical supply department) to project the outlets to the tile level.

✱ Designer's Tip

The tiles around your sink look best when they are the same width on all sides. The time to solve this problem is while you're laying them out. On a straight counter, lay out the tiles so that the first one is centered over what will be the center of the sink and work toward the ends. If the counter is L-shape, however, lay out the tiles with a full tile in the corner, as shown in Step 10. If placing the tile there creates problems at the sink, slightly reposition the sink opening before you cut it to make sure you have equal widths all around the sides.

Prep Work for...

Tiling the Backsplash

The section of wall against the counter covered with countertop material is called a backsplash because it protects the wall from splashes, bumps, and spills. You can make the backsplash a few inches high, or run it to the cabinets above, as shown on page 400. However you extend the backsplash, put up backerboard before you tile. Follow the same procedure as for the countertop. Put mortar directly on the wall, put backerboard over it, and screw it to the studs. Leave spaces between the edges, fill with mortar, and cover with fiberglass tape.

Dealing with ...

Plastic Laminate

To replace existing plastic laminate countertop with tile, don't tear out the laminate. You can lay tile over plastic laminate countertop—as long as there are no loose areas. Edges that have lifted should be glued down with construction adhesive and clamps. Then screw down cement backerboard and follow the steps on these pages. Tiling over existing countertop will make counter edges thicker and may affect sink and faucet installation.

13 **Tile the edge.** If you use edge bead, cut the tiles so they bridge the grout lines on the main countertop, as shown. Apply grout, put the tiles tightly against the bead, and tape them in place to hold them while the mortar dries. If you use edge tiles, you don't need to tape them because part of the tile sits on the countertop. Space edge tiles so the grout lines between them match those on the counter.

14 **Grout the tile.** After the tile has completely set (check mortar instructions), apply the grout. Mix the grout following the manufacturer's directions, and dump some onto the counter. Spread the grout using a rubber tile float. Work the grout into the joints by moving the float diagonally across the tile. Once all the joints are filled, remove excess grout by wiping diagonally with a wet sponge. Rinse the sponge frequently in clean water. Remove the excess grout from the surface of the tile, and leave the grout slightly depressed in the joints. Let the grout dry, and rub the tiles with burlap to remove the remaining grout.

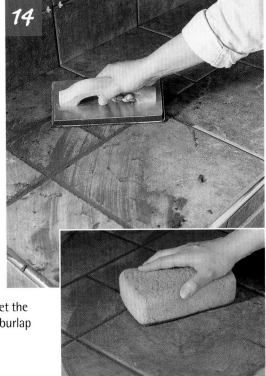

15 **Seal the grout.** Because grout is prone to staining, seal it with a silicone grout sealer after it has cured completely—about 30 days. Apply the silicone grout sealer to the grout lines with a foam brush or applicator, let it soak in for a few minutes, and wipe away the excess.

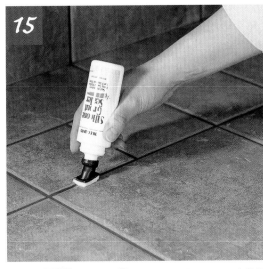

And Finally...

Stained Glass with Glazing Paints

The best windows are those with outstanding views. Most homes, however, have at least one window with a less-than-wonderful vista. These are good candidates for stained glass or (at far less cost) a technique that imitates that traditional craft—painting with glazing paint. The paint filters and diffuses sunlight pouring through the glass. Darker paint and flexible plastic strips suggest traditional leading.

You'll need a good design and a clean window that will provide a durable ground for the paint. Manufacturers caution that water-based paints will not hold up well if subjected to splashing water, heavy condensation, or long hours of direct sunlight. Use paint made specifically for the job, widely available at arts and crafts stores in kits that include several patterns.

When considering designs, keep in mind that you can leave the central portion of the window untreated to take advantage of the view. By decorating only a border, you'll also have less work ahead of you.

Stained-glass windows are a centuries-old way to turn golden sunlight into a kaleidoscope of color. For less cost, use glazing paints to turn ordinary windows into convincing versions of genuine stained glass.

STUFF YOU'LL NEED

✔ Glass paint
✔ Masking tape
✔ Black transfer paper
✔ Leading paint
✔ Pattern
✔ Scissors
✔ Tape measure
✔ Razor knife

Prep Work

Glass is not the friendliest surface for paint; it doesn't have "tooth" to help film adhere well and it subjects paint to moisture, UV light, and temperature extremes. Clean the window well before applying paint. Use low-tack masking tape to protect the window frame. If possible, remove the window from the frame to make painting easier. Throughout this project, remember that glass is fragile and that broken glass can cause injuries.

1 Draw the pattern.
Use this technique for a single large pane or for a window divided by muntins into several panes. For a divided window, choose one or more small motifs and repeat them in each pane. Get ideas for stained glass windows in books on crafting stained glass and on Victorian and Mission-style houses. Or choose a ready-made pattern from books sold with glass painting kits. Adapt a design by eliminating part or all of a border or by adding borders at top, bottom, and along the sides.

2 Attach the pattern. Tape the pattern to the outside of the pane. If the pattern is creased from folding, iron it so that it will rest flat on the glass. If you can't get to the outside of the window to attach the pattern, tape black transfer paper to the front of the window; tape the pattern on top of that, and trace the design onto the glass. This method is helpful if you work with a double-paned window that places the pattern at a distance from the inside pane of glass.

3 Make the "leading."
Areas of the design are divided with lines that resemble lead channels used in stained-glass windows. Make lines by drawing them with special-purpose leading paint on a sheet of nonstretching, nonclinging plastic wrap; then peel them off for use when dried sufficiently. Or purchase packs of ready-made plastic leading strips. Follow the manufacturer's directions for using either product.

And Finally...

Stained Glass with Glazing Paints

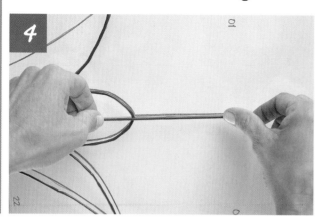

4 **Apply the leading strips.** Run the leading along the lines of the design, pressing the leading so that it adheres to the glass.

5 **Trim the strips.** Make precise cuts with a razor knife where leading courses meet. The strips should not overlap. Fill gaps with a dab of leading paint.

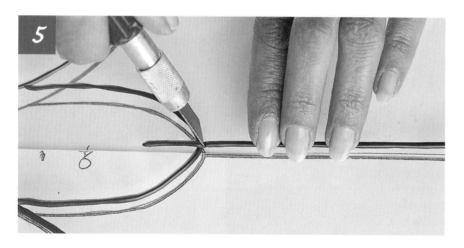

Bursting the Bubbles

Bubbles sometimes appear in the glazing paints as you apply them. In genuine glass, some bubbling is normal and is common in old window panes. If you have more bubbles than you like, pop them with a toothpick.

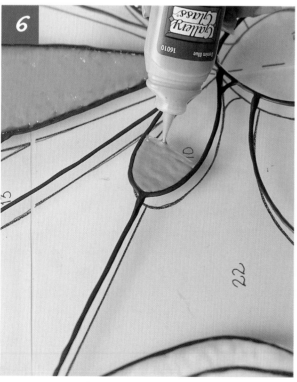

6 **Apply the paint.** Apply the glazing paint directly from the squeeze bottle. Start from the top of an area and work down, taking care to avoid puddling the paint along the bottom edge. Darken any shade by applying a second coat after the first has dried. To lighten a color, mix it with clear paint. Combine colors to make custom hues either before application or on the glass itself (see Step 7).

✱ Designer's Tip

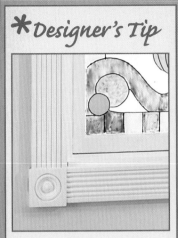

If the window generates condensation or goes through extreme temperature changes, apply the design to a panel of acrylic plastic and install it inside the window. Drill holes at the top of the panel and hang it with cup hooks, or install the panel with triangular glazier points driven into the wood of the window sash. Leave an air space between the panel and glass, and allow small gaps around the panel for ventilation.

Window Care

If your prep work is thorough, the painting should be quite durable. Clean by spraying a fine mist of plain water and going over the panes very lightly with a soft cloth. Do not use solvents.

7 Ripple the glass. To make an area ripple like traditional stained glass in cathedrals, apply the paint from the bottle so that the nozzle travels up and down within the area, leaving an uneven surface.

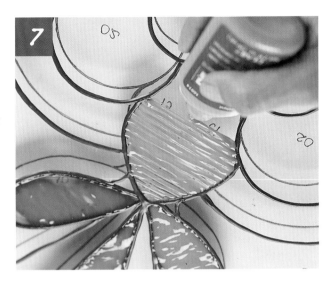

8 Marble the glass. To give an area the marbled, variable look of true stained glass, begin by randomly applying dots of a colored paint in the area. While this paint is still wet, surround the dots with white paint, allowing the paints to mix.

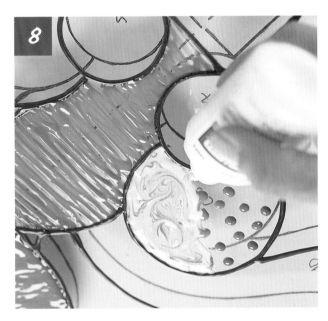

9 Remove flawed areas. This is a forgiving technique. If you don't like the look of a painted section, peel it away when it dries. Run a razor knife around the perimeter of the area, lift an edge with a finishing nail, and strip off the thin layer of paint.

And Finally...

Stained Glass with Glazing Paints 409

Index

Index 413

ACKNOWLEDGEMENTS and RESOURCES

We greatefully acknowledge the help and support of The Home Depot and the following corporations and individuals in the production of *Decorating 1-2-3*.

Photography Production: Woolly Bugger Studios; 520 East 6th, Des Moines, IA 50309; (515) 244-1140 To a great crew: Arends Productions, Lawrence L. Gilmer Builders, Anne Holtz Design, Marie McCartan, Cameron Sadeghpour, Dallas Hallam, Ann Wolf, Cindy Cohrs, Greg Scheidemann, Roger's Paint and Wallpaper, and John Hallstrom.

Special thanks to: Barbara Koller; Nathan Ehrlich; Rebecca Tainter; Ann Reissing; Hugh Miskell (The Home Depot)

Paint and Glaze: Behr Process Corporation; 3400 W. Segerstrom Ave; Santa Ana, CA 92704; (714) 545-7101; Fax: (714) 241-1002; www.behrpaint.com (All paint palettes used in this book are from Behr color sample books available by name at The Home Depot paint department.)

Wallpaper: Graham & Brown; 2031 Route 130; Suite K; Monmouth, NJ 08852; (800) 554-0887; www.grahambrown.com

Blinds: Levolor; 4110 Premier Drive; High Point, NC 87265; (800) LEVOLOR (1-800-538-6567); www.levolor.com

Frame and Panel Wainscoting: New England Classic; 465 Congress Street; Portland, ME 04101; Toll-free phone: (888) 880-6324 (NECI); (207) 773-6144; Fax: (207) 774-1685

Architectural Salvage and Reproductions: Salvage One, Inc.; 1524 South Sangamon; Chicago, IL 60608; (312) 733-0098; www.salvageone.com

Architectural Salvage Inc.; LaMill Street; Exeter, NH 03833; (802) 863-7832; www.oldhousesalvage.com

Heartland Appliances, Inc.; 1050 Fountain Street North; Cambridge, Ontario N3H 4R7; Canada; (519) 650-5775

Columns: HB&G; 1015 Brundidge Blvd.; PO Box 589; Troy, AL 36081; (334) 566-5000; www.hbgcolumns.com

Inlaid Flooring: Historic Floors of Oshkosh; 911 E. Main Street; Winneconne, WI 54986; (920) 582-9977

Speciality Doors: La Puerta, Inc. Architectural Antiques; 1302 Cerrillos; Santa Fe, NM 87501; (505) 984-8164; Fax (505) 986-5838

Laminate Flooring: Pergo, Inc.; 3128 Highwoods Blvd.; Raleigh, NC, 27604; (800) 33-PERGO; www.pergo.com

Section I - Color and Style:
Contemporary Home
Interior design by:
Projects, Kelli Linnemeyer IIDA
Teachout Building, Suite 100
500 East Locust
Des Moines, IA 50309
(515) 557-1833

Southwestern Home—Santa Fe
Interior design by:
Pamela H. Duncan
Wiseman & Gale & Duncan Interiors Inc.
150 S. Saint Francis Drive
Santa Fe, NM 87501-2445
(505) 984-8544
Pots: Lonnie Vigel
Dolls: Rhonda Holy Bear
Figurine: (Santo) Felix Lopez
Paintings in Bathroom: David Bradley
Painting in Foyer: Marcyne Johnson, Tucson
Mural: Elias Rivera

Southwestern Home—Adobe
(fireplace and nooks and crannies)
Interior Design by:
Mori Bergmeyer
Bergmeyer Manufacturing
229 North Highway 33
Driggs, Idaho 83422 (800) 348-3356
www.bergmeyermfg.com

Colonial Homes
Interior Design for both homes by :
Nancy Kalin Antique Interiors
PO Box 1
Middlebranch, Ohio 44652; (330) 877 3501
Thank you to: Robyn Stoney-Cordier (homeowner)

Country Home
Interior Design by:
HIKCHIK Design
417 Maple
West Des Moines, IA 50265
(515) 255 0588
www. HIKCHIK.com

Victorian Home Interiors
Thanks to:
Peggy and John Forbes, Marietta, Ohio
Larry and Grace Gilmer, Minneapolis, Minnesota
Lawrence L. Gilmer Builders, (612) 823 8454

Chapter 2 Painting—Stenciling, p. 56
Woodmaster of San Antonio
(877) 583-9742
www.uffos.com
Products used: Blanket box-#7006, 43-W2 drawer; Beaded Sleigh Bed-Model 416

Stencil:
The Stencil Shoppe
Olde Ridge Village Shoppes
Ridge Road & Route 202 S.
Chadds Ford, PA 19317

Southwestern Texturing:
Max Olivas and Cesar Olivas and Associates
Building, Remodeling, Lath and Plaster
Santa Fe, New Mexico, 87500; (505) 820-6147

Chapter 3 Wallpaper, p. 122
Ron Fisher Furniture
(800) 231-7370
www.ronfisher.com
Product used: #299 Custom English Cottage Round Table-32"; Old World Double Cracked Sage over Barley

Chapter 4 Molding and Trim-Installing Beadboard Wainscoting, p. 154
Babcock Lumber Company
(800) 454-5022
Product used: Premium Poplar 8" board w/accompanying cap

Products for Wainscoting Lead Photo
PALECEK
P.O. Box 225
Richmond, CA 94808-0226
(800) 274-7730
Product used: Sienna Side Chair-7162-83h; Side Chair Upholsterred Cushion-7374-66 Turkish Chenille C Fabric; Sienna Arm Chair-7163-83h Umber; Chair Upholstered Cushion-8605-66 Turkish Chenille C Fabric

Chapter 4 Molding and Trim-Creating a Custom Bookcase from Stock Molding, p. 159
Unfinished Furniture Factory Outlet Store
2611 Hwy 23
Oskaloosa, IA 52577
(515) 673-8433
Product used: Pine Bookcase

Chapter 4 Molding and Trim-Faux Plaster Rosettes and Cornice Molding, page 200
Balmer Studios
271 Yorkland Blvd.
Toronto, ON M2J 1S5 Canada
(877) 999-7019
www.balmer.com
Product used: Egg & Dart (T300) w/accompanying blocks

Chapter 5 Tiling Around a Fireplace Mantel, p. 171
Stiles Tiles
4140 Grand Ave.
Des Moines, IA 50312
(515) 277-7770
Product used: Silverado Apache-custom cut

Chapter 6 Installing a Tin Ceiling pp. 193-195
aa-abbingdon affiliates inc.
2149-51 Utica Ave.
Brooklyn, NY 11234
(718) 258-8333
www.abbingdon.com
Product used: #205 6" Multiple Plate; #4574 Molded Filler 24"x48"; #705 Cornice 5" Projection, Length 48"

Chapter 7 Ceiling Lighting-SBS, pp. 212-213
Ron Fisher Furniture
(800) 231-7370
www.ronfisher.com
Product used: Dresser in background-#573-Town House 5 Drawer Chest-Old World Cobalt; Blue Case & Knobs w/Old World Pine Top and Drawers

Elkhorn Designs
165 N Center Street
Jackson, WY 83001
(307) 733-4655
cherokee@elkhorndesigns.com
www.elkhorndesigns.com
Product used: chandelier

Chapter 9 Blinds and Shutters, page 237
Kestrel Shutters
(800) 494-4321
www.diyshutters.com
sales@diyshutters.com
Product used: Operable Louvered Shutters

Chapter 9 Blinds and Shutters-Installing Horizontal Blinds, p. 242
Graber by Springs Window Fashions
(800) 221-6352
www.springs.com
Product used: (2)-73-1603-10 2" wood blind, Snowflake

Chapter 12 Dressing a Door, p. 289
Locks and Pulls
6990 W. 105th
Overland Park, KS 66212
(800) 381-1336
www.locks-pulls.com
Products used: Custom Ironworks Collection #1-12

Rockler Woodworking and Hardware
4365 Willow Drive
Medina, MN 55340
(800) 279-4441
www.rockler.com
Product used: 13724-14" Hinge strap

SEGO DESIGNS LLC
(307) 739-0393
sego@wyoming.com
Product used: Palm Pull #2484

Chapter 14 Wooden Floors—Wood Floors w/Inlaid Border, p. 298
Strip Flooring
Bruce Hardwood Floors
www.bruce.com
(800) 722-4647
Product used: Gunstock -3/4" x 2 1/4";
Natural-3/4"x 2 1/4"

Inlaid Border
Historic Floors of Oshkosh, Inc.
(920) 582-9977
www.oshkoshfloors.com
Product used: Medallion #305-30 in lead and SBS;
Border No. 130RO Rose(c) in lead

Chapter 14 Wooden Floors-Wide Plank Floorboards p. 306
Duluth Timber Company
www.duluthtimber.com
(218) 727-2145
Product used: Douglas Fir plank flooring, 1"x10"

Judi Boisson American Home Collection
134 Mariner Drive
Southhampton, NY 11968
(516) 283-5466
Product used: Windowpane hand knitted rug,
Home Depot

Ron Fisher Furniture
(800) 231-7370
www.ronfisher.com
Product used: #321 Ladderback Bench-Newberry with Teal Seat

Chapter 14 Wooden Floors-Pickling Floors, p. 309
America Heart Pine
www.americaheartpine.com
(800) 554-5765
Product used: 4" Select Grade pine board

Chapter 15 Painted Floor Cloths, p. 325
Kunin Felt, Foss Manufacturing Company
380 Lafayette Road
Hampton, NH 03843-5000
(800) 292-7900

Chapter 15 Installing a TileFloor, p. 340
Daltile (R)
(800) 933-TILE
www.daltile.com
Product used: Special Patterns & Murals-1" hexfield (ordered custom pattern through Home Depot)

Chapter 15 Laminate Flooring, p. 334
Pergo, Inc.
3128 Highwoods Blvd.
Raleigh, NC 27604
(800) 33-PERGO
www.pergo.com
Product used: PO2330 Tuscany Stone

Chapter 18 Two-Coat Faux Finishes, p. 364
Woodmaster of San Antonio
(877)-583-9742
www.uffos.com
Product used: front/footboard: Model 177 Alamo w/Blanketroll; middle/headboard: Model 370 Cannonball; back/headboard: Model 327 Shaker Headboard

Chapter 19 Replacing a Faucet Lead
Babcock Lumber Company
(800) 454-5022
Product used: Premium Poplar 8" board w/accompanying cap (for wainscoting)

smith + noble
(800) 765-7776
www.smithandnoble.com
Product used: Top down shade, white and blue ragatta fabric

green home
www.greenhome.com
Product used: towels

Kohler, Co.
(800) 4-KOHLER
www.kohlerco.com
Product used but not seen in lead shot: Toilet:
Memoirs Bowl-PT-4257-0; Memoirs Tank/Classic-3452-0; Lustra Seat/Closed Front-PB-4662-0

Daltile
(800) 933-TILE
www.daltile.com
Product used: Special Patterns and Murals-1" hexfield (custom pattern ordered through Home Depot)

Plus: Plumbing fixtures supplied by Sign of the Crab (information below)

Chapter 19 Replacing a Faucet, page 383
Strom Plumbing by Sign of the Crab
(800) 843-2722
www.signofthecrab.com
Products used:

        P0060C- faucet/sink
        P0403C-chrome shower enclosure
        P0087C-chrome 90 degree brace
        P0342C-P11C + (2) P55C in chrome
        P0007BC-chrome waste & overflow
        GB0946C-chrome tub shelf
        GB0979C-chrome bookholder for tub

Chapter 19 Refurbishing a Tub or Shower, p. 392
Strom Plumbing by Sign of the Crab
(800) 843-2722
www.signofthecrab.com
Products used:

        P0154C-P6 w/PORC H/H shower
        P0342C-P11C + (2) P55C in chrome
        P0007C-chrome waste and overflow

Chapter 19 Knob Spread, p. 396
Home Embellishments
102 Main
Parkville, MO 64152
(816) 505-1022
Products used):

        1-Photo knob-insert your own photo
        2-fork
        3-pewter shirt
        4-wrench
        5-handblown glass

Chapter 19 Countertops, p. 400
Kohler Co.
(800) 4-KOHLER
www.kohlerco.com
Product used: Revival Kitchen FCT/LVR W/SPY-16109-CP

Wallcoverings used throughout projects:
York Wallcoverings
750 Linden Ave.
York, PA 17405
(800) 375-YORK

FSC Wallcoverings, A Division of F. Schumacher & Co.
www.villagehome.com
www.decoratewaverly.com
(800) 988-7775

Many thanks to the following employees of The Home Depot® whose "wisdom of the aisles" has made Decorating 1-2-3™ the most useful book of its kind.

Romeo Julian
Chicago, IL

Edna Atkins
Willow Grove, PA

Jerry Brennan
Westminister, CA

Debi Peoples
Rancho Cucamonga, CA

Ed Czyr
Landsdale, PA

Jerry Allen
Tustin, CA

Terri Sanders
Geneva, IL

Dale Solomon
San Diego, CA

Greg Korczak
Lodi, NJ

Erica Barrett
Downers Grove, IL

Dionne Collins
Woodland Hills, CA

Terry Clayton
Upland, CA

Jim Pelligrini
Jericho, NY